Published by

Hygge Media

www.hyggemedia.com

The Toss of a Coin: voices from a modern crisis

Written by Rory O'Keeffe

Cover and Illustrations by Shay O'Donnell

A catalogue record for this book is available from the British Library.

ISBN 978-0-9932729-0-5

Published by Hygge Media
For more copies of this book, please email: info@hyggemedia.com

www.hyggemedia.com

The Toss of a Coin
voices from a modern crisis

For Tracy, love of my life
without whom this would not have been possible

Contents

Prologue
The Road From Carthage 1

The Toss of a Coin. Tunisia, November 2011
The Toss of a Coin Part One: My Grandmother 7

**Choucha Refugee Camp. Tunisia, November 2011:
Moments from Lives on Pause**
Life on Pause 15
The Musician 21
My Mother 31
My Father 41
The Doctor and The Photographer 43
Choucha 47
The Dancer 55
The Toss of a Coin Part Two: Fifteen Days in the Desert.................61

Libya, November 2011 - April 2012: Sirte
The Mexican 67
Entering Sirte 81
France 85
'We Must' 89
The Clinic 91
Ehemmet's 97
Ibn Sina 103
The Journalist 107
A Good Man 113
The Palestinian...117
Brothers in Arms 121
Mantika Ethnaan 123
Reading, Writing and Rebuilding................................131
Ghosts (Sarna Yousseff) 137
Khaleeg Thaladi (from behind a wall) 141
Al Bayan..143
Haldoon (the 'weapon store')......................................147
My Brother 151
The Green Book Building..155
The Green Book Building: postscript 163
Parklife 165
University 169
Ghaddafi's cousin 177
New Year's Eve 179
New Year's Day...181
Television 185
Febriar 17..187
Guns and Politics: Part One 193
Guns and Politics: Part Two 197

Libya, November 2011 - April 2012: Tawergha
Tawergha I 205

Libya, November 2011 - April 2012: Misrata
Misrata 211

Libya, November 2011 - April 2012: Benghazi
Security 219
Second Amongst Equals..223
Turn Left 231
Tawergha II..237

Libya, November 2011 - April 2012: Bani Walid
Bani Walid 245

Libya, November 2011 - April 2012: Zawiyah
Zawiyah..255

Libya, November 2011 - April 2012: Tripoli
Guns 263
The Toss of a Coin Part Three: Days of Life in Libya.......271
Security 279
Janzour 285

Libya, November 2011 - April 2012: Leptis Magna
Leptis Magna (Turn Right)...291

The Toss of a Coin Part Four: The Toss of a Coin 301

Postscript

Tunisia 2014

Choucha...309
Tunisia: The State of Things to Come 311
Election, 26th October 2014 319

Libya 2014

A St Valentine's Day Charade..325
The Law of the Trigger..329
The South: Oil and Water 339
The Constitution..343
The 'Free Ones', the West, and the Oilfields 349
Morning Glory: The Rise and Fall of Cyrenaica................353
Morning Glory: Repercussions...357
Al Thinni..359
Libya's Future and Libya's Past 365
Haftar's Return...369
25th June 2014: Voting Under Fire 373
War I: Deja-Vu (July-August 2014)....................................377
War II: Airstrikes (17th and 23rd August) 381
War III: Recriminations and Retaliations 383
Matters of Legitimacy, 6th November 2014.......................389
Sirte 393
Failure?...395

Prologue

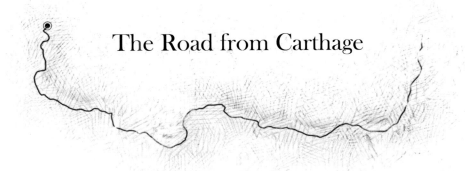

The Road from Carthage

This began as the story of the 'Arab Spring' – at least the way in which the events of early 2011 shaped the lives of people within the state where the first of the sequence of uprisings began, and its neighbour, where international armed forces united to depose North Africa's most powerful man. But in the course of writing it, I have discovered that it is other things too.

Although it is by no means comprehensive, this story touches on every armed conflict in Africa within living memory – in part because of Muammar Ghaddafi's involvement in so much of the continent's recent history, but also because Choucha refugee camp, as representative of the diversity in the Libya Ghaddafi built, also served as a cross-section of the African diaspora.

It is also the story of a road.

Many of us experience a certain sense of excitement and potential in a map. Unfolding a representation of something new – or something very, very, old – is to experience temptation and enticement, almost hearing it calling you to enter.

In North Africa, I discovered there is another thing which can inspire the same dizzying, almost breathless magnetism: a road.

There are many things to do in Tunisia. There are beautiful white beaches, the churning, swirling mass of people within the Tunis souks, even Tatouine, the 'planet' on which Luke Skywalker began to develop the skills he used to overthrow the Galactic Empire.

But there is also Carthage. And its road.

Long after the days of Carthage's imperious command over large swathes of North Africa, and long after the glorious defeat of Hannibal, whose tactics – and elephants – almost dealt defeat to the world's major military power, Rome's Emperor Claudius built a road.

In fact, like other emperors in other times and places within the vast Roman Empire, Claudius did not build as much as 'develop' his road.

Starting with a Carthaginian path, he paved and extended his road west, through what is now Algeria, to modern Rabat, on Morocco's Atlantic coast. In the other direction, he rolled his road through Tripoli, the vast city of Leptis Magna, and as far as Alexandria in Egypt.

Today, the road leads you (wars and politically-imposed blockades notwithstanding) for around 8,000km, skirting desert to the South, and flanked by the Mediterranean to the North, from Morocco, through Algeria, Tunisia, Libya, Egypt, Palestine, Israel, Syria.*

* If one were so bloody-minded, it would be possible to continue further still – following the complete 13,000km path all the way to Rome itself.

In short, the road's original starting-point and its Eastern progression laid out almost the exact course followed nearly 2,000 years later by the protests and rebellions which are now known as the Arab Spring.

Wherever you stop on this vast artery, which links all of North Africa, and curves up the Eastern shore of the sea at the heart of the Classical world, the view is almost identical: sea to your left, desert on your right. And while you are upon it, it stretches, in front and behind, grey and black, wide and straight, as far as the eye can see.

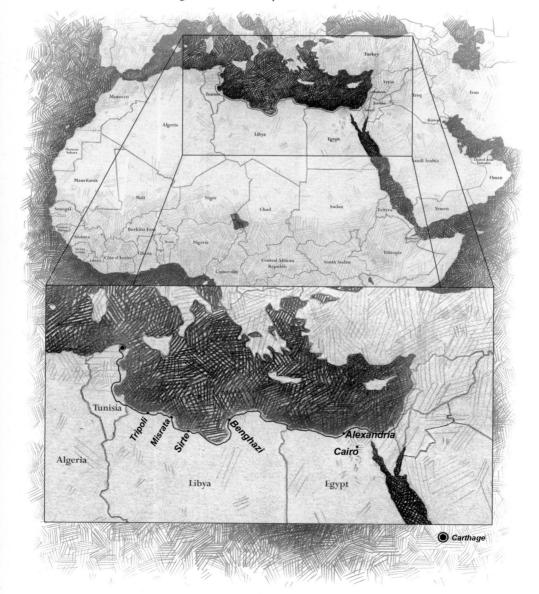

Whether you are alone, racing past desert dunes under an endless blue sky, or sharing coffee and conversation with Arab and African long-haul drivers.

Whether you have paused – in solitude, to take in the sheer scale of what surrounds you – or surrounded by camels, gazing blankly as they chew whatever food they can find in the sand at the roadside.

Whether you are in a line of cars, HGVs, farm haulage vehicles and bicycles, all heading to some destination you do not know, or taking part in a (certainly illegal) race with a cab driver who shouted something unintelligible before speeding up and waving you to follow...

... it is always magnificent.

There are moments when the history of the road itself is almost overwhelming: the Carthaginians who used its earliest section more than 2,200 years ago; the Romans developing and using it, imposing their brand of order and law, the Arabs travelling south and west, dispensing their fiery faith, their learning and culture, and their ornate, beautiful, fragile and imposing mosques as they went.

Africans from across the continent have also gravitated towards the road, for work, safety and for the chances to take what many see as the final step to a better life – the sea-crossing to Europe.

Recently, Westerners have returned: for sun, seas, souks and shawarmas, and of course for the new, undisputed queen of the desert, oil.

Others have used it too: many millions of tribesmen, farmers, long-distance drivers. Not, perhaps, for reasons of international upheaval, or which have been recorded for study by later generations, but just people living their lives, ensuring the world – and history – also keep travelling.

This was a road at the centre of the Ancient World. And it is the pathway at the centre of most of modernity's greatest – and gravest – issues.

It is also breathtaking.

Travelling slowly, or stopping, you fancy you hear a whisper on the warm breeze: 'Keep moving, keep moving, keep moving, keep moving...' The more you listen, the more you are driven along, the more you come to believe this is not the voice of the Romans, the Arabs or the Africans, it is the call of the road.

For that reason, this is not only the story of the roots and consequences of a revolution which sent ripples around the world.

It is not only the story of two states and the people within them.

It is, to an extent, a story of the recent history of vast swathes of the world's largest continent.

But it is also the story of a road, which has connected all of North Africa to the rest of the world for thousands of years. It is an important story. And it is a remarkable road…

Tunisia, November 2011

Choucha Refugee Camp

Choucha Camp

The Toss of a Coin
Part One: My Grandmother

Fifteen years ago, when I was seven, I was playing in the garden when soldiers ran into my grandmother's house, put a gun in her face and killed her. Then, they set fire to the house.

I started to run inside, but a woman had seen what happened and had come into the garden.

She grabbed me and held me to her, saying in Somalian: 'Don't go to the soldiers. They will kill you too.' It is not quite my earliest memory, but it is the clearest.

This happened in Ogaden,* in Ethiopia, where I was born. But I didn't always live there. Only a few months before I watched my grandmother get shot and burned, I lived with her, my father and mother, and my brother and sister in Kenya.

Ogaden is a region the size of Germany, with eight million inhabitants. It is in Eastern Ethiopia, and stretches the length of the border between Ethiopia and Somalia, all Ethiopia's Northern border with Djibouti and a small part of its Southern Border with Kenya.

Historically, it was a part of the Somalian Sultanate, and is known today by Somalians as 'Somali Galbeed' or 'Western Somalia'. It became part of the British Empire, but the British handed it to the Ethiopian emperor Menelik in 1897, as a reward for his assistance in helping them resist Somalian raiding clans. It passed back into the hands of the British, who ceded it again to the Ethiopians following WWII.

The British requested that Ogaden's 'Somali' majority retain their autonomy, but Ethiopia claimed the region outright. Perhaps out of guilt, Britain tried to buy Ogaden from Ethiopia, in 1956. It failed.

In 1960, perhaps having overcome its guilt, Britain handed the Northern Frontier District – situated at Somalia's South Western tip and also containing a large Ogaden population – to Kenya, even though a plebiscite of the region voted overwhelmingly to be part of Somalia.

Now, I am the only one still alive.

When we were in Kenya, my grandmother got a phone call from a hospital in Ogaden to say that my auntie had been shot in the breast and the leg. There was a war in Ogaden. I did not know why. But she had been shot by soldiers who were fighting there.* It was an accident, but she had still been shot.

* *In 1977, eight years after the assassination of Somali President Abdirashid Ali Sharmake in a coup which saw the leader of the country's military, Mohamed Siad Barre, seize the presidency, and three years after the Ethiopian Military Council, The Derg, had overthrown Ethiopia's Emperor Haile Selassi, Somalia invaded Ogaden.*

In the years preceding the invasion, the USSR withdrew support from Somalia, and transferred it to Ethiopia, which it had previously opposed. At the same time the West, led by the USA and UK, switched support from Ethiopia to Somalia, which it had previously opposed. Egypt, hoping to remove Ethiopian 'interference' in its control of the Nile Delta, also offered support to Somalia.

The majority of people in Ogaden welcomed the Somalian 'invaders', with whom they shared a language, the Islamic religion, and claimed a shared heritage and tribal belonging. Though some preferred the idea of an independent state, many were prepared to accept Somalian rule.

Somalian forces penetrated a long way into Ogaden, but in February 1978, in the campaign's decisive battle, Cuban and Ethiopian forces moved on Jijiga, a large town in northern Ogaden close to its borders with Somalia and Djibouti. They killed 3,000 Somali soldiers.

Within a month, Ethiopian troops operating a 'scorched earth' policy of poisoning water, killing cattle and strafing settlements, 'cleared' the country of Somalian troops. But violence in Ogaden continued.

The Western Somali Liberation Front, and later the Ogaden National Liberation Army, entered a prolonged struggle against the Ethiopian government, with sporadic battles and incidences of torture and war crimes committed on both sides.

For its part, the Derg – though still supported by the USSR, Cuba and at times North Korea and Ghaddafi's Libya – had little capacity to wage a full-scale war in Ogaden, as it was also fighting a nationwide civil war against, amongst others, Eritreans attempting to regain their state's independence after Ethiopia annexed it in 1962, Tigray, and seven other political and/or separatist organizations.

As a result, ethnically-Ethiopian police officers and military battalions were effectively left to their own devices in Ogaden for long periods.

In 1988, Ethiopia and Somalia signed a treaty which officially brought the Ogaden war to an end. By this point, 14 years of civil war had almost destroyed Ethiopia, resulting in hundreds of thousands of deaths by violence or through famine. It would last three years more.

Somalia's own decades of strife continued, with years of warfare over the country's leadership opened in a 1986 rebellion against Barre. The violence continues to the present day.

Ogaden remains a disputed territory, though still under Ethiopian rule.

My grandmother – all my family – was worried. So we decided to go back to Ogaden, to be with my auntie. We travelled north and west to enter Ogaden. I was in the first car, with my grandmother. My father, mother, brother and sister were in the second car. My grandmother and I crossed the border with no problem. But the second car, with the rest of the family, was stopped by the Ethiopian soldiers on the border. I have never seen or heard from them again. I have been told by many people that they are dead. I think that is true.

I travelled in the car with my grandmother to Jijiga, where my auntie had been. We stayed for two days but we found out she had been moved to a hospital in Addis Ababa. We were staying two days drive from Addis Ababa when the Ethiopian military came. It was a white house, but I don't remember a lot else about it.

The woman who had grabbed me took me to some Somalians, and told them to take me to Addis Ababa. I met some men, one of whom took me in his car. We drove for 46 hours, without resting. But we were stopped at the last road-block, where soldiers controlled who could enter the city. We were caught.

A man asked me questions. But I was seven, and I did not speak their language. I didn't know what they were asking me. The man who drove me knew, but he was hit in the mouth with guns when he told me what they were saying.

They asked me my name. They hit the man. I didn't know what to say. I said 'Ogaden' to explain I couldn't understand, but they hit me on the back. They asked me where I was from. The man was hit again. They told me I was a Somalian. The man was hit again. He was bleeding. I said, 'No. I am from Ogaden.' They hit me, this time, and then the man.

One man pulled out a bullet. He showed it to me. It was pointed. He didn't smile. He didn't look angry, either. I didn't know what would happen next. I didn't think he was going to shoot me. He did not.

Another soldier grabbed my right arm.

The first one took the bullet, and pushed it, point first, slowly, but strongly, into my arm. It went in almost up to the bottom. It made a very deep hole in my arm. I still have the scar. It's here.

It hurt. So much. I cried and screamed and I shouted 'Please! Leave me!' But I did not understand their language, and they did not understand mine.

They asked us more questions. But I did not understand them. And the man who drove me was quiet. I still don't know whether it was because he could not speak because he had been hit with guns so often, or because he knew they would hit him again if he did.

They would not let us into the city. But they did let us go. The man who drove me took me to a garage. He told me to sit on the step. I was still crying, because my arm hurt and was bleeding. I could see the bones, and I could not make my right hand work.

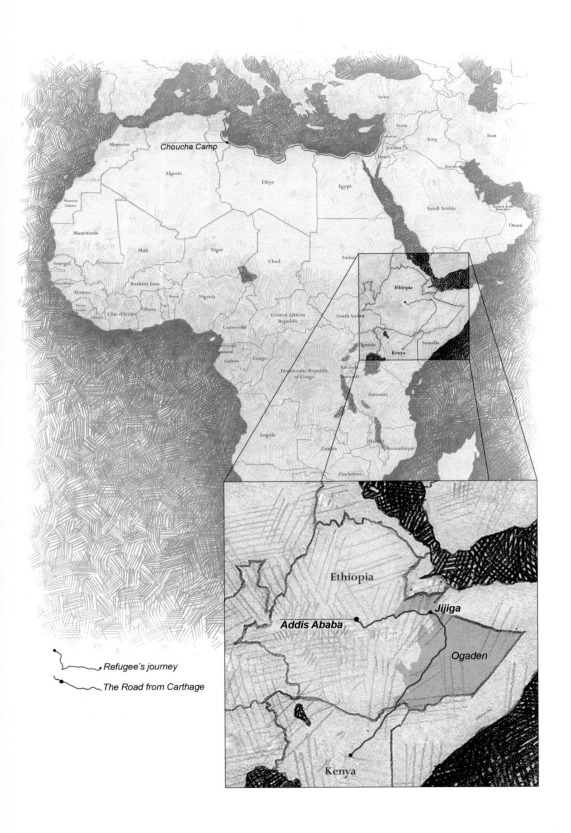

Choucha Camp

Ethiopia

Addis Ababa   Jijiga

Ogaden

Kenya

•———• Refugee's journey

•———• The Road from Carthage

The man told me to sit and wait, and a doctor would come. He drove away. I do not know where. I hope he went home. I never saw him again.

The manager saw I was there. He nodded, but he did not talk to me. I walked into the garage, and I found somewhere to lie down and sleep. My arm hurt so much I thought I couldn't sleep. But I was very tired. I went to sleep.

The next morning I woke up cold and hungry. My arm still hurt. It still had the bullet in it, and I still couldn't make my fingers work, or make a fist. The manager of the garage came, when he saw I was awake. He spoke to me, but I could not understand him, and he could not understand me.

He went away, and the other man spoke to me. I didn't understand what he said, but he showed me he would take the bullet from my arm. It hurt and I shouted and cried, but he poured very cold water on me, and he held a bandage against me to stop the blood dropping on the floor. When the blood stopped flowing as much, he wrapped another bandage around my arm. It hurt, but I could move my fingers a little bit again.

The manager came back, then. He gave me tea and bread, and he held my bad hand and spoke to me. I couldn't understand him, and he did not speak my language. I finished the tea and the bread. He brought me some more bread, and I ate it, and some water which I drank.

Then, he looked serious and talked some more. I didn't understand and in the end he sighed and pointed outside. He held my left hand and we walked to the church, where he showed me to sit on the step, and then he went back to his garage. I never saw him again, either. But I hope he went back to his garage. I think he was a kind man.

I sat on the step for three days, I think. I slept there, and one morning the priest came and saw me. He could speak my language, though not very well. He told me I could sleep inside, where it was much warmer. He brought me food. He did bring me that, and I was very hungry. And he also brought me a shoe-brush, and some shoe… cleaner? Polish. He brought me a shoe-brush and some shoe polish.

He told me that in the daytime I should go out and clean shoes. He said to charge five (cents) for every pair I cleaned, and if someone asked to say I was living at the church. He didn't take any of the money. I think he was a good man because he gave me the brush and the polish and he didn't take any money from me. This was my first money and I was proud to have money. I was very hungry, but I kept the first coin I was paid. Later, I cleaned a lot of shoes and I could sleep in the church, so I didn't have to spend money very often. I still have the coin now.

My hand did hurt, still, but it was much better. It worked again. I could bend my fingers, even though it hurt.

Some of the people asked me about my hand. Some would give me more money when I told them what had happened, but some would walk away without paying if I did. So I tried to make sure people wouldn't see I was hurt, so I didn't have to tell them why I was.

I stayed a long time living at the church, cleaning shoes. But when I was 15, an Ethiopian festival came, with drums and music and people marching and dancing. I was very interested and I watched and I walked and danced with some of the people.

In the road I found an Ethiopian boy. He was a student, called Hauptame. He was older than me, but we talked and I liked him and he liked me. He didn't speak my language, but I had learned to speak the Ethiopian language, because I had been cleaning shoes for a long time.

He said to come with him, so I went to his house close to the centre of Addis Ababa. I was part of the festival so nobody asked me who I was. I stayed with him, and he taught me to speak English. It was the first time I had learned English and it helped me.

When I first arrived there, he laughed and asked if my job was cleaning shoes. I told him not to laugh at me, and I said it was my only job and it meant I had money. He gave me a bucket, and told me to use the freezer they had to take ice to schools. I could sell ice for five cents per piece.

I went to the schools. It was strange for me. I was making money, which made me happy, but also I saw children in the schools and I thought about how it would be good if I had friends like they were friends. But I carried on. I cleaned shoes sometimes, and I brought ice to schools.

A little while later, Hauptame told me he could find me a better job, but I would have to work very hard. I told him I always worked hard, but I didn't understand. He found me a job at a Tae Kwan-Do club in Ethiopia. I was a security guard, but it meant I had to learn Tae Kwan-Do. It was hard to learn, but I enjoyed it and I made friends with the owner.

I worked from six pm to midnight and I lived at the same house as Hauptame and his friends. But sometimes I stayed at the club and slept there, too. I liked Tae Kwan-Do, and I was good at it, and people liked me there too. Soon, I became a teacher of Tae Kwan-Do at the club.

But one night I was there alone, and the police knocked at the door. I told them it was time to lock up, but they said I had to show them ID. I didn't have any ID, and I told them, and they asked where are your mother and father? I told them I didn't have a mother and father. They said 'Where are you from?' I said 'Ogaden.' One policeman said 'We will take you to prison' then they hit me and took me to the police station.

At the police station, they asked me questions. But I couldn't answer a lot of them, and when I did answer they said I was telling lies. They showed me a fire, and they put nails into the fire. Every time I didn't answer a question, or they didn't believe me, they took a nail in clamps and they pushed it into my leg. You can see the scars here.

I screamed, but I couldn't tell them the things they wanted because I didn't know what they wanted and I didn't know all the answers to their questions.

I sat in a chair, with hot nails in my legs and they said: 'Who are you?' I told them my name, but they put another nail in my leg, so I said I didn't know who I was. They said 'Where do you live?' I didn't want to say I lived at the Tae Kwan-Do club, or at Hauptame's home, so I said I lived at the church.

In the end, they pulled the nails from my leg, one by one, handcuffed me, and they made me stand in one of the toilets, in the bowl of the toilet, for two days. I slept, standing, when I could, but every so often they would come and hit me. They didn't ask me any more questions. They just hit me and injured me, in many places.

They kept me in prison for one and a half weeks. In that time, they made me clean the prison, but at least it meant I wasn't standing in the toilet any more. It was hard work, but I was allowed to walk when I cleaned. My legs hurt, but it was less painful to move than to stand in one place all the time.

They let me go. I think because I couldn't tell them anything they wanted me to say. So they set me free and I continued my life.

Things were the same until they held an election. In two departments of Ethiopia, including the one where I lived, people were unhappy with the result. I don't know why. I couldn't vote, because I had no papers, but the police started to fight people, and then people fought one another.

More police and army arrived. I think they were sent by the government.

They came to the Tae Kwan-Do club, and told me I had started the fighting. I told them I hadn't started it. I hadn't even fought. I told them I didn't know anything about the election, but I didn't tell them I hadn't voted because I had no papers.

It didn't make any difference. They didn't believe me. They said I had started the fighting and they arrested me, again.

They kept me in prison for seven months. They tied me up, and beat me many times. I was injured many times, in many places, but they did not put nails into me, or push a bullet into me. It hurt, but I had a board to sleep on and it was better than before.

But I was angry and unhappy, because they did not arrest me to ask questions or find anything out. They just kept saying I started the fighting, but I didn't. The police started the fighting. And I didn't fight. I just sold ice, and worked at the Tae Kwan-Do club, and cleaned shoes to make money so I could eat and buy clothes. But they hit me and kept me in prison.

When they let me go this time, I was angry and afraid. I knew they would keep arresting me, and I knew there was nothing I could do where I lived, that they would beat me and no-one could help me.

When I got back to the Tae Kwan-Do club, I spoke to the manager: 'Please help me,' I said. 'I like to live here and work here but the police and the army arrest me and hurt me. Please help me, I need it.'

But the owner of the club didn't know what to do. He said I could live there, but he didn't know how to help me. And he couldn't protect me from the police or the army. I understood.

Later that day, when I was cleaning shoes, a man said if I had a home, I could get numbers and papers. He said if I had papers I could show who I was and maybe the police would leave me alone and stop hurting me.

When I came back to the club I saw the owner again. I told him he could get me papers if I paid him, and then my life could be better. He told me he would help me to do this.

I gave him money, and he came back later with a number and a passport for me. He told me because I didn't live in the home he had got the number and passport for, it meant I would have to leave. He said he was sorry, because I worked hard for him and I was good at teaching people Tae Kwan-Do.

But it was alright. I thought it would be better to live somewhere else, because I was beaten and arrested many times in Ethiopia. So I said OK, I would go. It was in Spring 2009, when I was 19 years old.

I was going to go to Sudan. I needed a visa, but they asked me 'Is there someone you know in Sudan?' I didn't know anyone there, so I said 'no.' They asked if I had a job there, but I didn't have one, so I said 'no.' But the Tae Kwan-Do club owner had come with me. He told them he had a friend there who would find me a job and a home.

He called his friend on the phone, and he said he had a home for me, so they gave me a visa so I could go to Sudan. Before I got on the bus I told the Tae Kwan-Do club owner I would remember him, but he said: 'No. Only look after yourself.' He gave me money so I could pay the bus driver to take me to Sudan, then he went back to the club. I never saw him again.

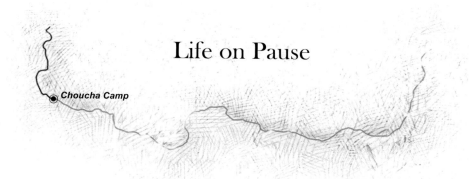

Choucha Camp

Life on Pause

One Autumn morning, a man in a refugee camp asks you for something to kick.

He's lived in a tent for more than eight months, so you can forgive him some a desire to get some frustration out of his system.

But it turns out that the refugee, one of thousands living in a tent-city situated on the Tunisian border with Libya, is just trying to ensure he could practise Tae Kwan-Do.

It's your first meeting on the first morning of the first day you have ever set foot in a refugee camp. And so far, it is shocking.

Not in the sense that you are rooted to the spot, mouth wide open, eyes bulging, but in a more gradual, creeping sense. As you go through the day, it works its way, slowly, steadily, through you, finally taking full hold only hours later.

By then, you will be in an office which would be ordinary were it not for the fact that conversation centres on distributing clothes, soap, water, food – the things which are necessary to survive anywhere, let alone in a camp on the northern edge of one of the world's great deserts.

From a distance, approached on one of the world's great trunk roads – a tarmac and concrete path from North West Morocco, through Algeria, Tunisia, Libya and onward through Egypt, into Syria, and eventually Rome – Choucha Camp looks almost inspiring.

Its tents, white canvas standing out against the yellow sands of the desert and a clear, intensely blue sky, appear to sparkle, pristine under the early winter sun.

The effect is intensified at moments when you swing north on the carriageway, bringing into view glittering salt flats. And at times as you have sped along it this morning, the road itself has seemed almost to be alive.

You have travelled on it through a major port and tourist centre, where a vast horse statue commemorates Carthage's greatest ancient hero Hannibal, and sits in the shadow of towering cranes feeding the cargo ships modern Tunisia hopes will deliver it new glories.

Further on, approaching the town's Southern outskirts, you passed a football stadium, a few small factories and loading yards, before breaking into the countryside beyond.

As it cut its way east and south, the road carried you through open country, at first green patched with small flashes of yellow, then, after a few miles of olive groves mainly yellow dotted

with patches of green until you entered a region where it was hard to imagine anything much exists anywhere in the world, but sand.

Closing on the Tunisian border with Libya (Choucha Camp is just nine km from the states' main crossing point), traders jostle with one another, in front of cafes and stalls selling pottery and fruit, to win custom exchanging one state's dinar for the other's.

Where there are fewer roadside stalls and money-changers, passengers in the seemingly endless, fast-moving train of cars, vans, trucks and other vehicles pass almost within touching distance of solitary herdsmen and their camels. The animals look up, gazing dully at the travellers, who in turn gaze at them.

As you get closer to it, Choucha Camp demands a more critical evaluation. Its golden floor is, after all Saharan sand. And the clear blue skies simply mean that the sun is beating relentlessly upon it – and on people who have now been trapped here for nine long months.

The tents, meanwhile, are far less white than they had appeared from a distance, though this is far less important than that on the one short period when rain did fall, the water was able to enter many of the tents, which had suffered damage either in transit, or at one of many previous locations for those who have been forced from their homes, and can do nothing but wait for another.

Of course, an observer may well ask themselves: 'This is a refugee camp. What did you expect?'

It's a fair question. The only answer you can give with any certainty is: 'Not this.' At least, not exactly this.

Perhaps, you think, struggling to remember a time before you had visited Choucha, what you had expected was desperation – even panic. But that is not what you have found here.

In fact, most of the people who remain at the camp have adapted to their awful situation, as anyone must to survive.

What is overwhelmingly clear, what can be tasted in the hot, dust-sprinkled air, seen in the eyes and heard in the speech of almost everyone you meet, is that here, in a hastily-thrown together community of close to 20,000 people (though that number does not remain steady for long), life is on hold.

Compared to the war crimes delivered by human beings, or the unthinking, unfeeling massacres forced upon people by natural disasters, that is neither a tragedy nor even tragic. But it is mind-numbing.

Across the world, people have celebrated the toppling – and death – of Libya's ruler; either a vicious, egotistical dictator without a single positive achievement, or a murderous torturer who incidentally delivered improvements in health, welfare, education and agriculture within his own borders. In the end, it matters little which side people are on: Ghaddafi is now dead, and for much of the world, that is cause for celebration.

Perhaps in some places, the celebrants pause, allowing a few seconds to remember those who died helping to bring this about. Some may even remember also those who were killed while they attempted to protect the regime.

But who remembers those who, terrified by a war which was nothing to do with them, and which in a distressingly high number of cases was merely the second, third or fourth armed conflict which broke around them, fled to save their own lives?

Those who had already given up their homes, families and lives in far worse regimes – or failed states –even than Ghaddafi's Libya, to try to find security, a job, a family-life, only to be forced once again to leave, to cross deserts and borders carrying false papers or no papers at all?

Who remembers those whose first escape from blood and bullets brought them to a new country, and whose second, the only way to be sure of escaping bombs, chaos, and the real, looming threat of an early death, has delivered to them only to the desert, to a life on hold for nine months or more, awaiting a decision which will shape the rest of their lives?

Under these circumstances, a kick-bag to help a few refugees retain the Tae Kwan-Do skills they learned before they were forced to leave their real world, and enter the seemingly-endless holding pattern of life at Choucha, may seem a trivial, unnecessary thing.

But walking past groups of youngsters being shepherded into makeshift schools, where fellow refugees and aid workers teach them English, Arabic, French, and IT, and watching queues of people from across the vast African continent waiting patiently for their daily food ration, you understand why this request, in particular, will stick with you.

Because it is an attempt by somebody surrounded by desert, whose life had stopped the moment they entered Choucha and could not truly begin again until they were allowed to leave, to continue some small part of the life he had led before, outside.

In a small way, it is a heroic act.

And there is little else left, when the world simply stops.

Choucha Camp

The Musician

February 17th 2011 was an important day for us in Tripoli. We had printed posters, made leaflets, everyone knew what we were going to do and they were going to join us.

But we were never able to do it.

I am a Somalian man. When I was 12, I left all of my family and travelled 6,000 miles to Libya. Now, I am 16 and I live in a refugee camp in Tunisia. I do not know what will happen next. I was born in Mogadishu, where I lived with my father and mother and my seven brothers and sisters. I love my family, but times were very hard for us.

One day, I decided I had to leave.

There were a few different reasons, but mainly there was one reason: my country had no government and people were being killed every day. Some of the people being killed were soldiers, but some of them were not.

It was a strange thing because on TV you see wars and the people are fighting one side against another. But where I lived, it was not like that. There were six groups sometimes, all fighting against each other.

When I was there, I didn't think about this, but since I have left Somalia I sometimes wonder how they knew which side was which.

Other times it was more normal. Just two sides fighting against each other.

My family was close and we were kind to one another, but we were very poor. My dad was a mechanic, but it was hard to get work because of the fighting. He had to pretend always to be friends with the people who were winning battles, which I think was very hard to do, and he also knew that mostly people did not need a mechanic, or could not afford to pay one even if they did.

Also, my father was trying to have another family, so the money he earned was divided between my family and his other family. It meant we were very poor.

One result of this was that I was the only member of my family who could go to school. It cost $10 per month and this was too much for my sisters and brothers to be able to go as well. That made me very sad.

Many times, even I could not go. I would get up and walk to school but while a lesson was happening I would be called to see the manager of the school and she would say that I had to

go home because my father had not paid the money that month. I know he tried to pay. But sometimes we did not have enough to eat.

But because my brothers and sisters could not ever go, I was sad and one day I decided I would have to leave home, leave my family and the city and country where I was born, to earn money so they could learn.

And there was another reason. Ever since I was very little, I loved to sing. I still do. It was always my dream to become a singer.

At home, my mum and dad liked to hear me sing. Sometimes my brothers and sisters would join in and they listened and they told me I was good at it. So I loved to sing. I think I was eight years old when I decided I would try to become a singer. I listened to the radio and heard singers and I thought: 'I want to make my dream come true.'

But in Mogadishu, the most powerful armed group was a group called Al Shabaab.* They would walk around the city and if they heard you singing they would pull you out of your home. People said they used to beat people for singing, but that was not what was happening at that time. They did not beat people for singing. They pulled people from their homes and shot them.

Formed in 2004, Al Shabaab began as the youth wing of the Somalian Islamist Courts Union. But when the Union was defeated by the Somali Transitional Federal Government and its Ethiopian allies, Al Shabaab continued as a military organisation opposed to the government.

It made vast gains across the south of Somalia, including in Mogadishu, where it was strongest. A fundamentalist Islamic organisation, it affiliated itself in 2012 with Al Qaeda. Its leaders call for global jihad, but most members are focussed on local and national issues, including a desire to impose sharia law across Somalia.

They would even do the same thing if you listened to the radio. A person who lived near me was killed for listening to his radio. I did not know him, but it was a very frightening thing.

This was the other reason I had to leave.

I was 12, so I could not go alone. I heard my neighbours talking about leaving Somalia, so I went to speak to them about it.

They told me they were going to go to Ethiopia, so I said I had to go with them. I said I have to leave this life. They said what about your family and I explained that I was going so I could earn money to make my family's life better. They knew my brothers and sisters could not go to school. They agreed to help me and they promised not to tell my family what I was going to do.

I travelled by car with them to Ethiopia.

I lived with them at their house for one month, but then they left. Their relatives had sent them invitations so they could go to join them and live where they lived in Europe. But because I was not part of their family, I could not go with them.

Before they left, they introduced me to another family, and said 'look after this kid'. It was kind of them, because it meant I was not on my own when they went to Europe.

I don't think I can describe Ethiopia. It was better than Mogadishu because there was less fighting. But people were always scared there, and I was still young so I don't know what it was really like in Ethiopia.

I stayed only for two months. I met some people who said they were going to go to Sudan and it felt like Somalian people were unhappy in Ethiopia. I told them about my life and they said they would try to help me, so I said 'let me come' and they said 'yes', so I followed them to Sudan.

Because they looked after me, I did what they said. I wanted to get work, to send money home, but they said 'No. You are too young. You must not work.' So I did what they said. But I lived there for eight months, and I did look for work.

But I failed.

Everywhere I went people said: 'You are still young. You should not work.' But I had left home to work, so my brothers and sisters could go to school. I was sad because I was away from them and also I was not helping them. That was all I wanted to do. I didn't think then that the people looking after me had told people about me to stop me from working. But that might be true. I wish they had not.

I called my family for the first time when I was in Sudan. The people I was with in Ethiopia had said I could not call. They were afraid my family would try to come to bring me back. That could cause my family trouble, and the Ethiopian people trouble, and it would mean I couldn't raise money for my family, so I did not want it either.

But I was very lonely. I felt very sad because I could not see my family and that was what I wanted. So I called in Sudan. It made me very happy to speak to them, but also a little sad because I had never been so far from them.

They were very worried and I said I was OK but my mother was crying. I thought my father would be angry with me but he was crying as well and said he was glad to hear my voice. I was glad to hear their voice as well.

When I finished speaking with them, I felt more lonely than before. I sat down, alone. But I thought about why I was there and about my family's life in Mogadishu and I felt less alone because I knew I was going away for them, to earn money to send home.

I met another group of people who were Somalian people and they wanted to go to Libya. I understood Sudan and I did not know Libya, but I could not find work in Sudan and I thought I could earn money in Libya, so I talked to the Somalian group and they accepted me and said I could follow them to Libya.

I wanted to go to Libya to earn money, but also because in Sudan people said Libya was a good place to go to earn money and then get to Europe. They said to go to Italy, then I wanted to go to Scandinavian countries from there. I thought I would become an asylum seeker. I didn't know what that meant, but I heard people talk about it. I believed in it. Because it was a hope. It was something I could do and I was sure because I knew Somalian people had done it. It showed me it is possible. I believed in the idea: get to Libya, then cross to Italy.

On the way, travelling from country to country, it was hard for lots of people. We had to try to work for money to carry on – most of the time, they said I was too young – and we worked hard. We did not sleep very much or eat very much and it was not always easy to get enough water to drink.

But we were a group together and we met people who would help us. Along the way, there were lots of Somalian people who had stayed in Sudan, and some who worked helping asylum seekers like us. The Sudanese people we met were kind to us as well, and many rented out rooms or let us sleep in their houses.

We told each other stories in the night time. About our lives, where we were from and what we had done, and about what we would do in the future. I told stories about where I lived, and my family, and about the music I love and how I would be a singer. People liked to hear the stories. So even though I was young and maybe some thought I was extra trouble, I was looked after when we travelled.

Thirty of us crossed into Libya in 2008. We arrived in Ajdabiya, but we had no documents and no passports. We were arrested and put in jail for six months. Because I was young, they treated me in a good way in prison. The soldiers asked me 'You are so young, why did you leave your family?' There was nobody there with me, so they took care of me and made sure I was OK.

But they beat the others and treated them badly.

After six months they let us go free. They made some people pay them money, but they didn't ask for any from me, they just said 'You can go.'

We met some Libyans in Ajdabiya and asked them if they would drive us to the capital city. They said they were not going to Tripoli then, but they would take us to Benghazi first. The driver told me it is the second capital of Libya.

We did not stay very long in Benghazi. We wanted to be in

Tripoli and it was easy to find people who would take us there, so we travelled by road across the north of the country. The sea was to our right, and often we could see it as we travelled west, but we did not think to cross it then. We needed to get to Tripoli.

When we arrived, I tried hard to find work. I needed to send money to my family and I had to save to get on a boat. But it's hard to imagine what it is like. We were very afraid that the police would catch us and make us go to prison again. I had been lucky in Ajdabiya but I might not be lucky again, and the others had been beaten and had their money taken from them.

I did find work sometimes. It wasn't good work, just cleaning people's houses sometimes for some money they had. I could not save because it was only a little money. But I sent it to my family because I knew it would help them.

But I was also afraid of Libyan people. In Tripoli, it was not like it had been in Sudan. We were not surrounded by people who helped us and who we understood. I did not understand them and they did not understand me, and it was hard. I felt alone and we heard stories that some people would blackmail other Somalians, saying they would take their money and send them to prison. So it was hard for me. For all of us.

The group I came with did not like it. They left as soon as they could, by sea. I do not know why I did not go with them then. I felt I wanted to stay and see if I could live in Tripoli for a time. I still wanted to go to Europe, but Tripoli was a big place and it was interesting. It reminded me a little bit of Mogadishu. It did not look like it, but it was big. And there was no fighting.

I was scared, but I thought 'if I can get a job and earn some money I can send money to my family and I can save money and go to Europe later'. I was still only young, 13 or 14. I thought I wanted to see if I could live in Tripoli.

I have not heard from any of the group I travelled with. I am sad because I think they may have drowned. Lots of people drown when they try to reach Europe by sea.

For me, after one year, things were different.

I could speak the Libyan language, so people understood me more and I understood them. My skin colour was different from theirs but it seemed not to matter as much as it had when I arrived, I think because I could speak to them and we could say hi and joke with each other.

So I met with Libyan people, and made friends. I also met with Somalian people and I made friends with them as well. It was a good time.

Near the end of 2010, some of my Libyan friends and some of my Somalian friends agreed to be in a group together. We practised and made songs, based on Somalian music, Libyan music and hip hop. It made me very happy. We had fun together and we were making good music. It is what I had always wanted.

I didn't forget my dream of getting to Europe. Most of the group, even the Libyans, wanted to go to Europe. But I think for all of us, working and making music made us happy and we enjoyed doing it.

We met some Sudanese people in Tripoli, who were like us. They made music based on hip hop and Libyan music, but also Sudanese music as well. We worked with them and learned about their music and they learned about our music. I also used to listen to American songs and Sudanese songs and I would change them to the Somalian language. We met up at least once a week, every week and created new songs.

It was good because we understood each other and I wanted us to play so other people could hear, so that people in Tripoli could understand each other and know about each other's culture. Because we were Libyans and Sudanese and Somalians working together I thought we could play and everyone would understand.

We got better and better and soon we were sure we could play to other people. We saved up and bought a guitar and keyboards and then we prepared to play live. We thought we could get people to buy tickets and the money we made could be shared out for the Somalian community, Sudanese community and Libyan community.

We arranged to rent a hall, we had our instruments and we had a lot of songs to play. It was going to be our first show, so we made posters and we advertised it around the city. We were excited. Our first ever show was going to happen soon, on February 17th, 2011.

It did not happen. That was the day that the trouble started. It was in Benghazi, but everything changed in Tripoli as well.

That evening, people were too scared to come out and the people who owned the hall said we couldn't play – we had to cancel the show.

Things had changed. The fighting had not started properly, but all the Somalians and many of the Sudanese people knew we had to escape.

It is hard to understand why. It is hard to explain. It was not because of the fighting itself. The fighting was not bad at that time in Tripoli, but we all saw the news and we thought it would get worse in Tripoli.

But for most of us, fighting was normal. We were used to being woken up, and trying to go to sleep, with gunfire in our ears and heads.

It made us sad because we had travelled so far to get away from that and because it had been good to live in a city where that did not happen. But that was not why we had to escape.

In my country, after 1990, we did not have a government. The war and the fighting meant that there was no law, no police, no courts, no governments. There were prisons but they were not used for criminal people they were just used for people the strongest soldiers did not like. Mostly, the prisons were empty, because the soldiers just shot the people they did not like.

And in Somalia, where I grew up, you would watch all sorts of people, Italians, Tunisians, Ethiopians, everyone, being shot in the road. And there was nothing anyone could do. You could not talk to the police because the few police who were still there were really soldiers.

You could not talk to the soldiers because mostly they were the ones who did the shootings, and even when it was just single people with guns, the soldiers were sometimes pleased, or said they did not care.

There was no law because if people broke the law nothing would happen. There was no government to make a law and there was no police or soldiers to make people obey a law.

The reason we wanted to leave was because we had lived like that.

We had escaped it because it is not a way people can live. Even when you did not notice you were scared, you were afraid every moment. We had escaped from that. We left everything we had known and the people we had loved so we could earn money for them and escape a life that was terrible, and we saw that it could happen in Libya. That the fighting would make Libya like Somalia.

We were not afraid of the war. Even though that was frightening. We were afraid of what would happen after the war had started. We did not run from bombs and battles, even though no-one should stay for those things.

We ran because we knew what a country without governments and laws was like. We knew the Libyan government might fall, and we knew what that could mean.

So, we decided to leave. We thought about going by sea to Europe, and we argued about it. But I said we should not. I said we had to try to go to Tunisia, because I had watched the TV and saw there was a camp there run by UNHCR where we could stay and be safe from the war and the things it would cause.

But lots of the group argued. They said we should go straight to Europe. That we would be together and find work and continue to make music. I refused. I said 'There is a big sea to cross. We might not make it.' I was scared, because I knew people died in the sea.

Four of them decided to leave. When I heard they had gone I was so angry that I broke my guitar. I was very sad, too. I knew I would never see my friends again.

We left early in the morning, six of us, and arrived by road at 5pm. It was the same road I had travelled from Benghazi to Tripoli and this time I went west again, to a new country.

We couldn't get a tent that day, so we slept next to the road. It was not bad. The road was busy but people knew why we were there and they did not bother us when we were asleep.

The next day we spoke to people who already had tents and found out where to register, and we stayed here ever since. Several months later, we got refugee certificates and that's how it is today.

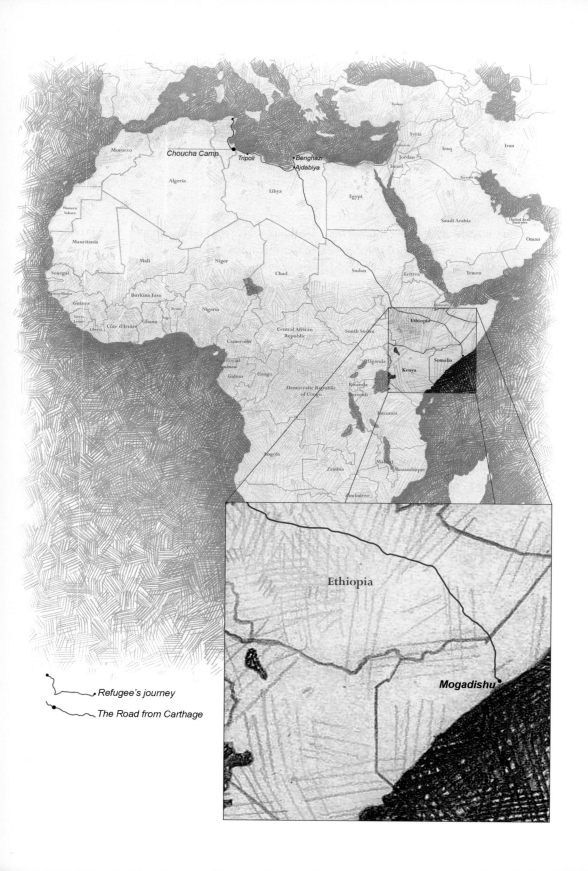

Choucha Camp

Tripoli · Benghazi
· Ajdabiya

Morocco

Algeria

Libya

Egypt

Western
Sahara

Mauritania

Mali

Niger

Chad

Sudan

Eritrea

Senegal

Guinea-Bissau

Guinea

Sierra
Leone

Liberia

Côte d'Ivoire

Burkina Faso

Benin

Togo

Ghana

Nigeria

Cameroon

Central African
Republic

South Sudan

Ethiopia

Somalia

Uganda

Kenya

Equatorial
Guinea

Gabon

Congo

Democratic Republic
of Congo

Rwanda

Burundi

Tanzania

Angola

Zambia

Malawi

Mozambique

Zimbabwe

Turkey

Syria

Lebanon

Iraq

Iran

Jordan

Israel

Kuwait

Saudi Arabia

United Arab
Emirates

Oman

Yemen

Djibouti

Ethiopia

Mogadishu

Refugee's journey

The Road from Carthage

I live alone in my tent. It is OK. I have friends here and it is safe. But it is not a life I want to live. I wake up early each day to queue for food. For some people, food lines are the biggest thing of the day. But there are other things to do. There are lots of communities here, different country groups and lots of people take part in running them. Some community leaders help new arrivals to settle down and feel safe.

But for me, the best thing is that I can now go to school. I have not been to school for nearly five years (my 17th birthday is very soon) and I have missed very much. I did learn things and I did not miss school, but now I have the chance to take lessons I really like to.

I have learned most of my English here, Geography, History, computers and some French.

I love to learn English. But my real favourite is Music. I take part in Music lessons in a different way. I help the teacher and teach the younger children how to play and sing, and how to make songs. The centre is only open some of the time, but if I could be, I would be here 24 hours a day, every day.

Because of my role here, I have helped children to perform for the rest of the camp. And I have performed too, with my friends in the camp. We have had some celebrations. It's nice to play, but it does remind me sometimes that we were supposed to play in Libya, the day the fighting started.

My family knows that I am here. They are OK. But at Eid, when I was about to perform, someone came to tell me that there was a phone call and that my mother had been taken to hospital. I dropped my microphone on the ground and ran to the phone.

She is OK now, but it reminds me why I went away, to make life better for my family, and it reminds me to work hard and to keep trying.

The rest of my day, I queue for lunch, come back to the education centre, then at 5pm I queue for dinner. If there is a performance coming, I will help the children in the day and practise my own things in the evening, with my friends. If there is not, in the evenings I go to friends' tents or I invite my friends to my tent.

I am waiting to see what happens next. We all are.

There are 51 Somalian people here in the camp at the moment and 30 young people have been resettled in Norway last week. But I have not been. I do not know what will happen. I do ask but I am not loud because other people are desperate to leave and I want to help.

I like to teach the younger people and I like to learn, so much that I sometimes forget about my rights and I do not go to the office to make sure I get a new home. I feel it is destiny.

But sometimes I am afraid. What if there is a conflict between UNHCR and Tunisia? What if they say everyone must go back to where they came from?

It would be very bad for me to have to return to Somalia. It would be good to see my brothers and sisters and mother and father. I would like that very much. But our lives would be very bad. If I stay alive, I would like to make my dreams come true.

It is a strange life here. It is a strange life everywhere, I think.

I would like to make a video about it, showing what I do every day, so that wherever I live in the end, I can show my children and grandchildren, and they can believe me and they won't ever forget.

I want to let them know about the world and this life. I would call it 'Hope'.

My Mother

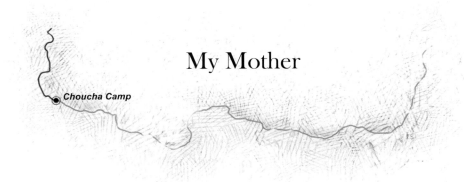

Choucha Camp

I have not seen my mother for eight years. In two weeks' time, I will leave this camp to visit her. I am very excited. I cannot remember what she looks like.

Last week it was my birthday. I was 17. My mother called me to wish happy birthday. It was the second time I heard from her in one month. And also the second time in eight years.

The first time, I did not believe it was her. But I knew it was her voice. I cannot remember what she looks like, but I can always remember her voice.

I was born in Chad. When I was a child, I lived with my father and mother, but they opposed the government. My father had opposed the government* and it meant we were split apart.

* It is hard to escape the feeling that history, geography, religion and global politics have conspired to deal Chad one of the world's unluckiest hands.

In common with many states created in the colonial era, Chad's population is disunited within its own borders, in its case between an Islamic north and centre, and a Christian south.

It is the fifth largest state in Africa, but almost all desert and therefore struggles to provide itself with food even in peacetime – and there has been very little of that in Chad's 55-year history.

It is totally landlocked, and along with the Central African Republic and Democratic Republic of Congo, it has been at the centre of struggles for influence by states including its immediate neighbours Libya, Sudan, Cameroon, and Nigeria.

Added to that, regular emergencies in Sudan, the Central African Republic and Niger have often sent refugees – and warfare – across its borders with those states.

Finally, and perhaps crucially, it was the state chosen by the US as its major proxy in its efforts to topple Ghaddafi's Libya.

As a result of each of these factors, it has experienced fewer than four years of peace in its brief, bloody history, and suffers the ignominy of having a former President – Chad's main recipient of US aid and support – now facing trial for crimes against humanity.

There are reasons for Chadians to be proud: their state can lay claim to being the wellspring of all Saharan language groups, and in 1940, after France fell to the Nazis, Chad was its first colony to rejoin the Allies. Its troops fought alongside British (and Libyan) soldiers in Libya, and captured Kufra from German forces.

It also has some reason to be optimistic about the future, after the discovery of oil – and rather more importantly the means to extract it – within its borders.

But Chad was not a nation born in peace, and its own history – even more than its geography – may be the greatest challenge it now faces.

In 1960, when the French ceded control, the state was led by the left-wing, radical, Chadian Progressive Party (PPT). Its leader, Francois Tombalbaye, the first President of an independent Chad, set the scene for all politics within his state for five decades to come.

He was a dictator who in 1962 banned all political parties other than the PPT, and filled Chad's jails with thousands of political prisoners. As a Southerner, he was also accused by residents of Chad's north and central regions of discriminating against them, and in November 1965, the population of Geura Prefecture rose in revolt against what it thought were unfair taxes.

Tombalbaye's military crushed the revolt, killing 500 people in the process.

But across Chad's eastern border, in Sudan, the National Liberation Front of Chad (FROLINAT) was set up and trained. It invaded Chad in 1966, sparking nine years of bitter warfare.

Tombalbaye first turned to France, whose troops had limited success against the invaders and insurgents, and then to his fellow left-winger, Libyan leader Muammar Ghaddafi.

Ghaddafi, in a stance against the colonial influence of France on Libya's southern neighbour, had been supplying some rebel groups with arms and financial assistance. Tombalbaye's alliance with the state cut that supply, and gave him an advantage in the struggle.

But although it was enough to keep him in power, the alliance between Libya and Chad was not enough to end the war, and the emnity it generated from other states proved to be the most important single factor of the next four decades in Chad.

In the relatively short-term, it was Tombalbaye himself who caused his regime most problems. As a Southerner, he had deliberately promoted people from the South of Chad to all positions of public responsibility: the army, the civil service and the PPT were entirely run by Southerners.

His alliance with Ghaddafi, who sent troops to quell uprisings in the north of Chad, meant that even under attack from FROLINAT, Tombalbaye's position was secure as long as the South remained loyal to him. But in April 1975, after his hardline policies began to bite even in the south, the armed forces rose in a coup, killing the President and replacing him with the junta's leader General Felix Malloum.

Malloum's position was little more secure than Tombalbaye's had been. Hissene Habre, a former commander of FROLINAT, and by this time leader of the Forces Armees du Nord (FAN), launched a series of attacks on the Chadian capital N'Djamena, destabilising and threatening to destroy the Malloum government.

In response, in 1978, Malloum appointed Habre as his Prime Minister. But Habre was unsatisfied. A year later, during an internal governmental dispute, he sent his forces once again to attack the Chadian army, sparking a three-year Civil War which saw 11 Chadian groups, plus forces from several other states, struggle for power.

Late in 1979, seeing that the state's government was all but powerless, the Organisation of African Unity set up talks designed to bring the Chadian Civil War to an end.

The talks appeared successful, with a new transitional government set up under Northerner Goukouni Oueddi as President, Southerner Colonel Kamougue as Prime Minister and Habre as Minister of Defence.

The government lasted fewer than three weeks. In January 1980, Habre again attacked the state of which he was a high-ranking government member, and it took almost an entire year for Oueddi and the Chadian army to regain control of N'Djamena.

The Libyan government under Ghaddafi had armed and assisted Chad's army to enable the government to regain control of the state, and Libyan forces were as a result effectively in control of large sections of the north of Chad by this point.

In January 1981, Oueddi and Ghaddafi issued a joint statement that they were working together for the complete unification of Chad with Libya.

Ghaddafi's plans have, in the West, been systematically attributed to megalomania and military expansionism.

It is easy to understand why: he was a man who referred to himself as 'Colonel' even though the title was at best a 'gift' from his own military. He had seized power in a coup and spoke of leading a unified, socialist, Africa.

But Ghaddafi was also a politician who believed much of what he said.

He had deposed a corrupt and tyrannical monarch in his own country, used its vast oil income to attempt to help his nation's poorest improve their health, education and prospects, and envisaged for Africa an opportunity to unite and develop, away from the intrigues, financial shackles and outright demands of former and potential future colonial powers.

There are entirely appropriate questions about whether he was the right man to lead that process – or even whether his view was right at all. One could also ask whether his own later economic co-operation with China could be seen as allowing a new colonist to access one of North Africa's wealthiest markets.

But there are alternatives to the Western view of Ghaddafi – that he was, or was solely, a mad, militaristic dictator – and there were reasons why many people in an Africa staggering out of the dark years of colonial rule saw him in a different light.

One man who did not hold a positive view of Ghaddafi was Habre. And his outlook was strengthened by the entrance into Chadian politics of the capitalist West's richest and most powerful state.

At this point, late in 1981, the former PM and Defence Minister was camped on Chad's border with Sudan. His forces had been defeated – though not routed – by the united troops of Chad's government and Ghaddafi's Libyan forward guard, and he had fallen back to regroup, retrain and strengthen his army.

It is impossible to be sure whether he could ever have delivered his planned coup d'état alone. He arguably faced more challenges than reasons for optimism, not least a growing sense of his inability to prosecute a successful campaign following two failed attempts to seize power.

But at this point, the CIA stepped in and offered him a 'golden ticket' – the full assistance of the US government.

Alexander Haig, the US Secretary of State, was on record that his country wished to 'bloody Ghaddafi's nose' and 'increase the flow of pine boxes to Libya'.

In Habre, it believed it had found its opportunity. The CIA's Khartoum station chief visited Habre's camp and promised US assistance for his coup, as long as the new President agreed to support the Reagan administration's desire to embarrass and destabilise Ghaddafi by killing Libyan servicemen.

Weapons and cash duly delivered, Habre succeeded where he had failed twice before, and seized power. It was for him third time lucky. It was to prove a less celebrated chapter in the history of Chad.

With American dollars and American weapons, including 12 'Stinger' systems – shoulder-mounted anti-aircraft weapons never before used in Africa – delivered by US C141 Starlifter aircraft, Habre set about attempting to remove Libyan soldiers from northern Chad. At the same time, the US recruited from within Chad a small group of Libyans – mainly armed with Warsaw Pact weapons – who formed an anti-Ghaddafi force, the Libyan National Salvation Front.

At this stage, the group was little more than a token 'Libyan anti-Ghaddafi' addition to Habre's offensive. Habre never fully succeeded in expelling Libyan troops, but his initiative did kill 10,000 uniformed soldiers from Ghaddafi's regime. As well as the US weapons, this was possible in part because of the increased mobility afforded his forces by Toyota Hilux 4x4s provided by the CIA. The vehicles' descendants are now favoured by international aid organisations across the Sahara region.

The success of the campaign earned Habre an invitation to the White House, where he met and discussed African affairs with a delighted Reagan.

Nobody can say whether Reagan or his administration were aware that at the same time, Habre appears to have been using his US-provided power and weapons to crush people within his own borders.

Human rights organisations estimate that in his eight years as Chad's President, Habre used weapons and starvation to kill 40,000 Chadians – four times more Chadians than the 10,000 Libyan deaths for which he was congratulated by Reagan's regime. He engaged in periodic ethnic cleansing of tribal groups including the Sera, Hadjera and Zaghawa.

Human Rights Watch described him as 'Africa's Pinochet' and a senior US official told the US newspaper the Washington Post in November 2000 that: 'Habre was a remarkably able man with a brilliant sense of how to play the outside world. He was also a bloodthirsty tyrant and torturer. It is fair to say we knew who and what he was and chose to turn a blind eye.'

It is notable that the only discernible differences between Habre's crimes, and those for which the West castigated and claimed to oppose Ghaddafi is that the Chadian dictator killed more of his own people, and had the support of the US government while he did so.

In July 2013, Hissene Habre was arrested in Dakar on charges of crimes against humanity. At the time of writing, he is still awaiting trial.

Even with US assistance and the violent repression he used to retain power, Habre's dictatorship was never completely secure.

The Southern-based rebel commando groups known as Codos who had fought against him remained a powerful force for two years after he seized power, and were only broken up in 1984.

In 1985, Habre rebuilt relations with the Democratic Front of Chad, the Coordinating Action Committee of the Democratic Revolutionary Council and even with Oueddi – which enabled one of Habre's most successful periods against Libyan forces, pushing them almost over the border into Libya. But this was a short-lived peace, and regional tensions between Hadjerai, Gorane and Zaghawa tribal groups led to the uprisings which finally ended Habre's rule.

In April 1989, General Idriss Deby, a Zaghawa from Northern Chad, left Habre's government and camped in Darfur, Sudan. From there, he launched a series of attacks on Habre.

The US government supported Habre's attempts to resist the attempted coup, but in December 1990, with the help of Libyan troops – and after the French government ordered its own soldiers not to intervene – Deby's forces marched on and seized N'Djamena.

In 1991, Deby was confirmed as President, and his Patriotic Salvation Movement (MPS) as Chad's government.

In the next two years, Deby escaped two attempts on his life, battling with four armed groups within Chad.

In 1994, the same year the International Court of Justice demanded Ghaddafi's Libyan troops leave Chad (they left before the year's end), a short-lived peace deal was struck – only to be rendered almost meaningless as new groups formed to strike at Deby's Presidency.

In 1996, two elections were held, confirming Deby as President, and MPS as the main party of government. These were Chad's first elections since 1960, and the first time the state had allowed more than one political party since 1962, but the results were strongly contested, with international observers noting serious irregularities at polling stations, during vote counts, and in the announcement of results.

The election did little to calm the violent resistance within Chad. Each time an armed group was defeated or agreed to end hostilities, as in 1997 (the year the Cameroon and Central African Republic-backed FARF and MDD, as well as the National Front of Chad and Movement for Social Justice and Democracy all accepted defeat and/or agreed to end violence) then an agreement elsewhere would fall apart, or a new group would rise.

Deby made some economic progress. The discovery of oil in the 1990s and its exploitation since 2000 generated badly-needed cash, and in 2001, he secured debt-relief for the state. But fighting continues to this day, and has killed hundreds of civilians, rebels and government forces.

In May 2001, Deby won a second Presidential election which was as widely criticised as the first, and had six opposition leaders arrested for accusing the government of fraud. One opposition party activist was killed after the election results were announced.

In 2003, fighting between government forces and rebels in Darfur, Sudan, caused more than 200,000 people to flee across the border into Chad.

In some cases, they brought with them the battles which were being fought in Darfur, and it is believed – at least by Deby's government – that the Khartoum-based Sudanese regime deliberately planted its agents, along with disaffected Chadians, within Chad to incite further unrest, in order to gain influence over it.

In 2005, an attack on Adre, close to Chad's border with Sudan, inspired Deby's government to declare war on 'the common enemy'. Deby's regime believed the Sudanese government had attacked Adre, and chose to attack the Rally for Democracy and Liberty.

The Rally was a resistance group based in Chad, but funded from Khartoum and which included members of the Janjaweed, a Sudanese militia which had been used by the Khartoum regime to crush resistance – and commit genocide – in Darfur.

Sudanese Foreign Minister Jamal Mohammed Ibrahim almost denied his government had anything to do with the attack on Adre, saying: 'We technically deny involvement in Chadian internal affairs.'

As the war continued, several different rebel groups became involved, including Islamic groups declaring jihad, as well as political and tribally-motivated forces.

Early in 2009, eight rebel groups which had united behind Deby's nephew and former chief of staff Timane Erdimi, attacked but were repelled from N'Djamena.

Just over one year later, in February 2010, under pressure from the UN, Deby met Sudan's President, Omar al-Bashir, and one month later, the border between Chad and Sudan opened for the first time in seven years.

But though the war had ended, within Chad things were little more stable. In April 2011, as Tunisia and Libya embarked on what later become known as the Arab Spring, opposition groups in Chad boycotted the general election. Deby was re-elected.

The US government, meanwhile, proved it was not yet finished with Chad.

The Obama regime responded to the Libyan uprising by flying the members of the Libyan National Salvation Front to enter battle against Ghaddafi.

In July 2011, Senegal, to which Habre had fled when removed from power in Chad, suspended his repatriation to the state, where he was to face charges of crimes against humanity. Twenty five months later, the US-backed dictator was arrested on charges of crimes against humanity.

I was left with a family. I did not know why. My father was already gone, and my mother was very sad. She said she loved me and I had to go away with my uncle. She said I could never return to my home again. She said she had to go away as well and she would come to get me, but she did not come.

Ever since she left me, I have had one dream. I have just wanted to ask her, why did you leave me? Why did you leave me alone and not come for me? I have wondered all my life, since I was nine.

My uncle took me away. He was scared. I did not know why, but he gave me to another family, who he knew would be going to Libya. We went by car, to a place called Sabha. It is in the South of the country, near to my home country of Chad.

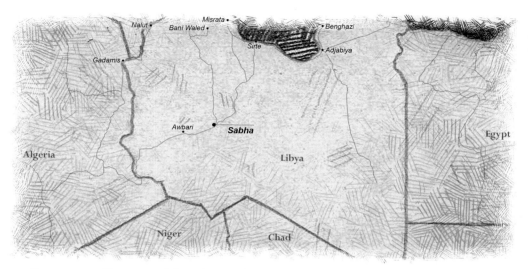

I was very sad because I did not know where my father was, and I did not understand why my mother was not there. But the family was very kind to me, and that made me happy. They would not talk to me about my mother or father, but they were kind and they treated me well.

We got papers to live in Libya and I think the way we lived was good. The adults worked and me and the two children went to school. But one day they left. They were afraid of the revolution in Libya, so they went back to Chad.

I was afraid as well, but I was more scared of Chad. I knew I must not go back there. It is something my mother said, and my uncle, and the family I lived with: 'You cannot go back. The government will find you.'

But I was afraid of the revolution in Libya. I had been nine when a revolution happened in Chad and I had lost my father and mother and uncle and my whole country, Chad. And in the new revolution in Libya I already lost the family who cared for me and my life in Libya.

So I ran away. I had papers so I could travel through Libya and the family left me some money so I could pay people to drive me. It took a month because it was a long way and because there was fighting. I could hear bombs, more when I travelled further north. And some drivers were too scared to drive.

But in June, I got to the border and I walked the last few miles to the camp. I knew there was a camp because I had been told by people on the way and because I saw it once on the television. I think being on my own in the journey helped me because I had never been alone before but I arrived here alone and I live in a tent by myself here.

The first few weeks were hard. They asked where I was from and I didn't say Chad, I said Libya. It meant some people hated me and they hit me sometimes and used to wake me by shouting outside my tent and throwing things.

I did not say anything but people from UNHCR found out and they moved me to this part of the camp where I live. It is better because there are people here from Chad and no-one is violent or angry with me.

I also met some people from Save the Children. They asked me 'Where are your family?' and I said 'Chad' because I didn't know where my mother and father were and I told them about the family who looked after me. But then they asked me 'Why did they not come to the camp with you?'

So I told them about my father not being there and my mother disappearing and my uncle giving me to a family and then the family running away from the revolution.

I told them about my dream, to speak to my mother again and find out why she had left me.

They made me write my name and some other things.

One month later they asked me to see them. I thought I was going to be moved away from the camp. Lots of people have left the camp since I came here.

But they asked me to sit down and they explained a man had come to the camp with a message. He said my name and said my mother wanted to speak to me. He said the woman had seen the revolution on the television and knew I had been in Libya, so she wanted to see if I was in one of the camps.

He gave them a number. They had called the lady and she said she was my mother. When they told me, I thought she was here and I looked around and they said 'No, she is not here. She wants to come but we think it would be good if you can speak to her on the telephone first. Do you want to?'

I said 'yes' and then I thought I did not want to. I was too nervous. I was afraid to ask her what I wanted to, why she had left me and not come back. I was afraid of what she would say, or if it would make her angry. But I had already said 'yes' and I did want to talk to her very much, so I did not tell anyone I was nervous. I sat down on the ground and talked.

It was my mother. She talked to me and said the words she said when she left, that she would come to get me. She said she had come to get me. She was crying. I cried a little as well. I tried to stop myself, but I could not.

I asked her why she left me behind, and why she did not come back to find me.

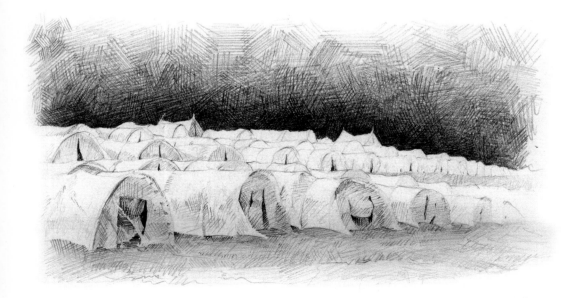

She cried some more. She told me that in 2003, things had been very bad for her and my father. They had arrested my father for opposing the government. I said I thought he worked for the government, but she said he had worked for a previous government.

He had spoken out against the new government and so when the revolution started they had arrested him. My mother knew that they would arrest her as well, soon, because she had opposed the new government. So she gave me to my uncle and told him to make sure I went to Libya.

Then, she escaped to the Central African Republic.

After the revolution ended in Chad, she had contacted my uncle and he explained where I had gone. Then, when the revolution happened in Libya, she came to Sabha, to find me. But I had gone. In the town, they told her I had gone to this camp, so she sent a man to find out whether I was here.

We had to stop speaking after that, because I was crying and she was too. She called me again on my birthday and she explained that I could leave the camp when I get a paper to say I can, and that we could meet and be together again.

I am very excited. I am really eager to meet my mother. We have a lot of things to say to each other. I have so many questions to ask her. I cannot remember what she looks like.

Choucha Camp

My Father

When I was 12, I left school to become a painter. I wanted to leave school, because it reminded me too much of my father.

He died of a heart attack when he was driving me and my brothers to school. I also had to leave school because when my father died, my family had no money. So I became a painter.

My father and mother are Palestinians, and so am I. They met in Jordan at a camp like this one and they married.

They left Jordan just after I was born and we moved to Zawiyah in Libya.

We were not happy there, because we wanted to live in Palestine, but we could not because the land we lived in was taken away by Israel. So my parents had lived in tents. Libya was better than that, but although I had friends and went to school, for my family, Libya could not be home.

When I was 12, my father explained to me that I should be pleased to live in Libya, which was a good place, but that he could not because it was his second choice. He chose to live there, but he could not live in the place he loved, because the land had been taken away.

He did not seem angry, just sad.

He wanted to return to Palestine with us, he told us.

He worked as a mechanic, and he earned enough money, so we had a house and a car and we could eat enough food. I went to school and played with people. My father told me it was important to go to school, but I liked it anyway, so even if he had not told me, I think I would have tried hard to learn.

We used to like to have breakfast together, my father, my mother, me, my sister and my brothers, and then before he went to work he would drive us to school.

One day, he pulled over to the side of the road and I asked what was wrong. He was hurt and said to call a hospital. So I ran to a house and called for an ambulance.

It arrived and took him to the hospital. We went to school, but my father died.

It was four years ago.

Because of this, my family had no money. I tried to go to school, which my mother wanted. She knew that would make my father happy. But I could not be there. I hated it. It just reminded me of my father.

It made me feel angry because I was so sad and I didn't want to be there and I knew that my father would want me to be there and to learn, but I could not. I was too sad, and too angry.

Also, we had no money. So someone had to get a job. My sister is older than me, but she was married and so she lived with her husband. So I had to work. I did not mind.

I became a painter. I would paint people's houses for them and sometimes I also painted cars at garages. They are different jobs but I liked to do them. I earned money, but now I think it would have been better to go to school. I couldn't go there at that time, though. I had to earn money and I was too angry and sad about my father.

When the trouble started in Libya, my mother wanted us to go to Jordan. But she asked us whether we wanted to go. I was 15. I am 16 now. I said I wanted to try to stay in Libya. We were sad, but she agreed and she left for Jordan. But things became worse in Libya, so my sister and her husband, their baby and I came to the camp here.

It is better here. At first, I found it hard. I was quite angry with other people and I tried to fight with them. But I went to the Save the Children centre. It is good there, because there is a school. It is not the same as the one I went to when I was a child and I like it very much. I like to learn French, because it is a new language to me, and I also like to help the younger children with Maths and with problems.

It is better because I am not alone any more. So now, I hope I can learn enough. My teachers say I am doing very well, and I want to learn enough so that I can run my own business. It would be decorating people's houses. I think that will make my father proud and I know my mother would be happy. That will make me happy as well.

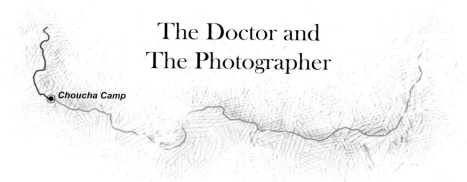

The Doctor and
The Photographer

Choucha Camp

One afternoon, some of the staff at the Save the Children centre at Choucha Camp are making fun of you for your poor performance in a volleyball game which is still going on behind you.

They do not notice you looking over their shoulders, through the wire fencing into the camp's vast living area.

A small boy picks up a rock, walks once around the family tent of another boy, raises the rock above his head, walks to the entrance and…

… by then you are there. He looks up into your face, surprised that the rock he was holding is not now hurtling into the tent to strike his foe, then looks at the rock, which you and he now both hold. He glares at you for several seconds, then turns and walks purposefully away.

You had spoken to the boy for the first time only that afternoon. He is a very quiet (child protection staff tell me he said his first words to them only two weeks earlier, after three months of silence) and self-possessed boy, stocky, strong, but almost always alone.

He came into a supply tent where you had just been speaking – in fact listening – to a young man who told you the story of how he lost his family, his homeland, his wife and several times his freedom, of being tortured, and of how his life had been saved in a way nobody would expect.

He had finished, thanked you, clenched his fist, thumped his heart twice, kissed his hand and clasped it over yours, then walked out to play volleyball with the shouting, laughing youngsters outside on the Saharan sand.

By contrast, you were left behind, attempting to collect your thoughts and process what you had just heard.

A shaft of light enters the tent as the boy pulls back the entrance flaps, silhouetting him against the sun, sky and sand outside. He looks around, walks over to a box, and tries to lift the lid. Finding it is locked, he takes the padlock in his hand, and examines it, slowly turning it over.

The first time he gives any indication he has seen you is when he walks over to the bench where you are sitting watching him, and holds out his hand.

You do not understand. He shows me the padlock. And points to a group of youngsters playing football outside. 'I want to play', he says.

You open the box, he leans in, picks up a ball, and walks outside. In the doorway, he turns and looks back. 'No problem', you say. He steps out, and begins kicking the ball to himself, until, moments later – and perhaps exasperated by his continual infringement onto 'their' pitch – the other footballers invite him to join them in their game.

It is only later that you realise it hadn't even occurred to you to ask him why the other children had not let him play right away. It is several hours later that a member of the child protection team explains that he had not asked them to.

He is six, although in his silence and self-containment, he seems considerably older than that. When he was eight months old, a baby in Somalia, where his parents were born, his mother died.

It is impossible to be sure of the effects of a mother's death on a boy so young, but his father confirmed that from that day, he was a different child: 'He had been happy. He smiled a lot, for a baby. And he liked it when other people were nearby. But suddenly, that stopped. He became tearful, and when other people were there, he would be silent.'

At school, he remained withdrawn. Though he was able to read and write, he sat in silence while other children played and learned around him.

His father, having experienced years of war, lawlessness and danger, decided they would have to leave their homeland, and so, in 2009, they arrived in Abu Salim, a district of Tripoli.

His father had planned to stay there. He had found work, they had a home, and while nobody pretended the boy enjoyed school, he was performing well, overcoming the language and cultural differences he faced without ever seeming to notice they existed.

But in early 2011, faced with revolution, a potential Civil War, his father, who in common with many of his countrymen and their fellow emigrants to Libya had experienced the grim consequences of years of war, escaped.

On 6th March 2011, with the help of the Somali Embassy in Libya, the boy and his father entered Choucha Camp. It was the third place the boy had been supposed to call home in just six years.

His father is open about the choice he took: 'We had to leave,' he said. 'But when we arrived I feared for my son. It was chaotic here. The camp was almost all single men, refugees. I was a single man and a refugee myself, but I had lost my wife and I had a small boy. How would other men be able to relate to that? How could my son be safe?'

Every day, father and son walked to the Save the Children centre, a group of tent classrooms and play spaces pitched around a central space for outdoor activities for youngsters. The boy never came alone, because his father feared he would not be comfortable, but also because he wanted to ensure his son would be safe at the centre.

The boy was no more convinced than his father. He said: 'It was strange, so I did not want to leave my father. I did not want to be alone with these other people.'

He was quiet, withdrawn and alone. He sat alone during lessons, and refused to answer questions. And when other children played, he sat in the sand, appearing not to watch.

But he is a six year-old boy. Despite seeming to want to stay alone, he has worked out ways to be allowed to play. And, it turns out, he is a keen photographer.

Handed a camera, he stalked the camp. He took photos of other children, of adults he knew and liked, of himself, smiling, and most often, of the sky.

'I like the sky most of all,' he said. 'I like it when people are in the camera. But most of all, I like it when I can see the sky when I look up, and when I look at the camera.'

There is another boy who visits the centre every day and grabs visitors' attention.

At ten, he is only slightly taller than the photographer, and unlike him, he is always surrounded – or more accurately followed – by others.

He is always on the move, three or four boys of a similar age in tow, covering every square inch of sand, seemingly driven by some irresistible urge to reach a new destination, helping a smaller girl climb the ladder of the slide here, pushing a younger boy on the swing there, and on occasion lifting distressed toddlers with one or more of his friends, and carrying them to the nearest member of staff.

He seems to be consumed by an unquestioning – in fact subconscious – self-confidence.

A journalist visiting the Camp remarked that he could imagine the boy in 20 years, wearing military fatigues and waving to crowds from the balcony of a palace he'd recently liberated from a previous dictator. You were surprised to admit you could imagine the same thing.

In fact, his aim is rather more peaceful: 'I want to be a doctor,' he said, hands flat, palm down on the table, and flanked by two companions. 'It is a good job. People say you can be rich, but I would like to make people better. That is why I would like to do it.'

He is from Sudan: 'But I was born in Libya. My family moved to Libya when my sister was very young, so I lived in Libya all my life. I went to school in Libya. I like Libya, but not as much as Libyans do.'

He arrived with his family, his father, mother, one brother and one sister, on 6th April.

'I was nervous,' he said. 'Because it is a new place for me. I needed to make new friends. My mother and father said we should come to this education centre every day, and I am glad. It means I have friends, and I like this school. It is good. It does not have every subject and I want to learn all subjects, but there are things to learn and to do. It is interesting.'

He says his favourite subjects are Maths and English, and his teachers, stood nearby, nod in agreement when he says he has improved at both (his English is close to flawless).

'I am glad we came here,' he said. 'Though I do not know why we did. But I am glad, because I have made very good friends here. My friends here are like my brothers, and we help each other. We help other people as well. That's why I want to be a doctor, to help people.'

Later that day, as the 'photographer' walks away from me, and the tent outside which he had stood with his rock, the 'doctor' appears, stands at the tent doorway, looks at him, then at you, holds up his hand, smiles, and slips inside.

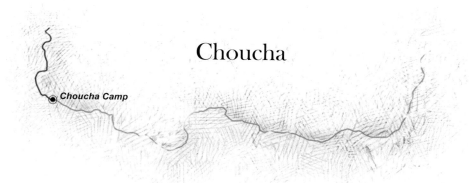

Choucha

Choucha Camp

Although there is no such thing as a 'right' place for a refugee camp, there are certainly criteria to make a wrong one – and Choucha Camp's location fulfils them all.

In the last weeks of 2011, the camp contains slightly more than 7,000 people, mainly sub-Saharan Africans, and the majority of those from Somalia, Eritrea, Ethiopia, Sudan and Chad. It is a familiar list to people who work in international aid, international news reporting and – very likely – international arms dealing and people trafficking.

But though the number of its inhabitants and their nationalities are not unusual, the camp's position, and as a result its brief history, are.

In part, this is because the first people to set up a camp here knew they were not likely to stay here long.

And so it proved. Egyptians based West of Benghazi, where the first exchanges of the Libyan Civil War took place, found themselves trapped behind an active war frontier, with their homeland and safety (however temporary that was to prove), beyond.

Leaving by the quickest route, across the Eastern border and directly into Egypt, was not an option. Instead, they went West, crossing into Tunisia, from where they knew they would be flown home within weeks.

Crossing the border on North Africa's great Roman Road, they travelled just 9km before stopping to await word from their government, head West to Tunis and other airports, and fly home to Egypt.

From their point of view, the location was perfect: close to the border, so they did not have to travel any further than necessary before settling, immediately beside North Africa's major road to make travel easy, opposite a military hospital to ensure treatment was on hand in the event of any emergency, and just 20km from the nearest town, ensuring there would be no shortage of food, clothing and water during their brief stay.

For the 80,000-100,000 people who passed through the Camp in the first month it existed, the arrangement worked.

But Egyptians were by no means Libya's only immigrant population. And they were followed to Choucha by its sub-Saharan Africans. For them, destined to be trapped at Choucha for many months, the Camp's location proved an increasingly large problem.

Refugees had arrived in Libya throughout the previous 40 years, seeking safety from war, terror and torture in their own countries of birth.

They were not exactly illegal. Libya's leader Colonel Muammar Ghaddafi had expressly invited people from across the continent he hoped one day to lead – especially those threatened at home – to settle in the North African state. But they were also not exactly legal, as few had identification papers, official visas or passports.

Seeing the outbreak of a Civil – and to an extent an international – War, they recalled the worst days of their homelands, and with grim determination, prepared to flee once again.

The route East remained largely cut off: if there was a single 'front', it was at this stage close to Benghazi, Libya's second city, where one man's sacrifice had sparked a city-wide uprising against Ghaddafi's premiership, and saw the city effectively remove itself from his command.

Ghaddafi's forces battled to regain entry to and control of the city – only foiled in the end by NATO air and sea strikes – at the same time as attempting to crush armed and peaceful protest.

As the country's 'semi-citizens' prepared to flee, they knew they must travel West, and on TV they saw images of the camp the Egyptians had made: Choucha.

They streamed across the border into Tunisia; mainly men at first, but later on families, single women and in many cases youngsters who had been separated from their parents, or had never left with them to begin with, came in increasing number.

Some experienced harassment and detention by soldiers and armed police as they attempted to enter Tunisia, but in most cases they crossed without difficulty: the officials were increasingly focussed on the likelihood they would be called to fight, so why should they care about forcing those fleeing war to remain within Libya?

Even for those who did care about such a thing, how could so small a number police an entire desert border?

Exhausted, hungry, and in many cases suffering as a result of the beatings and other torture inflicted upon them on their long march from Libya, the refugees settled at Choucha.

Unlike the Egyptians, who had only to await government-funded aircraft to take them home, these people knew there would be no quick resolution to their struggle for survival.

Most of them could not go 'home' – what awaited them there was war, torture or death, if there was even a state or government recognisable as such to which they could return.

But Choucha is vulnerable. So close to the border, it was a potential target for armed raiders –revolutionary khetibas fighting against Ghaddafi's rule and soldiers fighting for the leader alike – to lash out against people they could argue were different from them.

The possibility of such raids succeeding was increased by the fact that Tunisia was itself struggling to realign itself following its own revolution – the uprising which had sparked the entire 'Arab Spring'. That it was doing so remarkably swiftly (a democratically-elected government, charged with creating Tunisia's new constitution, was in place just weeks after Ghaddafi was shot in Sirte) was of little consolation, or reassurance, to those within the camp who noted with alarm the inconsistent policing of the border by Tunisian officers.

In common with many new democracies, Tunisia had produced a government containing several groups with divergent outlooks – ranging from Islamic hardliners to secular politicians of left- and right-ist persuasion.* This increased the pressure each group felt to be truly 'representative' of the Tunisian people.

* Tunisia, in common with much of North Africa's West Mediterranean coastal region, reflects a cultural duality which may be the result of Western – largely French – influence on previously Islamic, Arabic-influenced states, but could equally be the product of societies which have learned to pick and choose between the cultures of invading groups, from North and East, which have settled there over the past 2,000 years.

France ceded the state in 1956, leaving Habib Bourgiba as leader. Bourgiba swiftly strengthened his position, becoming in the process a virtual dictator, but also introduced compulsory free education, abolished polygamy and extended women's rights in the state beyond those enjoyed in any of what is misleadingly known as the 'Arab World' – except perhaps in Libya.

Many Tunisians are truly faithful and ardent Muslims, but Bourgiba insisted on an anti-fundamentalist version of the faith throughout 'his' state. He also – largely through making the most of French tourist potential – created a relatively strong economy, though it must be noted that 'relatively' here means by African rather than global standards.

As a result of these factors, most of the population regularly meets and interacts with Westerners, particularly tourists from France, and while it is unusual to see Tunisian women – outside of perhaps the largest resorts in the state – in swimming costumes, Westerners stroll topless along beaches even where the local community is made up of a mosque, 20 houses and a coffee shop. This is not protested, or even mentioned, by the Tunisian population.

The Tunisian elections of 2011 reflected the nature of such a society, with votes won by 'secular democratic' parties (who did not necessarily agree about how the state's economy should be run), and 'fundamentalist' Islamic groups, who desired a state run with their religion as the main inspiration for laws and social structure.

The largest proportion of votes – equating to 90 out of the 217 seats on the new Constituent Assembly – was won by Ennahda, a part of the international Muslim Brotherhood movement.

Ennahda presented itself as a 'moderate' Islamic party, believing in Islam's importance to the state, but committed to laws and 'codes of behaviour' based on secular, rather than religious, ideas of society.

Because the election had given no true mandate for any one political party or organisation, most parties urgently sought an issue around which the public would rally. Many eyes, sadly but predictably, turned to Choucha's population, fleeing a war they did not start, played no part in, and fled because they had already experienced warfare and societal breakdown elsewhere.

From October 2011, when the Assembly first met, and many of the refugees had spent close to 250 nights under canvas, there were consistent messages from elected politicians about 'resolving the problem' of the 20,000 or so homeless men, women and children tucked just inside the state's Eastern border, on the edge of a vast, inhospitable desert. This had not been a major election promise of any party. But such proposals seemed to reflect the attitudes of many of the people living in the nearest large town to Choucha Camp, Ben Guardane.

Ben Guardane had a largely deserved reputation as Tunisia's most politically active town. If there was a rebellion, a revolt or any serious political protest, it generally originates, or plays itself out in, Tunisia's easternmost town. The people of the town revel in their reputation, and some seemed to feel genuinely confused and unhappy that it had been a man in Sidi Bouzid, rather than one of their own, who sparked the revolt which brought down the government of Zine al-Abidine Ben Ali. But the issue primary to their assessment of Choucha Camp was more prosaic: road access to Libya.

Ben Guardane relies much more on Libya, just 29km to its east, than on other parts of its own state for trade and employment. Its people need the Roman road, upon which Choucha Camp also sits, to cross the border for income.

At first, many within the town had hoped the Camp would generate new employment. But as it became clear that the international aid organisations who responded to the Camp's urgent food, medicine, education, hygiene and water supply requirements were not employing solely from the immediate area, the town's mildly optimistic attitude towards Choucha changed.

And by May 2011, parts of its population were ready to take matters into their own hands.

At 4am on 24th May, several days into a simmering dispute between members of Choucha's Sudanese and Eritrean communities, four Eritrean refugees were burned alive in their tents.

It is still not certain exactly who was responsible for this crime: agencies within the Camp investigated, but never revealed whether they had found the people responsible. No arrests were made.

The Eritrean community was furious, blaming the Sudanese people within the Camp for the attack, while the Sudanese community strongly denied any responsibility. Leading members of the Camp's Chadian and Somalian groups mediated with the Eritreans and Sudanese, respectively, and a wider conflict was avoided – though four people were dead.

But the incident had other effects: the Nigerians within the Camp, increasingly distressed that they were being told they could 'go home' and that therefore they were not considered a priority for international resettlement, were also now alarmed at the prospect that they may be forced to spend years in an enclosed space in which ethnic tensions would lead to an ever-greater number of violent incidents.

Making demands which included greater consideration of their country's situation, and a restructure of the Camp on national and cultural lines, instead of the simple division between single men and families which was then in place, the Nigerian community launched a concerted protest.

Within Choucha's boundaries, this took the form of disrupting food queues, noisy protests outside the offices of some of the international organisations working at the camp and marches through its living areas. But the community believed its actions would have no effect if restricted solely to Choucha itself.

In the hope of 'encouraging' Tunisian authorities to force change to the way the camp was run, the protestors took their campaign to the wider community, by blockading the Roman road outside.

The road was blocked for just two days, but for the people of Ben Guardane, already increasingly angered by Choucha's existence so close to their town, and disappointed that it had not delivered them the jobs some had hoped it would, even two days of being unable to travel to trade and work was too much.

On the second night of the blockade, while the refugees slept, arsonists burned down two thirds of Choucha, killing hundreds of people, forcing hundreds more to flee, again, from mortal danger, and leaving thousands without even a tent to call home. It was disquieting to hear this story and realise that this inferno, which killed so many and destroyed the precarious feeling of security the second- third- and fourth-time refugees of Choucha had managed to snatch for themselves, was what young people and children had matter-of-factly mentioned only as part of their wider story.

Several times, a six or seven year-old would say something like: 'It was different before the fire. But then we moved.' Or: 'Where we used to live was good, but we moved to a new part of the camp when the new tents arrived.'

One girl, aged nine, did attempt to explain it: 'I woke up and people were screaming. I could see light moving through the tent wall and I could hear that it was fire. I came out, with my mum and dad and my baby sister. She was crying. So was my mum. But my dad didn't cry and so neither did I.

'People were just running around. They didn't know where to go. They were shouting out and falling over in the darkness. Some people tried to throw water on the fires but there was not enough water. It just wasted the water, my dad said.

'We stood still for some time. It seemed like a long time. My dad kept stepping forward but then stopping and looking at us. Then he picked me up. I cried out then because I didn't want to be picked up. But then I was quiet, because I could see that our tent was on fire as well, and I was very afraid.

'We went through the darkness, lit up by the fires everywhere and my dad left me and my mum and my sister in a safer place, where other people were. He went back to help people. Everyone was crying and screaming. It was very noisy and frightening and I think I did cry when my dad went away.

'All of the things we brought with us were burned and our tent was burned. We have a new tent but we have very few things now and it does make me feel sad. I am pleased that my sister, my mum and my dad are here and they are OK. The father of one of my friends died that night.

'For a long time after that I could not sleep, and sometimes I wake up crying. My mum tells me it is OK and strokes my hair. I know it is OK, but at night I am not so sure.'

A Tunisian working for an international aid organisation at the camp, added: 'People in Ben Guardane have a reputation for being out of control and this protest meant that they could not work and trade.

'But two-thirds of the camp was burned and so many things were changed. Lots of people died. It was hard for us to tell exactly how many because many people simply ran away, into the desert. Some of them came back, and we are sure some of them tried to cross to Europe by sea.

'Some of them may be alive still in Libya, or in Tunisia. But the desert is a hard place and some of them will not have survived it. The camp has not really recovered. We work hard, but things have changed a lot.

'Now, the camp is divided into communities, with fences between each area. It is only in a few places like the school where some people from different communities meet, when they bring their children. But even though we try to improve security with fences, people feel less safe than they did, and it is because everyone knows this is a collection of tents on the edge of the desert. The fences do not make it safe.

'The atmosphere is very different now, but our job is the same: to make sure people have somewhere new to live. We are working hard to make sure that happens, but we try to make their lives as good as possible as well.'

It remains impossible to say whether the fire which killed so many of the refugee population at Choucha was started by Ben Guardane residents, because even six months later, Tunisian police had announced no suspects, made no arrests and seemed not even to be investigating the crime. Despite repeated rumour and accusation, no-one in Ben Guardane has ever chosen to respond.

The Dancer

Choucha Camp

Before the revolution, I was a dance teacher.

Children would come to me to learn how to move to music, in traditional and modern dances. I loved to teach them and they enjoyed the lessons.

When I was younger, I had learned to dance at school in Tunisia. It was interesting, because at my school, in the same way as we learned and were taught in French for one half of the year,* and learned and were taught in Arabic for the other half, so we learned Western dance in one half of the year and Arabic dance in the other half.

The policy of teaching in French for one half of the year, and in Arabic for the other, is standard at all Tunisian state schools. It means that other foreign languages – including English – are taught to students in two extremely different languages. I did not see any evidence that this hampered people's abilities to speak several different languages.

It had not occurred to me to think it would be confusing, until I taught my own classes. I enjoyed it, and I found that what I learned in one style could help me in the other.

I taught at a small dance school on the coast, in a town tourists regularly visited. Life was good there. We would do the things we did every day, and many of the tourists were nice and made it a more interesting place to live. I think I would have stayed there a long time, until I married, or maybe even after then, if the revolution had not happened.

I have spoken to some people who do not know very much about what happened here in Tunisia. I can understand because things were not the same as in Libya, but the revolution here was frightening at times. At first, I think lots of us, even the younger ones, looked at Tarek* on the television and thought he was just another person who was protesting. But when you watched what happened next, you could see he was a different man, and what he did was so surprising that people took notice.

On 17th December 2010, Tarek al-Tayed Mohamed Bouazizi, enraged by what he saw as unwarranted harassment and mistreatment by police and government officials, set fire to himself in front of the offices of the governor of Sidi Bouzid. He suffered 90 per cent burns and died almost three weeks later. He was 26.

Bouazizi, who is now credited as the inspiration for the entire 'Arab Spring' was a vegetable salesman. He had repeatedly complained that he was being victimised by police and local officials.

On 16th December 2010, he had agreed to pay $200 for fruit and veg which he would sell in the next month from his mobile stand (after paying for the goods, he earned $140 per month, which he used to support his mother, uncle and six siblings. His father had died while working on a construction project in Libya). But the following morning, police apprehended him, confiscating his goods, stand and electronic scales. They said it was because he had no vendors' licence: Sidi Bouzid's state office has since confirmed he did not need one.

It has been suggested that the officers were looking for a bribe, but Bouazizi could not pay. Instead, he went to the municipal office, where he was refused the return of his possessions and, his family says, was insulted and beaten by staff. The latter claims are denied by the municipal office.

He went to the governor's office and when he was told the governor would not see him, ran to buy petrol, returned, and crying 'How am I supposed to make a living?' took the action which not only ended his life, but also inspired the overthrow of governments in Tunisia, Libya, and Egypt, protests in Morocco, Algeria, Palestine, Yemen, Oman, and the Syrian Civil War.

He was taken to hospital in a coma, and large numbers of Tunisians, mainly young people at first, took to the streets in angry protest. When he died on 5th January 2011, the crowds intensified their response. Within nine days, their entire government had been removed.

The Tunisian dictator, Zine al-Abdine Ben Ali, had come to power in 1987, when previous dictator Habib Bourgiba had been dismissed on the grounds of senility.

Like Bourgiba, Ben Ali was a strong opponent of Islamic fundamentalism. His regime introduced some press freedoms and freed a number of political prisoners, but won three elections with an officially-announced total of 99.9 per cent of the public vote. He also angered opposition politicians by altering the constitution to allow him to run for election again in 2004 and 2009.

Although a military autocrat, Ben Ali's immediate response to the violence, fires and angry protest on Tunisia's streets (French President Nicolas Sarkozy offered Ben Ali French troops to help 'retain order', i.e., enable Ben Ali to retain control; Ben Ali refused) showed some awareness of the underlying problems of his state. In a national address, he said: 'Unemployment is a global problem,' and attempted to assure Tunisians he was trying to help.

Commentators on the Arab Spring have suggested a variety of interesting factors in the causes and facilitators of the related uprisings.

Much focus has been given to the role of social media in enabling young people to organise and focus protests. This was a lesson learned well by UK PM David Cameron, who attempted to have young people prosecuted for their social media posts in the wake of the riots of Summer 2011, and it was certainly used to help organise Egypt's first public uprising.

But the basic causes of the revolution were rather less technological.

The three factors which led the majority of Tunisians to turn out on the streets were a vast rise in population – the Maghreb states' populations doubled in the period 1980-2010, and three fifths of their population was under 25 – combined with the global economic crisis, which increased unemployment to 20 per cent on average across the region (youth unemployment was significantly higher in Tunisia, Libya and Egypt), caused wages to drop and food prices to increase. The latter had led to the food riots of 2008, in hindsight, a kind of dry-run for the Arab Spring itself.

There is no doubt whatsoever that the final – clinching – factor was the lack of societal engagement in the political system.

Ben Ali may have been right to pinpoint unemployment as Tunisians' major concern, but he had effectively stolen power on at least four occasions, and had never attempted to unite 'his' people behind him. They had not chosen Ben Ali, so when he attempted to bring the nation with him, he discovered it had already chosen a direction of its own. Faced with this evidence of his inability to lead the country, he chose instead to flee.

However, the North African states share a great deal in common with those of southern Europe, and indeed both Morocco and Tunisia were, up to 2011, building increasingly convincing cases to be allowed to join the EU.

Because of this, to hide the economic roots of the Arab Spring is to obscure the truth of international geo-politics in the last decade: public demonstrations also spilled into riots across Europe in the wake of the global economic crash, and it is arguable that only the European Central Bank's intervention – and the fact that people had in some way 'chosen' the leaders of their states – prevented a 'European Spring' to match that taking place to the south and east.

Still, it was not clear that anything else would happen. In Tunisia, things were not as difficult as in Libya, I think. But in Tunisia, there were some very poor people, and nobody could have a say in how the government worked or who was in it. Many young people were unemployed and even those who had jobs, like me, knew people who did not. It was hard for people to have no money and no job, and a government they did not support.

So, there were some very angry people, and a lot of people who saw that life could be better for us if we had a new government. It was not a true Civil War. Two armies did not fight, as in Libya, and no-one came with powerful weapons, as Sarkozy, Cameron and Obama did in Libya. But there was some fighting and for a short while we wondered what would come next.

People fought in the streets – mainly police against protestors – but as we all began to speak up, and to stand together, the police seemed smaller. The government seemed smaller.

The revolution was not as terrifying as that in Libya and it seemed much faster than that of Egypt, but it changed us all. I would not be here at the edge of the desert if the revolution had not happened.

People here in Tunisia are proud of the fact that our protest and revolution helped other people to try to improve things in their own country.

But many of us were sorry when we saw what happened in Libya. Most people here do not like Ghaddafi, but the people in Libya are our neighbours, and they are like us. We were sad to see on television that they were fighting each other, and their homes and businesses were being destroyed.

Some of my male friends said they wanted to go to help. But I asked them how will it help? It will just be more people fighting. But I could understand. It was hard for us, to do nothing when we had changed our own country, and our neighbours were being killed.

It is part of the reason that when I saw people coming across the border and living in this camp, I decided I would come to help here.

I left the school and travelled east to get here. You will see that many people did the same. Many Tunisians work here from all parts of our country, as well as people like you from the West. It is a good thing that we can help people who have come to our country.

I came to an organisation here and I told them I wanted to help. They asked me what I could do and they were interested when I said I was a teacher. But I explained I was a dance teacher and I did not think children here would need to be taught how to dance. So, I do not teach. Some other Tunisians teach the children here, and some of the refugees teach, too. Many of them were teachers or experts in their own countries, so they can easily teach children here.

But I do have a job here, and it is something I love to do. Because many of the children who come to this education centre at Choucha have seen terrible things and some of them have lost their families. So I work with other adults to help make them comfortable here. I play with them and if they want to talk to me, I talk to them.

The centre is also where a lot of young people come if they are in trouble. So a lot of my work is talking to children and young people if they have a problem, and helping them. Sometimes a person comes who has lost his family, or who has no papers. In my job, I help to find them a place here which is safe, and people to look after them. If we can, we try to find their families, and we make sure the organisation in charge of the Camp knows who they are, and helps to find them a new country to live in.

We visit them every day and encourage them to come to the centre, because that way they have friends and people to talk to.

I do love my job now, and I don't think I will go back to be a dance teacher (though I have taught some of the children who go to the centre how to dance). Instead, when this camp closes, I hope to continue working to help children and young people who need help.

The job has shown me that people and their work can make a difference and can help to make people's lives better. I hope I have helped many people here. I think that I have. And I will continue to help more people. It has helped me as well, because I am very happy to do this work and to know I am making people's lives better.

For our country at the moment, it is interesting. I voted in the election and the party I voted for is not in charge. But no-one is really in charge at the moment.

But I do not think we will go back to how it was before. We do not want to. The government is having some troubles but this was our first time. It was our first try.

We will stay with this system and make choices for ourselves. If we sometimes get it wrong at first, that is OK. We will keep trying, and our lives will be better. It is our first time and we will get it right.

The Toss of a Coin
Part Two: Fifteen Days in the Desert

I travelled to Gondar, where I stayed for one night in a hotel. I paid for a driver, and at 12am, we left to travel towards the border. But the soldiers caught me again. This time, we had to get out of the car, and they made us hand over our passports. When they opened my passport, they said my name was from Ogaden.

I said I wasn't, and I didn't understand the Somalian language. It wasn't true, but I didn't know what I could do. I needed to get to Sudan because I couldn't stay in Ethiopia to be injured and arrested again.

They said I was a translator for Ogaden people, and I was helping them to fight. But I said 'no'. I wasn't. I was trying to live in Sudan. They hit me, and brought me inside a building, to the toilet. They hit me again. It was 1am.

They made me stand in the toilet and they sprayed it with acid. They said it was to clean it. It hurt me and burned me, and it didn't clean the toilet because it made me bleed on it. It damaged my legs and my head.

At 11am, they came and hit me again, and took me out of the toilet. They took me to the border prison, and kept me there for a week. They hit me, and asked me questions. They bit my right arm and cut it to the bone. I have still got the scars here. They also cut my left arm open with a bayonet. It hurt and I bled a lot.

But they couldn't prove anything because they didn't know me and I hadn't done anything wrong. So they let me go free.

I was free again, which was good. But I needed to find a job so I could buy food and find a place to stay. I went to the Somali people in Sudan where I was, but they told me not to stay there. They said it is better in Libya, that there are jobs and work there, and that most important, from Libya, I can cross the ocean, then be in Europe, and build a real life there. They said it as if it's a door to open.*

The island of Lampedusa, owned by Italy, but separated from mainland Africa by just 70 miles (Sicily is 109 miles away) is a target for African migrants from both Libya and Tunisia.

The sea is never any deeper than 120m between Tunisia, Libya and Lampedusa, though bitter experience proves that is more than enough to drown in: clothes, shoes, and occasionally wallets are washed up almost every morning and evening along the Tunisian and West Libyan coast, and fishermen along that coast confirmed the 'trade' which made them most money was attempting to deliver migrants to the Italian island.

The reason for this desire to flee is simple: the only African state with a higher average annual wage than the EU's state with lowest earnings, Bulgaria – where the average annual wage is equivalent to $9,000 per year – is South Africa.

To put that figure into further context, of the 1.1bn people who live in Africa, 90 million people – just eight per cent of the population – earn $5,000 per year or more.

And there were, in March 2014, 16 wars and armed conflicts causing 1,000 or more deaths per year in Africa: in the EU, there were none.

In 2004, Libya and Italy entered into a secret agreement which obliged the former to accept all African attempted migrants who arrived in Lampedusa. The EU criticized and reversed the measure when it was brought to light.

Lampedusa, and the continual perilous transport of – mainly sub-Saharan – Africans from Libya and Tunisia to Europe, was brought to the attention of many Europeans for the first time when 359 out of 514 people packed into a 20-metre fishing vessel were killed on 3rd October 2013. The boat was less than a quarter of a mile from Lampedusa when its engines cut out and it began to sink.

Onboard, a blanket was set alight to attract other vessels who could rescue the crew and passengers, but instead, it set the boat alight. As flames engulfed the boat, some threw themselves overboard, but others attempted to run from the flames but remain aboard the boat, causing it to capsize.

I asked him, 'How can I get there? I have no money.' He said: 'Don't worry. I can give you food, money and get you into a car.'

I travelled in a huge lorry. There were 200 people in it. It was very big, long and tall, but I don't think so many people should have been in it. There wasn't much space inside for us all.

Then, when we had been driving for a few days, the lorry broke down. We never really knew why – there were no mechanics who knew how to fix a large lorry engine. The driver just said it was a problem with the motor.

We were there for many days. Five people died.

Some people wanted to try to walk to a village, but there were no villages. At least, we didn't know where there were any villages near to us. We stayed inside the lorry. It was hot in the day, but not as hot as in the sun. And it was cold at night, but not as cold as in the desert outside.

Soon, some of us said again that we should try to walk, but the others said the desert was too big to walk through and we would be lost. They were right. I didn't know about the desert because I grew up in towns and cities, but we would have been lost and died.

After 15 or 16 days, some Libyan people arrived and brought us out of the desert. We were so happy to get in their cars. We were never sure how they found us. The lorry driver was very happy, and he pointed to his phone, but I don't know how his phone could even have still worked after that long.

Maybe he called and it took 15 days to find us.

Libya, November 2011-April 2012: Sirte

Sirte

Sirte

The Mexican

'I was here…'

THE last time I was here, I could not leave this courtyard.

My fellows and I were heavily armed, but trapped by others, equally well-equipped with weapons.

Every few minutes we would shoot, then they would return fire. But with no effect: the entry to and from the square was narrow, and to avoid the others' bullets each of us just had to take two steps backwards.

We shouted to one another through the night: we called for them to leave, they for us to surrender. Of course, neither of us took any notice. We were there for many hours, and then…

… I am crouching, shaking my head. My companion touches my shoulder: 'You were here?' he says.

I nod. 'I was here.'

'I'm sorry. Do you want to leave?'

I shake my head. We have work to do here, today.

He and I approached this school together.

He hopes to visit every school in my city – the 19 which are still standing, at least – because he fears they will not be fit for the children to return to in a few weeks.

I think he is right.

We work together, but we are also friends, I think. I have invited him to come to drink at my house. I know he would like to come, but he cannot. The people he is working with forbid it.

It is very funny to me. I am a Muslim and have brandy and vodka to drink, and he is a Westerner with no religious beliefs and yet it is he who refuses to drink because the people he works with fear it will offend Muslims here if he does.

I think it is very funny. I do not think he does. I find THAT very funny, as well. We are friends, I think, because we agree, at least on that.

The gates were locked when we approached this school. He looked around and climbed over. He stands out, a man in a Western suit and shirt, climbing a school gate in a city in the daytime. But as he says, other men in this city wear Western suits, and I am dressed in a jumper, jeans and a jacket.

In any case, he tells me that it is good for him to stand out here, that he wants people to notice him, and to remember him. He says it is better for him to be recognised wherever he is in the city, so that people know who he is, and are familiar with him, rather than just an anonymous Westerner, here by accident.

In that, so far, he has succeeded. People do know who he is, and though they talk about him when he is not there, they do not do so with anger. But I believe he developed the argument after wearing the clothes.

I, too, looked around, and climbed the gate after him.

He lands in the school playground, and immediately starts to take photographs. In many places, the school is not too badly damaged: the windows are all gone, of course, and the classrooms are black with fire damage and contain large pieces of broken glass, but there are no missile holes and only 40-50 bullet holes in each of the outside walls.

As he walks around the walls, I turn right and enter the covered courtyard…

… When I was a child, I went to school near here. Not at this school, but only a short distance, less than two kilometres away.

I liked school. I did not find it difficult and I played with my classmates in the day, and friends from my neighbourhood in the evenings.

We played football, ran through the streets, climbed and hid. We did what all children do when they are little. But we played a game which I do not think every child played – especially not every child in Sirte.

When the police – or soldiers – were here – we would march behind them. Whoever got closest and best made fun of their walk was the leader for the day. The soldiers sometimes turned around and would swing an arm at us, or chase us.

Other times, we would take green coloured paper and hold it in water, until it fell apart.

We didn't think about it at the time. At least, I didn't. But now, it is interesting to consider what we did, and why.

In 1975, the police killed my Great Uncle.

On the street, in broad daylight, police officers killed him.

My father and uncle were at home when officers came to tell them he had been murdered and that the police would find his murderers. But the police were the murderers. Other people had seen what had happened, and the police had grabbed him, beaten him and jabbed him with a poisoned needle. They dropped him, and he was dead by the time people got to him.

They did it because he was a critic of Ghaddafi and they wanted to show other people what happened to people who did not like the government. But because they acted for the state they could say anything, lie about what happened. And they did. They said someone else had murdered him.

My cousin was killed, also. The police came to tell my uncle. They delivered a note which just read 'he is dead'. I do not know why anyone would deliver a note which said that.

He was my uncle's son and that time my father and uncle thought he had been killed not only because he had been attempting to make people stand up against the police, but to show my uncle, too, that it was dangerous to speak out.

Some of my family, including my father, mother and uncle, had supported Ghaddafi in the early years. They had believed he was better than the King. But although the King had been a bad man, life under Ghaddafi was also much worse than we deserved.

My father used to say that he was glad the King had gone, but that Ghaddafi had failed us all.

But even after my cousin was killed, my uncle was the most outspoken against Ghaddafi. He said we must rise up against him, that people deserved to be free.

Sometimes my mother said what if he did not know how things were for us. But my uncle said that is no excuse. They are his soldiers, he said. And his laws. If he does not know, he is incompetent. And if he knows, he is no better than the King he removed.

Sirte was not a bad place before the war, as long as you agreed with everything you were told. The streets were clean, the buildings were new, people had jobs and most of the time there were things in the shops.

The schools were good – and free – and the hospitals were good, though not as good as in Europe. I know that compared to most of Africa, we were lucky. There was food to eat and the shops had goods to buy. Religious groups existed who wanted to force everyone to be like them, but the government did not want a religious state, so people could decide whether they believed strongly, or just a little, like me.

If you were very careful, inside your own home, you could even sometimes watch Western films. When I was a boy, one film I saw was The Good, The Bad and The Ugly. It was a great film. I still love it today.

My favourite part was the Dance of Death at the end, where all the characters are in a circle, none of them wanting to shoot because if they do, they think the others will kill them. But they know that if they don't shoot first, they may be killed by one of the others if they are faster. It is a standoff.

I loved the film, and I watched it even when my parents were not at home. I learned English at school, and I learned to do a Mexican accent. I made the other children at my school laugh.

But I did not say everything just to make people laugh.

Once, I said in school that I could not understand why people were arrested not by police, but by soldiers, and why we did not have more than one political party, why people could not vote for the best leader.

I do not know whether it was because of this, because of my family, or because my friends and I behaved as we did, but from then things got harder for me.

At first, I felt like I was being watched. Then, I knew I was. The police would follow me to school. At lunchtime, soldiers watched me.

One day, I was walking home, and was arrested. The police took my identification and passport, and told me they would decide whether I would ever be allowed to have them back.

They took me into a cell, left me there for several hours and then began to question me.

They told me they knew that I was working for Al Qaeda, and the CIA. They said they knew I was working for arms dealers. I was not working for any of them – and how could I be working for all at once? They all hated each other. It was ridiculous.

It was also confirmation of what my uncle and father had said. I had been watched for years – everyone had – and then arrested having done nothing, by armed police who took away my identification then lied to me about what they said they had evidence I had done and why.

I knew worse things were happening to other people, but this is not how a country should be run. In the middle of the night, I was allowed home. I walked in the darkness, still followed by police, past the school we are now in…

The courtyard is empty now, as it was then. The plastic roof is allowing light through to the concrete floor only where missile and bullet holes have been punched through it.

It is funny.

There were no bullet holes, and certainly no missiles fell on the night I was trapped here with my friends by Ghaddafi's soldiers…

… Here in Sirte, things were not the same as in Benghazi. There, there was an uprising, and things moved swiftly from it. I do not know whether there were resistance groups who had prepared and took advantage when something happened, or maybe in Benghazi everyone was a resistance person. Benghazi is like that.*

* Benghazi, Libya's second most populated city (roughly 1m people), is regarded by much of the rest of Libya as a 'rebel' outpost.

As one of the state's farthest Eastern settlements, at the opposite edge to Tripoli of the huge bay which runs along most of the north of Libya, some (though only a minority) of its citizens believe the East of Libya should secede, feeling unity with only a few fellow tribe members in other parts of the country. Almost all of its citizens have also felt unjustly overlooked in Tripoli's favour.

The years since 1969, when Ghaddafi seized power, intensified this feeling of neglect. Since then, not only Tripoli, but also the tiny fishing town of Sirte, close to where the dictator was born, where he attended school, and where he was assassinated in October 2011, had money poured into them for construction projects: the former as Libya's current capital, the latter as Ghaddafi's proposed new capital not just of the state, but a unified Africa.

That Tripolitans and Benghazans regarded the plans for Sirte with almost equal disdain and horror did little to bring them closer together, as Benghazans now felt they were no longer even second, but a distant third in the government's pecking order.

Under such circumstances, it is not entirely surprising that it was Benghazans' outrage about lack of investment which led to the city sparking the national revolution. From 13-16th January 2011, protestors in Benghazi, as well as in Bayda, Derna and some other places in East Libya, staged sit-ins at unfinished government housing sites. They called for political corruption to be stamped out, and for an end to delays in the completion of house-building.

By 27th January, the government promised a €20bn investment to complete housing and start new developments, but in the wider atmosphere of the 'Arab Spring', this was to prove too late.

Around the same date, Jamal al-Hajji, a political commentator, called online for Libyans to rise up and demand greater freedoms. Perhaps inspired by events in Tunisia, this was nevertheless not a clear statement of a desire to overthrow the Ghaddafi regime, but many – including the regime itself – took it to be so.

Al-Hajji was arrested on the 1st February and charged two days later with injuring someone with his car – a charge Amnesty International regarded as false.

Next, Ghaddafi – on behalf of the Jamahiriya, the government he had set up in 1977, two years before he claimed to 'step down' as President into a purely ceremonial role – met with journalists and known political activists, warning them they would be dealt with harshly if they took actions to destabilise the regime.

The warnings were – at best – ill-judged. Although Ben Ali in Tunisia had tried a more restrained approach (though police battled demonstrators in Tunisian streets) and failed, it is possible to imagine Ghaddafi – once described by US intelligence services as an 'unusually gifted politician and negotiator' – could have clung to power had he attempted a more conciliatory approach.

That he did not may be because he regarded Benghazi as a 'lone dissenter', that he believed his repeated declarations that Libyan people 'loved' him, fostering overconfidence, that police in Benghazi had – as he claimed – acted without the regime's permission by arresting lawyer Fathi Terbil just a fortnight later, that this was just Benghazi acting again as the state's 'rebel' city, or that he was as unsure as everyone else of what the revolutions in Tunisia and Egypt meant for Libya.

Terbil, who was arrested on 15th February 2011, represented the relatives of 1,270 people Human Rights Watch claims were killed at Abu Salim Prison in June 1996. In the incident, security forces had opened fire on prisoners who had stolen arms from guards and were attempting to escape.

Ghaddafi's regime claimed in 2005 that far fewer had been killed. It said that most of the 1,270 escaped before and after the 29th June incident. The arrest led to hundreds of people – some armed with improvised explosives and stones – protesting outside Benghazi police HQ.

As the demonstrators marched through the city, they blocked roads, before throwing some of the devices when they reached a city centre square. Police opened fire on the crowd, using tear gas, rubber bullets and water cannon. 38 people were injured.

In Bayda, also in East Libya, and Zintan, in the country's far West, protestors set fire to police buildings and barracks, and the following day armed protests continued in Benghazi, Derna and Bayda, with deaths reported in each city.

A 'Day of Wrath' had already been called for by Libyan residents and exiles on social media, scheduled to take place on 17th February 2011.

The date had been set to mark the fifth anniversary of another Benghazi-based demonstration.

That protest had seen a large, peaceful, march through the city, against the Ghaddafi regime. But somewhere close to the city centre, a smaller group, estimated by police to be 1,000 strong, broke off, surrounded the Italian consulate, and pelted the building with stones and burning missiles.

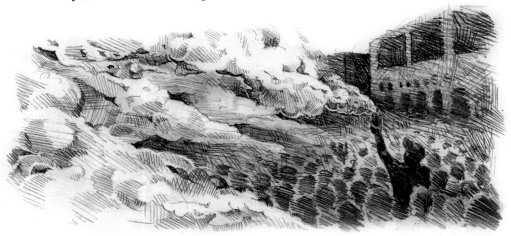

This smaller protest took place because Italian Minister without portfolio for Legislative Simplification Roberto Calderol – a member of the separatist Lega Nord – wore a t-shirt containing several cartoon 'images' of Mohammed which had been printed in a Danish newspaper in September 2005.

In the ensuing violence, ten people were killed by Libyan police and security forces.

On February 17th 2011, the Day of Wrath called for by Libyan nationals and exiles to mark the 'ten martyrs' of five years before, street protests took place in Benghazi, Zintan, Bayda, Ajdabiya, Tripoli and Derna.

Soldiers and police fired on the crowds, this time using live rounds, and government buildings were set alight. In Tripoli, protestors attacked TV and radio stations and set fire to the People's Hall, Revolutionary Committee offices, the Interior Ministry and security buildings.

The 'Day of Wrath' delivered what its name suggested it might – lethal violence from both 'sides', and a burgeoning revolution. Though the protests began in January, and Libya now marks February 17th as the day the revolution began, it was really the next three days, in which many rebels had by now armed themselves with looted weapons from military stores, which signified that this was not simply a series of violent demonstrations met by lethal retaliation.

On 20th February, after three days of fighting in which many police and soldiers joined protestors, those who remained in service to Ghaddafi withdrew from Benghazi.

The previous day in Bayda, local police and riot-control units were reported to have joined protestors. Some eyewitnesses claimed government helicopter gunships had fired on the public in the town. But despite this alleged attempt to smash the protest, the army was also forced to withdraw from Bayda.

Here, we had talked, but no more, when things started to happen. I was stopped on the street on 3rd February by a man. He was not in uniform, but I thought at first he must be a police officer. Instead, he just stooped, asked me if I was the student. I said 'Yes, I was at the University.' He told me a time and a meeting place. I was worried, but I went along to see what was happening. In a room behind a coffee shop, there were maybe 25 people. We talked about plans to overthrow Ghaddafi.

I was very excited. I returned home as soon as possible and my uncle was there. I told him what had happened. He told me that such an uprising was impossible, but I could tell he was excited too, because he told me to keep him informed about everything that happened.

We had hoped to hold a protest in Sirte, but in the end that never happened. Here in Sirte, there are many people who supported Ghaddafi. It is in the area where he was born, so there are many members of his family and tribe here.

At that point, they drove around in fast, expensive cars, telling everyone else they could do what they liked. It was true. While everyone else lived anonymously, the police ran the city and everybody else was just somebody else, Ghaddafi's family lived in the biggest houses, and they watched the police, rather than the other way around.

Some others who lived here but were not in his family supported the regime, too. Sirte was not a big place when Ghaddafi took over, and it had grown, with new buildings, schools and hospitals.

For those people, it was enough. As long as they asked no questions, didn't try to do anything new, or stand out, perhaps for them life was better. The regime ruled with an iron fist, so why risk being crushed?

I could understand. It was not fun to be followed and harassed by police, so I could see why they preferred to stay quiet and try to enjoy the little they had.

For those reasons – too few interested people, fear of police, tribal loyalty and fear of Ghaddafi's family and tribe – there was no demonstration in Sirte at that time. Later, I found out that people thought what was happening elsewhere must be an invasion, because they couldn't believe people would stand up against Ghaddafi from within Libya.

So even though I wanted to help Sirte, and my uncle was desperate to see a demonstration here, instead we went to Benghazi on February 17th.

We wore yellow hats, and we were armed. But unlike the soldiers and police – and some Benghazi protestors – we carried sticks instead of guns. When we began the march, the violence started, and some people were hit with weapons. I was not, but I helped to get people out of the water cannons' range, and to try to help people who had fallen and were being struck by rubber bullets.

We left that night, before the city was taken from Ghaddafi. At that time, I regretted it, but later I was glad, because I was here to help my own city through its own changes.

Now? Well, now is… more difficult. There is good and bad in all things. I don't think I noticed that before. In my city, now – my home city, not Ghaddafi's any more – I see people arriving from wherever they fled to in the last days of Ghaddafi's Sirte.

It is good to see them return. Then I remember that they fled not only Ghaddafi's soldiers who were arriving, but also me and my friends who had always been there, and the battles we would fight. That is bad.

I see them approach their homes. That is good. Then I realise that most likely their home will have at least one missile hole, from Ghaddafi's men or from NATO, or bullet holes, or will need complete rebuilding, or that they will open doors and find their home has been ransacked by either Ghaddafi's troops, or the khetibas who were our allies but thought that Sirte opposed them. Soldiers and khetibas alike stole from people's homes. Again, that is bad.

Then I remember that Ghaddafi is gone. That is good. And I think about what might happen next, which is bad and also good.

I remember all that we lost, and that we also removed Ghaddafi and I think of what happened to get us here…

…when we returned home, my uncle looked at me. He told me he knew I would be sensible about what I said, and to who, and he told me we must wait.

In March, he was contacted by Benghazi revolutionaries, who shared a plan with him. In the months that followed, I slowly built up a group with friends who I knew I could trust, and we did jobs for my uncle. Sometimes we played small tricks in the city, creating symbols like freezing green flags in water, so that at first they stood up, but then as the ice melted they collapsed and drooped, too heavy even for the wind to catch them.

But we were also preparing, bringing weapons into the city from Benghazi. We dressed in hoods, with our faces covered, because we knew that police or soldiers would kill us if they saw us and found out who and where we were.

It was strange in the city, then. Things were quite quiet. We heard about the fighting elsewhere from our contacts, and from people escaping from the battles, but here, we were quiet. The only signs of trouble were that the police and soldiers were nervous, and they were changed often.

On one night in May, we were spotted coming into the city. We had dropped off some weapons already, but we knew that the police would make us return to where we had hidden them and many others if they caught us.

The police chased us. If it had been two weeks before, we would have been caught, but by then the police were taken to other parts of Libya so often that most of those on duty in Sirte had not grown up here.

Because we knew the city better, we knew where we could speed up and where speeding would damage cars. And we knew which turns could take us far away, and which led to dead ends.

We needed three different cars, but we escaped, and laid low for days. Friends brought us food. We jumped even when we expected it was them at the door.

In June, things changed again. As fighting spread further, and more refugees came into Sirte, soldiers arrived, and many people helped them to build roadblocks at all the entrances and exits to the city.

By this time, most of Ghaddafi's family had left, because they had enough money to escape. But his tribe was still there, and many people who were afraid of Ghaddafi and his soldiers, so they wanted to help them so they would not be suspected of anything.

But it was the first time that I saw that there were people who were helping who were not afraid of the soldiers or Ghaddafi, but who were helping because they were afraid of what would happen if the war came to Sirte. They were afraid that if khetibas came who opposed Ghaddafi, they would simply shoot at everyone in Sirte. I understood.

In the days before the war, if you went to Tripoli or Benghazi and said you were from Sirte, everyone would look at you strangely.

People who secretly opposed Ghaddafi would think you must support him because you were from Sirte, and people who supported Ghaddafi hated you because they thought people from Sirte were proud of their links to him, and how rich and new their city had become. I could understand why some people tried to build roadblocks to stop anti-Ghaddafi troops coming into their city with guns and missiles. But we hated the roadblocks. We attacked them. It was the most dangerous thing I had ever done, and it changed my life even more.

My uncle had a farm tractor, and every time it got dark, we would drive it as fast as we could and smash the blocks. It was exciting, but also it was frightening. I had been threatened with guns before, but this time people were shooting at us. The bullets sounded strange when they passed us in the darkness.

Later that month, a man who lived near us came to the house. He did not knock or wait. He was a man we knew from when we had been children and we knew he supported Ghaddafi. But he left a piece of paper, which he had taken from the police. It was a list for the death squad, and it had our names on it.

We talked about what to do. We could not continue to attack the roadblocks, and we could not stay where we were. But we also did not want to leave Sirte. This was a time when we knew things would change. When the war would come, and could be won.

The people who wanted to returned to their families elsewhere in the city. They gave us their money, but then they went home to be safe. Those who stayed with us were the ones who said they would stay with us to the death.

We found a new place to stay. We realised we needed somewhere where Ghaddafi's people, and also our families would not know, because we didn't want to be in a place where our families could come to us and be seen.

We chose a place where there was only one road entry, so that we could see anyone approaching, and if we had to escape, it would be on foot in a direction cars could not follow. But we also had machine guns, RPGs and grenades, so we felt we could defend ourselves if we had to.

In August, we were attacked. A group of people dressed as civilians, rather than in police or soldiers' uniforms, came up the road and opened fire.

At this point, the government still felt safe in Sirte and it wanted people to think that this was not an attack by soldiers on revolutionaries, but by civilians on civilians. We were prepared for the attack, but until something like that happens, you cannot know what it is like.

We shouted to one another – and they shouted at us to surrender. A lot of the time it was hard to hear because of the shooting but I think at that point we both knew there was no point being quiet. Each group knew the other was there.

So we shouted to make it seem like there were more of us, and also to make sure no-one forgot he was not alone. They shouted also to make themselves seem more, and to see if they could make us surrender. But we knew we could not surrender: we would die. I did not think I would survive the night, because there were so many bullets and explosions, but I knew it would be better to die fighting than to be tortured and then killed.

There was one moment I remember. An explosion, close to where we were, lit up my friends around me and I looked at their faces. For a second I thought it was like a scene from a film. It seemed like it might not be real. But then the light dropped, and fear and concentration took over again.

Despite my fears, we survived that night. We managed to escape through alleys and narrow streets and found another safe place.

We discussed what to do. Some of us wanted to attack the people who were trying to kill us, but we agreed not to. We could see that if people in Sirte thought we were revolutionaries who were killing civilians – even though they were really soldiers and police – they would hate us and they might kill us instead of Ghaddafi's soldiers.

So we stayed safe and waited. During this period we laid low, and my uncle spent all of his remaining money on making sure we had food brought to us, and preparing for what might happen next.

Bombings by NATO started close to the end of August. The noise was like nothing I had heard, and even after bombs stopped, children screaming and adults calling and crying kept the city awake at night.

Very early in September, Ghaddafi's forces arrived and began to set up camp within the city. There was a particularly strong presence in Area Two, where most people traditionally supported Ghaddafi. Around the same time, small groups of the revolutionary khetiba groups also arrived, but most of them were fighting outside the city, unable to enter unless they defeated Ghaddafi's forces in the East, South and West.

On one morning, rockets fired from the ground struck buildings in Sirte for the first time, and that was when the first children were killed. Three children were killed in that first rocket attack.

I don't think that is what anyone wanted. When it happened, Ghaddafi's supporters said it was the revolutionaries. But we were with the revolutionaries and they showed us it was not them.

The missiles were launched from a park in the city, where Ghaddafi's soldiers, not revolutionaries, were based.

I think as well Ghaddafi's soldiers wanted to use the missile attacks to make people in the city

try to throw us and the khetibas out – to take revenge for the children's deaths. But it did not seem anyone believed it was us. They knew as well where the rockets had been launched from.

It was a mistake, I think. They didn't mean to kill the children. But it was a mistake which was their fault and it stopped people supporting them. But the revolution was now in Sirte. Gun battles raged all day, and missiles fired by Ghaddafi's soldiers and khetibas on the ground were joined by rockets launched from ships and aircraft from NATO.

Planes flew from navy ships in the sea north of my city and shot bullets and missiles into

buildings and onto streets. At that point it was clear that although we fought for the revolution, the planes, their bullets and rockets, did not know or care who we were. Anyone could be hit, and many people were.

On the streets, it was different: you knew who you shot at when you shot, and who was shooting at you. And from Ghaddafi's troops and the khetibas on the ground, you could see that they were firing rockets at particular buildings where maybe one side or another could be based.

But from the air, it was harder to understand the targets.

It was as if NATO was trying to destroy Sirte even though we were here and we had been joined here by other revolutionaries who had travelled and fought against Ghaddafi all across Libya.

It was not a good place to be. I was, by this point, a soldier. But for civilians, it did not matter anymore if you were for Ghaddafi or against him – though it mattered to both groups which they were. Whichever you were, you were being attacked and every day you might be killed.

I left Sirte at this time. I was not sure whether this was a good idea, but I had met with my mother and father, and my young brothers, sisters and cousins.

They asked me to help them escape from Sirte, so I agreed.

On Monday 12th September, at 6am, we left in two cars. I drove one, my father the other. I drove the car which had the six youngest children in – the youngest was one, the oldest, 12. The 12 year-old was helpful and helped the other children to stay calm, by telling them we were all going on a holiday.

On the way out, I was shot at. I do not know whether it was by a soldier who recognised me.

Of course, I was scared. But it is a little bit different after you have already been shot at many times. You are scared, but you know that you must just continue to do what you are doing. If you stop, or panic, you will be shot.

The children did not realise I was the target, I think. And the shooting stopped soon.

We drove a short distance to a town where we knew people, and which was strongly against Ghaddafi. I knew that here, my family would be safe. But I could not stay. I knew I had to return to help Sirte be free from Ghaddafi.

By now, the city was different. It was not a place where people lived, even though most people had not yet left. Walking in the streets, there were damaged buildings and roads – and it was getting worse every day. My uncle had also returned, and I met up with him. I joined some khetibas from Misrata, though I knew there were others who had come to the city from the East. By now it was late September.

The days settled into a kind of pattern. Wake up, run a mission – whether attacking the soldiers, or delivering weapons to other small groups. Eat, another mission, eat, sleep, wake to the sound of plane engines and bombing all night, try to sleep again, wake, start again.

We were active. I brought weapons into Area Three, including heavy machine guns, hand grenades, anything that could help, because there were many soldiers there, armed with mortars, rocket launchers and many other types of weapon.

At this time, I was given a sniper rifle, an SVD, which I called 'Katy'. I was able to use her at night, because she had night vision, and that was better for me because it was better to be awake at night hearing the planes and seeing the bombs fall than to be trying to sleep, unsure what would happen that night.

I was based with Katy at the covered courtyard of the school when I was joined by some khetibas I knew, the night Ghaddafi's soldiers found us and pinned us down with gunfire. But all the time, I was waiting. Everyone was waiting. Even when we fought, we were all waiting to see what would happen outside the city.

Sometimes, we would hear that the revolutionaries had won a big battle, and were about to enter the city. But they did not come.

Other times, we heard stories from people in the city that the soldiers had heard their friends had won a battle and they would soon be reinforced here in Sirte. But that did not happen either.

Instead, we continued to exchange fire, blasting bits out of roads and buildings, watching as NATO dropped bombs on us, and both groups knowing that what happened outside Sirte could change everything at once.

Things got worse. Both sides had snipers, like me, but in late September, when the money ran out at the banks, Ghaddafi's troops started shooting at civilians to take their money. We were angry, but we had fought each other to a standstill. We could not stop them shooting at civilians, and they knew it.

Unarmed people tried to carry on as normal, but they could not. If they were not shot by soldiers, or their homes were not hit by missiles from NATO planes, they could not get any money from the banks, and they could not buy anything because the shops were empty. People still went to work, and were still paid. But they could not get their money because there was no money.

Then, things started to happen quickly. On 21st September, we and Ghaddafi's troops agreed a ceasefire for one day. Not because we were friends, but because both sides knew things were changing outside the city.

The only radio station started broadcasting a message, and we and the soldiers knocked on doors throughout the city, all telling people, 'Get out. Things are about to get much worse.'

Most people did leave, and for the next days the city was almost empty. Just the tired soldiers

and the tired khetibas.

Now planes flew overhead every day as well as every night. They did not seem to be dropping more bombs, but they were using their machine guns in the daytime, striking buildings, roads and people.

On the 13th, people began to arrive from outside. Khetibas. It meant we would win, we knew. But they also brought news that my uncle had been killed. He had been fighting on the front, trying to attack soldiers and help bring people and supplies into Sirte, and he was shot, twice, by a sniper. He was hit in the stomach and the chest and he could not survive. He was 41.

Within seven days, almost everything was finished. The city was almost torn to pieces, by guns, grenades, bombs and missiles.

Khetibas from Misrata and Benghazi fought to help us, but also stole from the houses left empty by the people who had been told to leave the city.

Soldiers fought to kill us, and also ransacked homes. One of my friends joked that they and the khetibas might get together at night to choose which houses they could each steal from.

I just kept working, shooting when I had to, running when I had to. I was tired. I was not there when Ghaddafi was killed. I was only a couple of miles away, but I had a post and a job and the fighting was not over yet. It was enough for me to know he was dead. I did not have to see it.

The soldiers disappeared quite quickly, but there were lots of people in Sirte still loyal to Ghaddafi and they kept fighting. I don't know whether they wanted to see if they could still win, or thought they would be punished if they were captured. But it was days before I first woke up, did not feel I had to pick up my gun, and could walk out into the sunshine.

Was it worth it? Yes. But it cost very much indeed. Sirte is in ruins, the streets are flooded, people are dead and my uncle is one of them.

I never thought I would survive. I spent every day 99 per cent certain that I would be dead by nightfall. But we did win. Ghaddafi is gone, and it is worth it for that.

But I also feel that I survived where my uncle did not. I stepped into the sunshine after being pinned down by enemy fire, and that means I have to help to make things better now.

In this city, there are many who still support Ghaddafi. But it is strange. Now he is dead, we respect their belief, and they respect ours. We live together and we must make things better, because they are terrible.

And on the side of those I fought for, there are some who want to do their own bad things.

Not here in Sirte, where we are just desperate to rebuild and live, but in Libya.

It is our duty, who fought and won, to make sure we do not build a state where a new man is a dictator, or where a religion is. We have to make sure Libya is a place where people are really free, and where they can make their own decisions.

Later that day, the Westerner and I climb to the roof of another school, picking our way through broken glass, reading the graffiti the khetibas and Ghaddafi's troops have scrawled on the walls.

We look out, above the burned remains of tables and chairs piled here, across my city. In every direction, there are ruins. Buildings with holes where missiles have struck, others, less fortunate, simply piles of stone.

I look across Sirte. 'What have we done to our city?'

He looks at me, smiles sadly, and shrugs: 'The buildings can be rebuilt,' he replies.

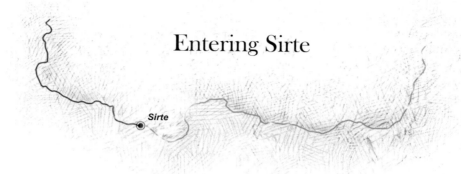

Entering Sirte

It's 5.30pm.

In the late evening sun, a man washes the white people-carrier parked outside his house.

As you watch, he bends to scrub the tyres, the water sparkling as it runs off the rubber and splashes the surface of the road.

A few yards further on is an HGV cab. You get the feeling it will be a much longer time before anyone comes to clean this. The cab has been peppered with bullet holes, including several punched into the front and back windscreens, both of which remarkably remain in one piece, and the rest through the doors, engine bonnet and wheels.

Behind the cab, a front garden wall contains yet more bullet holes, and the house it stands in front of is, if anything, more a collection of gaps to the desert sands beyond than any longer a structure in the generally understood sense.

But this is at least recognisably 'home-shaped', unlike its neighbours, now piles of rubble, bricks, tile shards, concrete and wooden struts – laying prone on this side street of the worst-hit of Libya's many stricken post-war towns and cities.

Welcome to Sirte…

Sirte is by no means a large place. Though referred to as a 'city' by people throughout the country, it is in fact only a third as big as Misrata, the closest city to it. With 500,000 or so residents, Misrata is just a quarter the size of Libya's capital Tripoli.

It was built as a port in the centre of the north Libyan coast by Italian colonists, near the site of the former Qasr al Zaafran (Saffron Fort). It remained so small that, during World War Two, a German officer reporting to his superiors described it as: 'a shabby village of mud huts by a foul-smelling stream'.

Yet, in the late summer and autumn of 2011, Sirte became the focus of international politics and warfare, with 452 'targets' 'successfully struck' by NATO airborne-missiles. Quite an achievement for a 'shabby village'.

By then, Sirte had around 120,000 residents, making it roughly the size of Banbury, England. Its first stage of growth began in 1959, when oil reserves were discovered nearby, but its major expansion was down almost entirely to its most famous – or infamous – son, Muammar Ghaddafi.

Ghaddafi was born ten miles south of Sirte in 1942 – around the same time as the Nazi officer's short, spiteful report was drafted – and attended school there until he was ten.

His affiliation with Sirte went even deeper than the memories of his formative years, however, because Surt, the region in which the town sits, is also the 'homeland' of the Qadhadfa tribe, to which the Ghaddafi family belongs.*

* *Within Libya there are 140 tribes, each tracing their histories back through more than 1,000 years. Though almost all consider themselves 'Libyan' almost all of the time, rivalries between tribes are often based on geographical location and the Roman states of Tripolitania (in the West), Cyrenaica (in the East) and Fezzan to the South, whose unification created modern Libya.*

The first two states, which would today be based around Tripoli and Benghazi, respectively, roughly match the major power groupings of modern tribes within Libya today.

But the vast majority of modern-day tribes were not in North Africa during the years of Roman rule.

Although 90 per cent of Libyans are now known to be genetically of Berber descent, the major era of tribe formation took place around 1,000 years ago, when Arabs arrived from the East.

As a result of the Berber traditions (in which tribes traversed the Sahara and met only occasionally to set laws in large gatherings of tribal representatives) and Arabic people's arrival long after the three Roman states had ceased to exist, many tribes – including the Qadhadfas – were not confined by the ancient borders.

In some ways, this has helped Libya to remain united. Unlike in many sub-Saharan African states, most people regard themselves as belonging to Libya, rather than to a group which considers itself more racially or linguistically linked to 'fellow tribespeople' across a border drawn hastily by retreating colonialists.

For example, the Masrata tribe, largely based around the town of Misrata, between Tripoli and Sirte on Libya's Mediterranean coast, recognises a historic link to Egypt (Misr in Arabic) but does not consider itself 'un-Libyan'. By contrast, in common with many other tribes, its members often see themselves as 'the most' Libyan, foremost amongst all their also Libyan peers.

Equally, when any tribe decides it wishes to 'break' from Libya, as some Benghazan groups have most recently expressed a desire to do, their aim is generally independence and seldom, if ever, to join with another state, or with tribes across a border.

But while it has assisted Libyan unity in some ways, the tribal system also creates some serious difficulties.

Because each family belongs first to its tribe –its children learning the names and deeds of the tribe's founder and/or most celebrated member – and only second to Libya.

Although the Berbers arguably used the same system to ensure all groups had representation in the wider 'Sahara state', in Libya it has served to weaken and in some cases replace central government and the law with a system based on tribal loyalty.

Every tribe pledges to ensure its members behave with honour and do not break laws, but in practice what this actually means is that if a tribe member breaks a law, their tribe expects to be able to bring them to 'justice' rather than relying on – or allowing – police officers to do the job.

In turn, this leads to feuds developing over single incidents between individuals, and escalating into long-term battles.

In light of this, though many of Ghaddafi's crimes – real and alleged – were a product of his own personality, his practice of appointing his own 'relatives' to positions of power (though few outside of his immediate family held any single post for a long period, and positions also went to the Qadhadfas' allies, the Warfalla and Magarha) and focussing investment on his tribal and actual hometown can perhaps be regarded as the product of the place and time in which he lived.

As one UK observer asked – perhaps too loudly – in a small café on the Roman Road: 'Is it so different from any government which appoints its friends, is advised by its friends and makes laws for its friends?'

Over the next four decades, Ghaddafi poured millions of dinar into Sirte.

He moved government departments from Tripoli to new buildings within the burgeoning city, staffing them with Qadhadfa tribe members, built three new suburbs (Manitika WaHid, Mantika Ethnaan and Mantika Thalaata'a, or Areas One, Two and Three), new roads and an international exhibition and conference centre (the Ouagadougou Centre).

Ghaddafi made no secret of his intentions for Sirte: he wished to make the former fishing village not only capital city of 'his' Libya, but also of a united Africa, led from the North by him, with other state leaders gathering regularly to debate and create policies for a continent he sincerely believed must act together or fail.

Under such circumstances, it is hardly surprising that so many people in the rapidly growing town declared themselves the leader's 'cousin' (a phrase which is less a declaration of family relationships than tribal belonging and loyalty), and forgivable that some – though by no means all – walked a little taller than they had before. But Tripolitans, whose city accounts for around one third of the entire six million population of Libya, were at first confused, and then angry that such a tiny town was being built up to 'usurp' their home's place as Libyan capital.

The one million Benghazans, whose own man Ghaddafi had deposed (King Idris had risen in the East of Libya as an opponent of Italian rule), were angered by what they viewed as a continued neglect of the city which led the state's manufacturing and technological development. And across Africa, it became clear that Ghaddafi's view of 'unity', though sincere, might only come at the price of Libyan lives. In 2010, it was as far away as it had ever been.

In short, Sirte's gains, while real, came at a cost: increased regional and tribal rivalry, jealousy and contempt from almost all other areas of the state, and association with a scheme whose worth was questioned even by its supporters.

In reality, the only true support Sirte had was Ghaddafi, and those who relied on him for the power he granted them.

From this financially privileged, but otherwise hopelessly weak position, the forces of change began to march, and the bombs began to fall, on Sirte.

Entering Sirte from Tripoli weeks after Ghaddafi's death, the West-facing wall of the first building you see had a huge missile hole blasted through it, enabling you to see into the former home.

It is immediately followed by a series of mangled street-lights that have been bent and mutated so that their bodies twist and bend and their lanterns sit, still connected by threads of metal, in their own pool of broken glass, on the roadside. You will realise only later that aircraft bullets are responsible for this eerie, mangled scene.

You see bullet shells, thousands littering every road surface, rusting slowly where they lie, rolling under your wheels as you drive, and waiting to be kicked aside by pedestrians should any arrive.

You see shops with every window shattered, but shards of advertising posters for bride and bridesmaids' dresses fluttering, pointless but oddly pretty, on the breeze.

To your left – taking your eyes from destruction which at first seems the greatest outrage possible – you see buildings.

Or at least what were once buildings, now simply shells.

They had been shops and houses, but are now so degraded, pockmarked, scarred, with holes so vast that they now resemble skulls in a particularly advanced state of decay. Skulls so denigrated that they must have belonged to some particularly shamed or hated group, victimised and punished horrifically and left, grimacing horribly, as an example for any who follow. Behind that, as you approach what appears a city of the dead, there is simply more of the same.

Precisely, crushingly, unjustifiably, horrifically, identical, with only one difference: further down the street here, bombs had split water pipes, meaning at this moment, on this street, the destruction, mindless, inescapable, concrete and crushing, is doubled, reflected in the flood waters under an early evening sun.

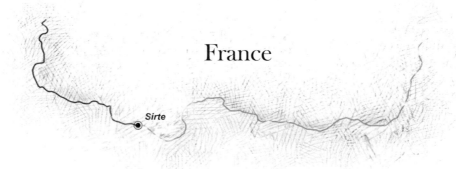

France

Here in Sirte, we used to have trees.

They were green in summer and winter and they helped to make the city a good place to live in. Now, most of the trees are gone. And most of those still standing are dead.

I have lived here all my life, in Area Two. My father ran the electricity company, and I was a student here. I study French, and I hope to do a Masters in French also.

When I finish, I want to live in France. I enjoy the language, and the philosophy, and I want to see what it is like to live there.

But I love Sirte. Or, I used to.

When I was younger, it was a clean city, the cleanest in all of Libya, and far less busy and full than Tripoli and Benghazi. It had several parks and in the summer all the families would go to spend time on the beach. It was a lovely place to live.

Today, the parks have been destroyed and you cannot go near the beach.*

Sirte's beach, which had for months been skirted by NATO warships, was inaccessible for many months after the Libyan Civil War ended, because three de-mining agencies had been forced to use it as a dumping ground for the live missiles and other explosives they had been urgently clearing from the streets.

Despite their best efforts, unexploded ordnance on Sirte's roads – and in buildings – caused injuries and deaths for months, new cases occurring well into February and beyond.

The toll was higher in December and January 2011-2012 than at any other time, largely because this was the period when most of those who had fled the worst of the fighting returned to what remained of their homes.

The de-mining agencies were the first international aid organisations to arrive in Sirte, and for many weeks the only reassurance available that a street was safe to walk down was their spray-painted symbols on walls and doors.

The agencies left, job still incomplete, when a missile was thrown over one of their office walls, into a courtyard where staff were relaxing post-shift. The attack coincided with the arrival in the city of a number of 'security groups', rumoured to have come from outside Libya, and promising to bring 'Law, religious order and safety' to the streets.

It is not a surprise. Many things have happened here that it is hard to accept.

Sirte is an unusual town. Before the war, many people were in favour of Ghaddafi here. Even when the revolution was happening, most people did not want anything to do with it. And so for many people the early months of the revolution made no difference. People went to work as usual, they ate at home as usual and they saw their friends as usual.

It is a strange feeling. The country was at war, it seemed all around us. Yet in the middle of it all, we just carried on as if it wasn't there. In fact, it was not. We all knew, of course, that something was happening, but no-one did anything, because why would they?

The pro-Ghaddafi people had no need to do anything: Ghaddafi was in power. The anti-Ghaddafi people were unsure of how little support they had, so they prepared for the future, or did nothing.

And everyone else was too afraid to do anything, or too busy trying to look after themselves, their families, their homes – just getting on with their lives.

At University, we would talk about it. We were split. Many students supported Ghaddafi. Why? Well, why not? Sirte was a good town, Ghaddafi had spent money on it, and families no longer had to spend money to send their children to school or university, or pay for hospital treatments. There were no more water shortages and there was food on people's tables.*

From 1977-2010, Libya's per capita income rose from US$2,168 to more than US$13,845 per year, the sixth highest amount in any African state. In 2010, its Human Development Index was the highest in Africa, higher even than South Africa, the continent's richest state, and also higher than Turkey, Mexico and the economic 'miracle' state of Brazil. Literacy rates rose from ten per cent to 88 per cent, life expectancy increased 20 years, to 75, and equal rights were established for women.

Free education and healthcare were introduced, unemployment benefits provided, and financial assistance was given to people who could not afford to buy a house.

Starting in 1983, one of the largest and most complex public water supply systems ever created, the Great Manmade River, was built, delivering fresh water from vast untapped reserves under the Sahara Desert. The US$25bn construction ensured the inhabitants of a country which is more than 90 per cent desert had access to clean, fresh water, free of charge.

Up to 2010, Libya remained debt-free, having funded almost all of the above by international oil sales.

Many of the people I knew at University were from families who were from Ghaddafi's tribe, and others who had supported Ghaddafi since he came to power.

They had done well from Ghaddafi and some of them definitely could not have stayed at school or afforded to go to a University without his policies. It may not be right, but it is easy to understand why people supported him.

Those who opposed him had many reasons to do so. They said his preference for his own tribe ahead of others was unfair, that his plans for Sirte were stupid when two million people live in Tripoli.

They said that he had assassinated people, that his police state was not good for anyone, and that people did not have any economic opportunities.*

* In 1973, four years after he had seized power, Ghaddafi announced the suspension of all existing Libyan laws. He told the nation he was stepping aside, to become a 'figurehead', but in fact remained in overall control, with the added 'right' to personally order executions.

In the same address, he announced the country would be 'delivered from' the 'politically-sick', and announced a state-run surveillance system, which from that point accounted for 10-20 per cent of all Libyan employment.

In 2010, execution was the official punishment for 'High Treason', 'Premeditated Murder' and 'Attempt to Forcibly Change the Government'.

That year, 18 people were killed by the state, the highest number in Africa, with executions broadcast and repeated on television. It is also almost certain that Ghaddafi-appointed diplomats and other international employees were responsible for assassinating Libyan refugees who had publicly criticised the state. Amnesty International declared it believed 'at least' 25 assassinations had taken place between 1980 and 1987.

Finally, although Ghaddafi's regime – unlike Mubarak's Egypt, or Ben Ali's Tunisia – provided free education and unemployment benefits, what it had in common with its neighbours were the effects upon it of the global economic crisis: as 2011 began, unemployment was at 30 per cent, and the cost of basic foods including rice, flour and sugar, had increased by 85 per cent in the previous three years.

I could understand both points of view. I opposed Ghaddafi, but I do not believe revolutions should be based on violence and terror.

I think the way to change society is through education, showing people how they can live, and how you plan to serve them, not by killing and hurting civilians. But at the University, I was not the loudest voice. In Sirte, in all of Libya, I think I was almost alone.

And then the bombs started falling.

At first, we were not afraid. The bombs were more annoying than frightening. They kept us awake at night, and we would each count the explosions, 50, 60, every night. But at the University, we would laugh and joke, pro- and anti-Ghaddafi people the same. We called it the sound tube, like a stereo with loud bass.

People's homes were hit, and more and more people 'disappeared' – as their families left, or they were injured, or they went to fight on one side or the other, but it was a little while before things really changed for many of us.

But every night brought the same pounding and, when bombs fell closer to us, the crying and screaming of those they had hit. And every morning, a little more damage had been done: another house, or shop, or school, or health centre had been hit.

It carried on like this, more and more buildings crushed and damaged, fewer things to buy in the shops that remained, but still people continued each day.

In August, the banks ran out of money, but people had to eat. So they kept working, and paid by bargaining or by leaving notes to say what they owed.

It was not until late September that things really changed in Sirte. By then, many people had already gone, their homes impossible to live in, their businesses destroyed, or just because they had decided they must join one side or another to fight. And we knew that things could not remain as they were. Our town was ruins and no-one could continue.

My family left about a month before the end. We went to a town where we had friends, to wait and see what would happen, and we returned as soon as it was possible to do so, in late October. I do not know whether it is because the memory does strange things, or because it was true, but Sirte was much much worse after that month away.

The buildings were ruined, the streetlights had been blasted away, there were missile holes in the roads, and where pipes had been damaged, deep water on the roads. This town, my home, had been ruined, and some people will never return to it.

I hope the revolution was a good thing, but I don't know yet. I can't say anything more than that I will work to help Libya recover from what has happened, I hope for the best, and I know that a revolution with guns is the worst kind of revolution there is.

'We must...'

Sirte

After about a fortnight in Sirte, things change.

Looking at a house punctured by 75-100 bullets, you one day catch yourself – astonishingly – thinking 'there's a lucky one'. You had never before thought anything that had been shot 75-100 times was lucky. You do not understand why that is what you now you seem to believe.

Then you turn a corner, and realise you expect – rather than are surprised – to see sub-Saharan Africans and black-robed Egyptians performing their daily ritual of waiting at the roadside in the hope of being taken by van to a building site, where they will carry bricks, then argue for two hours for a fair day's pay, settling for something less than that, but far more than their gangmaster originally tried to get away with handing over.

You keep walking, noting with concern that you are now using the bombed-out school, the crushed coffee shop and the burned car with the unexploded, intact, but inexplicably-declared 'safe' rocket in what remains of its engine, as landmarks by which to remember where you are, rather than as horrific reminders of where you are.

At this point, when you feel the stiffness in your jaw subside, as your face recalls that there are more expressions than its recent favourites 'wide-open mouth', and 'teeth-tightly-clenched', you begin to notice other things.

There is graffiti, everywhere. On every wall, on every gatepost, everywhere anything still stands. Some of it, strangely, is in English, but most is in symbols you still do not yet understand, and must ask translators to decipher for you.

Benghazi, Free; Misrata, Free; Tripoli, Free; Mukhtar, Free; Zintan, Free; Libya, Free; Libya, Free; Libya, Free.*

* After arriving in Sirte, 'Libya Hora' (Free Libya) was the first Arabic phrase you learned to read. 'I am not from NATO' was the first you learned to say.

It looks like celebration, but standing in the ruins of a South Mediterranean town, it feels like something else. Because as you talk to people in this town, you hear more and more about how the people of Sirte dropped everything and ran, to save themselves and their families from the worst NATO, Ghaddafi's troops and the khetibas had to throw.

You hear how when they returned, their business was ruined, their children's school was rubble, their favourite café no longer existed, their home was holed by missiles, and the door was open because, as they saw as they walked back inside, their house had been ransacked, turned upside down and emptied of all possessions, from televisions and computers to cots and children's games.

This was done by Ghaddafi's troops. But it was also done by the same khetibas who have written their messages all over the pockmarked, missile-strewn, ransacked, devastated town.

When you come home to that, what difference does it make who you supported, or even who 'won'?

How could you ever feel secure again?

But as that thought strikes you, you look around.

Over there, a man is using a house broom to sweep pieces of his own broken home, and machine gun bullet cases, from outside his front door.

Here, a woman is using a dishcloth to scrub dirt from the cracked, but still legible, sign bearing the name and number of her home.

The rubbish trucks have all been 'commandeered' – stolen, in less cushioned and more accurate language – by the victorious khetibas, so that today, Sirte's litter-collection vehicles are in Zawia, Ajdabia, Misrata; anywhere, in fact, other than the place they are most needed.

Perhaps they drive past a home in which a child is completing a jigsaw she neither knows, or would really understand, belonged to somebody else, a toy once loved by another boy or girl, here in Sirte.

But people are still clearing their homes, and their streets, bagging rubbish and rubble, and carrying it to collection points, where those whose cars are not burned, or smashed, or riddled with bullets, load it up and drive it to the town dump.

As you walk, you see more and more that, though it has been smashed, though the 'victors' have more in common with the losers here than they have with any of their fellow revolutionaries elsewhere in Libya, and though its people believe their home town's association with Ghaddafi means they are condemned to be abandoned by the nation which surrounds them, Sirte and its people are finding ways to begin again.

Returning home, you pass the entrance to Area Two, the junction where its main street meets North Africa's major road.

Area Two is still flooded. Its buildings remain so mangled and distorted by bombs, missiles, shells, rockets and fire that they still resemble nothing more than supernatural, horrifying, gargoyle guardians of a forbidden vision of a nightmare future.

But on a white bedsheet stretched between two poles, someone has erected a call to arms.

In red paint, it reads: 'Where are the journalists? Where are the politicians? We must rebuild our city.'

The 'Clinic'

Sirte

When somebody has fallen, and lies bleeding on the ground, you do not check his wallet, to see what he can pay. You help him. If you see a man dying, you check to see how you can help him, and whatever it is, you do it.

I have lived in Sirte all my life. Before the revolution, I was an engineer. Now, I run a health centre in my ruined hometown. It is free, because no-one has money here now, and because people need urgent assistance. We have to help one another now.

I am an adult. I have a wife and a young child, and when the revolution began I still had a job to do, and a family to feed. Many of the khetibas were younger men, without families, and without money or jobs. They went to fight. I can understand. But I wanted to look after my family, and I could do so because I had a job.

It is not about whether I wanted to fight because of politics, or whether I needed to – because I did not need to. It is about whether I wanted to fight to change Libya, or work to look after my wife and my child. I chose my wife and child. I will always choose my wife and my child.

Many people here did the same. We went to work because that is what you do. In that way, sometimes you could almost believe nothing was unusual in Sirte.

But we knew that the city was under siege, from March onwards. And although we did not often discuss it, everyone had an idea about what they thought would happen, or what should.

When people were not at work, you would quietly wonder whether they had fled, or joined an armed group, or were just unwell. It was a strange time to live in, working, eating, sleeping, meeting friends, but knowing that your country was at war with itself, and wondering how soon the war would come to meet you.

In August, everything changed. All the banks ran out of money – the last two because people rushed to them when they realised they were the only places left with dinar.

It was not economics, just physics: everyone went to work each day, and earned the same money as before. And everyone's company continued to make payments electronically into our bank accounts.

But no deliveries of notes could get through to Sirte by road, and no aircraft – except those of France, the USA and the UK – were allowed to fly.* They did not drop bank notes on Sirte. So, there was just no money. Nothing at all.

* UN Security Council Resolution 1970, passed unanimously on 26th February 2011, imposed legal penalties to be used against Libya if violence continued against those rising against Ghaddafi's government. It also imposed an arms embargo, which Libyan militia leaders later confirmed had been broken first by the French, who parachuted assault rifles, anti-tank missiles and machine guns to rebel forces.

On 17th March, UN Security Council Resolution 1973 was passed with ten votes in favour, and five abstentions. This resolution demanded a no-fly zone in Libyan airspace, an immediate ceasefire on the ground, and included a 'Responsibility to Protect' Libyan citizens from attack, by any means short of an occupying armed force.

The Responsibility to Protect, passed by the UN Security Council with specific reference to Libya, set out to enable outside forces to protect Libyans from genocide, crimes against humanity, war crimes and ethnic cleansing.

In circumstances where such things are threatened, this is an admirable and excellent commitment. But in the case of Libya, where there was little to no evidence that any of the four crimes were planned (and certainly none had been committed) by the government, the danger is that it can become a self-contained loop: that is, a state or states intervene, despite the fact that there was no prior justification, but then justify their actions in retrospect because none of the four crimes were committed – even though of course that does not serve as proof that the intervention was necessary to begin with.

In Libya, where the only acts of ethnic cleansing and crimes against humanity during the Civil War were committed by the Misrata khetiba which was supported by extensive NATO airstrikes, the repeated bombing of schools, hospitals, universities, homes and health centres 'to force Ghaddafi out' of regions – as if this is what was meant by Responsibility to Protect – must stand as one of the worst distortions of international policy ever committed.

Ghaddafi claimed to accept and welcome the ceasefire, but did not halt his forces' advance towards Benghazi.

On 19th March, in clear breach of the no-fly zone, French aircraft entered Libyan airspace to attack government armed forces' land vehicles. It was the first documented instance of what would be many hundreds of bombing raids and weapon drops in direct contravention of the no-fly zone NATO states called for and voted in favour of – and which only the Ghaddafi regime complied with.

Using Responsibility to Protect as a cloak, despite no accepted evidence that its criteria even applied to Libya, NATO proceeded to act, as Noam Chomsky put it, as 'the unofficial airforce of the Libyan revolutionaries'.

Whatever the strengths of the case for removing Ghaddafi, Responsibility to Protect, in Libya, became simply a justification for regime change. It was used to excuse acts designed not to protect people, but to attack Ghaddafi and destroy his regime – on the entirely unproven and unprovable grounds that one was the same as the other. It was a cheap street-magician's sleight of hand at best, a flagrant breaking of international law at worst.

Some people left then. After all, why keep working if you cannot spend the money you earn, to buy clothes, petrol, food or items for your children?

And at the end of August, the bombing started.

It is hard to explain what it is like to be in a city that is being repeatedly bombed. You know how this town is – from the highest points, you can look out to sea. We knew that NATO ships waited there, carrying the aircraft which every night flew over Sirte, dropping bombs and firing bullets at buildings, roads, trees, streetlights, wrecking parks and striking schools and hospitals.

The luckiest of us were kept awake at night by the noise and shockwaves of each explosion, and of the crying of frightened children, and cries of the injured. The less lucky were woken by bombs punching holes through their homes, by fire, by shrapnel and collapsing homes. The unluckiest did not wake up at all.

Early in September, one very bad night, I could not sleep. I did not want to remain at home, wondering whether a bomb would fall on us, so I went out walking.

It was dark, and the noise was far worse outside even than it had been in our house. Fires glowed in each direction, crashes and explosions, whistles of missiles almost drowned out the bangs of gunfire and bullets striking concrete, metal, wood and dirt. But on the street, more than any of these things, you could hear the crying of children and adults.

The next night, I went out again. On the third night, close to my home, bombs had fallen and people had run from their homes, only to be hit by bullets as they ran.

I knew that people were dying, and that there were few supplies in the city, anywhere. We had no telephones, or other means of communication. At that moment, in that place, where people were scared, injured or running, there was just me.

I walked into the street. I could see that people were losing blood, fast, and some would die. I ran to my car and people helped me get the injured men, women and children inside, then we drove to the hospital.

At the hospital, things were in chaos. Nurses and doctors were running between patients, but there were too many. They could not cope. I stayed for a short time with the people I had driven to the hospital, but a nurse told me she feared they would die without blood transfusions, and they had run out of O Negative blood already.

I drove home, and walked from street to street, calling for people to come forward for blood transfusions. Most were unsure of their blood type, but many of them agreed to come with me. Then, a cousin of mine stepped forward. He told me he had the right bloodtype, and that he would donate blood. We drove back to the hospital.

It is hard to know how we continued after that night, but we kept on working, helping one another when bombs fell and people were injured. It would have been harder if my job was still open, but as the bombs fell more, and the fighting outside Sirte came closer, and as more people left the town for safety, or to fight, or because they had no money, most companies and organisations stopped operating.

So, in the night-time, we worked. We escaped the bombs while we helped the people who had not been able to escape them.

Our work became harder, more serious and urgent, when the hospital was bombed. I do not think it was an accident. And I do not know why anyone would bomb a hospital.

But in Area Three, it meant there was a serious problem. The hospital was already unable to make everybody better and suddenly it had lost rooms and the medicines and machines which had been kept there.

We arrived on the night it was bombed with six people. There was a fire. We knew we would not be able to help them there, so we drove back towards my home.

On the way back, I thought I might be able to help them. I could not perform a blood transfusion, but I realised that if I had bandages, I could bandage them. If I had the right materials, I could clean their wounds. And near my home was a health centre.

I knew the health centre had not been open for several weeks. And when the hospital was open, it was much better to take people there. The health centre was just a small clinic, with a doctor, a dentist and some nurses.

But it had some machines, some medicines, and I was sure it would have the bandages and cleaning materials we needed.

If we had not broken in that night, maybe I would have left Sirte with almost everyone else on 21st September. When the soldiers and rebels knocked on doors, and the radio broadcast the same message 'Get out. Things will get worse', I was tempted.

But we did break in. And that night, we bandaged cuts, cleaned wounds, and helped people to recover from the shock of being bombed.

The next day, a woman came to my door. She was a nurse, she said, who had worked at the health centre. She lived nearby and she saw lights on. So she asked people whether the clinic had re-opened, and someone said I had been there.

She told me the other nurses were still in Sirte, and they would work with her, if the centre was open again.

In only two nights, we had seven nurses. We went out, as we had done before, to help people who had been injured, but now, instead of taking them to the hospital, we took them to the centre. So, when the soldiers and the rebels knocked at doors, and the radio also said we should go, I stayed here in Sirte.

Through those days, life was sad. I had never seen my home like this, almost completely empty,* and every day seeing more buildings damaged and destroyed. There were many more missiles in Sirte then than people, and thousands more bullets.

An estimated 400 of Sirte's roughly 120,000 residents remained in the town between 21st September and 21st October.

We went out, day and night, to make sure we could care for people who were injured. Here in Area Three, things were not as bad as in Area Two, where most of the fighting was. But bombs fell here, blowing holes even in the health centre, as well as people's homes and shops, and gun battles went on throughout our streets.

The hospital closed when people left – many of the doctors and nurses felt they must leave for their own safety, especially after NATO missiles struck it while they had been working – but some nurses remained in Sirte, and they worked with us, using their skills to help people who were injured.

It was also good to have them because they could help people who were sick, rather than simply wounded by weapons or falling concrete. It was a strange time, with so few people here, but so much noise day and night. I do not think I could have stayed if I had not had work to do. I think I would have gone mad. I still believe I could have.

People began to return here after Ghaddafi died. They came back to a ruined town. Houses, shops, offices, roads, everything was ruined.

About 60 per cent of the city was rubble. Almost every building still standing had missile holes in them, and some had unexploded missiles still sticking out of their walls. Every wall has bullet holes in, and of course many homes are badly damaged by fire.

It is not a place anybody would want to live in.

The hospital was still badly damaged, but it was one of the first places to reopen its doors, and as a result, I planned to close the centre here.

But I could not. Every day, I received calls from people who were ill, or injured by bombs exploding, or buildings collapsing. Also, I feared that water and sanitation equipment had been badly damaged. Many people still have no money and too little food.

There was real potential for epidemics, and apart from the bomb-damaged hospital, there were no clinics or health centres which had re-opened elsewhere in the town. There were serious problems, and too little medical support for people.

We closed for just a few days, and then on 1st November, I reopened the centre.

We have been lucky, here. Including me, there are now 31 volunteers who work here. Most of us are not qualified in medicine, but we have one children's doctor, one general doctor, some qualified nurses and dentists. And the volunteers here work hard and they have learned quickly. We all have.

People have been generous. We have had many donations of medicines and equipment, though we always need more. I had no experience of work in a clinic, but this had to be done. It was just a matter of organisation. In the first month, we saw and treated 7,500 people.

We also run programmes to help people. We have a breast-feeding programme, helping young mothers to eat as well as they can. We have 1,100 mothers who have come to take part.

But even with our help, they cannot breastfeed for long, because people's diets are too bad. There is food in the shops now, but there is still no money in the bank, so what can people do? How can they get enough to eat? We try to get them supplies, but we have no money either.

We have too few medicines here, too. And too little equipment. There are all sorts of things we need, even scissors.

And we are all tired. We live in homes which have been damaged by war, we walk streets which have missile holes in, and we are surrounded by the results of months of bombs and fighting. It is exhausting.

We cannot do enough here each day. Every night, we receive urgent calls from people who have heard about us. We can take them to the hospital, but that is all. It means we are working all day and most of the night, too. We work hard, but we can't really help people who have life-threatening illnesses.

I am very pleased to help the people living here, but sometimes I wonder why we are having to do so much without help.

We are all doing what we can, in different ways, just to help one another. The clinic helps to keep people alive and healthy. I am very proud of that. Elsewhere, people are doing other jobs, like rebuilding. We work for free, and we do not ask people who come here to pay, because we all have to help one another now.

Ehemmet's

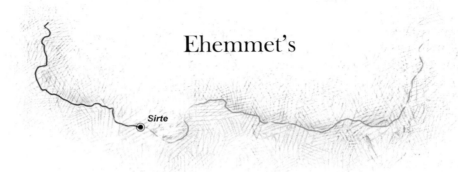

Sirte

In many small towns, there is a central meeting point. In some, even when they grow, it remains the main centre of the local social scene. And in every war, there is a location where an opportunity is wasted, or an avoidable mistake is made.

In Sirte, that point was Ehemmet's café.

Ehemmet's sat on the northern side of the main road running East to West through Sirte – and East to West from the Eastern Mediterranean, across North Africa, to the Atlantic coast.

When Sirte was a small town, Ehemmet's was where the sailors and their friends met. When oil was discovered, the sailors were joined there by engineers, and when Ghaddafi attempted to make Sirte a capital of Libya and a united Africa, the officials and office workers he sent added to the crowd.

Simply by being there, remaining where it was as Sirte grew around it, and continuing to excel in the short, thick, sweet coffee preferred by Libyans, Ehemmet's became the town's focal point. Entire generations, grandfathers and granddaughters, business women and fishermen, visited, watching the traffic zip by, talking to some people, and talking about others.

In October 2011, Ehemmet's is a pile of shattered stone, topped by three huge, broken slabs of concrete, and decorated on three of its four sides by crushed, burned cars.

If you stop, on your journey through Sirte's centre, or to Benghazi, Egypt, Gaza, Lebanon, Syria, you can see inside to the café's bar.

It is covered in brick and concrete dust, but saved, for now, from destruction by the almost forty-five-degree angle at which the roof, smashed here, here, and here, by missiles and their shockwaves, had collapsed, creating a makeshift and accidental shield.

In the garden, umbrellas, material burned from their charred limbs, remain standing and open, as if vainly attempting to shelter their tables, which sit hopelessly mangled beneath them.

And across the road, a horror you have so far been fortunate enough to miss: a block of flats struck from above by NATO missiles as its inhabitants slept. It is still too unsafe to retrieve the bodies, meaning it now belches out the stink of rotten flesh.

Unlike the apartments it once faced, no-one was killed when NATO bombed Ehemmet's café. But its bombing prevented an early end to the Libyan Civil War, arguably causing many more unnecessary deaths and certainly causing the ruin both of Sirte and the lives of many hundreds more of its people. A student from Sirte – a revolutionary who had borne arms against the soldiers loyal to Ghaddafi, and had been a translator, guide and friend – explained: 'It may seem strange, but the coffee shop was important to Sirte. We had been a small town, and we grew very quickly. In that time, Ehemmet's remained important to us all. Everyone knew it, everyone visited. Even people who did not like coffee would go, to see their friends and to talk.'

As a result of its popularity, its position as a 'shared meeting place'* – and perhaps because the drinks were good – Ehemmet's had, during the Libyan Civil War, become the location where the town's future was debated and discussed.

*It is a particularly bitter irony – the kind in which Sirte seems to specialise – that Ehemmet's café was arguably the best-known, and certainly most popular, point in the town, despite Ghaddafi's years of investment. Only metres down the road, Sirte's Green Book Building and Green Square (Saha Khedera) – identical to those in several of Libya's largest towns and supposed to serve as Civic gathering points and symbols of the dictator's new model state – occasionally attracted more people (not least because poorer members of the community were paid to attend, and cheer at the appropriate moments of, Ghaddafi's live speeches at Green Square). And as an ornate, wigwam-shaped building and a concrete square painted entirely green, they certainly stood out more than Ehemmet's. But it was the café which served as Sirte's central point.

In the weeks after the Civil War ended, almost every town and city in Libya renamed their 'Green Square' 'Martyrs' Square', after the ten killed in Benghazi in 2006, and those who had died removing Ghaddafi from power. In Sirte, where the Green Book Building was then a charred, punctured shell, most people just called it 'Saha Markazee', or Central Square.

And early in September, with the war edging ever closer, the discussion achieved more than speculation. Representatives of the leading families of Mantika WaHid and Mantika Thalaata'a – Areas One and Three – met at the café, agreeing that if either suburb was attacked by Ghaddafi's forces, they would unite to defend one another and rid Sirte of government forces.

Areas One and Three were not strongholds of pro-Ghaddafi sentiment, however, and they were separated by Area Two, where a large proportion of people felt either tribal loyalty to the leader, or gratitude towards him for being allowed to live in Libya, having fled violence and torture in their birth countries.

So, while the suburbs' agreement to support one another was reassuring to both, it was both predictable and – without support from elsewhere in the town – unlikely in itself to have a decisive effect on the fighting to follow. But within Area Two, the realities of the situation – Ghaddafi's failure to retake Benghazi, his imminent loss of Tripoli, Sirte's banks running out of money, ever-increasing NATO bombing raids and the advance of the khetibas on the town from West, South and East – had helped to shift attitudes.

'Loyalties had been divided in Area Two to begin with,' the revolutionary explained. 'Many were pro-Ghaddafi, some were against him, but even among those who supported him, there were some who were unhappy at some of the things he had done.

'And the people in Area Two were not bad people. They just disagreed with people like me. And most of us understood why the other group thought the way it did. We were not enemies. We were just in disagreement about Ghaddafi. And they were also not stupid. Many of them supported Ghaddafi, but Sirte was their home, where their friends lived, as well as their families. They knew the bombing would continue until the war was over. They cared about their city, and their friends, and so they wanted to protect them by helping to end the war as soon as possible.'

As a result, the agreement between Areas One and Three was supposed to have been only the first step in an historic pact: the morning after it was made, representatives from both suburbs were set to meet with their contemporaries from Area Two, to forge a similar agreement to defend one another from attack by pro-Ghaddafi forces.

Ehemmet's café was the obvious meeting point for the deal to be struck. That night, NATO launched raids which destroyed the café, and with it any chances of a swifter, less wasteful, end to the Libyan Civil War.

'We cannot be sure about why NATO planes hit the café,' the revolutionary said. 'I have heard people say that maybe some of the khetibas told NATO there were meetings between people happening there. But it was a bad mistake.

'The café was more than just a café. It was something people thought of as being a part of Sirte. When it was destroyed, the leaders from Area Two were furious, and they were also worried. They said they could not make any agreement now, because how could they support anyone who would bomb a café? People tried to convince them. Some said that NATO had made a mistake. But Area Two asked how you could trust somebody who would bomb a place where people met to talk and spend time together. The agreement was not made.

The war continued almost 50 days after NATO's strike.

Ehemmet's café is not the only incident people in Sirte raise when they want to explain why they are suspicious of NATO. They show where its aircraft bombed schools twice on consecutive days, the second strikes risking the lives of those who were attempting to clear the most dangerous results of the first. Many mention, too, a strike on a car on Sirte's main road, in which a second missile was fired only after bystanders had flocked to attempt to help people from the burning vehicle. That had killed 20 people outright and injured many more.

Nor did the destruction of Ehemmet's café end resistance to Ghaddafi, even in Area Two. The notorious – and powerful – Safframi family campaigned for its neighbours to unite with the rest of Sirte against the government's forces. But with general agreement shattered by the bombing of Ehemmet's, hopes of a Safframi-led Area Two resistance were killed – along with one of the family's youngest sons – by a sniper's bullet, fired as the boy raised the green, black, white and red flag of the 'new' Libya on the roof of his house.

Nonetheless, the destruction of Ehemmet's café is the only single strike to which everybody refers, and which is necessary to understand why, even among Sirte's 'victorious' anti-Ghaddafi combatants, the Libyan Civil War is not a simple, clear-cut choice between 'good' and 'evil', or even between common-sense and stupidity. And it is the only strike which can fairly be argued to have, by itself, lengthened Libya's Civil War, ensuring even greater destruction of its homes, schools, roads and hospitals, and increasing the number of its dead.

Days later, passing by the café on the way to an interview, another student, a Syrian who speaks excellent Russian, stops you. He waves at the café: 'What do you think?' He says. 'Is a café a legitimate target? Is it dangerous enough to smash with missiles?'

Ibn Sina

Sirte

We stayed for as long as we could. We are nurses, we work hard to make sure people are well, and if they are not, we work to help them get better. We cannot go away during a war.

It did not matter to us that we could not get money from the bank. It was hard, but people knew us, knew who we were and so we could eat. And we cannot leave during a war. It is when we are needed most. It is not just people who were injured by bullets, or grenades, or bombs. When water pipes were broken, people came with diseases.

When electricity was cut off by bombs, people were hurt by being shocked, or because they had injured themselves trying repairs, or working in the dark. And people do not stop becoming ill just because there is a war. A hospital is needed when there is peace, because people catch a disease, or hit their head and are unconscious, or have a heart attack.

That does not stop in a war.

So a hospital must not shut, and a nurse must be at work. It is what we are here for. But when the missiles struck, it was harder for us to find places within the hospital for us to do our jobs.

The first time, it was at night. We were glad, because some people had already left Sirte, so there were fewer people.

It is strange to be in a hospital at night when bombs are falling. They make a noise outside but at first, because there are machines here, you do not hear that. Then, when you hear, you know it is because they are close. So, you hope they will not hit you, or your ward, or your building, or the hospital.

That night, they hit here. This children's ward. The bed which was here was destroyed straight away. These beds on the other side of the room were on fire, and had pieces of the roof on them.

Next door, glass shattered into beds, and fire devastated the ward.

We were lucky.

Normally, that ward was full, and one of us would have been in the ward, too, because we stay there to look after the children.

That night, it was empty. Because some of the sickest children had been taken away by their parents to find a place they could get well in safety. So we, also, were away from the ward, down the corridor, where the small kitchen is, and close to the other wards.

We jumped when the bombs hit, and screamed. And at first we ran towards the wards. We thought there were children caught there. We remembered. But only after we had reached the burning wards. We backed slowly away.

A few nights later, another ward was hit. We were lucky again. Not because the patients there had gone away, but because we had taken them to another part of the hospital to get drinks. They were frightened of the bombs they could hear, so they cried and woke us up.

We held their hands as we walked down the stairs, and we clung to the bannisters and to the walls as the whole building shook when the ward we had left a few moments before was struck.

There was no-one to put out the fires, so we left the children with some of the other nurses in another part of the hospital and we went upstairs with some other staff to throw water and to do what we could.

At that point, we were told we did not need to come in any more. The managers said that the hospital was too damaged, and that we could not do a job even if we were not in danger ourselves.

Some of us, those with families, did leave Sirte that night.

But others came back the next morning to our hospital, Ibn Sina, dressed in our uniforms, and started to work.

The managers smiled, as we worked with them to help some of the patients to cars and other vehicles, so they could be taken away by their families, and as we tried to clear the rubble and debris so it would not fall through the floor while we were gone.

I do not know why people would bomb a hospital.* I think I had thought it would not happen. In the end, it happened twice more, but we had gone before then.

But we survived the first two attacks on Ibn Sina, and Ibn Sina survived two more.

* The official and semi-official explanations given by NATO and the khetibas (pro-Ghaddafi forces also attacked a variety of buildings from the ground, but few of them were around – or admitted that they were – to offer excuses for their behaviour) for strikes within Sirte was that targets were chosen 'because they were tactically sensitive'.

The khetibas who agreed to be interviewed revealed that in many cases, this meant they contained – or were rumoured to contain – snipers. There is no doubt that khetiba snipers did position themselves in schools, apparently making those schools 'legitimate targets'. It seems impossible that pro-Ghaddafi fighters did not take up similar positions.

But it is equally inescapable that, in Sirte at least, NATO's 'legitimate military targets' included the city's University, several health centres, its schools and its sole hospital, Ibn Sina, even when staff and patients were within it.

The Journalist

Sirte

When we returned to Sirte, this is what we found: everything ruined. Our town destroyed by weapons and fire. Everything stolen. But why?

We trusted the rebels, we left our homes in their hands, and this is what we got in return. And so we hope to live in peace, but if that is impossible, then life is done. We do not care.

I have lived in Sirte all my life, in Area Three. My father was also born here. Before the revolution, it was a unique place, like nowhere else in the world. A great place. I really liked to live here. Everything was new and clean: new buildings, new parks, new roads. Everything was new and clean. Nobody even dropped litter. Now, there are bricks and lights smashed all over the streets, papers and books scattered on the roadsides.

It wasn't like that before. It was a very very good place to live. It was a friendly place as well. It was growing bigger but because it had been a small town everybody knew each other. The new people who came could make friends very easily here because it was a place where people were friendly and welcomed the new people.

Now, it is not so good.

Most people here were like me. Before the revolution, we did not think too much about rebellion. We knew some things were wrong, but it seemed far away – a problem between the government and some of the people in Libya, but not between Ghaddafi and everyone else. We just lived our normal lives and most of us did not get involved.

But when the rebels attacked military places in the East of the country, and took weapons, when they started to shoot the police, and set fire to police stations, it became more serious. People had to have an opinion, because it was clear that this might happen everywhere.

Life still continued, though. Things got harder, and the streets had fewer people on them, but life here in Sirte went on. What else could it do?

When the rebels came here in September, many people welcomed them. We were expecting it. We knew things would happen. But not the way they did.

They said they were going to liberate Sirte, but they didn't. They behaved like animals, attacking us with everything, destroying everything, stealing anything, killing everybody who moved.

Ghaddafi's troops were no better. Not at all, except in parts of Area Two. But we expected that. The khetibas were supposed to be liberators, an army of people fighting for freedom, but they were thieves and robbers.

When I returned to Sirte after the khetibas and Ghaddafi's soldiers told us to get out and then robbed our homes, I saw all of the town, very quickly, because I went to volunteer with Radio Sirte.*

Prior to the Libyan Civil War, Sirte had, along with two newspapers, two radio stations and a TV studio. The television studio was struck several times by missiles – from above, indicating NATO strikes, as well as from ground level – and everything of any value, from electronic equipment to tables and chairs, had been stripped from the site.

Both radio studios had been ransacked, but a group of students and former government-employed broadcasters cobbled together a makeshift set-up on the outskirts of the town.
Given Sirte's post-revolution devastation, the perceived (and actual) lack of outside interest in its situation, and its position perched alone between the Sahara and the sea, it would not be completely inaccurate to describe Radio Sirte at this time as a lone voice in the wilderness.

Two weeks after the interview with The Journalist, the station's 'studio' was broken into, and all of its equipment stolen.

Rumours in the town were that the station had been 'closed down' by a group of khetibas, angered by reports updating Sirte residents on its whereabouts, activities, and alleging some members had been engaged in ethnic cleansing during the Civil War.

No khetiba ever commented on the allegations they were behind the closure of Radio Sirte, and the station, unable to broadcast any longer, wound up.

I chose to work for the radio station because it was not political. It said it would not broadcast messages in support of the khetibas or in support of Ghaddafi.

This was vital to me. I did not want to work for someone that supported Ghaddafi. I would not have chosen a career before the revolution working to support Ghaddafi, and I certainly would not after the revolution, when he was gone and no-one was forced to support him.

But I also could not work for the revolutionaries. I felt they had made us all victims, killing us and stealing from us in our own homes.

As a result of my job, I was here in the early days, before most people returned. I saw all of the town, and what I saw horrified me.

Everything was destroyed. Every home, every building, empty, hit by bombs or bullets, set fire to or allowed to burn. Everything stolen from everywhere, every home, shop, office, school, clinic, the hospital, empty. Cars and vans stolen, the whole town, ruined. And why? We did not trust Ghaddafi's soldiers, we knew what they would do. But they were nowhere to be seen. Most of them had been killed.*

* Relations between residents and the khetibas in Sirte was deeply uneasy at this time. Though claims that 'a majority' within the town supported Ghaddafi during the Civil War were incorrect, the level of pro-Ghaddafi feeling – around 40 per cent of people held pro-Ghaddafi or anti-revolution views, though a far lower percentage took any part in the Civil War – was unusually high.

And pre-war attitudes to Sirte (one man taxiing passengers between Tripoli and Sirte advised them all – with genuine concern as his motivation: 'The people in Sirte are bad people. They believe they are better than others in Libya. We used to have to show our passports to be allowed to visit and it made them not Libyan.'), combined with greater than average resistance to the khetibas within the town, led to a feeling that Sirte was a major centre of resistance to the revolution.

Ghaddafi's use of the town as a hideout after the fall of Tripoli, though hardly welcomed or even known about by the vast majority of Sirte's residents, understandably strengthened such feeling.

From the point of view of Sirte's own residents, the town's relative proximity to Misrata meant it had an arguably less positive experience of 'liberation' than other parts of Libya.

Misrata was the closest major town to Sirte on the Roman Road, which meant that members of the Misrata khetiba made up a large part of the 'Free Libya Army' which entered Sirte first. But the khetiba was widely-reviled, among revolutionaries as well as those who supported the Ghaddafi regime. Misrata had endured a long and damaging siege by Ghaddafi's forces, and the khetiba – rumoured to have 40,000 members – was renowned for its unusually harsh treatment of both 'enemies' and those who were simply not engaged in the revolution.

The people who accurately described themselves as 'ethnically cleansing' Tawergha, a small town between Misrata and Sirte, publicly stated they were part of the Misrata khetiba. In the post-war period, the khetiba's members were still 'active', rounding up Tawerghans from the places – including internal refugee camps overseen by Libya's transitional government forces and by other khetibas – to which they had fled during the war, and transporting them to Misratan prisons.

It was in this highly-charged atmosphere that on 20th October 2011, Ghaddafi was captured and then shot dead – though the then leader of the National Transitional Council, Mustafa Abdel-Jalil claimed within a week that: 'Those who wanted him killed were those loyal to him or who had played a role under him. His death was in their benefit.'

It was also Sirte, at the Mahari Hotel, which the Misrata khetiba had taken control of after heavy fighting, where 53 Ghaddafi supporters were massacred.

Their bodies, which were discovered in the gardens of the hotel, overlooking Sirte's Mediterranean beaches, were examined and estimated to have been killed between 15th-19th October.

Many had had their hands bound with plastic, and several wore bandages, leading to people in Sirte to speculate that they had been patients at Ibn Sina hospital, which had also been taken over by members of the Misrata brigades.

Human Rights Watch reported in 2012 that 17 of the 53 had since been identified as part of the Ghaddafi convoy, which had been attacked by NATO aircraft as it attempted to flee Sirte – a strikingly different account of the dictator's capture than the one told at the time of a search which led to Ghaddafi being pulled from his hiding place in a drainage pipe, and a reminder of how far NATO managed to stretch its UN-sanctioned 'Responsibility to Protect' the people of Libya.

Although the Geneva Convention specifically outlaws the killing of captured combatants, nobody has ever been arrested or charged in connection with the shooting of the Libyan head of state, or the massacre of 53 prisoners of war.

But the revolutionaries, the winners, we trusted you. We left our homes in your hands, and what did you do? You took everything you could steal, and ruined our homes. You were not dead when we came home, but the only ones we saw – the only ones we see now – were the ones who sit at the armed roadblocks, checking to make sure who travels and why.*

* *It was impossible to avoid khetibas anywhere in Libya in the months following the war – especially if you had to travel.*

There were more than 40 'brigades' of men, who had taken part in active combat and contributed to the demise of Ghaddafi.

Most had been unemployed, or worked in low-paying roles with little or no potential for improvement or promotion. Though 'khetiba' means 'office worker' – in part a reflection of the 'pro-business' attitude by which some of the revolution's leaders claimed to be motivated – the vast majority of their number had never worked in an office.

And after the Civil War, these young men looked at Libya's immediate prospects for economic improvement and decided to stay with the only secure job many of them had ever had: the khetibas remained after the war not just because their leaders craved power, but also because their 'rank and file' required jobs.

Their members stood, only occasionally uniformed, but always heavily armed, at 'checkpoints' all along the Roman Road, and at every entrance and exit to still-inhabited towns.
Where city 'gates' did not exist, the revolutionary forces had used cargo containers, piled on top of one another, and often painted in the red, green, black and white of the 'new' Libyan flag, to build passable substitutes.

Where such containers were not possible to find, the presence of 8-12 heavily-armed men, and a rocket launcher mounted on a pick-up vehicle proved sufficient to encourage traffic to stop.

For a white Englishman with papers in order, the khetibas were generally polite, good-natured and, considering that most of them were men aged 16-24, with little prospect of work or comfort, and armed with high-calibre assault weaponry (it was never possible to check how much of it was French), extremely, remarkably calm, collected and careful.

In the sunshine of Libya, asked by smiling people about football, the UK, and my impressions of Libya, the khetibas almost seemed a normal part of life. But for black Africans, the Roman Road between Tripoli and Sirte (the 'Misrata' section) was off-limits, and to the residents of Sirte, the khetibas posted at the entrance and exits to the town, and who were not slow to fire weapons as warnings where perhaps words would have achieved the same purpose, felt like a containing force rather than a 'security team'. And at every moment at which I was obliged to deal with them, however easy the conversation was, I could not help but come back to two points:

First, that in December 2011, the National Transitional Council had announced a law outlawing the khetibas – demanding they disband and trade their arms for money or jobs in the armed forces – and that months later, these people, still heavily armed, were illegally 'patrolling' Libya's major transport routes;

And second, that in the words of the DJ, the Somalian refugee at Choucha Camp: 'I fled because I knew what a war leads to. In my country, people could be shot on the street, in daylight, and nothing would happen. There was no law, because there was no-one to make laws. I did not fear the war, I ran from what would come next.'

The khetibas were good-natured, if you were the right colour, or from the right region. In truth, many of them – though certainly not all – would have been good-natured regardless of where you were from, or the colour of your skin. But they were a constant reminder that the government had already failed, and a constant warning that things could – and under unfortunate, but worryingly possible circumstances would – spiral into chaos at any time.

I could not work for the revolutionaries, any more than for Ghaddafi's men. I do care for my country, and for my town. It is why I chose the volunteer job I did. We worked night and day to tell people what was happening.

We warned people if places were dangerous, and explained over and over again what had happened, so that people coming into the town, feeling shattered and angry, and realising that in Libya, Sirte was alone, would know what was happening and that in Sirte, they were not alone. I am proud to have done that.

About the revolution, I do not know any more. I opposed Ghaddafi because for some people things were very bad, and he was the leader. He should have done better.

But I supported the revolution. I wanted it to happen, because people talked about a new start, about a new Libya, about the country working better. But instead, we got death, violence and robbery.

I wonder whether we should have got rid of Ghaddafi, if those were the only people who could replace him. We needed changes, and a constitution. But not this way. Maybe we should have tried to force him to listen, to see what was happening to us all, so that we could have avoided this. Maybe we would have fewer people dead, fewer homes destroyed if we had.

Now, my hopes are that the rebels in my town will all leave. Then, I hope there can be forgiveness here and across Libya between those who fought for Ghaddafi fighters and those who fought against him, to increase – improve – my country.

I hope to live in peace. We all hope to live in peace. Right now, it is all we can hope for.

A Good Man

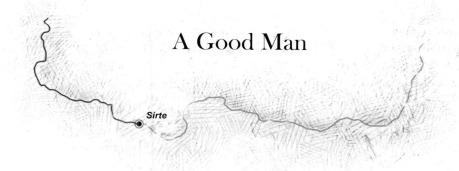

Sirte

'He is coming today. I have not seen him in a long time. We are going to meet and have coffee. He is my friend. He is a good man. You can come and meet him today.'

You are sat with your Sirte 'fixer' in the room you use as an office. He is a local man, whose job before the War is now gone – though he hopes to build a new business as soon as things start to improve.

He has driven you all over the town, translated for you when you needed it in shops – and proudly, beaming, declared 'He has a book!' when shopkeepers have gaped, astonished on the few occasions you have managed to use Arabic without his help, even though he taught you the only two phrases you use there 'Mumkin ashtaree?' ('Can I buy?') and 'Bi kam?' ('How much is it?').

He has shown you the best places to get coffee – and the worst places to be seen alone as a white man, day or night. And today, he is very, very excited.

His friend is coming from 'over the sea' to visit Sirte and to meet him. They were at school together, but the friend left Sirte to live elsewhere (you never have been able to understand where he went, or why) and is returning to visit family and friends in the aftermath of a war which has destroyed most of his hometown.

'Hiya Nadhab!' ('Let's go!'), he calls, and walks towards his vehicle.

He drives past the twisted, distorted, former buildings of Area Two, still looming as if a warning of the horrors of war created by a deranged sculptor, past shops, many now open even though their upper floors and street-level windows no longer exist, and up to SaHa Markazee.

'He wanted to meet at Ehemmet's,' he said. 'But I explained why that would not be possible.'

You wait, leaning against his pick-up, watching the rags of the old regime's green flags, tormented by the wind, slap against the flag poles which line the green-painted public space.

A car pulls up nearby, and you and the fixer walk towards it.

'I am glad you are here!' the friend beams to you. 'This is a good place. It is not always like this, and it will be better again very soon!'

You walk together across the Square, you, the fixer and the good man, as he tells you about his parents' home (badly damaged, but he will pay for people to help them fix it) and asks where we can buy a coffee now Ehemmet's has gone.

Across the road from where you now stand, you see another man you have met before, a Ghanaian who had worked in Sirte before the war and who remained here rather than returning 'home' when the fighting began.

He smiles, and comes over to say hello.

The fixer introduces him to his friend. The fixer and the Ghanaian have met before, dancing and pretending to be superheroes during a break from working to help repair a youth and social club near the Square.

The friend looks at the Ghanaian, smiles, and says: 'Where are you from?'

'Ghana, and where are you from?'

'It is clear I am from here,' says the friend. 'So, when will you go home? When you have taken enough of our money?'

The Ghanaian laughs: 'We all need to make money,' he said. 'But I will be here as long as people need me.'

'Nobody here needs you,' the friend replies.

At this point you open your mouth to speak. You know the Ghanaian. You know that he has a family to whom he sends the money he earns as a carpenter and construction manager.

You know that he, like everyone in the town, has for seven months only had access to money on the rare occasions he can find someone able and willing to pay him in cash (though ironically and fortunately his family in Ghana have access to the money paid into his bank account).

You are about to tell your fixer's friend that in fact, this man, his skills and his character, have proved just as vital to Sirte as the commitment and hard work of those born here.

The fixer has also started to speak, but the Ghanaian cuts you off.

'It is OK,' he says. 'Some people have not had time to get used to people who do not look the same as them.'*

> * *Race relations had been fraught in many regions of Libya since well before Ghaddafi took power in 1969 – indeed, it could be argued that he went some way to increasing racial equality in the state.*
>
> *Though slavery had officially ended in 1853, black Africans were long regarded as second class citizens – at best – in parts of the country, and in 1930, a Danish Muslim traveller claimed in his travel diaries that it was still possible – and easy – to buy a sub-Saharan African girl as a slave for £30 at the Thursday market in Kufra.*
>
> *To this day, the word for slave, 'abd', is the same as the word for 'black person' in Libyan, though it must be noted that to use this word to describe a black person is understood by all to be particularly offensive. A more usual term would be 'abid', which takes the diminutive, therefore friendly, form of the same word.*
>
> *In Arabic, this is regarded a more important difference than it would be in English.*

'It is not your colour,' says the friend. 'It is that you are in the wrong place. You should go home. You are not a Libyan. You cannot be. Your children will not be. You and people like you are why Libya has fallen apart. Libya does not need you. And you should go home before you harm us further.'

'I do not believe that is the case. I came here to work hard and I do work hard.'

'You came here to take advantage of our kindness, our good nature, and you came here to take advantage of our great country.'

The Ghanaian laughs, sweeps his arm about him, indicating the shell of the green book building, the missile-holed hotel, the shops without windows or roofs, and the apartment blocks crumbling as we watch. He shrugs.

'You know that is not what I mean,' the friend smiles, but speaks through gritted teeth. 'If you were prepared to work hard, you would make your own money, in your own country. You would not need ours.'

At this point, you cannot take anymore.

'Yejib edhab. I must go. Ana oreed edhab ila maktab. I want to go to the office.' It is the best you can do to try to end – or at least leave – this conversation.

'You see,' the friend says. 'He has been here a short time, but speaks Arabic better than you.'

You open your mouth to speak again. This time, neither the carpenter, or your fixer's friend, even notice.

The conversation continues in Arabic, as you turn to your fixer, he shrugs, embarrassed, and apologises, and you walk across the Square, away from a man who moved away from his country arguing that he deserves it more than a man who moved to live in it.

The Palestinian

Sirte

When bullets are shot into your living room, you have to escape.

I have lived here in Sirte for most of my life. My parents are Palestinians, but they left rather than live in a camp in their homeland. I think when I was a child I was proud of being Palestinian, but my mother and father always told me and my brothers how lucky we were to be here in Libya, in Sirte.

I liked it here.

But in September, I ran away with my family. If I had been able to get to Egypt, I think I might have stayed there. This is not a good place to be in today.

I don't know. I know I must help to rebuild Sirte, but I am tired, I am scared and I am sad. The city has been ruined. My home has been almost destroyed. Nobody has any money. I have two children and I am desperately trying to find food, milk and clothing for them. But it is so hard.

We left on 18th September. The money had run out in August, and bombs fell every night, but we stayed. This is our home. We did not want to leave it. But late in August and then in September, the gunfighting got worse. At night, the explosions of the bombs, and the sound of the plane's engines woke us, but it was the gunfire that kept us awake.

It was a very bad time. My young children would cry and scream at night, afraid that the gunfights they could hear meant that men were coming to kill them. They could not sleep at night and they cried all day and all night.

I told them that they were not in danger, but then on the night of 16th September, a bomb hit the house. We had to run, because it was on fire. We threw water and the neighbours helped, and the damage was not as bad as it could have been.

Our bathroom was destroyed, but I thought how lucky because the girls' bedrooms had not been hit and they had been inside them.

But when we went into the house again, we began to cry. There was fire damage everywhere. The roof had a hole in it, which went through the bathroom floor into the kitchen. One side of the house looked like it would collapse, and all of the windows were broken.

We started to gather our things, but we had to stay for one more night. The girls would not sleep without us, so we all stayed downstairs together.

The room was continually lit by flashes of bombs and fires across the town. We did not sleep at all. The girls wanted to get up, they were crying and they said they could not sleep. I am very glad I told them to stay where they were because we soon heard gunfire outside the house.

We huddled together, scared. I said to the girls to be quiet. It was not really because I thought anyone would want to come inside our house, but because I did not want the girls to cry. I was afraid myself and I did not want them to see that I was.

We stayed lying on the cushions on the floor of our living room, and as the sounds of the fighting came closer…

I do not know how to describe what happened. We could hear bullets pass above us. I think we could see them glowing above us. I believe even that I can remember feeling the air move in the room as they passed above us.

It sounded like a hum, and then a crash as bullets struck the walls. The bullets were coming in through the windows and through the outside walls, and they were flying over us and into the walls on the other side of the room.

I tried to think what to do. The girls were screaming, and my wife was shaking and crying. I tried to think but there was nothing I could do. I put my arms over the girls and my wife. I think I wanted to protect them. But it wouldn't have protected them from bullets. How could I have done that?

But with my arms over them, at least they did not stand up.

I do not know how long that continued. Maybe only a few moments. Perhaps the fighting moved past our home very quickly. But it seemed like a very long time, with bullets crashing into our home as we lay below them, and we thought one would hit us and kill us at any moment.

When it got light outside, we sat up. We were shaking. My girls had stopped screaming but they were making little high noises and my wife was crying and crying. I walked to the walls, which had maybe 80 bullets in them, and ran my fingers against the splits and cracks.

I walked to the window, and ducked when I saw someone walk past. But it was not a fighter. It was a neighbour of ours.

He came to our door to see if we were OK and all alive. I nodded and put my hand to my face. I noticed it was wet with tears.

We put more of our clothes and some food into our car and we drove to Misrata, to escape.

We stayed there for two weeks, but it was hard there. We were running out of money so we decided to go to Benghazi, from where we hoped we could get to my cousin in Egypt.

We drove across the country. It was strange. We were stopped many times, but I do not remember what happened. I spoke to the soldiers of both sides but I cannot remember what I said. I think they must not really have been interested in us.

We arrived in Benghazi with almost no money left at all. I decided we must sell our car so we could get to Egypt. We left with many other people, but at the border I was refused entry to Egypt.

I explained about my cousin, that I had family in Egypt who we could stay with. But the soldiers there said my girls and my wife could cross because they were Libyans, but I would not be allowed without a visa because I was a Palestinian.

I told my family to cross without me, but they would not go. My girls hugged me and my wife held onto my arm and although I was angry they would not do what I said, and sad because it would be better for them in Egypt, I was also happy because I would not be alone.

We came back into Benghazi, and stayed for two nights in a camp in the city for Libyans who had lost their homes.

There were many people there from across Libya, including lots and lots of Tawerghans. We told stories about what had happened to us. I do not know whether what they said about Tawergha was true. I hope it is not.

The people working at the camp said lots of people were in other camps, as well, because they had come when Benghazi was freed from Ghaddafi. And after two days they told us Sirte was free, too.

We decided to come home, back here to Sirte, and we have come back to our house.

We are trying to rebuild it, now, but it is not easy. The girls still do not sleep. They cry and scream out in the night, they say they can hear gunshots even when there are none* and they say they can see people in the darkness.

In Sirte, gunshots were heard regularly even months after the end of the war. Most adults had learned to tune them out, but the children often flinched or cried out when they heard them.

My wife and I lie with them and hold them tight, but they do not sleep for very long. We are trying hard, here. We are working to make things better. But it is very hard. There is no food, and we cannot rest. I say to the girls that now there is peace and things are going to be much better. But then I look at my home, and at my town, and I realise I do not know what will happen next.

Brothers in Arms

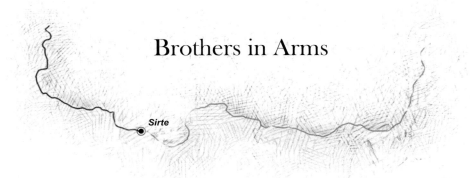

Sirte

Standing on Sirte's main road, where you are scribbling notes and taking photographs of shattered windows, broken buildings and mangled metal lampposts, you are approached by two men, who are walking together, arm in arm.

You exchange greetings and explain what you are doing to the more talkative.

'Where are you from?'

'England.'

'Oh, I have been to England. I lived in Manchester! It was very rainy.'

'In Manchester?' You are interested, having lived there yourself for three years. 'Whereabouts?'

'In Didsbury, on Clyde Road.'

You had lived one road away from Clyde Road.

'When were you there? I used to live on Old Lansdowne Road.'

'Ah yes! I had a friend who lived there. There was a café at the end of the road, did you go there? It was six or seven years ago. I was a student there.'

It is one of the more surreal moments of your life, standing in the winter sunshine of a ruined town, talking to a man you have just met about a café in a pleasant suburb of a rainy city some 1,800 miles away, where you and he lived, at the same time, within yards of one another.

'Yes, I went there. Many times. What did you think of Didsbury?'

'It was nice. Though it was too cold for me. I was pleased when I came home to Sirte. But I think Didsbury must be better than this.' He motions to the crumbling brickwork beside you.

You glance at the man's companion, still linked arm in arm with the former Mancunian. He has so far said nothing. He remains silent, but meets your eye and nods.

'Oh! Forgive me. My friend does not speak English well. He has not been to a University like I have and he does not understand most of what we say.'

'Anyway, he may not like to talk to you, because he is a supporter of Ghaddafi.'

'Really? How does he feel about what has happened?'

'Like any defeated soldier. He is tired now. He has laid down his gun, as I laid mine down too, and we are trying to live in the world again.'

'You both fought together?'

'Ha! No. We both fought, but not together. He fought to save Ghaddafi, and I fought to destroy him.'

'But, um, look, I'm sorry to ask, but you're both walking down here arm in arm after that? You might have been shooting at one another a few weeks ago.'

He nods, vigorously, grinning as he says: 'We were! We have spoken about where we were during the revolution. We did shoot at each other! Only a few yards away from here!'

'And now you are arm in arm?'

He smiles even more widely: 'It is strange, isn't it? I do not know if I would have expected it, either, to be friends again with someone who I was in a war against.

'But really, he was not fighting me. He was fighting to save someone and something he believed in. And I was not fighting him. I was fighting to free my country from a bad man.

'Now, one of us has won, and the other has lost. But that is not what is important. We were at school together. We have been friends since we were young children. When I went to Manchester, he was one who wished me well when I left and came to meet me when I returned.

'We are friends. That is what is important.'

They turn to leave, walking, still arm in arm.

'Goodbye my friend!' He calls. 'It is great to have met someone I lived so close to, so far from where we are now! I will tell all of my friends about you!'

You will tell all of yours about him.

Mantika Ethnaan

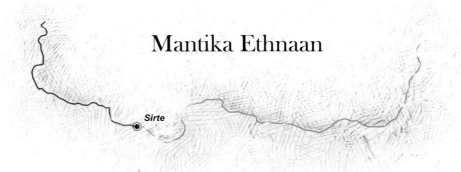

Even in the warmth of the afternoon sun, Area Two makes you shiver.

You walk past the call to action at the suburb's entrance intersection with the Roman Road, past buildings destroyed by gunfire and missiles from the air and street-level.

A shop on your right has re-opened, selling flat-screen televisions. You mention to the owner your surprise that he is open: surely no-one has any money to spend on a television?

He laughs: 'And there is nothing to watch here if they did! But at least it means that no-one will steal from my shop.'

It is just as well. His 'shop' has no front windows, no doors and no roof. A child could wander by in the evening and remove every single television, if they had the mind to. But this is Sirte, Mantika Ethnaan, Area Two. Things are not the same here as everywhere else.

You had been warned not to come here alone. Indeed, you will shortly be warned that if you ever do this again you will lose all protection from a group you have been working with.

But this is why you are here. This is the centre of the final battles which decided the future of a nation. It is where one of the world's most notorious dictators spent his final days, where a state's armed forces tried and failed to hold out against the same state's civilian militia, where NATO unleashed its dreadful firepower from the air, even as the revolution stormed the streets.

It is also where you can learn the darkest, starkest, most terrifying and unpleasant lessons about what war is, and what it does, not (just) to those who fight, but also to the civilians forced to live through it, and who have no choice but to try to continue living when it ends.

All of Sirte is like this. But Area Two is where the experience is concentrated.

This is why, you are beginning to realise, it is so dangerous.

You continue up the small 'hill' which hides the Mediterranean from most of Sirte, passing heaps of rubble and rubbish on every street corner.

You pass near to the house in which Ghaddafi lived out his final days, now largely shattered stone and broken glass, in common with every other building you can see.

You have already seen the building once, but it is, after all, just a smashed construction in a town where that is now the standard.

There is no blue plaque here to note the famous – infamous – man who 'rested' here, nor shall there ever be. It is simply another sorry, smashed mess.

At the bottom of the road, the sea dashes against the sands.

But today, rather than sunbathers, the inhabitants of the beach's higher reaches are missiles – hundreds of unexploded bombs which have been gathered and left here by de-mining agencies fighting desperately to clear them from residential streets, to reduce the daily injuries from youngsters playing with the enticing, mysterious, shiny metal forms.

To your right stand the seafront homes of Qadhadfa tribe members, those people most closely related to Ghaddafi.

Though the grandest of Sirte's seafront buildings, they stand empty. Their owners – some of Libya's wealthiest people – have not returned. In Sirte, few people believe they ever will.

To your left, an open area contains the burned and broken remains of cars, pick-ups and vans, and behind them stand apartment blocks, punctured with vast, gaping missile holes, black around the edges, making these homes appear similar to 'scientific' drawings of decaying teeth on TV adverts for dental hygiene products.

You walk West, with the sea on your right-hand side, the town to your left, following a row of street lights, smashed, snapped and mangled out of shape by bullet-fire. They lie prone, or bent almost double, as if to touch the carpet of rusted bullet casings which covers the road's surface.

Apart from the sound of the waves, and the wind which whips off the sea to 'play' the damaged buildings as a musician would a flute, or a drunk a beer bottle, producing low, almost impossible bass notes, Area Two is almost silent. It is two pm.

But there are signs that life continues, even here, where the war has had the most devastating and crushing effect.

You cross the street, where, improbably, a shop stands open, even though the entire top floor of its building has been completely smashed away.

You intend simply to ask the shopkeeper, a youngish-looking man, whether it would be possible to photograph his store from the outside, but as you enter you catch the aroma of freshly-baked bread, and decide also to grab some fruit juice and olives.

'Where are you from?' He asks.

'England.'

'Ah, David Cameron. He is a good man.'

Looking around Area Two, it is hard to believe anyone could seriously believe this to be the case, but he appears to be sincere.

'No. Sarkozy, Cameron, Obama, bad men.'

You had not seen the second man when you entered the store, but he appears from behind its only central row of shelves.

'That's not true,' the first man responds. 'They helped us to be free.'

'We are not free. They gave us nothing. Look around you.'

Both turn to you, and smile, as if awaiting your decisive insight into the recent history and immediate future of their nation.

You smile back.

'Your store was lucky,' you say, immediately regretting telling a man whose home may have been destroyed and whose shop is only half the building it had been eight months ago how fortunate he is.

'People have to eat. When I saw my shop was not destroyed, I put plastic on what had been the floor upstairs, and started to stock food. People are busy here, they work hard and they do not come outside very much, but they need to eat. We all do.'

You smile, glad not to have offended the man, and to have avoided attempting to find a middle-ground between a man who believes Cameron has magnanimously aided his country, and another who believes he has selfishly destroyed it, in a language neither speaks as a native, and walk back out onto the street.

Perhaps because it has now been confirmed that they are there, you begin to notice signs that people have returned to Area Two. A mother calls her children on the second floor of one block. In the garden of another, washing hangs on a line.

You kneel down, attempting to find a position from which you can photograph the bullet casings on the road and the missiles on the beach, and as you start shooting, you hear a shout.

A small boy runs towards you. He calls 'Halloooo! Meeester!', grabs your camera, smiles, takes a photo of himself, and hands you the camera back. You show him the shot he's taken, and he beams back at you.

His English is at about the level of a four year-old. It is vastly superior to your Arabic.

But you spend some moments exchanging information about your names, ages (he is eight) and where you are from.

'I went away,' he says.

You do not understand at first. He grabs your pen and pad, and after a few seconds, you see what he means. He, his mother, father, and a baby are in a car. Behind them, billowing with smoke and with a large hole in its roof, is their house. The family smiles out at you, waving.

'Do you live near here?'

He nods, and points. He says something in Arabic you cannot understand.

He sighs, and sits down. You sit, too, and he taps your arm.

He puts his head on one side, closes his eyes and mimics being asleep. You nod, so he stands, puts his arms out to one side and makes 'plane engine sounds.

You nod again.

He sits down next to you, and makes another noise. You have never had to lie awake, listening to this noise and wondering what it will mean for you, your friends, your family, so it takes a couple of seconds before you realise that the noise the boy is making is an eerily accurate reproduction of the sound of a missile falling.

The sound continues, and continues, and continues, the boy carrying on for longer than you would expect from a young boy telling a short story, getting louder and louder, until 'Boooooooom!'

The boy jumps up, runs around in a circle, then sits, out of breath, and points back to his drawing.

You let out a long breath, which you realise only then that you have been holding for several seconds, then slowly unclench your fists and ungrit your teeth.

The boy smiles, shakes your hand, says: 'Goodbye Meeester!' and runs back in the direction he had come from.

Further West, a large pile of rubbish alongside a stretch of relatively undamaged wall turns out in fact to be a well-organised collection of military paraphernalia.

Guns, bullets, missile launchers, boots, a helmet, ammunition straps, a jacket and some grenades have been laid out on the pavement, and around them, police tape has been strung to prevent anyone walking on them, or grabbing them to take home.

This is the place the khetibas, which had advanced on Area Two in a pincer movement, met again for the first time, symbolising victory – or at least its imminence – in Sirte as a whole.

A car engine, the first you have now heard in two hours or so, distracts you. The man in the driver's seat of a blue pick-up is shouting and gesturing to you.

'What are you doing?'

The man is in his mid-thirties, in his car alone. He is frowning. You hesitate. But there is no way you can avoid answering.

"Anta tekellum inglisee, do you speak English, min fadlik?'

'No.'

'OK,' you smile. 'I am sorry.'

He frowns again. 'Anta tekellum arabee?'

'Laa. Ana ooreed, laakin laa.'

Forgetting himself, he smiles, then quickly composes himself and returns to frowning.

'What are you doing here?'

You talk, in English, for a moment. You explain that there is no sensible reason to be here, that you are trying to find out what has happened, why it happened, what the results are and what will happen next.

It sounds stupid, as you say it.

He visibly relaxes, offers you a cigarette, which you light and begin to smoke.

'What will you do, if you find out?'

'Tell people, I guess.'

He looks at you.

'This is not a good place to be, any more. There are no children here, any more. The children are dead.'

He offers you his hand. You take it, then he drives away. Behind you, on the beach, hundreds of missiles lie, silent but almost tangibly malevolent, in the sand.

Across the road, two houses, empty, and collapsing on themselves stand, just about, as if they have been exhausted by keeping watch over the missiles, to prevent them fulfilling their sole destructive task.

On their front walls, graffiti reads: Misrata Khetiba, Zawiyah Khetiba, Libya Hora, Libya Hora, Libya Hora.

This, it seems, is freedom.

At the end of the coast road, you turn left, back towards the town.

West and north of the part of town in which you have been staying, this is a part of Sirte you have so far seen little of.

To the right, there are few buildings. To the left, there are few that remain in the shape they held six months before. Instead, there are garages, collapsed on cars. Roofs, smashed through the first floor, into the living rooms of the houses they were designed to shelter. In what was once the last coffee shop before the beach, a Pepsi fridge lies mangled under chunks of concrete.

At the crest of the hill, facing east, you can look across Sirte, noting the holes in the higher buildings which still stand, and the gaps where others used to stand.

You see the junction at which the gloved, uniformed, 'dancing' traffic officer, works.

Each day, dressed in black dress jacket, peaked white hat and gloves, he bows, smiles to the motorists in one lane, spins, left arm extended, hand up, to stop traffic, raising his right hand to beckon cars on from a second part of the crossroads.

You are pleased to be one of few people who know that he was doing this long before most people had returned to Sirte after the war – that the traffic is more an audience to an ongoing public show, than its cause. You are also puzzled, because the remnants of traffic lights stand at the junction: has this man just created himself a job?

The few cars on the road on which you now stand have no need of calming.

Three sit in a central pedestrian island, one leaning with its front wheels mounted on the street's sole standing lamppost, one without wheels at all, and the third balanced on its side.

None have windscreens, all are burned, are empty, are abandoned and all sit in an almost reproachful silence.

To the right, as you walk, a small boy is sweeping the step of a house which looks relatively undamaged. But it is the only one, and he is the only person you see.

The final five buildings on the left-hand side sit empty, looking in their dilapidation like part of the set of a Western, left outside the studio once the film was in the can, to decay in the elements for several decades. Perhaps, after 20 or 30 years, rain and wind could have bored the holes which gape from their walls. Six months ago, people lived here.

You raise your camera, gazing into the gaping holes, darkly recalling Neitchze's abyss, when your eye is drawn to a piece of graffiti.

In bright green, on a white wall which is punctured by 30-40 bullets, some of which gleam in the afternoon sun, it reads: Libya Hora.

Free Libya.

You put your camera away, turn left onto the Roman road, and walk back towards the town.

Reading, Writing and Rebuilding

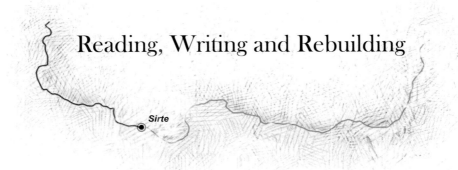

Sirte

'In the morning, I am a headteacher. But in the afternoon,' the man beams, tapping a wooden board with a finishing trowel. 'I am a worker!'

When the phrase 'military target' is used by smiling, celebratory, or even frowning, concerned, military personnel at press conferences, it's hard to know exactly what is being referred to. In Sirte, you can gain some insight by visiting the town's schools. The headteacher of Manara School, normally an all-girls establishment on the edge of Area Three, around 200m from Sirte's coast, is hard at work.

He's smoothing cement over a missile hole in the wall he has recently filled in. Across the playground, you see two other recently-repaired holes in the walls, three in the ground, and note that the basketball backboard has had three of its four corners shot off. Twenty of its windows have bullet holes through them, thirty have been recently replaced, and some fifty-or-so more gleam, having been replaced in the last few days.

'I am glad you did not come last week,' the headteacher nods, noticing the direction of your gaze. 'The school was in a real mess then.'

In the school's main building, every door has been smashed off its hinges. A total of six desks, out of a starting total of 288, remain unbroken and unburned. Holes have been smashed through the school's ceilings, and many of the walls have wooden boards nailed across circles 1-2m in diameter, where missiles have struck ('The ceilings and walls take longer than the floors to repair,' the headteacher had told you. 'But this way, no rain comes in.').

Bullet holes have been blasted into – sometimes through – every wall, and the school's electricity and water systems, which had been destroyed by missiles and later street-fighting, have been patched back together by the headteacher and some other dedicated members of staff.

'It is not ideal,' he admits, looking at the plumbing and wiring work. 'And the electricity often still fails. But we cannot have children here if there is no electricity for heating in the winter, and no water for toilets, washing hands, or to drink.'

Not only is Manara nowhere near the worst of Sirte's schools, it has in fact been chosen by the Ministry of Education as one of the town's best, and chosen to take in youngsters from schools which have been hit far harder by the Civil War's NATO strikes and ground battles.*

* Before the war, Sirte had 25 schools, serving a total of around 30,000 children.

Of those 25, two – Haldoon and Al Bayan – were destroyed outright by NATO strikes: the only possible way forward being to clear the rubble from their sites and rebuild them from the foundations up.

Six more suffered such serious structural damage from the air and the ground that it was dangerous to stand inside them. Basic security advice was not even to walk close to them, though most sites contained children and young people playing.

At best, they required serious extensive structural and strengthening work. At worst, they needed pulling down and rebuilding.

Seventeen schools remained standing and safe to enter. But of those, 15 had missile holes and bullets in their walls, almost every window broken, and almost all furniture and computers broken, stolen, or burned.

Fourteen had lost their supplies of either electricity, water, or both (one headteacher smiled grimly as he told you that it was fortunate the windows were smashed and the walls and ceilings holed by missiles, as this would make it easier to collect rainwater for the children to drink), and ten were suffering such serious drainage problems that their playgrounds, surrounded by walls, were permanently submerged beneath 30-50cm of water.

'We are preparing to take children in from another school, Al Afreakee.* They will come in the evening-time and study then, and our girls will be here in the morning.'

* The Libyan Ministry of Education realised swiftly after the war that in some parts of the country, children had missed up to nine months of schooling. In response, it pledged to ensure that all young people across the country would return to school in time for the start of the new school year, in January 2012.

With this in mind, it hurriedly arranged for the 'less damaged' schools to 'assist' those which in many cases continued to exist only in name. While understandable, and in some ways laudable, the effect was often that schools which would have been condemned elsewhere were passed as fit for use in post-war Libya.

The previous day, you had visited another school, Al Markazee, where another headteacher ('I am also a history teacher at Sarna Yousseff, but that will not open for a long time') was working on repairs in the hope of re-opening for 1,500 students. He said: 'We have been working for 15 days, and we have made some progress. Although the base of the school has been hit by rockets, and so there is very important strengthening work to do, we were quite lucky: the repairs will cost us 200,000 dinar* and much of the money has already been donated by supporters of the school.

*Ten Libyan dinar was exchanging for around US\$6.50 – available at jewellers and nowhere else – at this point. The average Libyan wage after the war was equivalent to almost US\$4,600 per year.

'But we were supposed to open days ago, and we cannot. We still need to replace 240 windows, the toilet block is unusable, and we have no water.

'We have to spend the money. The children must return to school, where many have not been for almost a whole year. You cannot simply miss a whole year of education. They must return as soon as they can.

'But children cannot study in classrooms with no windows, or in a place where there are no toilets and water. It is unacceptable...'

At Manara, the situation is identical.

The headteacher frowns, then shrugs: 'The work is not completed, but that is OK, because most of the children cannot yet come in any case.

'There is just not enough transport here in Sirte to get them to school. Before, we had buses, which would bring the girls here. But now, the buses have all been burned, or stolen.

'And the children cannot be driven to school, because in 90 per cent of cases, their parents' cars have been stolen.

'So, we miss the deadline for school starting, not because work is not done, but because all of the ways of getting to school here are burned, or stolen. This is Sirte, today.'

...Yesterday, Al Markazee's headteacher had walked you around the second floor of his school, where entire window frames – concrete supports and all – had been blasted out, leaving the charred remnants of desks, smashed school lockers, bullet-punctured walls and whiteboards bearing the ubiquitous 'Libya Hora' message in green, red or black, open to the elements.

He had said: 'We did open the doors two days ago. We felt we must, that it was important. We had failed to rebuild our school in 12 days, but that was not the children's fault. We wanted to open it for them, so they can try to continue their education, and make up time the war has taken from them.

'But only a handful came.

'It is not their fault. During the war they left their homes, with their parents, because they were told to. Because there was a war, and they were in danger. No child should be in danger.

'And when they came back, their homes had been destroyed. By missiles, by robbers and by fire. All of them suffered at the hands of at least one of those. Many from all three.

'The same thing happened to my staff – the bombs, fire, and the ransacking. What do you think if you are a child and return to that? As a parent, how do you explain it to the children you love and care about?

'So, we rebuild, and we prepare the school for the children, when they are ready, to return.'*

* *The readiness of youngsters to return to full-time education was a serious concern for the town's teachers.*

Several schools, including Sokor Khaleeg, also close to Sirte's centre, had recognised that not only could parents simply not buy schoolbooks for their children (almost every single schoolbook in Sirte had been burned or had been stolen and removed from the town. Books had been ordered from the Ministry of Education, but had not yet arrived) when they struggled to buy food or keep them sheltered from the elements, but also that the children themselves were simply not ready to return to learning.

Sokor's headteacher explained: 'We have opened. There are parts of the school with relatively little damage, and we want the children to come, so they have somewhere outside of their damaged homes which is comfortable and safe. But they have no books. Even if they did, I do not think they could use them yet. How could they sit and study normally, after all that has happened here?

'So we are running art classes, where they can draw and paint anything they want. Music classes, where they can play or listen.

'We have PE outside because children must play. And we give them pencils and paper so they can write if they want to. If they do not, they can talk about what they have seen and what they think, or they can play.'

Because most schools in Sirte were so badly damaged – by NATO, Ghaddafi's troops, and the rebels alike – the vast majority of children were not so lucky.

You look around at Manara again. You think of the progress at Al Markazee. The work that has been completed, though by no means enough to make them 'acceptable' by the standards of a nation at peace, is still impressive.

'I am very proud of my staff,' Manara's headteacher says. 'They left Sirte when they were told to, but they all returned, all of them, and they were some of the first people to return.

'They wanted to help the school. More than that, they wanted to help the children, to give them a place to be safe and to start to learn again. They have done an excellent job.'

He looks up again: 'We are paying for this,' he says. 'Me, the other staff and some funders. The Ministry of Education says it has funds available, but that will take a very long time, and there are other schools which need it more.

'But it is expensive. That is why we are doing the work ourselves. We have so far replaced 200 windows, at a cost of 15,000 Dinar. We cannot afford to pay workers to come and do it for us. It is a shame, because like all of us, they would be very pleased to be paid for what they do best.'

…At Al Markazee, you had been taken through a science lab, where a model head and torso stood alone after staff removed the shattered test tubes, chemical bottles and shredded text books which had surrounded it when they arrived. You were shown into a large, empty room.

The lock on its door had been shot out, but the door itself had been smashed off its hinges, as if those who looted the school simply could not wait for the lock to be disabled before plundering.

'Welcome,' the headmaster had said. 'To our computer centre.'*

* Every school you visited in Sirte had had at least one room which had been set aside for computer studies. Numbers of machines in each school had varied from five to 90, but every single one had been stolen or destroyed during the Civil War.

He looked at the floor, pained. 'This is one of the hardest things for us here,' he began. 'We are all saddened by the state of our school, but this was something of which we were very proud. We had 90 computers here at the school. Because computers and the internet are important, and exciting.

'They had cost very much money, but the children loved to learn to use them, and they were good at it.

'When we returned after the war, 75 had been stolen.

'Although 15 remain, each one has been destroyed with one bullet fired through the hard-drive.

'Even when the school is rebuilt, we have no money. Libya has no money. I fear it will take us years to reach the levels we were at here. Maybe we never will...'

In his school's own 'computer lab' – equally empty – Manara's headteacher agreed: 'We had fewer computers, 30 for students' use and another four for staff to run the school. But now we, also, have none.

'This was something all headteachers in the town had worked towards and were very proud of. Now, we are not sure what to do. We have certainly run schools without computers and we can do so again. But they are vital for our children. How can they grow up and work in a modern world without experience using computers?

'But the money does not exist. It is not here.

'Even if the Ministry of Education is able to give schools in Sirte money – and it has not been able to so far – that money must be spent on windows, water, electricity, and patching up holes in walls. And schools like us and Al Markazee are the lucky ones. How could we take money from Sarna Yousseff, or money that could be used to rebuild Al Bayan or Haldoon?

'Still, we are working. The town is not good.

'We can teach the children, and we can work with them to help them, and to continue to educate them, but to do this, we must have the chance to. That means the children must be able to come to school, and their families must be able to make that happen.

'I went to school here. I studied here, and I graduated here. I went to train as a teacher and I came back to teach here. Now, I am the headmaster. This is my school, and I look after it. This is our town, and its children deserve better than they have now. We will keep working to provide it. So, I am a headteacher in the morning, and a worker in the afternoon.'

Discounting the figures from the two schools which were bombed to the point of oblivion, or the six which were considered in too poor a state to open (this in itself indicated a vast amount of damage had been done: one headteacher proudly told you his school passed the inspection, but the building had three missile holes, each large enough for a child to fall through, on the second floor), the following is the basic damage count from Sirte's 17 surviving schools:

Windows in need of replacement: 1,906
Desks and chairs burned, broken or stolen: 2,458
Computers shot or stolen: 509
Electricity systems broken: 11 (two repaired)
Water systems broken: 14 (two repaired)
Missile holes: 74

Ghosts (Sarna Yousseff)

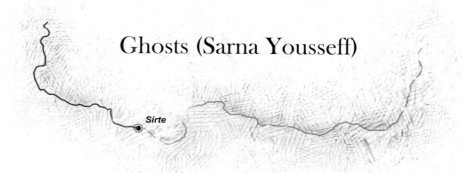

Sirte

From the front, Sarna Yousseff looks almost ordinary.

An orange coloured block, with red-framed windows. To the left, you can hear teenagers playing football on the five-a-side courts, as you walk towards the building.

As you approach, it could almost be a technicolour version of Grange Hill, or your own school, if not for the two broken windows, one – there – on the bottom floor, on the left-hand side, and another up a floor and further right.

The sun is beginning to set as you walk left, following the school wall, turning the corner and then…

On this side of the school, piles of bullet casings – some from guns, others far larger, from aircraft-mounted weapons – lie, piled up against missile shards, and its walls, which you look up to see are sagging towards you.

Every single pane of glass in every single window has been broken. If any had managed to survive whatever onslaughts were unleashed against the school, they would have been torn apart as the wall began to pull itself down and out, away from the rest of the building's structure.

You are used to this almost routine, seemingly meaningless devastation by now, but perhaps in the late afternoon light, or because the contrast between the school's front and its ruined back is so great, or maybe even because this is one of the moments where you realise this is a school and this kind of thing should never happen to a school, where children play and learn and meet friends and fall out with them and make up…

… You feel dizzy. And a little unwell.

To your left, the teens continue to play football. In your woozy, disturbed state, you wonder whether it is safe for them to be there. You glance up, then ahead and left, and decide probably it is. They would have to be very unlucky for a piece of falling stonework to strike the pitch from that distance.

You smile, realising that if anyone is in that kind of danger, it is you. You pass what was probably once the school's reception area and realise you are not the only person at risk.

At what was once a major entrance to the school from its playground, and is now, without doors, just a rectangular hole into darkness, six children are playing.

They see you. You wave, then stop waving. They call out to you.

'Kayfa hala? Laa takellum arabee,' you reply.

'Come inside,' one calls.

They disappear into the school. You run to stop them, but they are already inside. You catch sight of one of their hands as they disappear around a corner, behind a staircase which has folded completely over onto itself, and then, having lost them, you stop.

Inside, the light is different, orange, and heavy. The air is damp, and you can feel its moisture almost pushing against you as you walk. You look at the hole left by the crumpled staircase, and see the walls leaning in and over it. You are being stupid. You should not be here. No-one knows you are here, and even if they did, you would not survive if the building collapsed now.

You should walk outside, run to the gate and onto the road, but you do not. Instead, you pick your way around the staircase, turn right into a corridor, and walk. It is darker here, but there is still enough light to see and avoid a striplight, which hangs from useless wires from the damp, collapsing ceiling.

Strangely, the dead light makes you think of what the school had been like before, with youngsters shouting and knocking into one another, lights illuminating artworks, or school notices and messages.

As you walk, the ghosts of children probably still alive, who have been away from school for a matter of months but will likely never return, are surging towards and shouting all around you.

To the left, there is a doorway. Again, it has no door, but this is not unusual. You turn left, and step inside. The room is huge, but it is not possible, yet, to work out what it was, before.

To your right, floating in a pool of water in the corner closest to the door, there is a book cover – though the book itself is long destroyed – with a picture of a recorder on it. Probably a music room, then.

In the centre of the gloomy space, where a large light had once hung from the ceiling, shards of glass break the surface of another pool of water.

In this pool, a book shows an image of a colourful clock face, of the kind used by very young children to learn to tell the time.

The only furniture which remains are cupboards, some broken, some with missing doors, some overturned, but all empty of whatever – instruments? Sheet music? Test tubes? Text books? - they had once held. You feel, suddenly, short of breath, and drop, left hand on the ground, holding yourself in a crouch.

It is not the first time you have been overwhelmed since coming to Sirte, and it is not the first time you have considered that the only truly sane response to this is to cry.

But you have work to do. Like everyone else in Sirte, where nobody stops and nobody cries.

You stand, pick up your camera, shoot, and, stepping across what looks like the remains of a children's board game, walk back the way you came.

Outside, the football match continues, youngsters shouting and laughing while they play. You consider asking to join them, but it is late, and you have more to do. As you reach the school gates, you look back over your shoulder. The school looms out of the early evening light, and it occurs to you that you do not know where the six children have gone.

Then again, you do not know where any of the several hundred children – the ghosts of Sarna Yousseff, who played and worked here every day – have gone, or will go next.

Khaleeg Thaladi
(from behind a wall)

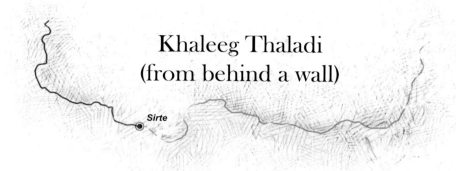

Sirte

Although many walls are designed for protection, or to mark the perimeter of something private, a certain type of person will always see them in only two ways: a mystery, and a challenge. The wall poses two questions: What is behind this? And how do I get to see whatever is there?

In Mantika Ethnaan, Area Two, the wall around Khaleeg Thaladi is around two metres tall.

It's still standing, with remarkably little damage considering its position. Like the wall surrounding a fort, its main entrance is a hole cut into the wall, with a large wooden gate.

Behind it, however, is desolation.

The school's cracked paving stones, concrete, and floor tiles are almost completely covered by orange and silver bullet casings.

To your left, its basketball court has been flooded by broken pipes and blocked drains, the mangled hoops standing alone, reflected in half an inch of still, leaf-strewn water.

Closer still, the charred stumps of what were once rows of thick trunked and green-leaved trees now sit, squat, black and forlorn between you and the school.

The school building, a three-storey block, which horseshoes around a concrete courtyard, looms over you. Most of its windows are broken, missiles have punctured two holes in the walls of the façade facing you, but its roof is largely intact.

In short, it is slightly better than average for a post-war Sirte school.

Inside, the electricity is working, cold strip-lighting illuminating classrooms which appear to have swapped tables and chairs for bullet-holes.

You start making a note of the actual number of windows broken, and later, when you arrive home, you will lose track three times of the tally you took – which stretches across a page and a half of your notebook.

On the third floor, you enter a classroom where a group of teenagers – all boys aged 14-17 – are reconstructing a section of the wall. It is dangerous work, one says (you peer through the hole they are attempting to fill with concrete, and are met with the familiar sense of dizziness which comes when all that is between you and the concrete floor is a 20ft drop), but this is their school.

No-one else is fixing it, they say, so here we are.

They are making slow progress, and none of them has any construction experience or training. But at least what they have managed – a strip of new windows here, a missile hole large enough for a child to fall through patched up over there – is making some difference.

Outside again, you stop to take pictures. You hear a noise behind you and see two men striding across the school grounds towards you. You can't see any way they could have entered – there must be a hole you had missed in the wall.

They glance at your camera and notepad. One man steps forward and demands: 'What are you doing here?'

You explain that you are attempting to ensure Sirte's schools are safe enough for children to return to, then the same man, slightly more softly, says: 'There are no children here, now. The children are all dead.'

The two men speak – too quickly and softly for you to catch – in Arabic. As they do, your translator glances from them to you, nervously, then nods to the boys who have come down from their work and are now standing behind you.

You smile to them, not wanting to provoke – or prolong – any confrontation, then the second man turns to you: 'My friend apologises,' he says. 'He saw you were a Westerner with a camera and a book and he was angry you may be here to list the achievements of the war.

'He wishes you to understand: he did not support Ghaddafi. He had no opinion, he did not know what would or should happen. He lived here, as we all do.

'One night, he went to bed, his wife and two children with him. He woke up when a missile smashed into his home, exploding and starting a fire.

'He ran to the side of the house where his children slept, and grabbed his first son.

'But his younger son was gone. The bomb had fallen on his bedroom. It had exploded there.

'This man is my brother. His younger son was my nephew.

'I found my brother, his wife and my surviving nephew sitting outside their home, holding one another and crying.

'I took them to my house. My wife and I looked after them, gave them food and drink, and the next morning, we left Sirte.

'He did not wish to return. But now we have come home, he wishes to protect his town. We hope that you can help the schools to open and to be safe. Not all of the children are here. But not all of the children are dead, either. Many will return.'

You are by now staring at the ground. The teenagers behind you murmur their sympathy.

The men shake hands with you, the first offering a thin smile as well as his hand, and turn back across the playground.

The lads slap your back, and shake your shoulders, then return to their work.

You lean for a while, against the two metre wall, looking first at the trees, then the school behind, and finally, focussing on nothing, at the sky.

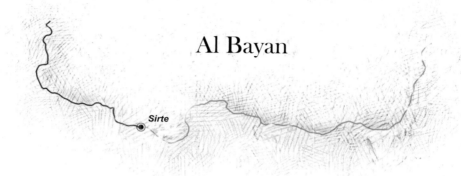

Al Bayan

As you enter its main gateway, Al Bayan appears to be bowing to greet you.

Its entire roof slopes towards you, front right-angle resting on the ground, as if in supplication to its latest visitor.

It is an effort you would rather it had not made, as it appears to have caused the entirety of two of its walls to collapse, scattering cracked concrete and shards of glass to the ground around it.

Now little more than an extremely dangerous curiosity, Al Bayan is one of two schools demolished by NATO attacks on 'military targets'.

You had not been sure whether to visit Al Bayan at all: you had already been provided with a photograph of the damage caused by NATO's 'legitimate' two-day bombardment upon it, and unlike 17 of Sirte's schools, this one was far too badly damaged for the local community to work desperately, day and night, to try to reopen it.

It would be easier – and quicker – to build an entirely new school on an empty plot of land.

But you were in the area – strangely, buying thread to sew a button back onto your jacket – and walked the short distance from the shop to visit the ruin.

There is something grimly gripping about a building which has been recently levelled.

The ruin has not yet fully settled into what would, if left to rest in peace, be its 'final transitional' shape before being reclaimed by the land on which it stands.

And the damage done is serious enough to shock, particularly when you consider that this is where 800 or-so youngsters played and learned months, perhaps weeks ago.

Here, where the roof is still propped up at the corner of two walls, you can see through widows into former classrooms, now coated in white dust, desks and chairs smashed into splinters by falling masonry, leaving twisted metal support frames standing, skeletal and forever useless.

To your left, as you near the end of a full circuit of the building, you can see what was once a sheltered area, a place where perhaps youngsters had worked, or eaten their lunches.

Now, it has been almost entirely crushed: a bomb from above simply smashing the roof onto the seats below, two picnic style benches, tossed by the explosion into the debris of the similarly ruined building behind it, the last recognisable pointers to what had once been there.

So yes, you are gripped. A little nervous about what you may see – even at this stage, some time after the war's end, not every body has been removed from buildings so utterly unsalvageable as this one – and a little nervous that the second you take your next step may be the second a section of wall finally gives way, crashing to the ground around you, but gripped.

More, you realise, you are feeling what the US President before the one responsible for the destruction of this school had wanted so badly: shock and awe.

Because this is shocking.

It was a school, and it is now nothing of the sort.

It is the wrong shape, the wrong dimensions.

At best it is like an unfinished drawing of a school, perhaps scribbled upon by an architect's youngest son or daughter.

Shock is exactly what you feel. How can you feel anything else when presented with something so utterly inexplicable, abnormal, unforgivable and unbelievable?

But as much as you do not wish to feel it; as much as you know it is what men like Ghaddafi, and 'organisations' like NATO want you to feel, making you want to fight it with every part of you, there is also awe.

Awe that something so huge and seemingly strong as a two-storey, concrete block, designed to shelter hundreds of children as they learn, could so easily and quickly be transformed into something so different, so sad and so much more dangerous.

When they announced their bombing 'statistics', NATO's spokespeople did not at first reveal that many of the 452 'military targets' they struck in Sirte in two months were in fact buildings not normally associated with 'military activity' at all.

They did not at first stand proudly and name the hospitals, schools, universities and TV broadcasting stations their missiles had hit. That revelation came only later, justified by statements such as 'weapons storage', 'improvised military base',* or, as in the case of Al Bayan School, 'hideouts for snipers'.

Ibn Sina Hospital, Sirte, was taken over by Ghaddafi and his supporters, a fact widely reported in October-December 2011 as if in justification of NATO's repeated airstrikes upon it.

In fact, NATO missiles struck the hospital twice; both times while it was still operating as a public treatment centre, while nurses and patients, rather than pro-regime fighters, were working and recovering there.

Those strikes, performed by NATO, forced the doctors and nurses at the hospital to evacuate the hospital's patients and flee, saving Ghaddafi's soldiers the no doubt tiresome job of terrorising them themselves.

It was left to the khetibas to make the final missile strikes and 'win' the hospital for 'Free Libya'. NATO's strikes came too early for that.

You stay for a short while longer, before your translator begins to complain that it is raining. As you walk back towards the car, he says: 'This made people particularly angry.'

You nod, thinking you understand.

'They bombed this school twice, on consecutive days.'

You nod again, though you now realise you do not understand.

He looks at you. 'When they bombed buildings normally, the day after, people would go into the building, to see if anyone was injured or killed,' he says. 'But here, this school, was the only place they bombed on the next day, when people were actually there.

'Those bombs could have killed people who were innocent, and trying to help. They knew that. Nobody understands why they did that.'

Haldoon (the 'weapon store')

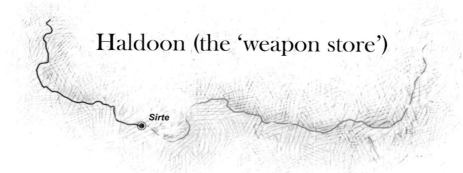

Sirte

'They said it was a weapon store. But then they bombed it, and it collapsed, and there was no huge explosion. So where were all the weapons?'

Haldoon school is a place you have heard about many times before you have seen it. It stands – those bits which do still stand – close to the law court, between Saha Markazee and the small slope between Sirte's centre and the sea.

On the occasions you have mentioned planning to visit, people have expressed fears for your safety, and in some cases for your sanity.

Almost all have told you it was bombed for being a weapon store and questioned why an airstrike failed to cause explosions when, in one man's words: 'When the ground fighters struck the fire station, the oxygen tanks blew up, but at what they said was a weapons store, nothing exploded. A school was destroyed.'

In part because of its relatively secluded, back-street location, the approach to Haldoon is quieter – and as a result more foreboding – than that to Al Bayan.

And as a more compact site, concealed to a large extent by an orange sandstone square arch, the tension grows – rather than reduces – the nearer you get to it.

There are two rooms within the arch, one to each side of the walkway through it.

Both contain nothing more than rubble – a sign that after the NATO strikes, Haldoon, in common with most large buildings in Sirte, was considered important enough for Ghaddafi's forces to fight khetibas to control.

Yesterday, you had told a boy you were going to visit Haldoon. 'The caretaker was there to clean up, last week,' he said, and laughed, hard.

Stepping from under the arch into Haldoon's main central courtyard, you can see why.

The first job for any caretaker here at Haldoon would be to find a single part of the school of which any care could still be taken.

Sixty or so days ago, Haldoon had been three connected rectangular buildings at the North, East and West of a central courtyard (the arch through which you entered is at the South, facing the centre of the town).

Today, the structure at the north end appears mostly sound, but its face is smeared with soot, pocked with missile holes, and every pane of glass is gone from its windows.

The two-storey building to the West comes to an abrupt, jagged, halt a quarter of the way along its original length. In place of its centre, there is now nothing more than a pile of stone, smashed into pieces. The damage to the Eastern building, however, seems almost perverse in both extent and appearance.

The front of the building has been peeled forward, torn away from the rest of the structure, and contributing to the courtyard's carpet of rubble. The roof has smashed to the ground, now resembling a raised floor more than any shelter or protection from the elements.

Inside the North building, it quickly becomes clear that severe damage has been done to the side of the structure you could not see from the courtyard.

You scramble over rubble, becoming covered in white concrete dust, and ducking and twisting to avoid the mangled metal building supports, which now, blasted and bent from their original positions, appear like vast, thick spider web threads.

This is no longer a building. There are no books, no clocks, no cupboards – not even really anything you could describe even as a room – to remind you of what Haldoon was originally for, of its staff and pupils and the activities they undertook daily.

But as you clamber up another pile of smashed stone and concrete, your hair, skin and clothes now so plastered in the white dust as to make you almost invisible against the rubble, you realise that to your left, you can still squeeze through underneath the top of a doorframe.

Inside the 'room', you are able to stand. A whiteboard, cracked but recognisable, has somehow remained attached to one of the few pieces of wall which remain vertical.

Some few desks have survived – like you, plastered in white dust– and still sit facing the board. But the half of the room behind you, is completely missing, open to the blazing sunshine outside, its white stone gleaming against the bright blue sky.

At this end of the room, large chunks of stone remain attached to the exposed metal building support rods, looking like small rocks caught in a net.

Strangest of all, also framed by the metal support grids, plants are growing and water flowing, creating an effect which reminds you disconcertingly of a mediaeval atrium, designed to be used for reading or contemplation in calm communion with nature.

You pick your way back over the smashed chairs, desks and stone, and step through the courtyard – now little more than a collecting point for smashed school parts.

As you pass under the arch, something catches your eye.

Half buried, just inside the room to your left, sits a small piece of white metal.

You pick it up to take a look.

It sits within the palm of your hand, a broken piece of missile casing, roughly the shape of a small fish.

Printed in black, on white, in English, reads: 'For use on MK 82 Guided Bomb'.

My Brother

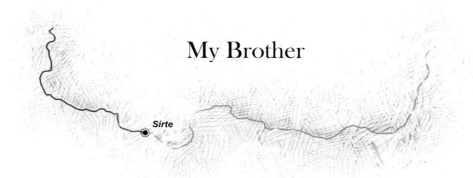

Sirte

An international organisation has set up centres in Sirte, for use by children and young people.

Equipped with table football (greeted by young people in Sirte as if they had awaited it with longing for every moment of their lives), table tennis, pens, papers, modelling clay, books and games, the idea is to offer youngsters from all over the city the chance to meet and play in safe places, away from collapsing buildings, and the unexploded ordnance which litters the city.

You are performing interviews for the organisation, finding out more about the youngsters who are using the centre.

Predictably, at first, none of them are interested. But once you have convinced the first child to sit down and talk, others ask if they, too, can be interviewed.

Finally, at the point of critical mass, even the teenagers volunteer to talk.

As you finish speaking to a boy about his school, and how he helped to save his sister when his house was bombed (his sister, older and taller than him, will later be at pains to point out that she carried him from the house, while he clung to her and cried, rather than the other way around. You conclude that perhaps she has the more reliable memory of this event), one teen rolls up his trouser leg and stamps his foot on the chair beside you.

'I love Ghaddafi!' he shouts, though you do not realise this until your translator murmurs it, almost too quietly for you to pick up.

He has a circular scar in his calf, which you recognise from other conversations, here and at Choucha Refugee Camp.

You look at him, and ask him to sit down.

'I love Ghaddafi. I am 17 and I love Ghaddafi. I wish he was still alive.

'What do you think about that?

'You don't have an opinion? You must have an opinion! I love Ghaddafi! You are a Westerner, and I love Ghaddafi!

'Why? Because Ghaddafi is a good man! He is the leader of my country! I fought for him because he is great! He was good for my family! He gave us money when we had none and he helped us to go to school and to learn new things!

'Yes! That is good! You are right that it is good! That is why I fought for him!

'How did I come to fight for him?

'I am 17. I come from Area Three. My brother, who is 25, he was a member of the Libyan army. He had a uniform and he would fight for Libya and Ghaddafi wherever he was told to, here or in other countries.

'When we were attacked by the rats, from France and the USA and the UK and here within our own country, he went to fight against the rats.

'My other brother is 19. He was not in the army. He was in University. It is where I will go, too.

'He had promised my mother that he would not join the army. Even though the rats were fighting against Ghaddafi and we had to help him, she was afraid that he would get hurt. She said that it was enough that one of her sons was being shot at, she did not want any more in danger.

'But one day, he left my house. He told me where he was going – to join Ghaddafi's soldiers. It was because we had the same bedroom and so he could not sneak out in the night without me knowing.

'He told me I must not tell my mother, and that she would be proud of him. I felt sad because I had to lie to my mother, but I thought about her being proud, and about him fighting the rats, and I knew it was the right thing.

'So, when my mother found he had gone, I pretended to be surprised.

'But a few days later, I felt bad again.

'My house was hit by a missile. It struck the front room and I was in the back room. I was scared. My mother was scared as well. But I was also angry.

'I could see that my mother wanted my brother to come home. She was scared like we all were about dying and wanted us to be together.

'I thought she would send me to get him back, but she did not. I knew that she would be happier if my brother came home. So, in the night, I sneaked out.

'I went because I wanted to find him and make him come home. I thought when I found him, I would tell him how our mother was sad and he would come back.

'So I went out into the town. I had to be careful. I knew where Ghaddafi's soldiers were, and where the rats were, but I did not know where they were fighting each other, and I wanted to find my brother.

'After a day, I could not find him. I could go home, but what would I say to my mother? She would be even more sad, because she had lost me, her last son, and she would not get my brother back.

'So instead, I went to a building where Ghaddafi's troops were.

'I went inside and told them my brother's name. I said that I had to get him to come home because my mother was sad. They laughed. They said they knew him, but he was not there.

'But it was hard for me. Because I love Ghaddafi. And I wanted to fight for him, against the rats. So instead of asking where he was, or going back to my home, I asked if I could fight with them.

'My oldest brother had told me about his training, but I did not get any training. I was given a gun, and there was a uniform for me. I put on the uniform and picked up the gun.

'The soldiers were nice to me. They were nice to each other. But it was not always a very good feeling.

'It was good to be a part of a team and to be defending my country and my leader with other people, but it was also sometimes frightening, and I sometimes wondered what the rats were thinking. Did they think the same way as me?

'After three days, I met my brother in Area Two. It was good to see him.

'I told him about my mother and he said he would come home if she was sad, but first he had to fight. He told me to go home, but I said I would not go back without him.

'He tried to make me leave, and told the other soldiers to take me home, but I stayed to fight that night.

'It was a long battle and it was hard in the darkness. I do not know who won. I was shot in the leg by a sniper. Yes, of course it hurt. It was a terrible pain.

'I did not think I would die because the pain was so bad. I had read a book that said if you are injured very badly, you cannot feel it because your body makes the pain stop. So I did not think I would die because it hurt me so badly.

'I was screaming and in the darkness I also worried that another bullet might hit me. But a soldier ran to me and lifted me up. He said stop screaming or he would be shot as well. He told me to bite on his sleeve. So I did that.

'He carried me to a car and then took me to the hospital. They told me the bullet had gone straight through my leg. You can see it on both sides, look.

'I was there for two weeks. My mother found me there. She was very sad, but said she was glad that I was alive.

'I wanted to know where my brother was, but he was arrested. He was taken to Misrata, but we have not heard from him since. My oldest brother was in prison in Benghazi. They have let him out, and he will come back to Sirte soon, but at the moment he has stayed there.

'He is working with people who have no homes because of the war. Libyans who do not have a place to live. He says it is a good thing to do. He says that the war means that he should help people who supported Ghaddafi, and even the rats, who had to run away and have no place to live.

'I told him I know that. Most people in Sirte had to run away. Even the rats. And I do think it is good to help people. There is not a war any more so we should all help each other.

'I love my home. I love Sirte and I love Libya. I love Ghaddafi.

'I am glad now that people have come back to Sirte. And I come to this centre, which is good. I have met new people and I like it here.

'But I am sorry that my house and the whole town is destroyed. Look around you. Everything is broken.

'That is what we must do now. We must fix Sirte and fix Libya. Now, the past is dead. We must live in the present and make a new future.'

The Green Book Building

'When the building was bombed, I was here. I watched the planes fly and I saw the bombs drop and crash into it.

'It was dark, in the evening time. I shouldn't have been here.

'I was supposed to be getting salt from a shop for my mother. But I wanted to play and so I came here to see if any of my friends were here.

'Then the planes flew across from where the sea is, and they dropped their bombs.'

You are standing in SaHa Markazee, formerly Green Square, listening to a seven year-old boy tell you about how he had stood in the same spot when airstrikes blasted the teepee-shaped Green Book Building, the remains of which stand 500 yards to your right.

'I didn't really feel anything,' the boy says. 'I just stood and watched the flames glowing. It was very pretty. But very quickly, stones started to fall out of the sky. I ran away then, back to my house.

'A few days later, we were playing here and a plane came in daylight and bombed the building again. It was not so pretty that time. Some of the boys were crying, but I did not cry. I just watched.

'I wasn't here when the rebels attacked the building the third time, because we had gone away to escape the war. But I heard that a tank attacked it and shot more holes in it.

'I don't know why, because it had already been bombed twice. People did not like that building.'

The boy's father arrives, shakes hands with you and takes him home, leaving you in the darkness, looking across at the building he had watched being destroyed.

Sirte's Green Book Building, or Centre for Recitation and Study of the Green Book, was one of five identical buildings (the others were in Tripoli, Benghazi, Sabha and Al Bayda)* built for the general public to learn about and discuss Ghaddafi's political manifesto, the Green Book.**

* As almost comically simple symbols of Ghaddafi's regime, the Green Book Buildings were obvious targets of the khetibas and NATO. They were heavily bombed, and destroyed in each town and city.

** *Released in three sections in 1976, 1978, and 1979, The Green Book was Ghaddafi's attempt to create a new politics – a 'Third Universal Theory' designed to supersede both communism and 'atheistic capitalism' (a name, and aim, which raises the interesting possibility that some 25 years later, Ghaddafi and Tony Blair compared notes on the 'Third Way').*

Though it has been fairly described as 'more entertaining than coherent', the Green Book's internal contradictions have been overplayed by commentators seemingly unable or unwilling to accept the strength of the fairest possible criticism of Ghaddafi – that he was a megalomaniac under whom Libyan citizens faced terror, imprisonment, torture and death.

To an extent, the greatest criticism which could be made of the Green Book is in fact more a criticism of its author: having written it, Ghaddafi seemed content never to put the majority of it into practice.

That is not to say its proposals would have worked – every politico-economic system has flaws which can overcome the whole: in our own Liberal, Representative Capitalist Democracy, people sleep rough and die from poverty-related conditions – but no system stands any chance if it is not even enacted.

From a Western perspective, one easy criticism of the Green Book is that it exists at all: Ghaddafi was a relatively-uneducated man, this argument begins, who seized power through a military coup of which he was just one of several architects: how can he justify then producing a book about the 'ultimate' political and economic system?

The idea that the book was written either as a reflection of Ghaddafi's arrogance, or to present him falsely as a great revolutionary leader is reinforced by its obvious inspiration, Mao's Little Red Book, which set out to 'replace' Confucianist philosophy in China in much the same way as Ghaddafi hoped to replace the Qur'an. But Ghaddafi's book is lighter in touch than Mao's work, and owes at least some of its inspiration to Rousseau, Engels, Egypt's General Nasser, Bedouin traditions and the wider tradition of Islamic rulers writing models for law and society.

Further Western criticism of the book's content often centres on what commentators regard as its 'inconsistencies', with one example often cited: the idea that he simultaneously calls for a socialist system and exalts the ownership of private property.

It is hard to reconcile this criticism with what the book actually says: 'Man's freedom is lacking if somebody else owns what he needs… All men need a place to live, a vehicle, and an income… There is no freedom for a man who lives in another's house, whether he pays rent or not… Your vehicle should not be owned by others.'

Whether workable or not, Ghaddafi's ideas here are at least logically-consistent: for freedom to exist, no-one's basic requirements can be owned by someone else. Therefore, no-one can own a second home to rent to another because they would then control another person's basic requirement of a place to live.

Ghaddafi regarded a 'housing stock' and a 'vehicle stock' as a 'commonly-owned whole', shared equally between the population, while Western commentators view home-ownership as a branch of individualistic capitalist endeavour.

The latter view was particularly understandable in the UK and US, where neo-liberalism was busy stoking unsustainable housing booms based on the very idea that home-ownership was a central capitalist tenet, but it does not 'prove' Ghaddafi's view to be wrong, or that the Green Book was 'illogical'.

Ghaddafi also wrote that no person should be a wage-earner because if someone pays another for work, they 'own' that person's inalienable right to an income. Again, this idea – which is arguably the Green Book's hardest to understand and to enact – is easier to grasp from a collective, rather than an individualistic position. Ghaddafi argues that everybody should work to produce goods or materials, all of which are to the wider benefit of the whole of society.

Under this system, everybody shares equally in what is produced, or the income raised by what is produced. In this way, Ghaddafi claimed – in a reflection of Engels' thoughts on the movement of money – that profit and wages will become unnecessary, and both will cease to exist.

Again, this may not be possible to enact – for example the book does not explain how a state would move from a model in which wages 'are exchanged for work and one in which all work for the benefit of all;' and Ghaddafi offers no definitive list of what is an 'acceptable' level of comfort and what items are 'unnecessary luxuries' – but the view is not internally contradictory.

The Green Book also criticises government systems, which Ghaddafi claims to believe are unrepresentative of the will of the people. He argues that representative democracies based on a constituency system encourage competition between politicians interested in their own areas, to the detriment of the country as a whole.

He is also suspicious of voting systems which enable 'up to 49 per cent' of voters' wishes to be effectively ignored for four or five years (in plural party systems, the number can be far higher), and that referenda are little – if at all – better, because they allow people only to vote 'yes' or 'no' and not to express their full opinion.

(As I was writing this book, a polling company contacted a friend of mine to ask 'are you happy with the <UK> government's immigration policy?' He answered 'no', but was unhappy to discover there were no further questions. A few days later, the London Evening Standard used the poll as the basis of an editorial claiming that 'Sixty per cent of the UK public feel immigration policy is too weak'. My friend had in fact hoped to express his opinion that the government's immigration policy was unnecessarily and detrimentally harsh.)

Ghaddafi adds that because political parties tend to represent only one class or social group, they are incapable of delivering a system in which the national interest is the priority, and that single-party systems are unacceptably undemocratic because they offer only one group the possibility of representation.

He argues that populations are too large for a true direct democracy, in which everyone's full opinion can be heard, and proposes instead a system of people's committees and popular congresses. Avoiding, for a moment, the massive, glaring question that this raises: what purpose can the congresses serve if there is no system of direct democracy in place? It should perhaps be noted that whatever Ghaddafi's educational achievement, legitimacy as a ruler, or intelligence, these are not unreasonable points.

And it is in this section of analysis that the Libyan dictator's thoughts have been argued to share ground with Rousseau, a true formative genius of Western political thought. Ghaddafi and Rousseau share a clear belief that sovereignty is inalienable, indivisible and infallible: that the 'general will' can be found, and must dictate the policy and direction of every state.

In fact, Ghaddafi goes even further, stating that: 'the outdated definition of democracy – the supervision of government by the people – becomes obsolete. It will be replaced by the true definition – the supervision of the people, by the people.'

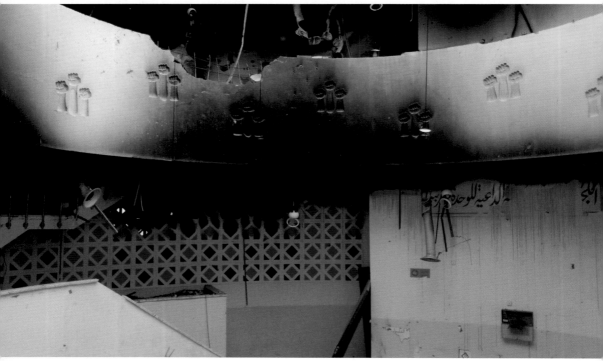

The problem with Ghaddafi's view is basic and simple: none of this happened.

It is tempting to write more, but it is also unnecessary: sometimes, things are so damning when expressed simply that little more is necessary. However good or bad Ghaddafi's model may be, none of it was delivered.

People's committees and assemblies were nominally created – indeed, many of the meetings held at the Green Book Buildings were officially named as either one or the other – but made no decisions, instead solely discussing the Green Book's contents.

The system Ghaddafi expounded and which he alone was capable of introducing in Libya was never introduced by Ghaddafi.

The Green Book also touches on nationalism – which Ghaddafi believes is vital, describing the nation state as: 'the real constant dynamic force of history.'

But here, again, Ghaddafi's actions seem to clash with his proclaimed ideas. Perhaps least problematic, the book claims all nations require just one religion, as more than one strong belief system makes internal conflict likely.

But within Libya, although Islam was by far the largest religion, not only was it not the sole religion practised, many Muslims felt that the faith was given too little importance by the regime. Indeed, a large minority of the khetibas were motivated not by the desire for free market economics, but by a desire to strengthen Islam and enable Libyans to live as 'better' Muslims.

From a Western perspective, religious plurality is not a negative characteristic for a state, but Ghaddafi's stated opinions and practise once again appear to have been in stark contrast to one another.

One driving factor in this contrast may have been Ghaddafi's attitude towards women. Across Libya, women were in work, and the Green Book is very clear that this is what Ghaddafi wanted for the state.

The clearest message on the subject reads simply: 'There is no difference in human rights between men and women.'

This statement is in fact completely in keeping with traditional Islamic thought: despite the laws laid down later by less enlightened members of the faith, Mohammed promoted the rights of women, stating clearly that men and women were equal in the eyes of Allah. And he lived his message, with women in advisory and evangelical positions in Islam's earliest years.

On the other hand, Ghaddafi also declares in the Green Book that it is a woman's 'natural role' to be a mother, and that children should be raised by their mother, rather than sent to nursery.

But this seemingly contradictory message is not dissimilar from the debates over women, work and children which were taking place elsewhere in the world at the same time, and even today in the United Kingdom newspapers and magazines consistently carry articles on the topic of whether women can 'have it all' (by which they appear to mean 'have a job and a child').

Ghaddafi's views on race also betray a gulf between his writing and his action. The Green Book talks about the 'difficulties' of a nation containing ethnic minority groups (the alternatives are that the 'group' fits into the 'social structure' of the nation, but risks losing its own 'social rights', or forms – or imports – its own 'social structure', retaining its 'social rights' but eventually forming its 'own' nation).

But in practise, Ghaddafi declared himself as the 'King' of Africa ('Emperor', though sometimes used in this context, is in fact not correct: Ghaddafi's hope was that Africa would choose to unify, and that he would become its leader, rather than that it would be unified by conquest from Libya, and he would be its ruler) and invited refugees from across the continent to settle in Libya.

Once again, this is not a negative factor: many thousands of persecuted human beings owed their lives to Ghaddafi's decision. But it raises, once again, questions about the gap between his words and his actions.

In part, Ghaddafi's view on the wider Africa, his role within it, and the need for a 'pan-African, pan-Arabic and pan-Islamic leader' came from Egypt's former leader, Gamal Abdel Nasser, who Ghaddafi had idolised as a young man.

Nasser had taken power in Egypt in 1952, ousting King Farouk, and set up a Socialist Republic with himself as its leader. As a teenager, Ghaddafi was captivated, and learned many of Nasser's radio-broadcast speeches off by heart. Indeed, much of his early life could almost have been a deliberate attempt to emulate Nasser's achievements in order.

But other factors influenced the Green Book as well. Ghaddafi looks to the Bedouins, traditional inhabitants of Libya, to inspire his ideal 'way of life'.

As well as praising the Bedouins' solidarity, Ghaddafi also compares the 'natural' Bedouin existence with the 'ills of modern' life.

This leads to some surprising positions. The Green Book, unlike both production-centric capitalist thinkers and supply-driven Socialists, argues against 'mechanised' farming and factory chicken raising, as wild-raised birds taste better and provide healthier meat because they 'grow naturally and are naturally fed'.

It is equally likely that Ghaddafi's belief in Bedouin traditions influenced his views on compulsory education, which the Green Book argues is a 'forced stultification of the masses… destructive to freedom… deprives people of their free choice, creativity, and brilliance.'

Instead, Ghaddafi proposed that all knowledge must be available to every person, and they should be able to learn what they choose to, 'in a way that suits them'.

On freedom of speech, the Green Book is also outspoken: 'Freedom of expression is the right of every… person, even if (they) choose to behave irrationally, to express (their) insanity.'

It states that freedom of speech can only be delivered if publishers, newspapers, television and radio stations are publicly-owned, as private ownership undemocratically allows only a few voices to be heard.

Once again, this simply did not happen. Ghaddafi had the opportunity to ensure the full public ownership of the media, and its freedom, but did not do so. Instead, his regime repressed free speech, used its media for propaganda and to display executions as warnings to the nation.

The major problem with the Green Book is not what it contains, but the fact that its own author ignored its contents so assiduously.

Like Green Square, which it stands beside, the building was also a clear statement from Ghaddafi, a centrally-positioned, imposing building representing the new Libya and the central part Ghaddafi and the Book should play in it.

Even holed and fire-damaged, it is reminiscent of a smaller 'Paddy's Wigwam' – Liverpool's Roman Catholic Cathedral – though in white and green (in fact, the comparison bears some examination: if the Green Book was, in some way, Ghaddafi's attempt to create a 'new', secular Qur'an, then the Green Book buildings could easily be considered its mosques or cathedrals).

In daylight, it is interesting – a new-ish building, badly damaged, but still standing, and in that sense doing considerably better than the regime it used to represent.

You approach it, coming closer to its dome, now just an empty shell of supporting wire, its glass shattered, and with holes punched through its sloping walls. Its green lattice-work remains relatively undamaged, but the building's concrete support spars – thick, white diagonal spars, reaching from the dome's peak down beyond the edges of the circular walls of the main structure – are scarred by bullet holes from aircraft, machine- and hand-guns.

On its walls, interestingly, along with the 'standard' graffiti – 'Libya Hora', Febriar 17, 'Free Zlitan', 'Misrata Khetiba' – is written 'Mahjooz', meaning 'reserved' in the sense of a restaurant booking. You do not speculate over its meaning for long, instead glancing behind you, to see if you are watched.

Though there are shops across the road, you figure you are far enough from them not to be seen, and enter the building through the remains of what were once glass and metal doors.

There are no lights, of course, and even in daylight, and despite the holes in the walls and roof, and the total lack of glass in the building's dome, it takes your eyes some time to become accustomed to the darkness.

You glance left, to an antechamber in which the ceiling strips are peeling away, wiring has dropped from ceiling to floor, the windows have been smashed – not just the glass, but the stone window-frames themselves have been blasted away by missile fire – the ground is coated in the white dust which seems to cover every not-yet-cleaned surface in Sirte, and all the furniture is melted, burned or smashed.

Well, not quite all: somehow, one desk, heavily varnished to the colour of oak, stands seemingly undamaged in the middle of the wreckage.

In the next room, the main hall of the building, one item also survives. Not the seven rows of 15 chairs: every single one is burned, leaving only the white metal bars on which the seats themselves had been mounted, almost skeletal, as if now, as you stand below the shattered, empty dome, you are regarded silently by bones. Not the vast majority of the items on the raised dais the incinerated chairs once faced: a lectern, papers, seats, smashed, shattered, torn, beneath a pile of rubble and broken glass. Nor the ceiling, sagging, collapsed, with sections now resting on the remains of the chairs, wires exposed and spilling out as if the veins and organs of a wounded animal.

A staircase on the stage's right-hand side, marble with metal bannisters appears undamaged until, eyes following its course towards the ruined dome, you see its top has been smashed from the balcony it once connected to.

On the lower rim of the balcony itself, raised fists are carved in the grey stone, in groups of three set equidistant from one another all around the circular ledge.

You imagine that before this building was hammered by aircraft, tanks, missiles, grenades and rockets, these fists, raised together, may have served the same purpose as the 'black power' salute – a defiant symbol against opponents, and a signal that together, those gathered under the symbol are strong.

Today, they are black in a more literal way, fire-damaged, covered in soot, as if the injustices and failures of the regime they represented can be righted or changed simply by recolouration, its problems solved by a change of shade.

One item actually in one piece and undamaged, however, is also the most obvious and simple, visual metaphor of all.

Atop the rubble and broken glass, at the centre of the stage, a globe sits, surrounded by the detritus and devastation of war.

Its seas remain blue and its land is still green. But it is inverted, so that Antarctica, dusky but still recognisable under a film of brick-dust, now sits at its top.

In the centre of Ghaddafi's hometown 'cathedral', surrounded by and carried on the detritus of war, the world has been turned upside down.

It sits, alone, in the gloomy half-light, waiting on events outside to decide its fate.

The Green Book Building
postscript

Sirte

Across the road from the Green Book Building, a shopkeeper and his customers stand chatting.

Mothers and children walk together along the pavement framing the Roman highway, while cars, bikes, pickups and the occasional long-haul truck, pass by in the afternoon sun.

None pay any attention to the destroyed structure across the road, and as you stand and take photographs, you wonder what, and whether, any of them think about it any longer.

In every place in Libya where one of these identikit centres existed, Tripoli, Benghazi, Al Baydan, Sabha, and across the road from you, here in Sirte, it was one of the first focal points of the rage of the revolutionaries.

In Tripoli, Benghazi, Al Baydan and Sabha, they were burned and smashed by the khetibas themselves, making you momentarily wonder whether NATO really needed to bomb the Sirte Building twice, and whether the khetibas here were unhappy the symbolism of their 'strike at Ghaddafi's heart'* had been stolen from them.

---

* *'By a T-72 tank,' as one beaming eyewitness later told you. 'I studied there myself, so I was interested to watch it. It took a long time to smash.'*

Outside each one, celebrating rebels burned copies of the Green Book itself, inspiring the New York Times to report: 'Small wonder, then, that… one of the first expressions of the will of the masses was to burn the very book Ghaddafi claimed would set them free.'

This may be the first time the NYT has ever unquestioningly justified mass book-burning anywhere in the world.

In truth, the Green Book Buildings were always destined to stand or fall with the leader whose ideas they were created to represent. As he fell under foreign missiles, national anger, flames and destruction, so, of course, did they.

The Green Book failed Libyans. Perhaps because even its own author made little effort to follow its strategy for a 'better' society, perhaps because attempts to force any set of ideas upon people who have not chosen them for themselves are always doomed – however eventually – to fail. But in spite of everything, you still wonder what happened there? What did those who visited it regularly do there? How did those who experienced the building not just as an abstract symbol, and the Green Book not only as a curiosity to be criticised from the comfort of a University residence, actually regard them?

'It is a good question,' says one of the customers of the shop opposite the Building. 'I supported Ghaddafi. Some of his ideas were good, and we were better off in many ways with him than when we had the King.

'But the Green Book Building was a boring place where people droned for hours and never said anything at all.'

He looks at you, sighs, and shrugs his shoulders: 'How can you have a political debate if nobody is allowed to disagree?'

Parklife

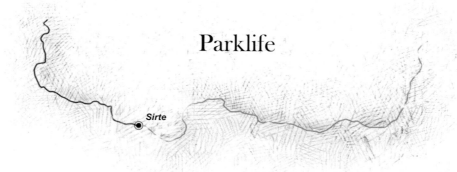

Sirte

You can still see what they'd intended.

Unlike Ghaddafi's tent-cum-exhibition centre a short distance away, which now resembled a tent less than a collection of hundreds of short steel rods covered in melted plastic, there was, even as you had picked your way through broken glass, bullet casings and artillery containers, no mistaking how nice – in the exact Middle-Class meaning of the word – this place had been.

Having asked your driver to stop on an overcast afternoon (he stayed in the car, having been given strict instructions by his company not to enter), you had crossed the road, at first keen to peer through the railings.

You were distracted for a few moments by the piles of bullet casings, shimmering in the drizzle which had just passed, and then walked alongside the ornate metal rails and sculpted concrete pillars, each slightly diminished by chips clipped out by gunfire, or chunks smashed away by rockets.

Eventually, noting that the gates remained locked even though several metres of railings had been blasted to the ground, you stepped inside.

You walked across lawns, only slightly overgrown even now, past large ponds, with islands whose burned stumps showed signs of once having been palm trees, but only tiny amounts of water.

Now on a boulevard where ornate lanterns had been shot into grotesquely-twisted poses, and where bullets, missile shells and artillery casings now clogged up what had once been a water-feature, you can still see what this place was supposed to be, and wonder whether the word nice was the sole inspiration for this park.

Even the way it had been designed, with a small incline upon which a café had sat, with the children's play area on the other side – almost an exaggeration of the Victorian ideal that children should be seen and not heard* – seemed to fit the term's reserved, genteel tones.

---

* In fairness to Libya, one accusation which could never be laid at its door was that it believed children should be seen and not heard. From riotous laughter as they picked their way through bombsites to singing contests across shops two metres wide, the one thing you could guarantee was that if you could see children – and often if you could not – you would certainly hear them.

You stop, almost overcome by a ludicrous image: men in top hats, dress coats, white britches and knee-length boots, ladies in bonnets and floor-length dresses, while children ran in caps, jackets, stockings and shorts, enjoying an hour together in Sirte's newest, and nicest, park.

Carriages drawn by horses rattle by, as in any English period drama. 'You must come and visit sometime, darling. It's really such a nice park.'

You smile to yourself. Nice Park. Even if there had been any plans to give the park such an awful name (and there had not), nobody could have called it that at this moment.

The park's central café, ahead of you, has had its roof burned, mangled, and partly blasted off. Missiles had punched holes through its side walls, through which you see that all that remains inside are collapsed ceilings, burned furniture and soot-smeared sections of walls.

Every sheet of glass (there are 30 gaps where they should have been) has been shattered.

You walk down into the children's play area. A lion's head lies on the floor, its flat body, some yards away, raised slightly at an angle thanks to its handle. Not far away is a horse body, at a similar angle, but with head still attached.

Several yards away stand the large orange springs which would – had the park ever had the chance to open – have enabled children to ride the lion, and the horse.

Instead, war broke out before the park was named, let alone opened.

No-one walked its boulevards, except some soldiers loyal to Ghaddafi, who chose this strangely exposed site as a base. It seems unlikely to you that any of them took time out to ride a lion on a spring.

You walked towards a climbing-frame, made to look like a miniature house. You note the countless bullet holes punched through its walls, which make it as accurate a representation of the buildings around it now as it was before the war, but some ironies are too sharp to enjoy.

In any case, you are momentarily distracted by a small crater, with a dead missile, head peeled back like a banana skin, still sat within it.

You understand that this was a war, that the park was not filled with children, and that in fact this was a battlefield upon which Ghaddafi's regime and the rebels who sought its overthrow fought one of the last major battles on the Libyan Civil War.

But it still seems perverse to be walking past decapitated children's toys and viewing bullet-holed children's play apparatus while stood beside a miniature, almost child-sized crater gouged by a rocket yards from a climbing frame.

All the more so as almost every day you watch children clambering up ruins, hiding in missile holes and swinging on the metal struts of buildings smashed by war.

Nobody had ever named 'New Park', and as the drizzle begins again, you realise with sadness that now, it would become simply one more public place named 'Martyrs' or 'Victory', to ensure Libya could never really make itself a nation at peace.

You walk back across the desolate, abandoned park, climb back into the car, and ride home.

University

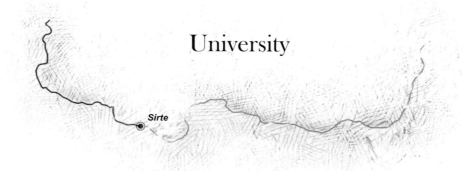

Sirte

As you sat at your desk, a translator for an organisation you were working for walked into the room. You nodded and smiled, asked how he was, and got back to work.

He hovered close to the desk for a moment, then murmured 'I did not think you would be at work', before placing two gifts on the edge of the desk.

You looked up, surprised. It is Christmas morning, but you had not expected to celebrate in Libya.

'I lived in the UK,' he said, by way of explanation. 'I will not forget how kind a family was to invite me to their home when I had no-one at Christmas time. Merry Christmas.'

You were immediately sorry. First, because you had not bought him a gift, but even more because you did not feel you knew him well enough to let him know how much the gesture meant.

'Chokran, thank you,' you said. 'Anta lateef. You are very kind.'

He shrugged. 'Afwan. It's nothing.'

So the day began.

In a foreign state, where you know next to nothing, and absolutely no-one, there are worse places to start than a university.

You have already met – and 'recruited', after a fashion – several students who, thanks to their study of English, French or multimedia communications have proven kind and useful contacts, allies and friends, but you have not yet spent any time at Sirte's University* itself.

* Prior to the war, the University – formerly a campus of Garyounis University but since 1991 an establishment in its own right - had been known as 'Altihadi' or 'Challenge' University. At the point of this visit, it was already unofficially being called Sirte University, the name it retains today.

It's a cold morning – by Sirte's standards at least – about 7°C, but the skies are clearing as you approach the university's white, blue, green and gold entrance gates.

It's busy – registration for courses opened yesterday – and students and prospective students head from department to department, meeting staff and catching up after their forced 'vacation'.

'I'm in charge of the repairs here. I am also a lecturer, but we are all repairmen now.'

The man has walked across the car park towards you, at first wondering whether you were a prospective student, now warming to your questions about his recent experience.

'Students are coming back every day now. And before them, the staff came. We have all worked together, doing everything we can.

'We have fixed most of the colleges and offices,' he said. 'Well, those that we can fix.'

He glances over his shoulder.

'That was the University hotel,' he says, indicating a formerly two-storey building. 'It's where students' parents could stay if they were visiting their child, in term-time or at graduation.'

You walk, together, towards the building.

Parts remain intact: pillars holding the roof above a balcony section of the white-painted stone building. Perhaps once, the stucco and pillar design might have invited accusations of pretension. Now, the bits which remain appear dignified, ornate against their surroundings.

To the right, several pillars have been knocked out of place – smashed aside, in other words, by rockets, causing the roof to collapse, sloping forward and right into the ground floor, where rubble, glass, metal and other detritus is piled against the wall.

To the left, there is no longer a ground floor, let alone a first. There are no pillars, no windows, no doors. Nor is there even really a roof – bombs from above ensured that is now simply a huge slab of concrete, which has smashed through all below it, crushing it to the ground. It now lies flat, at ground level.

It should be an outrage – an affront to mankind. Instead, it is just another of a multitude of similar wreckages, similarly devastated structures, similar destruction of the achievements, and aspirations, of humanity by humanity, in Sirte.

Even they are overshadowed by the unfathomable and inexcusable insults to the concept of humanity – delivered by the three 'players' in Libya's Civil War who have stained the state in blood, scattered victims of torture in its wake, and chased thousands of refugees across its borders.

The building's destruction, its current state, should be a surprise, at least. Instead, it is just another depressing pinpoint on Libya's map of devastation: a reminder that even in Guernica, outrage, horror and anger – the only appropriate, just, responses – eventually give way to numbness and resignation, hammer blows to the soul reduced to drips of water, tapping lightly but insistently on a windshield.

The man shakes his head, sighs, and steers you back towards the University's main entrance block: 'We have not yet fixed or replaced all of the glass, but we hope to do so soon. When we first arrived here, we had so much to do. It was bleak, and grim. But when you start to work, to achieve things, and to finish small pieces, day by day, it gets better.

'Best of all is when the students began to return. They are what makes the University what it is. Without them, it is just empty buildings. Things will improve now they have returned.'

The University's Chancellor stands as you enter his office. He is physically small, the top of his head slightly higher than your shoulder-level. But he has big plans for the future.

'The University is the centre of the community of Sirte,' he says. 'We are proud to have it, of course, but that is not all. What the University does is to show children and young people that there is hope for the future, that there is something to work towards and to achieve.

'It brings young people to the town and it helps those within the town to see who they are, where they are, and what can happen in the future.'

He explains that the University has 12,000 students, 1,300 staff, 13 faculties, 'more than 100' departments and that four faculties are based 250km away in Jufrah.

'The University was like Sirte,' he says. 'Very clean, very tidy, very well-organised. And it is still like its hometown. There has been almost total destruction.'

You decide to reserve judgement, having so far seen only the buildings closest to the Roman Road – a mix of the hotel's devastation and the relative 'fortune' of a generous spray of bullet holes and broken windows in the University's office buildings.

'But reconstruction is happening now. Life starts from the University. The life of Sirte begins here.

'Lots of people are still away, but if the University opens its doors people will bring their families home to study. Otherwise, people stay away. They see no future for their children. That is why our focus is to get open by all means.'

He claps his hands, seemingly overcome by his admittedly contagious enthusiasm.

'What they forgot, NATO, rebels and khetibas, is that we are a University. When we need people who know about construction, we can find them. When we need engineers, we know where they are. Because we train them!'

He pauses, for a moment downcast.

'The destruction is astounding. Astonishing. We cannot estimate the cost because how could we know? What similar situation could we base it on?

'But we are working. We are working not for ourselves, and not even for the University, but for our community, and our town. And because of this, and because of our expertise, and because of our commitment, we will be ready.'

The University, he tells you, was effectively closed by mid-August.

'The war really begins in Sirte in September,' he explains. 'There was a great deal of bombing before, but September is when the war arrives here.

'But in August, when Tripoli fell, it was clear to most people that Sirte would be the next capital for Ghaddafi, and that there was no way back. That Ghaddafi's Libya was over.

'So, in effect, most departments closed down here in August. The students have had a very long time away from their studies, so we must open soon and make sure we work together to make up for lost time.

'But we can also do more for Sirte. I would like us to try to help the children. I think our students might be able to help teach children things. I would like us to open our computer laboratories to the children of Sirte. But at the moment, like those of the schools, they are empty. We will restock them. We are part of Sirte, we grow with our home, and it with us.'

Back outside, you walk with another staff member, through the University campus away from the Roman Road.

'We had a journalist here soon after the war finished,' the staff member tells you. 'He had a camera, but I do not know what happened.'

The man shepherds you from place to place, making it seem at times as if you are taking part in the least persuasive University promotional tour ever undertaken. You visit a lecture theatre, where the graffiti on the tables (if you did not, by now, recognise the shapes if not every

sound they represent) could almost be the bored doodlings of students, but where a rocket has blasted the concrete from the wall in the lower left-hand corner of the room, enabling you to view the courtyard outside through the mesh of the metal wall supports, without leaving your chair.

Walking down a corridor, he points to a piece of graffiti: 'Libya Hora', he says. 'Free for what?'

Back outside you insist on stopping outside a faculty building. You can see inside to a large leather chair, over which a tutor's gown has been laid, black lined with green. A bookcase and desk sit close by.

The effect – of an almost clichéd example of a University head of department's campus office – is spoiled only by the fact that you are not viewing it through a window, but through a vast hole, larger than you are, smashed through its wall.

You are taken across a courtyard, towards the edge of the University's campus, and into another building. Much of the interior is relatively unscathed – bullet holes in walls aside – until you are taken upstairs, follow a corridor round to the right and step into…

… Nothing. This had been a room, but is now simply part of a floor, jagged at the edges, and two sections of wall.

Looking across to a car park, the staff member says: 'Over there, we used to have buses. They brought students up from the town, and schoolchildren to use the facilities here.

'Now, they are gone. I do not know who needed several buses, but they have them, now, wherever they are.'

And what of the damage to the room?

'The same as most places. They say there were snipers based here. Who knows if they are correct? There may well have been, or there may not. Whichever is true, who is paying for what was done here?

'It is not Ghaddafi's soldiers, who may have been snipers here, because they are dead, or hiding, or have just gone back to their lives. It is not the khetibas, because who can make them pay for anything? And it is not NATO, because NATO is celebrating a victory, without looking towards the country they have left behind. Who can afford to pay for all of this?'

You leave him at the building, and walk back across campus towards the car park. Before you leave, you notice three things, two of which you cannot understand how you could have missed before.

First, next to the Languages Faculty, is the ceremonial hall, where Sirte University's students celebrate graduation. It was an imposing building, its ornate, gilded features informing graduands and parents alike about the status of the University in which they sat.

Today, it imposes itself in a different way. Its huge arched windows are blackened, its white walls now loom menacingly in a coat of grey, its once strong-looking architecture now presents its holes as if proud of them.

Inside, it is worse. It is still possible to imagine how the main hall looked, just a few months before. You would be more comfortable were it not. For now, all that remains of the once-grand venue is a mangled wreck. Melted furniture, some now so dry and brittle a strong breeze would tear it apart, sits in front of a charred and soot speckled skeleton of what was once a stage. Once, students climbed the steps on the left, which have now been replaced with a pile

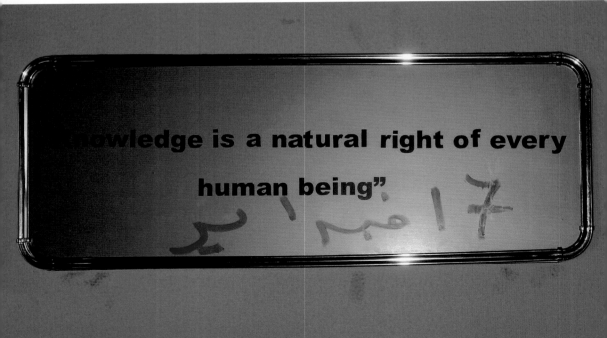

of ash, to receive their certificates at the end of their University careers.

Today, the hall resembles a macabre meeting-place of the long-dead, a celebration venue of the damned, and you cannot help wondering whether it was coincidence that this building appears to have been targeted in a way no other has, whether it was a deliberate decision to blast this symbol of Sirte's achievement and potential with flames, to change it into a literally hollow shell of its former self.

Yards from the wreckage, you are drawn towards a covered open-air area. You hear water running, and imagine for a moment that the sound comes from the fountain which sits a few yards away, uncovered, in the sunshine.

But the fountain is broken.

Instead, the water is flowing along the underside of the foyer's 'roof', some dripping from the ceiling, but much of it reaching its pillars at the end, trickling down to the ground and flowing into the square.

You stop for a moment to take it in: listening to the water flow, and noticing that plants are growing, thriving in the foyer's shade and seemingly unending water supply.

You have a photograph, now, of that moment in the South Mediterranean, when the sun glistened and shimmered off the moving water, the green leaves and red berries of a small bush sharpened by clear blue sky, on Christmas morning in Sirte.

It does not reveal that you are also surrounded by the charred ruins of the town's most prominent, once proud, centre of learning.

As you are leaving, you notice two signs, both in English.

The first, printed in black ink on standard printer paper, reads:

'Death is closer than it looks.

'Life is a trip that we shall enjoy, but without forgetting that it will, sooner or later, end.'

The second, etched on a gold-coloured plaque: 'Knowledge is a natural right of every human being.'

Underneath, a line of graffiti, written in marker by one of the many khetibas to have 'freed' Sirte University, reads simply: 'Febriar 17'.

You return to the car-park, where your driver – recently returned from fighting against Ghaddafi in his country's Civil War – is discussing with his tutor when he can sit his next Economics exams.

Ghaddafi's cousin

Sirte

There is a pizza shop open, maybe half a mile from your room in Sirte.

Unlike many other outlets, which have remained closed while attempting repairs, this establishment has somehow seen fit to open despite the fact that not only does almost no-one have any money, but every single piece of glass in its doors and floor-length windows have been blasted out by missiles, and not yet replaced.

Libyan winters – at least on the coast – are nowhere near as cold as those in the UK, however many times someone shivers in coat, scarf and gloves next to you, saying 'Takus Barrid' when the temperature is 7°C, but these are still December nights.

It is the busiest takeaway in Sirte. One evening you are leaning on the counter, back to the door, when you are tapped on the shoulder.

You look round and see a man maybe five years your junior, and a head shorter than you.

He is dancing from foot to foot, resembling no-one quite as much as Mickey Pearce, from Only Fools and Horses, and he smiles at you as he points one thumb at himself and says something in Arabic.

'Laa takellum Arabee,' you reply.

He looks at you again, translates in his head and says slowly, still smiling: 'I, am, Muammar, Ghaddafi's, cousin.'

'Oh,' you say. You look down at him – he is anywhere from an old-ish looking 16 to a young-ish looking 20. It is not the first time – nor will it be the last – that a young Libyan, seeing a Westerner, will try a little mischief to sow a little discomfort. On the other hand, as you look at him more closely, he does look a little like Ghaddafi.*

* *The term 'cousin' in Libya is used often to denote tribal ties, rather than any direct family relationship. However, as it is also used to denote 'son/daughter of your parents' sibling' it was not always immediately obvious whether there was any blood link between people who called themselves 'cousins'.*

Even so, why should you care? A relative of Muammar Ghaddafi is not Muammar Ghaddafi: 'Pleased to meet you. Kayfa hala? How are you?'

He pauses, confused: 'No. I am Ghaddafi's cousin. Do you understand? Muammar Ghaddafi. You know?'

He kisses his fist, then touches it to his heart.

'Hello,' you say. 'Ma esmuk? What is your name?'

He looks around him. 'I am Ghaddafi,' he says. 'Muammar Ghaddafi.'

You ask him what sort of pizza he has ordered.

Now, he looks confused: 'I have chicken and harissa with tomato ketchup and mayonnaise,'* he replies.

> * In this pizza shop every single topping comes with added tomato ketchup and mayonnaise, unless – in fact often regardless of whether – you make a specific request to the contrary. At first, you did not know how to ask why this is. By now, you are quite used to it.

'Great!' You say. 'I hope you enjoy your pizza.'

He looks crestfallen, as his pizza arrives, and leaves.

A few days later, you see him again, at the former Green Square.

This time, he is part of a large group of young men, carrying spades and brooms with which they are clearing the detritus of war from Sirte's central space.

'Saba Hal Heer,' he says.

'Saba Hal Noor. Kayfa hala?'

'Hamdullah!' he replies.

Then he breaks from the baby-level Arabic, guessing – correctly – that you will not understand what he says next if he uses his native tongue.

'I am doing this,' he gestures towards the pile of bullet shells and rubble he and his friends have cleared. 'For my cousin. Not for the West, or the rats! For my cousin Muammar Ghaddafi! It is his square, and this is what he would want me to do!'

'You have done a great job,' you say. It is true: it's still before 9am and the square is close to being clear – the first time you have ever seen it free of metal and rocks.

He looks sad, and walks away.

'Do not worry about him,' another boy laughs. 'He is a Ghaddafi, and he does not want anyone to think he feels the same about Sirte as everyone else. But he works to make the town better, the same as every one of us does.'

You nod, once. 'You do not have to tell him,' you say. 'But I do not care if he likes Ghaddafi or not.'

'He does care,' the boy replies. 'But it does not matter anymore. We are all together, now.'

You watch, for a little while, waiting to see if you can help. But there is no spade spare.

New Year's Eve

Sirte

31st December 2011 marked the end of a year among the most momentous in Libya's history. But only really for Westerners.

In Libya, the New Year – 1433 – began at midnight on November 27th.

In Sirte, that was rather too soon: most of the town's inhabitants had not yet returned to the wreckage which awaited them, and those who had were far too busy – and shocked – to celebrate, regardless of the side for which they had so recently fought.

So on 31st December, you marked New Year in a large room, sharing half a bottle of semi-illicit vodka* with a few other Westerners, who were working for one of only four Western aid agencies in Sirte, and watched the world's new year celebrations on Al Jazeera.

* Libya's laws on alcohol were ambiguous at best under Ghaddafi – part of the leader's attempt at 'compromise' between a truly secular state, and one united by one religion. In the early stages after he left, most laws were close to non-existent. In Tripoli, some streets were littered with empty beer bottles on Saturday mornings. In Sirte, far fewer people openly drank, if they drank at all.

It was not the liveliest New Year you ever had. But it might have been the strangest, which perhaps counts for something.

You stood, picking at snack-food and watching people celebrate across the world: in London, Paris, Madrid, Barcelona, Rome, Berlin, Tunis, Ankara, Cairo, even in Tripoli.

As each city's festivities were broadcast, even as you shared stories and jokes, playing music, singing and dancing, each of you found your thoughts wandering home, to families and friends, and to your hopes for the next 12 months.

Later, in bed, you lay awake as the wind howled through the town, amplified as it rushed across missile holes, windows empty of glass and roofs half or wholly collapsed, creating a haunted, deep soundtrack for Sirte – a semi-deserted ruin perched between the Sahara and the sea.

Occasionally, a gunshot was fired, echoing across town even over the howling.

In common with every other night, you could not be sure whether the shots were in anger, or celebration.

Sirte

New Year's Day

1st January finds you alone. You write a few e-mails, which you will be unable to send until either you leave the town, or Sirte's internet and other communications are reconnected (the former will occur far sooner than the latter).*

During the civil war, in an attempt to isolate the East of Libya (even as it claimed its soldiers were fighting to retain Libyan unity), Ghaddafi's government cut the physical communications links between it and the rest of the country. But mobile phone companies Libyana and Al Madar managed to retain service, and in fact for a short period after the Civil War, operated without any charge to customers, to ensure people could remain in contact across the state.

The networks of each were patchy, requiring users to use SIM cards from each at different times of the day, and no connection was possible to networks outside of Libya, but both companies provided a vital service in the immediate post-war period, when no internet or landline communication was possible.

Despite this, however, Libya's mobile phone user numbers remained below their 2010 peak (when a remarkable 10.9m contracts were in operation: 171.52 per 100 people) for more than two years (in 2012 the figure was 9.6m, equivalent to 148.19 contracts per 100 users).

An international connection – albeit far more limited than the one which had previously existed – was reinstated in April 2012.

Losing interest in the four walls surrounding you – even despite the maps of Sirte plastered across them, each detailing areas of destruction, school locations, clean-up projects and other points of 'local interest' – you head onto the roof. From there, you see a thick plume of greyish-black smoke. It is easy to follow it to its source, and as you arrive you see a small crowd has gathered outside a building on the other side of the Roman Road.

You had not paid it any attention before, as, like many of Sirte's larger commercial units, and unlike most of its smaller 'independent' greengrocers, shoe shops and even retailers of flat-screen televisions – it had remained closed since the war. But the Supermarket – its name illegible due to battle damage sustained when the khetibas replaced Ghaddafi's troops in Sirte – had been popular only months earlier.

And today, it has drawn a crowd to 'see it off' – one Westerner on a New Year's outing, and a crowd of children and adults for whom this is just another thing to see in a town struggling to stay alive.

At first, you wonder whether the fire was started deliberately – or by accident – by gunshot, bomb or firework. But the truth is rather more prosaic.

'It was just an electrical fire,' one woman says. 'I was in a shop over the road there, and we noticed the smoke from there, so we came over to see. No-one did anything to start it, it is just the sort of thing that happens when people cannot look after things.'

It is tempting to try to imagine the store as a metaphor for Sirte – once bustling and popular, now aflame, mourned by few and forgotten by most – or even to make some kind of weak comparison with New Year's celebrations the previous night.

But neither would be fair. As the woman said, this is simply what happens to a town when no-one remains to look after it.

No fire engine has yet arrived – the fire has been burning for 15 minutes and there is now only one engine left to serve the entire town* – and a group of children, who have been standing much too close to the burning building for your comfort, but have so far steadfastly ignored adults' calls to step back, decide to alleviate the boredom of the wait by speaking to the only stranger they can see.

A few days later, you happen to pass by Sirte's 'fire station'. It is empty, but clearly still in use, despite the two-foot wide missile holes in several places along its walls.

Outside, on a flooded stretch of concrete, two engines lie, never to move again under their own power. Both have been blasted from their chassis, one now stricken on its side, the other still upright, but both empty and hopelessly broken.

You had been told all but one engine had been stolen when the victorious khetibas left town: doubtless, that is the case. But at the fire station, the two which were beyond repair were left to decay, their uselessness guaranteeing an undisturbed rest.

As you walk back towards the car, you hope the helmet you step over was simply blasted from the seat of an engine, or from the station within.

'Who are you?' asks the boldest of the trio, and you exchange names, discovering in the process that two of the boys are eight, the other seven, and that they are bored.

'Will you take our picture?'

You do, and show them the result, foiling an attempt by the youngest to snatch the camera. You smile at the boys. They smile back, watching you put the camera in your pocket. After a few moments, Sirte's sole fire engine arrives, and the firemen set their hose against the flames.

The children watch as you take the camera from your coat pocket to photograph the dousing of the fire. Two start to talk to you about their school and what they do each day while it is closed (a mixture of going to the shops for their parents and playing on bomb sites, like many of the young people you have met here), while the youngest sneaks to the side.

You laugh as he creeps towards the pocket with your camera in, as he looks like Elmer Fudd, eyes narrowed as he attempts to sneak up on Bugs Bunny, and you smile at him as you put your hand over your camera, just in time to block his attempt to snatch it from your pocket.

The boy who is talking actually stops and says 'Oh!' as he sees this happen. His eyes are open wide, and he looks as if he is desperately trying to plan an escape.

You laugh, again: they are children, and you have met boys like them on the streets of Liverpool; bored, brave, clever, and looking for something to do to pass the time.

They pull themselves together. You shake each of their hands, tell them it was good to meet them, and they move on to their next adventure in their ruined hometown, seemingly having forgotten the fire altogether.

The fire engine is now winning the battle, the flames and smoke shrinking back from the jets of water, and people begin to return to their shopping, their walk around town, or their journey to wherever they are going.

After a few minutes, the fire extinguished, the engine retracts its hoses, starts its engine, and trundles on to its next assignment.

The supermarket, damp now, and still smouldering a little, looks surprisingly unchanged, the fire's damage just one more scar on what was once a bustling, noisy, living store.

You remain where you are, watching as the building once again loses its status as a centre for attention, conversation and human exchange.

As people hurry past it, on a cold, overcast afternoon on a New Year's Day few here even recognise as such, the former supermarket stands empty, abandoned, desolate, and all-but unnoticed once again.

You turn up your collar, and turn east towards the town centre.

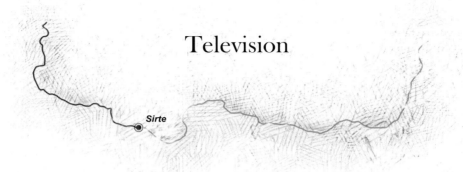

Television

Sirte

On your way to visit and photograph the Ouagadougou Conference Hall (created by Ghaddafi as a symbol of Libya's regional and global status, and Sirte's importance as a city, but today just another missile-strewn wreckage of a small South Mediterranean town) you stop outside Sirte's Libya TV studio.

It is not against international law to bomb media outlets during war, and it has become very much a standard NATO tactic, from the attacks on Serbia TV during the Balkans crisis (including one strike in Belgrade which killed 16 people and injured 16 more, for which only one person, Dragoljub Milanovic was ever punished, for failing to evacuate his staff from the building) to strikes on Al Jazeera's outlets in Iraq.

In the Serbian case, the attacks were justified by NATO on the grounds that the broadcaster was producing 'propaganda' and was helping organise Serbian military manoeuvres. It is more difficult to see either motive in the strikes on Al Jazeera offices.

In Sirte, the stories are jumbled. In this case, you are told, the TV station was bombed because it was spreading propaganda (though it is hard to see what part propaganda could have played in a war which was almost over when it came to Sirte, and when almost all of its residents had fled within weeks of Ghaddafi's troops arriving) and that it was being used 'by snipers'.

Either or both may be true. Equally, as when NATO bombed the Baghdad offices of independent broadcaster Al Jazeera, the bombing of a TV station also serves as a symbol of power, a message which states: it is us, not you, who control what will be said, when and to whom.

It is raining when you arrive. You pass an outbuilding, once perhaps a reception point, which is no longer capable of offering shelter to a registrar or security guard. Its varnished oak table is now crushed under what was once its roof, and is surrounded by the remains of what was once its walls.

You pass on, towards the main building. The station's broadcast aerial, once itself both a symbolic and a useful item, now stands part melted and twisted out of shape, bowing North and West towards the sea, as if using its final moments to point to the source of Sirte's destruction – and warning of the piled weapons of destruction now on its beaches.

The building itself has been struck several times.

Windows have been patched up and, remarkably, parts of the structure are still useable – Sirte's residents tell you that when the broadcasts stopped, thanks to a strike which destroyed the station's capacity to beam news and entertainment to the town, NATO's strikes ended too. Perhaps snipers were less of a concern here than at the hospital and schools.

Close to half of the damage – low-level missile holes, blasted by ground-launched rockets and tank-carried shells – was done later, when the khetibas rolled into town.

There are a few staff inside, one of whom stops to answer some of your questions: 'We cannot do anything here now,' she says. 'We have repaired all we can, but the building really needs more work.

'Much of it is not safe. We do not have the money for that, so we are just doing what we can with what we have.'

She concedes that this is very little: the khetibas took the TV cameras, editing equipment and other technology home with them to Misrata, Benghazi, Zintan, and there is no money to replace them, or to pay for the reconstruction of the studio itself.

'We worry about this because we are broadcasters. We have shown people in Sirte what has happened in other states when war comes, and we do not want to be used as a symbol of the damage done by one political group to another which tries to start a new war, or take power by force.

'But that is what we are now: we are ruined because of the war, and we cannot start again because of the war's effects. In each house in Sirte, there is a television which does not show any programmes. That is a constant reminder of how the situation is here, and we are here, in this ruin, a symbol of something we do not wish to be.'

Febriar 17

Sirte

You wake up, make a coffee, strong and rich, thickened with evaporated milk, and step into the courtyard of the building where you have been a guest for the last week.

As you raise a cigarette to your lips and reach for your lighter, a small open-topped jeep speeds round the corner. Its inhabitants, six young uniformed men, wave guns above their heads.

They shoot, and you drop behind the building's wall, getting back to your feet only as you hear the clinks and clangs of the bullets landing – they had fired into the air, 'happy shooting,'* rather than at you.

> * *'Happy shooting', which began as soon as the Civil War finished in 2011, was a major feature of any and all celebrations in Libya. This was entirely predictable, in a state where the population owned more than one gun per person, on average, and where those weapons had been used in anger so recently.*
>
> *But it was also spectacularly dangerous. Shooting bullets into the air in crowded places killed people celebrating on balconies above, and rained bullets down on people, killing and injuring hundreds in the aftermath of the hostilities.*
>
> *In late November 2011, one aid worker had grimly warned you that more people would be killed by the celebrations of the war's end than by the fighting itself: he was only half-joking.*

Nevertheless, you are acutely aware that this morning, you are the only Westerner in the whole of Sirte, and today marks the official first anniversary of the start of a war in which NATO played a large part in smashing the town.

You sip the coffee, light your cigarette, walk across the courtyard and poke at a newly-emptied bullet casing, still warm from the barrel, with your foot.

So begins February 17th 2012. In the run-up to the first anniversary of the start of the Libyan revolution, preparations have been made for parties across the country. But here, where so much has been destroyed, and where even those who 'won' the war have been left with close to nothing, seemingly abandoned to whatever the fates decide, the community has agreed that a celebration would be wrong, and impossible to enjoy.

Instead, Sirte will mark Febriar 17 as a 'commemoration'. Perhaps more an Irish-style wake than an English one, but a remembrance nonetheless. Even so, one dresses up and shares anecdotes, food and drink at a wake, and so it is in Sirte.

In the last few days, people have strung coloured lights across their roads, which will shine onto jagged streetscapes when the sun sets later today. Two days ago, you helped a group near your temporary home, first holding the ladder, later climbing it to adjust the display.

A little further away, you had helped erect what looked like the metal cone framework of a shopping centre's artificial Christmas tree, in the middle of a busy tributary of the Roman Road.

All over town, people have hung banners with messages of hope for the future, the new Libyan flag, and proclamations honouring those who lost their lives, those who survived, their hometown and the God they believe is watching over all.

They have prepared play areas for youngsters, cooking areas and speaking platforms for those who wish to speak on behalf of their tribe, or their area, in memory of those who have died or in hope for the future they are working – and desperately hoping – to make better than today.

The khetibas continue their careering circuits around town for most of the day. You see several different jeeps, many with machine guns mounted on their backs, and young men firing into the air.

It feels incongruous, when considering the mood of Sirte today – pensive, uncertain, reflective, with shades of happiness, but seldom approaching pleasure – to see these uniformed, armed men speeding like joyriders and firing skywards like Yosemite Sam. But it is not your place to blame them: they too fought a war, and are young men a long way from homes where the mood is far more joyous.

Nobody joins their raucous celebration, but nobody appears angered by it either. Some people wave and flash a brief smile – returned by the jeeps' inhabitants as they speed by. Others simply watch, impassive and unmoved. You are the only one, so far, from whom the gunshots have inspired a fearful response.

You cannot work, because you do not know how welcome your questions will be on this anniversary, and you cannot write because you cannot drown out the reports of the khetibas' happy shooting, which ricochet and echo through every broken wall, window and missile hole.

Instead, you spend much of the afternoon reading, smoking cigarettes and drinking coffee.

Around 5pm a light drizzle begins, but it is not cold, so you remain outside on the balcony, listening and waiting for the lights to come on for the first time. You had hardly noticed, but the shooting seems to have stopped now, minutes without a shot becoming a quarter of an hour, then half. You put on some music and watch as the sun sets, sliding behind the homes opposite, beyond that Green Square, and further away, Tripoli, Tunisia, Morocco, the ocean and the United States…

'Hey! Where have you been?'

You are shaken from your thoughts by the man who owns the house you are staying in, waving and smiling as he approaches.

'Kayfa hala,' you reply. 'What are you up to?'

'I came here to get you. To see why you are not with us this evening,' he said.

You are surprised. You had decided to be careful today, to avoid any possibility that anyone might feel you were intruding on an anniversary which marks the end of a chaotic, violent, blood-stained, hope-fuelled year.

'People kept asking me where you are,' he continued. 'They said they would like you to be there.'

You pull on a jacket and walk with him through the thick, slow, early evening light.

As you approach the small-ish square where the event is taking place (Green/Central Square had been considered too sensitive a site), you see why the gunshots of earlier in the day have ceased: khetibas have driven here to keep watch over the proceedings.

It is unclear whether they have come to prevent problems bubbling up from within the square, or encroaching from outside, but they smile respectfully as your friend walks through the gate, and they remain reserved and quiet throughout the evening.

This is more than can be said for the children of Sirte.

Faces painted, they are charging about, yelling and throwing water at one another, playing games, chasing and tugging each other towards the bouncy castle, ball pool, and other pieces of play equipment.

'It is a good time for the children,' says your friend, just loud enough to be heard over the noise. 'Many of them have parents who will never return from this war, and others still wait to hear from the prisons in Misrata and Benghazi. Today, they can play together, and enjoy themselves.'

You are handed a soft drink, and turn as a group of young men begin to sing. Not far across the square, a second group start a different song.

'This group,' your friend says. 'Sings a song which praises Ghaddafi and what he achieved. But the group over there is singing a song of resistance, which we sang when we fought against the Italians and again when we rose against Ghaddafi.'

Neither group, nor those watching them, seem particularly perturbed by the other, continuing to sing as if particularly good-natured and polite supporters of opposing football teams. As they finish, a ripple of applause and some cheers go up around the square, including from khetibas dotted around the square and at its entrance and exit points.

A man approaches you, hugs you and asks whether you are enjoying the day.

'Over there,' he points. 'Is the home of the Safframi family. It is because the home is here that we are here today.'

He tells you the story of how one of the family's younger sons – a supporter of the revolutionaries, like all his family – had been shot and killed while attempting to fly the 'new' Libyan flag, the black, green, red and white banner of King Idris, from the roof of the house.

'They lost a son, like many of us have,' the man said. 'Those who supported Ghaddafi, and those who opposed him, all lost someone or something. It is why we do not celebrate, but it is also why we come together to look forward after remembering.'

A group of children approach, with drawings and paintings which they are putting on the wall of the main tent in the square.

They show you pictures of doves, of tanks, of flowers, of fighter-planes, of their town as it was, and the ruins now in its place, of machine-guns mounted on jeeps and filled with khetibas, of relatives lost, and friends they see every day.

'It is something we thought would be a good thing,' the man says. 'To let the children draw and paint whatever they wanted, and to display their work, to show who we all are and what we all feel.'

One boy holds out his work to you.

'I drew a picture,' he says. In it, a man stands next to a river, under a tree. Birds sit in the tree, and a small animal sits on the other side of the river. You wonder if the man is his father, or an older brother. 'Who is this?' you ask.

'It is Ghaddafi,' the boy says. 'He is dead, but it is alright, because he is in heaven, and we are not in heaven, so we must work here to make Sirte better.'

At this moment, a jeep reverses slowly through to the centre of the square.

Tied down in the back of the vehicle, a camel stares blankly at the faces of the people now gathered around. A man steps forward with a machete and as the camel opens its mouth to roar its discomfort, the man slits its throat with one stroke. The blood gushes down the side of the jeep, and forms a red stream, flowing across the square. You watch in silence, as a cheer goes up, and fires are lit on which to cook the fresh meat.

Later, a series of speeches are made by men and women, recalling the glories of the 'old' Sirte, which existed only a few months before, remembering family members and making pledges for a better future.

A group of face-painted children sing in the darkness, a slow song none of which you understand, but which fits the mood perfectly, simultaneously sad but hopeful, notes rising from a depth you had known but not fully experienced, to a shivering crescendo you had not expected. Women cry, while men attempt to hide the fact they are wiping tears from their cheeks. The lights you helped put up are on as you walk home. Their beautiful reds, blues and greens cut circles of light through the darkness, with white bulbs creating the clearest, sharpest shadows of all.

It is almost dark enough to ignore the holes in the walls, and in the road, and the jagged edges where pieces of the tops of buildings have been blasted away. But as you know, you are used to the devastation by now: the beauty of the lights is the only thing new to you here.

You recall a story you once read, in which a British platoon 'liberated' a Nazi concentration camp at the end of the Second World War.

They were astonished and horrified to see the emaciated state of the prisoners within, and even more shocked that even though they had thrown the gates of the camp open, noisily announcing that everyone was free to go, those prisoners did not move towards the exits, instead shifting listlessly from foot to foot if they moved at all.

One low-ranking soldier pulled a lipstick from his bag, which his wife had given him as a reminder of her and her love for him. He tried to hand it to one of the women, then drew lipstick onto her lips himself.

Other officers moved towards him, thinking to prevent him from committing further outrages, but even as they did so, the woman grabbed his hand, and another smiled and took the lipstick from the soldier.

Within moments, many of the women wore the make-up, smiling and asking one another how it looked. The men who had also been imprisoned in the camp watched with interest, some smiling and began speaking to one another.

They all, men and women, helped one another then, to walk together towards the gates.

You realise, even as you recall the story, that the comparison is flawed for many reasons.

The situation is not the same, and the simile developing in your mind cannot therefore be completely accurate.

But despite that, you cannot fully resist thinking of the lights as make-up, masking damage and perhaps helping unite a community in a way that even recent shared experience and effort has not.

Weeks later, you will be shown images from Benghazi and Tripoli, where celebratory gunfire, dancing, and the release of thousands of Chinese lanterns marked Febriar 17 far more noisily, with less reserve, and arguably with more beauty.

But tonight, you pause for a moment, leaning in shadow against a wall. You breathe the cool air, and look at the decoration, sparse in its simplicity, the colours and light with which the recently strung bulbs cover ruined streets, and broken buildings.

You stand a few moments longer, on the quietest night Sirte has experienced in many months, silently watching the light's soft flow.

You are surprised when you realise that this place, at this moment, is the greatest tribute to Sirte, and the most beautiful way to mark Febriar 17 you can imagine.

Guns and Politics: Part One

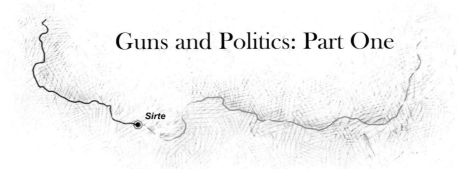

Sirte

On a Thursday evening, you walk through the darkness, weaving through crowds and ducking in and out of shops just off Sirte's main road.

You have almost completed your food shopping, and are wondering whether to talk more to the owner of a music 'store' (more accurately, a building which no longer has a front containing six tables piled high with CDs) about the relative merits – if any – of several Libyan ska artists, when a bomb explodes, creating a shock-wave which knocks a small child into your shins, and almost sends you sprawling against the closest wall.

The child runs, crying, towards her parents, and you regain your balance, looking around you in shock and confusion for the source of the explosion, expecting debris and flames (it is only when you are calmer, later, that you realise with embarrassment that you were dusting down your suit as you did so).

A hand slaps onto your shoulder, causing you to jump for the second time in as many seconds, and a voice says: 'It is OK, my friend. Do not worry.'

You recognise the owner of a shoe shop, a fan of an English football club, with whom you have spoken many times, though not, as you are sure he is aware, with much intention of actually buying any shoes.

He asks if you are OK: 'It is nothing to worry about, only a wedding,' he smiles.

In his shop, a few moments later, he hands you a coffee, and continues: 'It is a real problem here. We have had a war, which has destroyed our city. It has affected every one of us – how could it not? And the ones who pretend not to have been affected are the most dangerous of all.

'So everybody does their work, the children go to school, they go out shopping or stay home mending their houses and their lives, grieving for their dead, or worrying about those who are still in prison. And all worry about the fact that Sirte has been left alone, that the only people who come here now are the khetibas from outside, who sit and watch us to make sure we do not do anything to 'harm' the government – a government which we do not see, and which has so far done nothing.

'And we sit and worry that we are now alone, and what the future might bring.

'So when there is a chance to celebrate, a wedding, or a child's birthday, it is also a chance to forget. We prepare and look forward to being with friends and family, dancing and talking.

'And then what happens? Well, you have heard. The celebrations begin and someone explodes a bomb. A bomb! Here in a city which has seen more bombs than any ever should!

'How can we ever recover from what has happened here when we mark every celebration with an explosion, and gunfire?'

He pauses, takes a sip of his coffee, apologises: 'I am sorry. It is just that I was here when the bombs fell. We all were. And we do not need to hear more. Tonight, the celebrants of a wedding forced the whole of Sirte to remember the aircraft, the damage, the fires and the fear. They made children cry and adults jump. It is not right that this should happen.

'And then they fire their guns into the air. Who needs to hear more gunfire now? Who could possibly think that it is a celebration to shoot into the air when we have all seen so clearly what gunfire does?

'And how can it be anything other than stupid to be firing guns into the air, at night, in a town which is surrounded by veterans of a war, heavily-armed and in uniform, here from somewhere else to 'keep the peace'?

'Sirte is a sick place. In Libya today, there are more guns than people, and we cannot make a better future while that is true.

'The government should make it illegal to own a gun, but even if it did, no-one would do anything. The government and the army is weak and the khetibas are strong: people will do whatever they want. But it is our children who suffer, and our future.'

Like everyone in Sirte, you have seen this first-hand.

Weeks earlier, you had visited an organisation's children's centre, where the youngsters had written and were reading aloud their experiences of the war.

Each tale was much like the next – the TV news which parents worried about, the start of bombings by foreign aircraft making it increasingly difficult to go out safely, then the schools closing, bombs falling on homes, fire, dirt and damage, shortages of food, shooting on the streets, missiles exploding and buildings collapsing, a long journey to friends' or families' homes, or to the desert, days and weeks of hiding, then a return to a home in ruins.

Each time, whether told by the child of a pro-Ghaddafi or an anti-Ghaddafi family, the story was applauded softly by the other children.

Mid-way through the sequence, you realised some parents had arrived, and were now stood watching intently. As they took their children home, they embraced them, and one another.

And then, thankfully after many of the children had left, gunshots were fired yards from the centre's entrance.

The remaining youngsters looked at one another, wide-eyed, but stayed rooted to their seats. The centre's staff made sure they were OK, while you, your translator, and one of the centre staff ran to see what was happening.

Outside, a middle-aged man stood. 'I know him', your translator said, and ran out to remonstrate with him.

The man was the father of one of the boys. He had arrived to collect him from the centre, and had fired his gun three times in the air because he was overjoyed that his boy had somewhere to come to play and learn with other youngsters once again.

He stood looking at the ground, ashamed, gun in his right hand, as your translator shouted at him: 'There are no guns here! There are no guns here!'

The boy came out to meet his father, who had by now put the gun back into his jacket. They, too, embraced, and the man lifted his son into his arms. He had not meant to cause trouble, but every shot sent those children back to a world in which they should never have had to live, and you, too, had wondered what future there could be for a town – a nation – where the same guns which had weeks before snatched life after life were still on the streets.

Where those guns remained in the hands of men who meant little harm, but who were fresh from the horror of war and still clung to weapons which could kill at any second.

A few days later, during a sunny Spring afternoon, a man opens a conversation with you, in English, with a joke about a man drinking beer on other people's behalf: you know, immediately, that you will get along with him.

He is an accountant, born in Sirte, but who left as a teenager with his family, escaping the increasingly irrational and spiteful rule of Ghaddafi.

He returned as soon as the Civil War ended, to help his town, but also because, although he could not allow himself to admit it while he was in Europe, he missed Sirte every moment he was away.

He is pleased to have returned, but pessimistic about the future.

'Nobody has truly thought about it,' he says. 'Of course, all of the groups wanted to be rid of Ghaddafi, but their view that he was stupid is not as accurate as their view that he was bad – and some of them have less right to call him bad than others, when you consider what they have done, and their own views.

'Sirte is in some danger. The older people want a religious take-over. I am not so strongly religious as they are – though I am a Muslim, and I do believe it is the true faith – and I am afraid that what they want may be just as bad as Ghaddafi for the men, and worse for the women.

'The people who use economic reasons to justify Ghaddafi going must also be careful that they do not destroy the good things about Libyan life – the hospitals and the Universities and schools – while destroying the restrictions that they faced.

'But it is the youngest people I feel most sorry for. They risked their lives for this, and they did not do so because they wanted a stronger Islam here. And they did not do it because they wanted an economic philosophy. They did it because they looked at what was here and they saw it was wrong.

'They were the ones who did most fighting, and they deserve the chance to say what should come next – at least how it should come. Instead, they will be ignored by the people who are driven by religion, and those who are driven by economics. I believe we have an opportunity. But I believe it is being wasted.

'It is hard. We have a war, and we get rid of a man who has become something even I do not believe he wanted to be: a killer, and a person who crushes debate and disagreement.

'But then what happens next? The people who rule now are those who killed Ghaddafi, not the government they put in place.

'Everyone has a gun: the government cannot compete with that. It cannot be strong enough to pass laws that are not the laws which the people who have the guns want to exist.

'And this is not just individuals, though as you know there are many here, standing for what they say are their rights, and refusing to obey laws made for the good of the whole nation. It is also the khetibas.

'You and I know that the khetibas behave, mostly. But who is in charge of them? How can a government bring them and keep them under control? They cannot. They behave as they wish.

'This is bad enough with the Zintan, Tripoli and Benghazi gangs: at least they know who they are and what they want – Zintan and Tripoli will eventually join a strong government, and Benghazi will at least decide based on its members' view of what is good, even if they are wrong.

'But the Misrata khetiba is mad, now. It is out of control. It can never behave sensibly, as long as it exists. Because the Misrata khetiba believes it, more than any other, made the revolution happen, even though everyone did that.

'And the Misrata khetiba believes it is the only group which can decide who lives and dies, and what happens next in Libya. It is insane, and it is powerful. It is why I worry for Sirte, and for all Libya.'

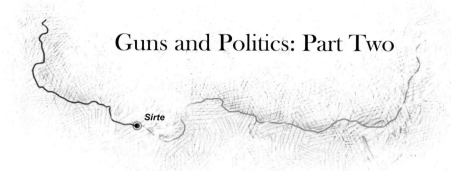

Sirte

Guns and Politics: Part Two

Your host gestures to the corner, where you at first assume you are to put your shoes. A single glance is enough to show you otherwise: propped against the wall are two assault rifles, with a scattering of handguns around them.

'Are they yours?' you ask.

'Ha! Not all of them,' your host replies. 'Most are theirs.' He flicks his head back, into the room where several young men – all students, and most already friends or acquaintances of yours – are gathered.

'I don't have a gun,' you say.

'I know,' your host smiles. 'But it would have been impolite not to show you where to put one if you did.'

The room behind him is huge, looking slightly empty even with ten people already in it. Against the walls are piled long, rectangular cushions, and in the centre, on a silver table, tea, coffee and sweets.

Although the wall between its courtyard and the road is peppered with bullet holes, the house itself has suffered remarkably little damage – its courtyard tiles are broken but remain in place, and some minor damage has been done to the plaster-work on the outside.

In other words, it would be considered in urgent need of repair in the UK, but remarkably unscathed here in Sirte.

You pour a coffee, smile and say good evening to the other guests, and sit down.

Two of the students come over and sit next to you. One, with whom you have worked previously, had taken part in the revolution, and whose uncle was killed while fighting against Ghaddafi's forces, introduces you to the other.

'Look at his watch,' he says.

The other shows you his wrist. He is wearing a white-faced watch, with Muammar Ghaddafi's face printed in black upon it.

The first student laughs: 'We are friends,' he begins, slapping the other on the shoulder. 'But he loves Ghaddafi and I fought against him.'

The second looks uncomfortable, but smiles and shrugs as you ask how things are for him now.

'It is… unusual,' he replies. 'But the people I was friends with before the War are still my friends now. And I still have a place at the University. We all lost someone or something and I think we all try every day to remember that.

'I am sad that Ghaddafi is not here any longer, but there are other important things, too. We all spend time on those things.'

As you speak, more people enter the room. It is a strange mix: linguists, economists, medics, mathematicians, one or two historians and a few people you have never met.

You are told that in the next room, a similar-sized group of female students are gathered. You ask why, when they study together, they do not socialise outside of University.

'We do when we can,' your host responds. 'But some adults prefer it if we do not. So, we are here, and they are there.'

You talk for a while, introducing yourself and being introduced to the students you haven't yet met, talking about football, music and how English people 'survive' the cold and rain.

Then there is a pause, which you would not have noticed or remembered if not for the question which followed it.

'We have just fought a war to be more like you,' one student asks. 'Yet we saw on the television that there was fire and rioting all across your country. Why is this? Why do people riot when they have the chance to live like you do?'

You take a breath. Perhaps the most 'sensible' or 'polite' response would be to quietly acknowledge the differences between Libya and the UK, and pretend that you think the riots were unjustified. But you have been invited here, and someone has asked a question about something in which you have some degree of expertise – in direct contrast to the majority of your experience in Libya to date.

And you do not feel this question was asked as a 'trap'. Everyone is now watching you, and even if they disagree with your response, it's clear that they are all interested – confused, perhaps, but certainly keen to know more about what could have led to UK young people taking to the streets when there was no Ghaddafi to depose.

'There were a number of things,' you begin. 'None of them individually so big as what you fought over, and in many cases not as clearly articulated. But together, they added up to something huge.'

You were a journalist when the riots began, and were in the office one morning as an economic update was shown on the same screen as images of cities aflame: on one side, numbers tumbling, on the other, buildings being consumed by flames. On both sides, grim-faced presenters commenting and updating.

'It looks like the end of the world,' one colleague said. And for a little while, it did.

By this point, the second week of August, the Libyan Civil War had been running for almost six months. Six days' unrest, compared to six months. But it was something unusual in Britain at that time.

'It started when a gangster called Mark Duggan was shot in North London. The police claimed he was carrying a gun: he wasn't. It wasn't the first time someone had been shot dead by police even though they weren't carrying a weapon.

'Mark Duggan was renowned for being a gangster, and the police also used that to try to explain why they shot him.

'But in the area where he lived, people came out onto the streets. It was peaceful at first, most people were carrying candles, and holding a vigil. But for some reason, fighting broke out.

'It's hard to say exactly why at that moment. People were upset and angry and police in Britain are often not very good in that situation: they get nervous, and there are few things worse in a crowd than nervous police officers.

'But that might have happened anywhere, at any time. People gathered, either the police or the crowd did or said the wrong thing and a fight started. It doesn't happen very often, but it does happen.

'The difference was that this time, TV cameras were there, because of the shooting earlier on, and across the country, people saw live on TV as police and people fought one another.

'In cities – and it was only large cities – across the country, other people got out onto the streets and started to fight, set things on fire and steal.

'Some of them had a definite motive, but most did not. They broke into shops and stole trainers. In one case, someone was filmed running out of a store carrying free samples of carpet. Who would need to steal free samples of carpet?

'But that meant the newspapers started to say that the only motive was theft. It meant that David Cameron and other members of the government were able to stand up and say they would have these thieves arrested and thrown into prison, without ever asking why it happened to begin with.

'But think about it. If your aim was to steal something, you would try to do it in secret. And you'd try to steal whatever was valuable. You wouldn't charge onto the street, throw rocks at the police, set shops on fire and then run away with carpet samples.

'Something else was going on. The thefts were only partly about stealing something valuable, like a flatscreen TV. And if anyone ever took the time to think about it, they might ask what kind of a society we have in the UK if in times of civil unrest, when streets are ablaze and the police are fighting the public on every street, the first thing you can think of is to steal something you can't afford to own.

'So, no. Theft has never been the main aim of rioting, no matter how much gets stolen.

'But you may not be aware of some of the things that had happened before – that had been happening for a long time before.

'In the UK, unlike Libya, we have spent a long time selling off things like our telephone system, our electricity companies, our gas and water providers, and our public transport. We used to have a lot of houses which were owned by the state and which could be given to people who were homeless. But we sold them all cheaply and now everyone in the country has to pay the private landlords who bought those homes to enable homeless people to live in them.

'The cost of everything went up, and it was harder and harder to own a house, or go to University, or have enough money to buy the things you all see English people with in films, without getting into debt.

'When the economy was going well, that wasn't so bad: you could earn enough to repay the debt bit by bit, and your life could be OK, as long as you had a job.

'But then in 2008, the economy crashed around the world' (at this point, some of the students murmured in agreement). 'It was worse in some places than in others. Here in Libya, people could not eat, and unemployment rocketed. In Spain, youth unemployment was at similar levels to Libyan levels, but at least people could afford food. In Greece, the people responded with violence, too.

'In the UK, things were hard, too. But people were able to continue more easily than here, or in Greece. People were angry, but rather than being solely angry with the government, like here, where you had a dictator who tortured people and you had never been able to vote, people mostly blamed the wider causes of the crisis – the politicians a little, but the international banking system as well.

'But in the General Election of 2010, a Party which blamed the government won 25 per cent of the total possible vote, 33 per cent of the votes that were cast. This Party had said it would cut services affecting the poorest. It's the main reason it didn't win enough votes to form a proper government.

'Instead, it did a deal with another Party, which won about 15 per cent of the total possible vote. That Party had said it opposed cutting services for the poorest, and people had expected it would join with the Party which had won 20 per cent of the vote. But it did not. Instead, we had a government which only a quarter of the people who could have voted actually voted for.

'And this Party started to take money away from the poorest people. It cut unemployment benefits, and took away services that the poorest people relied on. It cut wages – and food prices were increasing all the time.

'It tripled tuition fees, so that unlike here in Libya, where University education is free, people now have to spend £9,000 every year they study.

'In 2011, I had been at two rallies in London. One was when students marched to complain about the high cost of University fees. That ended in violence, which was instigated by some of the students, and saw the government's Party headquarters vandalized.

'The police were not really in the wrong on that occasion, but it was an example of the people fighting the police.

'A short time later, on a workers' march, I was there when people took over a famous London store, Fortnum and Mason. Very few things happened inside the shop. In fact, the customers who were in there said the intruders were very well-mannered and well-behaved. But outside, I was taking photos between a line of protestors and a line of police officers and again, violence broke out.

'It's hard to say for certain who struck first, but the police were using shields and batons to smash people to the ground, and people were throwing missiles and picking up pieces of wood wherever they could find them to attack the police.

'Both sides claimed they had done nothing wrong. The opposite is more likely to be true.

'And to make matters even worse, in May 2011, an inquest found that a man named Ian Tomlinson had been killed by the police on the way home from work, while a demonstration against the G20 meeting was going on.

'In fact, he had been pushed over by a police officer and died from a heart attack, but the police had originally denied any involvement and it seemed to some people that it was an attempt by police to lie about something serious.

'Finally, in the UK today, many of the poorest areas of the biggest cities are right next to the richest areas. The richer people sometimes live behind huge walls, with locked gates on their streets, meaning people cannot walk on roads they feel belong to their community.

'With a government which was making the poorest people pay for the criminal activity of the richest, that meant people were made angry every time they looked out of their window, or stepped out of the door.'

You stop, realizing you have been talking for a long time. You feel slightly embarrassed to have spoken at such length about a six day riot and its causes to young men who have recently been combatants in an eight month war, but as you look up to apologise, you see one of the former soldiers has his hand up.

'But you could vote. Here, we do understand that wages were low and there was unemployment and prices were increasing. And it is free for us to go to University, and water and electricity are also. And we could not get rid of him any other way.

'But you can vote. Why didn't you vote the government out?'

It is a good question.

'The problem is that in the election in 2010, only 25 per cent of people voted for the Party that was making all the laws. And that government passed a law which said there would not be another election until 2015, and then they started to do the opposite of what they had promised.

'So it meant that many people were suffering, and didn't trust the police, or the economic system we had, and they hadn't voted for a government which was making their lives worse and had changed the law so they couldn't vote again until 2015.

'When it came to it, people went mad because they couldn't vote to change anything.'

'Thank you,' the student says. 'It is something we did not know about, and it is interesting. We need to create a new country and lots of people think that the United Kingdom and the USA are good models.

'They are much better than ours was, and is now. But we must create a constitution for Libya which means the state works in the best way, not just in a better way.'

'The problem for Libya is not that there has been a war,' one student says. 'It is not even Ghaddafi, because he is gone now. It is what enabled Ghaddafi to happen.

'When he came to power, he was considered to be better than the King. I think most of our parents thought so,' (nods and general agreement). 'But as time went on, he was just a man who became worse and worse for Libya; he killed people and took money.

'But some things here seem to be better than even in the UK. People can be educated for free, which is a good thing, and people do not have to pay a private company for water.

'We should try to keep the good things, but prevent the bad.'

From there, something you had not expected begins to happen. One by one, these 19-21 year-olds, almost every one of whom has at least one gun stacked a few metres away, begin to chip in ideas to sketch out the basics of a new constitution for Libya.

A young man you have met before, but do not know well, speaks next.

'The problem with Ghaddafi was not only that he hung on to power without elections, it was that he took money, and gave positions of power to his own tribe members.'

'Would anyone else have done any different?' You surprise yourself by asking this, even as you do so. But the room is now a place where this is a reasonable question.

'No,' the student responds. 'Nobody would have behaved differently. Because tribes are more important here than government or law.' More agreement from around the room. 'Only a very unusual person would have done differently from Ghaddafi.

'If someone breaks the law in Libya, it is not the police who deal with it, it is the tribe. The person's tribe is expected to punish them. And if it does not, then the tribe of the person the crime was committed against will get revenge, either on the perpetrator or on the whole tribe.

'In this way, there have been a series of tribal battles across Libya in recent years. The police are only involved when things become too bad. And then it is too late. They are not keeping the law, they are just trying to enforce peace.'

Another student stands, a man you know had fought for Ghaddafi weeks before.

'The problem is deeper,' he begins. 'It starts at school and it continues throughout everybody's life. At school, children are taught about the history of Libya but they are each taught to look at what a member of their tribe did to create Libya, or to develop or defend it. It means they are proud of Libya, but it also means they believe their own tribe is responsible for what is good about it.

'It continues throughout your life. Your tribe says what is important, who is good and who is bad. People are Libyan. They are proud to be Libyan. But the tribe takes priority, because the tribe is your family, and your tribe built Libya.

'We must try to ensure that Libya, its rules and laws are the most important thing, not tribes led by people who care only about their tribe. It has to begin at school, teaching children history from the view of Libya or from the world, but it must also come from everyone: people have to stop teaching each other about their tribe and people have to stop being happy to act outside the law.

'To make that happen, we also need clear rules, and a police force which is Libyan, swearing to do what the constitution says, not what a leader tells them to.

'The police and the army must be made up of people from every different tribe, and the minority groups like Africans and the Amazigh,* so they represent everyone and everyone will be treated fairly by the law, as a Libyan, not just as a tribe member.'

*The Amazigh – Berbers who have not adopted Arabic-influenced Maghreb customs and language – are mainly based in the South-West of Libya. In part due to – though in no way justified by – their linguistic and cultural differences from the majority of Libya's six-million population, they were persecuted by Ghaddafi, and as a result joined the revolution against him in February 2011.

Since the revolution ended – and well into 2014, when this book was written – they campaigned for fairer treatment than they had received from Ghaddafi, and than they felt they were receiving from the new Libyan political system.

'Will it work?' You ask.

'We cannot know. Libya has a chance to be a new state today, and we do not know what would work and what would not.

'It would be difficult, to try to change people's minds, and to help children to learn about their home and their lives in a different way.

'But we know that the rule of tribes does not work. It did not stop Ghaddafi from happening, and it does not make people behave well towards one another. It does not encourage people to keep the law or to think about Libya as much as about their tribe. So it is something we must work to change.'

The conversation continues through topics including what sort of government should exist (a Republic under an elected President in charge of the police and armed forces, and a Parliament and Prime Minister which makes laws and carries out day-to-day tasks. You are half-joking when you ask 'Like Italy?' but the suggestion is taken seriously and most people in the room agree that an Italian structure might suit Libya) and how it should be elected (very strong support for full proportional representation: 'Local politicians will look after local interests and local people. National politicians have other things to do,' one former pro-Ghaddafi combatant said).

There is some discussion about issues of public versus private ownership, with most agreeing that 'the people' should own Libya's water, electricity, education, hospitals and crucially oil, but that private businesses must be allowed.

One man – who had so far remained silent – argues briefly that no-one should be homeless, and that although he had fought against Ghaddafi, all homes in Libya should belong to all the people.

Despite some debate about whether specific policies should be included in a constitution, the former soldiers and guerrilla fighters agree that the idea is good.

The student with the Ghaddafi watch speaks next. 'I want to know what the rights to vote would be in a new Libya. Do we all get to speak on everything?'

It's a controversial question, as everyone in the room understands the possible reference to Ghaddafi's Green Book proposals for people's committees and assemblies, but the student continues: 'We cannot have a system as in the UK, where people may vote only once every five years and then must suffer whatever happens to them next. Nobody fought their neighbours and tore our country to pieces because they wanted to have democratic power only once every five years. So how can we deliver real power to people?'

Another proposes that internet voting could enable every single decision to be made by all Libya's 3.4 million citizens of voting age (out of a total population of six million) because it enables immediate voting from across the state.

'But many people do not have a computer, and some parts of Libya have only irregular access to the internet.' One student comments.

You add: 'How can you help to ensure that people know enough about each issue to vote sensibly on it? How can you ensure people will be interested enough to find out about the issues?'

Your question is met by a mixture of blank looks and astonished faces. But the student with the Ghaddafi watch says: 'Now is the time to make sure of that. People here do care what happens next. They are engaged now with Libya and the future. Everyone is political, today. We have to enable them to vote, to make sure they have information to make their minds up. If we start very soon, then it will continue.'

Another asks: 'How do we ensure we are not stuck with governments who we dislike, who do not do what we elected them to do?'

'You can use the internet for that,' you say. 'Set a rule for a public vote of no confidence.'

Another student interjects: 'So that if the government does not do what the people want they can force a new election. So the people get to make sure that what they want will happen.'

'Exactly,' you say. 'You can set up a system whereby if one million people in Libya put their names to a petition online, a new election must be held. The current government might win that election, but it might lose it. Even if it wins, it will have had to explain what it is doing and why. At least politicians will understand their role in society, what they should do and how they should do it, including always being answerable to the people.'

The conversation continues on these topics for hours, constructing the basis of a constitution for a new Libya piece by piece, question by question, until one by one, the soldiers-cum-politicians begin looking at their watches, Ghaddafi-faced or otherwise, and preparing to leave.

They are enthusiastic about what could happen next, as most were when they left their homes and families with weapons to play their part in one of the defining moments of their state's history.

This evening, however, they pick up their high-powered guns with different hopes – not to destroy, but to start at last to build.

You know it will not be these people who build the new Libya, but you are certain that others – similar men and women, who gave up their lives to fight and create something new – are having these conversations. That across the state, over coffees and sweets, couscous and harissa, they must be coming to similar conclusions – that a state can be built, that it must be built fast, and that Libya has a rare – almost unique – opportunity to learn not only from its own mistakes, but from everyone else's too.

As you step out into the warm Sirte night for one of the last times, you realise this may be the first time since your arrival that you have felt genuine optimism for Libya.

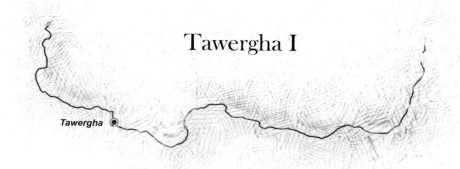

Tawergha I

Speeding West from Sirte towards Tripoli, about 30 miles from Misrata, you enter a ruin.

Your driver refuses to stop, instead, at your repeated request, finally slowing your vehicle to a crawl along the Roman Road, moving slowly enough for you to take photos, read graffiti and experience the atmosphere of desolation and desertion, but always ready to speed away at the slightest hint of a problem.

It is a ghost town, but you realise very quickly that your driver's fear is not ghosts: he is afraid of who and what may be living here now.

He needn't have worried.

The town, today, is completely deserted. The only things which move, as you lean from the vehicle's window to survey and photograph the dusty, devastated buildings, are grains of sand, and the wind which carries them.

Less than six months ago, this was a bustling town. Today, it is a collection of holed, parched, yellow ruins in a parched, yellow, deserted landscape.

It is unlike anything you have ever seen before, save perhaps in science fiction films: nothing walks, nothing breathes, nothing happens. Just the slow collapse of yellow buildings into yellow sands.

It is also the scene of the greatest war-crime of the Libyan Civil War – an episode in ethnic cleansing trumpeted and celebrated by its perpetrators, and rightly denounced as a crime against humanity by the few who know anything about it.

It is Tawergha. In Berber, its name means 'Green Island'.

As someone who by now knows Sirte well, there is something unsettling about Tawergha.

You are not new to the insane destruction rained from the sky by NATO and then compounded by ground forces defending and opposing Ghaddafi.

The destruction here is more complete even than Sirte, but there is nothing new to you (though you shudder to realise it) in the way the roofs of tall buildings seem to bow to meet you as you pass, or the way the homes, hospitals and offices sag, as if exhausted by the African sun.

You wonder whether it's the fact that it is the only modern town you have ever seen in which nothing is alive. Certainly, that's a factor, but there is something else.

Then you realise it: all of the buildings which are still standing bear the scorch-marks of fire damage. That's not so unusual in the many which have been bombed by NATO aircraft, nor even in those where bullet-holes suggest some kind of street fight.

But even those buildings with no bullet holes, and no missile damage – small in number though those buildings are – are covered in black, their interiors charred shells.

They are not simple 'casualties of war' – as horrendous and de-humanising as that phrase is – these buildings have been deliberately and systematically set alight, destroyed so they cannot be lived in again.

Tawergha first came to prominence during the Roman Conquest of what is now Libya, when its position on the 'sand road' – the Roman Road linking Morocco to Syria, meant it held a position of strategic importance: control of it meant the Romans controlled Tripoli to the West, and the route to Egypt in the East.

It is a bitter irony that after some 2,000 or so years of sleepy existence, engaging itself in fruit production and little else, the next time it became important its position (and some far darker motives) led to its obliteration.

The town had become a key point on the slave routes north out of Africa, and as a producer of massive quantities of dates, it also became a place where slaves were forced to live and work.

As a result, it became the only place on the Libyan north coast where black Africans were the majority, rather than a minority group.

Though they had lived there for hundreds of years, when Ghaddafi came to power many Libyans still regarded – and treated – the Tawerghans as foreigners and slaves.

Ghaddafi himself drew attention to this, stating in many speeches that 'no longer will the Tawerghans be treated here as slaves'.

Ghaddafi does not seem to have passed any law, or begun any initiative designed to put an end to the way Tawerghans were treated or regarded, but it is maybe a mark of how marginalised they felt that they responded to this minimum effort with loyalty and support.

When war broke out, the Tawerghans rallied to the leader they believed supported them. Many were already soldiers in Ghaddafi's army, others signed up to join the fight in his support.

In response, both the Misrata khetiba and NATO dubbed them (and all other black people in Libya who didn't oppose Ghaddafi, including guest workers and other black Libyans) 'mertezqh' or 'mercenaries': a transparently incorrect accusation, which NATO in particular should perhaps reconsider its eagerness to use in future armed disputes.

As the war progressed, it became clear that Misrata, a staunch opponent of Ghaddafi's continued rule, which sat between Tripoli in the West, the 'pro-Ghaddafi' town of Sirte and the 'first battleground' of Benghazi in the East, and which was 'independent' from Ghaddafi's rule from 23rd February, would be a major obstacle to Ghaddafi, and to the future of his regime.

As a result Tawergha, 30 miles East of Misrata, became central to Ghaddafi's war effort, becoming the staging post for land attacks on the rebel city, as well as being used to launch missiles directly towards it.

This was grimly predictable – and another dark irony of the War, as the closeness of Tawergha and Misrata had seen strong ties develop between the two places: many Tawerghans worked in Misrata, or had family members there. Less predictable was the response of the Misratans: they declared their intention to 'wipe Tawergha from the map'.

One Misrata khetiba commander, Ibrahim al-Halbous, told reporters as he led his brigade towards Tawergha: 'Tawerghans should all pack up. They must all leave here immediately. Tawergha no longer exists: there is only Misrata.'

At this point, Misrata was emerging from its hardest period of the war: it had been besieged by Ghaddafi's troops and pounded by missiles. Though not as hard-hit as Sirte would be in the following weeks, its citizens had suffered violence, fear and hardship beyond the imagining of most people in the developed world. But its response was to attack a town of civilians.

The khetibas – and indeed Misratan civilians – attempted to justify their efforts to wipe Tawergha out. For many months after the War ended, Misratan news broadcasts claimed Tawerghans had raped Misratan citizens, and that Tawerghans had chopped the penises from Misratan men.

They also claimed that when they 'took' Tawergha, they discovered Libya's largest mass grave of anti-Ghaddafi fighters. But the evidence for these claims has never been shown, and even if they were true, nobody could seriously have levelled the blame for this at Tawergha's civilians. Regardless of this, the Misratans called for air strikes on Tawergha, which NATO, described by Noam Chomsky as the 'air-force of the revolution' – and despite the no-fly zone its members had voted into place at the United Nations – duly delivered.

Western missiles hammered Tawergha for three days. NATO's grim 'battle update' press notices from 10th-13th August note a series of strikes, and travelling through the town now, you can see, in the piles of shattered bricks which were once homes, the collapsed roofs of former schools, and the ruins which only months ago were offices, clinics and a hospital, what those strikes were for.

Pounded into submission, the people of Tawergha faced, on 13th August 2011, the final day in their hometown. The Misrata khetiba swooped, shooting to maim and kill, 'arresting' men and forcing women and children to flee: those lucky enough to live and escape imprisonment have never been allowed to return.

As you ride, creeping slowly through the town, you see evidence of the underlying reasons for this outrage. One piece of graffiti, which your driver, embarrassed, attempts to avoid translating in full, reads: 'Misrata brigade: the brigade for purging slaves and black skin'. Another, even more stark, simply reads: 'Town cleansed'.

When Misratans – or at least the khetiba which represented them – entered Tawergha, they told reporters the town was now cleansed, and that Tawerghans would never be allowed to return home except 'over our dead bodies'. You can see that they were faithful to their declaration. Everywhere a building stands, it has been set alight, the khetibas having sought to erase any possibility of life here, unless at their express agreement, on terms they set themselves. Unlike in Sirte, the 'lucky' buildings are not the ones containing dozens of bullet holes, they are the ones with black smears betraying the fact that Tawergha is now a town – lifeless and empty thanks to the deliberate actions of its nearest neighbour – where fortune no longer exists.

Back in Misrata itself, the suburb of Ghoushi, where the vast majority – nearly 80 per cent – of people were originally from Tawergha, or were the children or grandchildren of people from the town, has also been emptied.

A bounty had been announced for the arrest and delivery to the khetiba of the Ghoushians. They were not even residents of Tawergha, let alone active combatants. They had suffered the

same punishment meted out by Ghaddafi, shoulder to shoulder with their fellow Misratans. Such is the mindlessness of racism, red in tooth and claw. This was not an act of 'war' or combat: it was, as its khetibas proclaimed, a cleansing of Misrata and its surroundings, a complete purge of anyone with black skin.

On such terms, there is no escaping the fact that the cleansing of Tawergha was a war crime at best, and given what followed, far closer to a crime against humanity. Because the persecution did not end there: the Misrata khetiba chased Tawergha's terrified natives across the country, attacking the tents and huts, refugee camps for those who had been forced forever from their homes, in Homs, Sabha, Benghazi, Tripoli.

More than 2000 men – of an original Tawerghan population of 30,000 people – are in Misratan 'prisons'* where they are tortured to 'encourage' confessions to acts the vast majority had no part in, if they even happened at all.

They remain there today (Spring 2014). The majority without charge, for once you have charged an innocent man, you may be forced to release him.

While this process was in its early stages, on 18th September 2011, the Prime Minister of Libya's National Transitional Council, Mohamed Jibril, announced that the Tawerghans would receive no protection from his 'government'. He said: 'Nobody has the right to interfere except the people of Misrata. This matter can't be tackled through theories and textbook examples of national reconciliation like those in South Africa, Ireland and Eastern Europe.'

You realise he was right: in Ireland, Eastern Europe and South Africa, people remained for a reconciliation process to begin. Here, there is nobody. You do wonder, however, why Jibril chose not to act to protect those who had already done as the Misratans had demanded, and fled from their homes. Not everybody stood by so meekly, or attempted to justify the khetiba's behaviour. In Benghazi and Tripoli, efforts were made to ensure people had places to stay – albeit only refugee camps – and that Tawerghan children received what education they could.

And on 26th January 2012, only a few weeks before your slow drive through Tawergha, Medicines Sans Frontiers, one of the few international organisations to have been in Misrata consistently from the moment it was safe enough to enter, withdrew from the city.

It announced that it could no longer remain in a town where people brought Tawerghans who had been so severely tortured they could barely speak or stand, who had had their teeth smashed out with rifle butts, the soles of their feet beaten with rope, ribs, arms and legs broken, to be patched up and made fit enough to be taken back to prisons and tortured more.

Its General Director Chris Jones appeared on Libyan television to say: 'Our role is to provide medical care to war casualties and sick detainees, not to repeatedly treat the same patients between torture sessions.'

As the wind blows sand and the dust of NATO and the Misrata khetiba's darkest Libyan achievement into your eyes, you note the blacked out road signs, with new words scrawled over them. Your driver translates: 'It used to say Tawergha,' he says. 'Today, it reads "New Taminj".'

Taminj is a suburb of Misrata. You find it hard to imagine it looks much like today's Tawergha.

Misrata

You stop in Misrata, glance around a store for notebooks, get caught up playing quiz games with youngsters, and then you do what you are there for.

You are reluctant.

You know about Misrata. About its khetiba and the crime against humanity it committed.

About the fact that its inhabitants are willing to believe the transparent lies they are spoon-fed by its media. About the base racism that was allowed to take over not only its armed representatives, but also its civilians.

You know about Misrata. And you are reluctant to allow anything new to influence your view of what the people of this city have done.

In the centre of the city, a museum has been hastily created in honour of the Civil War, and those who fought in it.

Two of its long interior walls are covered with photographs. Some are black and white, some colour. Some contain smiling faces, others serious expressions.

All are of young men, and every single one is now dead.

According to the museum's owner, 1,200 Misratan men were killed in the Libyan Civil War.* The walls contain fewer photos than that, but their sheer simplicity and impact – hundreds and hundreds of people, all now dead, staring at you as you pass, pause, and take another step - is overwhelming.

> * Misrata's local government reports that 1,083 men – some pro-Ghaddafi combatants – were killed, with around 2,000 people at that stage (September 2012) still missing.

And those deaths are nowhere near the whole story. Misrata is not quite a city of ruins. In fact, it is a great deal better off than Sirte, and of course Tawergha, which you promise yourself you will not forget whatever you see here, but that is not the point.

The point is that Misrata is a city of 350,000 people – Libya's third largest, but relatively small by Western standards – and the tallest building on its central street, directly opposite the museum, has had its front smashed off, as if by someone simply too lazy to open its doors to see what is inside.

Destruction is not all-encompassing, as it is in Sirte and Tawergha. But had you arrived here before those sorry towns, the sheer damage done to this place, where people live and work every moment of every day, would be astonishing: so shocking you would need to sit, perhaps for hours, just to try to take it in.

By any sensible evaluation, Misrata is both devastated and dangerous: you fear that falling masonry must claim more lives before long, as buildings appear ready to collapse at any moment.

And you feel slightly horrified – and nauseous – that you have met it with equanimity only because of the awful state of other Libyan towns you have already visited.

By this point on your journey, because of what you have already seen, what you have already heard, and where you have lived, it is hard to do justice to what was done to Misrata.

Its buildings were hammered: damaged in a different way from those of Sirte and Tawergha, because Ghaddafi's missiles were largely launched from the ground (the UN's no-fly zone was ignored only by NATO) and nowhere near in the same number, but pounded and smashed nonetheless.

Misrata was under siege from February until May – held at all times by Misratan opponents of Ghaddafi, but under attack from the dictator's forces.

By that point, Benghazi had declared itself 'free', but Misrata was the sole city in the west of Libya to have removed itself from Ghaddafi's rule.

As a result, the city was a major focus of Ghaddafi's war effort.

Nothing was allowed out, and the only things which entered were the rockets of a man who was supposed to lead the Misratans' homeland.*

---

* Ghaddafi's relationship with Misrata had not always been negative. The town's origins are unclear: the Romans built a fort here, named Thubactis, and several hundred years later, a town grew, this time using the Arab version of the name, Thubaqt. But Thubaqt, a thriving caravan and trading post, is believed by archaeologists to have been a 'new' town, named after the Roman site.

Its modern name comes from the Arabic Misr (Egypt) Ata (the one from) and refers to the Ottomans who arrived from Egypt in the 16th Century. It had profited from the slave trade, then from the unusually high rainfall which enabled extensive agriculture. But successive political and military intrigues between the city's leaders, the Turkish Empire, and later Italian colonisers, had left it relatively neglected.

During World War One its citizens managed to expel first the Italian army, then the German and Turkish forces, remaining as an independent 'oasis', but the war also altered Italian and Libyan ambitions in the region.

Despite its reduced national status, the city's outspoken, sometimes explosively-tempered, citizenry still influenced Libyan life.

Its political protests and riots after alleged vote-rigging in 1952 were a major part in King Idris' decision (or at least explanation of his decision) to permanently ban political parties in Libya, and when Ghaddafi snatched power in response to the King's increasingly ineffectual rule and repressive policies, Misrata seemed at last to have retaken a leading role in Libya's future.

Ghaddafi's development of the city saw its population increase hugely, and included the redevelopment of its port, the opening of new businesses and helped inspire its elevation to a major educational, economic and administrative centre. But the city never lost either its pride in its history, or its desire and ability to stand against injustices – real or perceived – which were committed against it. That pride and desire led it to its second defiance of a potential 'occupier', and the most vicious and bloody fight in its history.

On February 17th, in 'solidarity' with the people of Benghazi and other Libyan towns, a few dozen Misratans gathered in the city centre to protest against the excesses of Ghaddafi's rule.

In common with that in other towns, Ghaddafi's response in Misrata almost appeared designed to cause him and his troops the maximum difficulty: instead of simply ignoring the small, peaceful, demonstration, his soldiers arrested many of the protestors.

Predictably, Misratans came out in far greater number to protest these almost-certainly unnecessary arrests, at which point Ghaddafi's police and/or armed forces opened fire using live ammunition.

The earliest reported estimates of mortality were out by up to a factor of ten: original estimates of protestors killed in Misrata suggested 70 deaths, in fact six to 14 people were killed.

(This was a regular error in early reporting on the Civil War. In Benghazi, for example, reports suggested 519 civilians had been killed by police and soldiers, with no casualties on the government side. Human Rights Watch now puts that figure at 'at least 233', with 163 soldiers and police officers killed.

Also unreported was the lynching of 50 African men, mostly from Chad, in Bayda on 18th February. Most were killed by being locked inside a police station which was then burned to the ground. Fifteen escaped that grim fate: they were beaten, then hanged, in public. Their 'crime' was the accusation – they were not granted the honour of a trial – that they were 'mertezqh', 'mercenaries').

But nobody on Earth could justify or accept one death, let alone six, in a civilian protest in a town centre. And the people of Misrata did not accept it: they took to the streets, and by 23rd February, had driven the government's forces out of their city.

But Misrata, the largest city on the Roman Road between Tripoli and Benghazi – and sitting between Tripoli and Sirte – was too important a strategic point for Ghaddafi to allow to secede. His troops surrounded the city from February until mid-May, hammering it with ground-launched missiles and at times taking control of key sites within the city, including its airport.

During these long months, Misrata was assisted by ships from Malta, which carried vital food and supplies into the port Ghaddafi had built, and NATO, which used its seeming immunity from the UN-imposed no-fly zone to bomb pro-Ghaddafi strongholds from the air.

But throughout this period, Misrata stood defiant against Ghaddafi. Missiles struck apartment blocks, schools, businesses and health centres, and soldiers loyal to the regime launched wave after wave of attacks, but as against Italy, then Germany and Turkey, and in a small way, against King Idris, Misrata stood firm.

On 11th May, Misratan khetibas struck their final blow against Ghaddafi, retaking the airport and nearby military airbase. The three-month battle had cost the lives of 366 rebel combatants, and up to 862 civilians, as well as up to 545 Ghaddafi loyalists, but it was a central moment in the wider Libyan Civil War.

With Misrata safe in the hands of the khetibas, Ghaddafi's regime could no longer even connect all the nominally 'loyal' parts of Libya's North coast – its wealthiest area.

But you cannot help but feel uneasy about Misrata's response to its desperate – and eventually victorious – struggle against Ghaddafi.

Although you realise it is unfair, you nevertheless find yourself comparing the atmosphere of every place you have visited in Libya with the others. And it is not a comparison which compliments Misrata.

In Tripoli and Zintan, there is a feeling of aspiration – of the opportunity for improvement created by Ghaddafi's ousting and a reaching towards a new Libya, as yet unknown, but worth aiming for.

In Benghazi – a city where there is an almost tangible feeling of self-sufficiency – all eyes were on what might come next.

Even in Sirte, there was a grim determination to create something better from the ruins and devastation of the present.

Each of these places also held an undercurrent of sadness – sorrow at what, and who, had been lost in the preceding weeks and months.

Misrata shares that sadness. But here, it is weaved into something different.

Inside the memorial museum, the collection of photographs, a genuine, moving tribute to those lost, is surrounded by bullets, guns, missiles and rocket launchers – examples of the weapons used to kill those who supported Ghaddafi.

And outside its entrance, a huge statue of an eagle, with wings spread and painted in the colours of the 'new' Libyan flag, stands alongside tanks, armoured vehicles and vast guns, pointed skyward.

It is not an expression of loss, or of sorrow, but a loud celebration of victory, and of war.

It shouts that Misrata has won, that strength and bullets have overcome and that this city and its khetibas believe that might is right, that the finger on the trigger is what controls Libya.

It is anger which controls Misrata now.

The city suffered during the Libyan Civil War. However insensitive the comparison, it was hit harder, and for longer, than either Tripoli or Benghazi. But it is hardly alone in that.

All along the north coast of Libya, there are towns and cities in worse or similar condition than Misrata.

Yet it is Misrata, where citizens undertook ethnic cleansing, and from where the khetiba 'purged' its closest neighbour Tawergha of 'black skin', that shouts loudest, longest, until its voice cracks with the effort, that it is strong, that it is powerful, even that it – ahead of all other cities – 'won' the war against Ghaddafi.

It is Misrata where anger rules all, and as a result it is Misrata which now faces in the opposite direction to most of Libya – looking backward to its victory rather than forward to a new Libya.

Perhaps there is something else which helps explain Misrata's rage – frustration at always coming second. To Tripoli in the West, to Benghazi in the East, even, most humiliatingly, to Sirte under Ghaddafi.

But Misratan anger is dangerous: its khetibas still search out Tawerghans, arresting some and chasing the others from wherever they are attempting to build new lives.

Its khetibas are among those who sit, heavily-armed, at the roadblocks set up every ten km or so along the entire Libyan section of North Africa's great Roman Road, stopping traffic, 'checking' documents (what would happen if they were not in order? No-one you have asked seems altogether sure). And its khetibas are among those to have undermined the government by refusing its requests and demands to lay down their weapons and start to build the new Libya.*

The government had, at this time, requested khetibas leave Tripoli to return home on two occasions, and demanded their removal from the city once, threatening reprisals if they refused.

The khetibas ignored both requests, and reluctantly agreed to leave Tripoli airport, though not the city, only at the last moment before the deadline set by the government. No reprisals were taken. The khetibas continued to sit, armed, at roadsides and 'strategic' points, all across the country.

Misratans may have helped to end Ghaddafi's regime, but theirs is now a city of anger and bullets. You find yourself caught, for a moment, on Misrata's main street, between the Museum, with its glorification of violence, and the now-faceless building opposite, a stark reminder of its bitter, wasteful, shameful, unacceptable outcome.

And you wonder how much longer this city's love of weapons, defiance of the government and overwhelming anger can continue: how long can Misrata behave this way until it drags all of Libya back into bloodshed and chaos?

Libya, November 2011-April 2012: Benghazi

Benghazi ◉

Security

One night, in the darkness outside here, a man came with a gun and started shooting.

I am a security guard, and although this was not in the complex where I work, it was very nearby.

You know what it is like. You want to see what is happening, don't you?

So I went outside of my hut here, and outside the walls, and saw a man holding another man by the throat.

He had a gun, which he was pointing at the man's arm, and he was saying 'If you don't go home now, I will shoot you.'

I do not know where either of them is from. The man with the gun looked like me: he could be from here in Benghazi, or somewhere else in Libya, even in Egypt or an Arab state. The other man told me later on that he was from Pakistan.

I do not know whether the man with the gun wanted him to go home here in Benghazi, or home to Pakistan.

I stood and watched and the man with the gun turned to look at me. He was younger than I thought he was at first. Probably only 17 or 18. He turned away from the man from Pakistan, and looked at me. He lifted up his gun, but I thought he would not shoot. I do not know why, but as he raised his arm, I just thought 'he will not shoot, he will not shoot'.

I stood still. I did not move. He held the gun at arm's length, pointing at me. But he was shaking. He lowered his arm, and then he ran away.

I went to the man, who had sat down leaning on the wall. I brought him inside the hut I work in at night, and we talked a little.

I will be honest, I still do not know what he and the other man disagreed about, because I was not there to see what happened first. But I think the boy had a gun because of the war, which had only finished a few days before, and I think before the war, maybe it could not have happened.

That does not mean I think the war was wrong. It just means that I think Benghazi has changed. All of Libya has changed. Some changes are better, some others make life harder.

I came here to Libya from Kuwait. I lived in Kuwait with my mother and my father, but we left after Iraq invaded. Things were bad then, but they were worse after the war.

Because my dad was a Palestinian. He had come to work as a chemical engineer, and he was good. Kuwait was a rich state and he earned a lot of money.

Then Iraq invaded. Like all the children, I had been born in Kuwait and hoped he would leave. We could not go to school so I used to read at home with my sisters.

I remember that when the war ended my friends came and we all played outside together. We did not really celebrate the war was over, because we did not really know very much about it. But we were happy to be outside in the sunshine and all playing together again.

But very soon, we had to leave. The Kuwait government said that people like my father, who was a Palestinian, had supported Iraq in the war. But my father had not supported Iraq. They said that people like my father had stopped working to fight for Iraq, but my father had stopped working because his work place was closed. He did not fight anyone.

But the soldiers came anyway. They broke things in our home, and they held my mother and father against the walls and made us look while they said they would kill them. My father did not do anything, even when they had gone. But my mother and some of my sisters were crying.

We left, to start a new life in Libya. We lived in Brega. It was a long way from Kuwait, but it was a place where my father found work for an American company, and it was a place where we could go to school and work hard.

I became an electrical engineer. This job that I have now is not what I will do forever, though I am glad to have it. It is a job that I do until I can return to work.

Because after February 17th, things changed again for my family.

My father was at work, even though he is 70, and I was at work as well.

I came home before my father and called out to see who was at home, but I did not hear anything.

I looked into the main room of the house, and I saw that there was a man there, in uniform, with a gun. He did not shoot me. But he did not speak to me either. He had an army uniform, so I am sure he may have been fighting for Ghaddafi, but I still do not know for certain.

He pushed me out of the way, then walked to the door. He shot the doorframe three times and then walked out. I did not know what to do. I do not know why, but I went up to my bedroom first.

Everything was broken. There was a great deal of good furniture from Kuwait that we had saved and there was some from Libya, and a TV I had bought when I had earned enough money. But it was all smashed.

I walked downstairs again, and into the main room. On the walls the intruders had painted 'We will get your mother and your sisters. Palestinians are dirty. You must leave.'

I was angry, but I did not know what to do.

I went into the kitchen. There were plates and cups broken on the floor and I saw my mother sitting in the corner, shaking and crying with a piece of a plate in her hand.

This had happened to her before, to have her home broken into, and to be threatened, to see her life smashed by armed men.

But now she is old. She cannot just leave again. And I do not think she should have to.

My father came home a little later. He took me outside and showed me that a car belonging to my oldest sister had been stolen, and another belonging to my mother had been shot so that the engine would not work any more. My father had his car, and I still had mine, because we had been at work. But my father did not return to work. It is the second time this has happened to him, as well. And he is 70 now.

He stayed at home the next day, and the day after that. And then everyone had to stay at home because all the businesses closed because of the War. But after the War, he still did not return to work. All he does now is to sit at home in the main room and stare at his walls. I made sure I cleaned the paint away and repainted so he does not have to read what was written on them. He had only told me about Palestine once and he said it was a good place but that people had to leave it because they could be killed. On that night, he said very quietly when only I was there 'I wish I was at home.'

I nearly said that he was at home, or that Kuwait, which was my home, had been as bad as Libya. But I realised he did not mean Brega, or Kuwait. He meant Palestine. But he cannot go back there. Nor can he move anywhere else. He must stay now where he is.

When the War ended, my family was scared. I tried to return to work, but I could not. The company told me there were not any jobs for me. But I discovered another man was doing my job. He was a Libyan, and I was not.

So now, to support my mother, my father, and four of my six sisters (two have husbands who have jobs), I came to Benghazi. Things are different here for me. I was able to find this job.

It is not what I trained to do, or what I want to do forever, and it takes me six hours of driving to return to my family on my days off, but it is a job, and I do get to see my family sometimes, even though I am tired. I am working very hard to make sure my family is OK.

But I do hope to get a job soon as an electrician or electrical engineer again. I studied hard to learn to do that.

Many people in Libya think that Ghaddafi was too kind to foreigners and that now he is gone, the foreigners should go too, that they should not have jobs any longer.

But I do not believe this. Ghaddafi was bad to everyone. If he wanted to be bad, he did not decide to be bad just to Libyans. And if he was not bad, he did not behave more nicely to foreign people than to Libyans.

We live together in a new state, like we did in an old one. I hope that we can work together to make it a better place for all of us.

Second Amongst Equals?

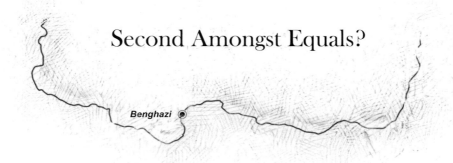

It has taken you a long time to reach Benghazi.

You entered Libya from the West, travelling on the Roman Road from Zarzis in Tunisia, past Ben Gardane and Choucha Refugee Camp to the border crossing point.

After three hours, a lone uniformed employee emerged from the hut where he had been 'checking' your passport, looked at your bag, picked it up, put it down, lit a cigarette, leaned against the baggage checking machine he had ignored, and nodded you through the gate.

From there, you continued East on the Roman Road, the towns becoming progressively less East Tunisian, and more West Libyan as you went.

And as roadside stalls selling pottery and fruit gave way to roadside shops selling clothing and coffee, you also noted something else.

Every wall, whichever way you looked, was totally covered with graffiti. A few pieces were eye-catchingly good, showing symbols, landscapes or scenes from wars. Most were caricatures of Muammar Ghaddafi painted by artists with greater or lesser ability, while many, you later learned, were eye-watering Arabic insults aimed at the deposed and recently-deceased ruler.

You had entered Tripoli on the Roman Road in darkness, on that first night, spending only a few hours there, experiencing the engaging chaos of the city's traffic, its horns blaring, windows wound down, as well as vast crowds of people, late-night food and coffee shops, music and engulfing, almost overwhelming, noise.

The following morning, you had thrown your bag into a pick-up, which had raced another on largely deserted stretches of the ancient highway, through desert sands, past sea views, slowing only for the road-blocks at the entrance and exit of every village and town. You arrived in Sirte by early evening.

Sirte gripped all of your attention, then, and has never really let it go. But Benghazi, the Eastern 'capital', industrial 'capital' and its nation's second city, is the originator of the Libyan revolution.

Though generally regarded second in most things to the Libyan capital Tripoli,* it had led low-level unrest against the Ghaddafi regime for many years, gaining a reputation as a 'rebel' town even though its 'rebellions' had been less 'civil unrest' and more 'public demonstrations of frustration'.

* *Benghazi's fractious relationship with Tripoli is rooted in the two cities' history as capitals. Benghazi, founded in 525 BC by Greek explorers, and named Euesperidies, likely after the paradisiacal garden of the Hesperides, was regarded for many of its earliest years as an object of conquest by Libyans, rather than a 'leader' of its nearest communities.*

In fact, in one of the earliest chapters of its history, told by Greek historian Thucydides, it was besieged in 414 BC by Libyans, and saved from being overrun only because Spartan forces, sailing from Sparta to Sicily, were blown off course and forced to land nearby.

Through such fortune – as well as more deliberate defensive measures – the city remained the capital of the Greek colony of Cyrenaica for three hundred years.

For a short while, it ruled a wider region, including the briefly Greek-ruled Tripoli, but the latter was swiftly conquered by the Carthaginians, who were building an empire which would stand until Roman incursions changed the face of the region again.

When Roman troops entered North Africa, Benghazi prospered, remaining the capital of Cyrenaica, which was bordered to the west by Tripolitania.

By the early Middle Ages, it was an important port, but as such also an object of desire for potential conquerors. The Ottomans seized it in 1578, and allowed it to be ruled by their clients in Tripoli.

It passed in 1835 into direct Ottoman rule, until 1911, when Italian troops invaded to carve a section of North Africa into an empire.

Led by Omar Mukhtar, Cyrenaica's population resisted Italian occupation. Mukhtar, leading a force largely made up of members of leading Cyrenaican tribe, the Senussi (Mukhtar was not a member of the tribe) and using desert guerrilla warfare tactics, kept resistance alive for almost 20 years.

Mukhtar was captured by the Italians on 11 September 1931, and publicly hanged five days later. He was 73.

All Libyans – not just those from Cyrenaica – regard Mukhtar as a hero.

Muammar Ghaddafi, on a state visit to Italy in 2009, brought the Senussist leader's son with him, and wore a photograph of Mukhtar, taken while he was imprisoned by the Italians, days before his hanging. This is all the more remarkable given that Ghaddafi's coup had deposed King Idris, the leader of the Senussi tribe.

It is hard to imagine what Ghaddafi felt about the khetibas fighting against him in the Libyan Civil War under a banner of Mukhtar, or the fact that one khetiba brigade was named after the Cyrenaican.

Benghazi changed hands five times during World War Two, but in 1949 became capital of the Emirate of Cyrenaica, which was founded by Idris Senussi I. Idris became King of a united Libya in 1951, when the Emirate merged with Tripolitania and Fezzan.

The King held both Tripoli and Benghazi as 'twin capitals' (he effectively governed from Tripoli, but lived in Benghazi, where his Senussi tribe remained the strongest social group), until Ghaddafi's coup in 1969.

Ghaddafi, with no Senussist ties or loyalties, and a belief – shared by most Libyans, including many Benghazans – that the King was both a dictatorial and untalented ruler, abandoned the 'twin capital' experiment, making Tripoli the sole administrative centre of the state, perceived by some Benghazans as a deliberate insult to them.

And pro-Senussist feeling – including a belief that the tribe was directly responsible for the liberty and existence of Libya – stoked further resentment of Ghaddafi.

The Libyan ruler arguably helped increase the city's antagonism towards him by focusing money on his plan to make Sirte the capital of a united Africa – a title Benghazans felt would be better suited to their own home.

It is very likely that this friction – which had led to regular street protests and violence against Ghaddafi's regime in the eastern city – explains in part the leader's inept response to the protests of January and February 2011, when some demonstrators were filmed carrying images of Idris I, a bad, but at least Cyrenaican, monarch.

And it had begun the Libyan revolution, winning its freedom from Ghaddafi's rule in the 'first battle' of Benghazi on February 17th, and arguably keeping the entire struggle alive by repelling Ghaddafi's forces in the 'second battle' just under one month later.*

* The first 'battle' of Benghazi did not begin as a battle at all. Neither did it end as one. It saw protests which had begun in January 2011 grow, following repeated arrests, to large demonstrations of anger at the Ghaddafi regime.

In February, matters became more serious, and on February 17th, police and soldiers opened fire on protestors using live ammunition, an attack estimated to have killed 14 people.

On 18th February, during a funeral procession for one of those killed the previous day, soldiers in the Benghazi katiba (the major Libyan army barracks in the city) opened fire. It is difficult to believe that they did so under direct orders from Muammar Ghaddafi, and there remains debate over whether the shots were fired before or after protestors threw rocks at soldiers in the barracks.

In fighting that day, 24 protestors died. Two policemen, accused of having fired on the crowd, were publicly hanged by demonstrators that evening.

By the morning of 19th February, almost all police and soldiers had withdrawn from Benghazi. Those who remained were members of the Khamis Brigade – in reality the 32nd Reinforced Brigade of the Armed People, but nicknamed 'Khamis' after Khamis Ghaddafi, son of the Libyan leader, who led the brigade – which had entered the city as police and other government forces left.

The Khamis Brigade was regarded as the state's 'elite' force, and based itself in the Benghazi katiba.

In the nearby towns of Derna and Bayda, both also part of the former province of Cyrenaica, police and riot control units joined protestors on the streets – in Derna, Islamist gunmen, led by a defected army colonel, seized 250 firearms and 70 military vehicles.

The same day, in Benghazi, reports claim that the Khamis brigade opened fire on another funeral parade. If this is correct, it means that either Muammar Ghaddafi ordered the shooting of funeral parades, as now two separate brigades had done so, or that soldiers in the Khamis Brigade were operating without, or in contravention of, orders.

Rebels turned bulldozers into battering rams, and one group raided an army barracks on the outskirts of the city taking every weapon stored within, and three tanks. These, too, were driven at the katiba's walls, but with no decisive outcome.

The following day, the actions of a lone car-bomber did what days of looting, shooting and military manoeuvres had not, smashing open the katiba's gates and enabling Benghazan rebel forces to overrun the barracks, forcing Ghaddafi's troops – who accepted a deal offering them free passage – out of the city.

The second battle, a month later, saw Ghaddafi's troops attempt to retake Benghazi.

On 19th March, having arrived the night before and dug themselves into position on its outskirts, Ghaddafi's forces shelled the city.

They sent in a column of tanks, which rebel troops – by now better armed thanks to French-airlifted weapons (the first of NATO's regular, systematic breaches of the UN Security Council Resolution 1973 which they themselves had called for and voted for just two days earlier) and the collection of those left when government forces had fled the city – met and repelled.

As the day's fighting continued, the Benghazan force managed to push Ghaddafi's troops back, though only amid some confusion and 'friendly fire'. A Mig fighter jet was brought down by Benghazan ground fire, but was flying on behalf of the city's – not Ghaddafi's – cause.

As a result, messages were broadcast from mosques across Benghazi: 'Do not fire on the aircraft – they are ours.' Whether through overconfidence in his 'superior' firepower, fear at the potential response of the UN, or respect for the Security Council, Ghaddafi was the only participant in the second battle of Benghazi who obeyed international law on aerial attacks.

At around 16.00 on 19th March, French aircraft – again in contravention of the no-fly zone over Libya for which the French themselves had voted – flew over Benghazi on reconnaissance. By 18.00, they had bombed several Ghaddafi-regime armoured vehicles and other targets on the outskirts of Benghazi.

The same afternoon, the US and UK navies launched cruise missile attacks on Libyan airfields across the state, and at 4am on 20th March, French aircraft spent two hours firing on a Ghaddafi-regime armoured column outside Benghazi.

Whether thanks to NATO's airstrikes and cruise missile launches or, as Mohamed Jibril of the Libyan National Transitional Council claimed, the bravery and diligence of Benghazi's own forces under General Abdul Fatah Younis, who had defected from the government to lead the city's resistance, Benghazi had twice defeated its government. It would not be challenged 'at home' again.

In terms of population, wealth, even fame, Tripoli deserves its regard as Libya's first city. But Benghazi is without question the First City of Libya's Civil War, and arguably of its nation's freedom from Italian rule.

You could not leave Libya without visiting.

In the event, you arrive in Benghazi in late afternoon, after a literally agonising seven hour journey. Throughout, a small black tomcat had alleviated its boredom and discomfort by playing a game in which it had hissed, leapt from one seat-back to another, using your face as a brief stopping point between each one.

This hilarity had been punctuated every half-hour or so by a second game, in which it would sit very still on your lap, before suddenly arching its back and pushing its claws through your jeans and skin, and into your thighs.

The third time this happened, the lady next to you, who owned both the cat and the car in which it was expressing its extreme displeasure, said softly: 'He does have a basket, you know, but he really doesn't like it in there.'

You cross the 23rd July Lake on Algeria Street, sunlight glittering off the water below. And from the road's highest point, you are given a brief view of almost the entire city.

Apart from the Benghazan Green Book building, which sits empty and still smeared with the soot marks and fire damage inflicted on it by the rebels after the first battle of Benghazi, it is in far the best condition of any place you have visited so far.

Unlike Ajdabiya,* for example, where you had stopped for lunch, the buildings in its centre are not holed by missiles, or partly crumbling as the weather takes effect on gaping impact holes.

---

* *Ajdabiya, 93 miles south of Benghazi, is a town of 73,000 people. It had grown into an important Roman settlement – one of the major trading points on the old Roman Road - in part because it had drinkable water, but also because it was the point at which the North Sahara route to the coast from the oases of Jalu and al-Ujlah met the great trans-Africa highway.*

Though never part of the original Cyrenaica, it is in the modern sub-region, and in common with many other towns in the region, declared itself 'free' from Muammar Ghaddafi's rule after protests on 16th and 17th February.

In Ajdabiya, it is claimed ten people were killed by pro-government snipers across the two days, while rebel activities included burning down the local government's offices.

But Ajdabiya's location made it as important in the Libyan Civil War as it had been to Roman and North African traders. For both Eastern rebels and Ghaddafi's forces, control of the town offered the opportunity to control the Roman Road, the most important land route to the 'enemy' – Tripoli for the Benghazans, Benghazi for Ghaddafi's forces.

As a result, when Ghaddafi's forces launched their major counter-offensive in March 2011, Ajdabiya was a focus of its campaign.

On 15th March, after defeating khetibas in the important oil-town Brega, pro-Ghaddafi forces arrived at Ajdabiya.

Fighting lasted two days, and thanks in part to Libyan naval ships shelling the town from the sea (Benghazan aircraft sank one ship, though rebel leaders announced they had hit three, sinking two, and rebel helicopters managed to strike government reinforcements arriving from Sirte, but to no immediate gain) the government won a decisive victory in what observers had claimed could be a pivotal battle in the Civil War.

From there, Ghaddafi's troops pressed on to stage the 'second battle' of Benghazi.

But fighting continued in Ajdabiya, which was held by the government for just 11 days.

Benghazan rebel forces, having won the second battle of Benghazi, advanced on Ajdabiya on 20th March. On 21st March, they were repelled by Ghaddafi's troops, but US aircraft struck the town by night, claiming its airstrikes were designed to force government troops out of the city.

The strikes struck the centre of the town, as well as its eastern entrance, leaving buildings smoking and ruined. On 23rd March, more strikes were launched by US 'planes on the government forces at the eastern gateway. On the same day, reporters from the UK's Independent newspaper reported that they had seen 'no evidence' of damage khetibas claimed government forces had done to the town.

Battles continued throughout the next day, enabling more khetibas to enter Ajdabiya, and that night, British 'planes launched strikes on the town.

On 25th March, the khetibas had taken most of the eastern section of the town, with government forces falling back to points in the west and centre.

Yet more NATO airstrikes – this time from British aircraft – were launched overnight, and after a few hours' fighting on 26th March, the Libyan Deputy Foreign Minister Khaled Kaim confirmed government forces had left Ajdabiya.

He said: 'NATO forces were heavily involved, so the Libyan armed forces decided to leave Ajdabiya this morning. NATO is now attacking government forces, instead of assisting the civilians in the town.'

When you stopped there, many months later, the marks of NATO's 'Responsibility to Protect' were prominent and conspicuous: buildings with gaping, blackened holes, others in states of actual collapse, and 'protected' people giving those in the worst condition a very wide berth.

But in the short time you were there, the people were warm and open, sharing food, drinks and stories with you and with one another. As you ate at a crowded café, one man told you that Ajdabiya's residents and politicians had agreed to name the city's largest square – formerly Ghaddafi's Green Square – Tim Hetherington Square, after a British photojournalist killed during fighting in Misrata.

As in every place that NATO 'visited', Ajdabiya's scars were impossible to hide, unavoidable, and horrible reminders of the recent past.

But it was also a town at peace, and the people you met were relaxed, kind and welcoming. You rather liked it.

In all the time you are here, you will never come up with an explanation for that which wholly satisfies you.

At this moment, you wonder whether it is perhaps because the city is simply richer than the rest of the state – Benghazi is, after all, surrounded by Libya's largest oil deposits – and so was capable of moving faster to make repairs.

Later, you will be told by one Benghazan that the city is more independent than others in Libya, that it acts for itself rather than waiting for orders, and so its people simply repaired their city themselves.

It is true that there is an underlying atmosphere in Benghazi of remoteness, a form of separation, but the populations of Tripoli and Misrata were working to repair their homes and businesses without 'orders', and Sirte's residents were doing so despite feeling deliberately and systematically ignored by the rest of the state.

It is perhaps ironic that one of the major things to connect all Libyan cities immediately after the Civil War is a sense of isolation, uniqueness and the necessity to work as a city, for the city, rather than as part of a wider Libyan state.

But though Benghazi's individuality and sense of separation prevail throughout the city, its challenges are those faced across the state.

'Benghazi's problems are not all the same as the rest of Libya, though some of them are,' you are told by the leader of an international aid organisation with offices in the city. 'Like Tripoli, there are a lot of internally-displaced people here, people who fled the war but came here instead of leaving Libya altogether. Many of them will start to return home soon, but some, like the Tawerghans, cannot.

'But the city needs less physical rebuilding than much of the rest of Libya. Its problems lie elsewhere.'

He explains that his organisation's work here has changed even as people have returned home, as it became clear that the emergency educational and health provisions it supplied were equally needed by people in small slum areas across the city – a problem you had not noted elsewhere in Libya.

But a central challenge was all too familiar: 'We set up school boards, in which parents and teachers can meet to set policies on how their schools should be run, and they report what they are doing to us.

'A major problem is that young boys, aged eight and older, are now coming to school with guns. I have worked across Africa and this happens everywhere there is a war: adults own guns, and they become normal to people. Children are seldom given guns by parents, but they are in their homes, and once they are normal, children bring them to school to show friends or sometimes even because they have been in a fight.

'Most children do not really know how they work. In the worst case here, a boy brought a gun to school and hit another boy with it. But the normalisation of firearms is very serious. It sets dangerous practices in place, as these children will grow up with guns as part of their lives, and gun violence as a normal idea in their minds.'

Later, you are walking around the city with the driver who has agreed to work with you for the next few days. It is a 'sightseeing' trip of sorts for you both, as he – a Tripolitanian – arrived here for the first time only a couple of days ago.

You are discussing the extent to which the fact that the Creation story of Adam and Eve is shared by Judaism, Christianity and Islam can be taken as evidence for its truth, when you look up.

Ahead of you, slightly to the right, a large number of buildings sit fire-blackened and part destroyed. You walk around the buildings, until you come to a pile of rubble, under which lie the crumpled remains of a car, and upon and above which graffitied slogans have been painted in Arabic. It could almost be Sirte.

A man walks slowly towards you both, introduces himself and shakes your hands.

'Welcome,' he said. 'Do you know where you are?'

You shake your head. 'This,' the man says. 'Is the Benghazi katiba, where Mahdi Ziu* struck to help the revolution.'

---

* *Mahdi Ziu was, by any sensible definition, a suicide bomber. One day, he pushed a copy of his newly updated Will under the door of a neighbour, loaded gas canisters and a small amount of explosive into his car, drove to the Benghazi katiba's front gate and sat for a moment while rebel snipers fired on the barracks, and soldiers fired out on those near enough to strike. He accelerated, and sped into the gate, the resulting fireball blowing a hole in the katiba's wall, killing several soldiers and forcing the others to retreat. Within hours, the katiba fell to the Benghazi rebels.*

Ziu was a middle-aged man. He worked at the Arabian Gulf Oil Company, and had a 21 year-old daughter. He regularly attended his local mosque, but had been known to turn away – even to leave – when extremists called for violence or the imposition of Sharia Law in Libya.

He launched his attack after seeing a young man shot and killed outside his front window.

His actions, which enabled the rebels to strike their first real blow of the Libyan Civil War, cost him his life. He was 48.

But the only term by which the English language enables us to describe Ziu is 'suicide bomber'. Sometimes, when we need it most, and for many different cultural and geographical reasons, language fails us.

The fall of the katiba was the decisive moment of the first 'battle of Benghazi'.

As a result of it, and in part also of the defection of Libyan Interior Minister Abdul Fatah Younis to the rebels, who was then persuaded to grant pro-Ghaddafi forces safe passage out of the city, Benghazi rebels won the first victory of the Libyan Civil War.

Mahdi Ziu, who had disliked politics, and whose main interests were surfing the internet and reading books, was a suicide bomber. He struck a blow against Muammar Ghaddafi from which he and his regime were destined never to recover.

He and the driver talk for a few moments more, as you take photos.

When the man leaves, you and the driver stand in silence for a moment, at the spot where a nation's history was turned by the suicide of one man.

You are both moved, for the same reasons, though perhaps to different extents.

And at that moment, perhaps inspired by the site's similarity to the destruction you have lived with each day in Sirte, a third possibility occurs to you.

Maybe the reason Benghazi is now less damaged than Sirte, than Misrata, Tripoli, Ajdabiya, Zawiyah and many others is that the city repelled Ghaddafi early (and then a second time). Almost immediately, you wonder whether the reason this matters is not because of Ghaddafi's forces, but NATO.

Without need to 'flush out' Ghaddafi's troops, NATO did not deliver on Benghazi its systematic approach to warfare, bombing repeatedly to attempt to break its foes' cover.

The katiba remains as a symbol because it is unusual: the rebels struck at the single stronghold of Ghaddafi's power, rather than at everything, all at once, to 'destroy' an enemy.

Its destruction is a landmark, a testimony to Benghazans' bravery. Here, its disarray makes it stand out. In Sirte, where NATO focussed its 'Responsibility to Protect' for two months, rubble and devastation are the standard; crushed vehicles nothing special.

Perhaps, it occurs to you, the mark of NATO in Libya is not 'protection' or the 'new Libya' – or at least not either of those things alone. Perhaps NATO's most visible legacy to Libya is the chaos, and the wreckage, it has left in its wake. Perhaps this is why a job should not be left half-done.

And perhaps this means that buildings which have not been destroyed are the equivalent of a graffitied message reading simply: 'NATO was not here'.

Your driver looks across at you as you think. He walks closer to the rubble, pointing to the graffiti: 'This one reads "Mahdi is hero", and this one "Mahdi, liberator of the katiba".'

Turn Left

Benghazi

'The airport camp is a very interesting place. It's a pocket of poverty which really seems to have been overlooked by everybody so far. In the South of the country, that might be understandable, though unacceptable. There are communities there which exist for short periods away from everything else, because it's desert.

'But here, it's very unusual. Children at the camp have little to no education, and people are scratching a living out of whatever they can. We first came to work here because a large number of Libyans came here when their homes were being attacked. They have gone home now, but we have stayed because the people who actually live here are in a desperate situation.'

You are in a pick-up with the local manager of an international aid organisation, heading for Benina Airport Camp.

It's a strange journey, a six-lane road, populated by speeding cars and haulage trucks, which runs just 20km from the centre of Benghazi to the city's international airport.

Though short, the road carries you from the built-up, urban environment of Libya's second-largest city, into the northern reaches of the world's largest hot desert.

As you approach its end, with the walls of the airport towering ahead, and the small village of Benina to the left, you are aware that this is the edge of 3,600,000 square miles of sand.

You watch the steady flow of traffic slow, then turn right. Almost alone, you head left. You rattle around on a strip of stones and sand, after a couple of minutes coming to a halt. Within yards of the airport's perimeter wall, on four very short 'streets' a collection of buildings sit.

Each is single-storey, made of a mix of stone, plastic and metal sheeting, small, close to destitute, but with touches – dabs of paint, hand-carved wood used as decoration – which show their owners care about them. Most also have a small wooden shelter nearby which, the sound and smell reveal, contain chickens.

The effect is not so much of a tiny village as an allotment containing some well-painted sheds. In some ways, this is the most remote, least well-connected community you have ever visited.

To the east, it is isolated by the high wall of an airport its inhabitants have too little money to use, to the north, it faces desert, then sea, to the west, a strip of sand cuts it off from Benghazi, and to the south, the vast trunk road, populated by thundering metal juggernauts, is more a barrier than a link to the rest of Libya.

Twenty families live here, a relatively small distance from a city of 1,000,000 people.

For all their contact with Benghazi, they might almost as well be on the Moon.

The charity manager walks with you to the Airport Camp centre – a space for young people to play, learn and draw.

It is almost identical to each of the 'buildings' which surround it – corrugated iron roof, single-storey, small windows and rugged stonework – but painted white, and with a small sign reading 'NO – to violence against children' next to its front entrance.

Inside the front door, a colourful poster is pinned to the wall. It is nicely drawn – an image of Muammar Ghaddafi, with a child stood nearby, and writing underneath.

Before you have the chance to read the words, a small girl grabs your hand and pulls you to where she is playing with a small doll. Beside her, other children, most aged 4-7 you would guess, play with toy cars, plasticine, and teddy bears which look like they have been played with many times before.

You ask the girl her name and where she lives. She stares blankly at you. A woman comes over and asks her again, still in Arabic. The girl smiles, then looks quizzically at you, and tells you her name, and how old she is.

The woman says: 'The children do not expect you to speak in Arabic, and they find your accent strange. So they do not understand. Do not worry.'

The girl tells you she lives nearby and does not go to school, even though she would like to.

But she also tells you that her favourite thing to do at this small centre is to play with this doll, and that she does not like to learn English or Arabic, so you wonder, smiling to yourself, what she believes she would like about attending school.

As it turns out, she is alone in her (understandable) preference for toys.

Another small girl, holding a pen, pulls you towards a table. She sits and writes the numbers 1-10, which you have fortunately just learned to read in Arabic.

You smile, and count in Arabic with her, then pick up the pen and write 1-10 in European figures: 'Ingliziyah, English' you say.

She frowns, takes the pen and points to the figures she has written: 'Laa, Arabee, No, Arabic,' she replies.

This is the kind of conversation for which your Arabic-speaking ability was made, so it is almost a shame when the woman comes over again to sit with you, speaking English to a level far beyond your capability in her language.

'She comes here every day,' the woman says. 'But she says she was on holiday for the last two months. It was one week, though. And she was not really on holiday, she just had to work with the chickens at her house.

'She enjoys it here. She goes to the other school nearby, though most of the children do not, but here she says she learns English best.' (At this point, the girl writes bnIna, the name of her home. Given the difference between rules on vowels in written English and Arabic, it is a good effort for a girl who claims to study one hour per week).

She looks up: 'I like it here. I like to live here. I like everything about it. I like English and I like to see my friends.' The woman smiles: 'Before the centre opened here, the children used to play on the street. It is not that they did not want to go to school, but that it is dangerous. The highway out there is so dangerous that many parents will not cross it with their children. It means they do not go to school.

'But parents need to have time to think, and children must have time to play, where it is safe. That is why I came to work here as soon as it opened.'

A second woman, also a teacher, play-leader and child-minder combined, as this situation appears to demand, introduces herself: 'This is a good centre,' she says. 'We were lucky to live here after we had been to school. Some of these children have never been to a school, even once.

'So as well as giving them a place to play, we teach them to read and write, and we teach Arabic and Mathematics.'

She explains that she has worked at the centre since it opened in March 2011: 'Lots of people arrived here after the second battle in Benghazi,' she said. 'They came from all over Libya, because there was war where they lived. They expected their children to learn even though they were far from home, and when the centre was set up, parents who had always lived here started to send their children here to learn and play because they could not go to school because of the road.

'I wanted to help people who needed help, and I was very happy that at last the children here could learn like other children. I work all the shifts I can, morning, afternoon and evening. It's very rewarding and I enjoy it very much. Now, all the people from other parts of Libya have left here, but it's good the centre keeps going, because the children need it.'

At the next table, a boy sits drawing with chalk on paper. He tells you he is 13 and says: 'I have a book at home. It is my only book and it has artists from France, Egypt, Jordan and Yemen. I would like to visit those places and draw what they have drawn.

'I would also like to go to Tripoli, Misrata and Benghazi. I would like to see what is there and I would like to see if I can draw it.'

He shows you his picture, which is of several people, each coloured to match the flags of a different country. It is a nice idea, and the people are sketched accurately, in chalk. You tell him the drawing is good, and he looks embarrassed, but smiles.

He says: 'I wanted to go to school. My father taught me to read and to write, but it is not the same as a school. Before this was here, we would just play. There was nothing else to do. Just playing. But I like to read and to draw. I like to come here. I know that this is not a school, but there are things to read, and there are friends I can meet. I am learning English and I have paper to draw on. Also, there are marbles here. I like to play marbles. I had not played before.

'I am glad to come here.'

The first teacher, slightly the older of the two, comes over and praises the boy's work. He looks embarrassed again.

'He is quite a good artist,' she says. 'I attend Benghazi College and I am studying History, but there are some artists there studying and I showed them a drawing he did in pen, and they were quite impressed. They said he should work and he will become very good. So I intend to keep working with him.'

At that moment the second teacher claps her hand, says something, and every child in the room turns to face you.

They file out, in silence, and you wonder whether you have done something wrong.

The History student looks at you, smiles and says: 'You did not understand?' You shake your head. 'Oh, I am sorry,' she says. 'You asked earlier if you could take photographs and asked in Arabic, so we thought you would understand. The children would like a photograph with you.'

As you reach the entrance, she points at the painting you had looked at on your way in.

'He did that,' she says. 'It says "Ghaddafi in nature". I think he means he is dead but not in heaven, instead with animals and birds. I do not know why he thinks that. Here, it says "I promise to forgive. I promise to forgive everyone. I won't hold a grudge. I won't be angry. I want to be a new child in a new Libya".'

She pauses, wipes her eyes, then raises her head: 'Asif, sorry,' she says. 'It makes me a little bit sad. It is odd to say, but I think what has happened might have helped these children in a way nobody expected. It is why I am so happy to be here.'

You walk out, and pose for a photo with 30 smiling children. You have had worse days in Libya.

Tawergha II

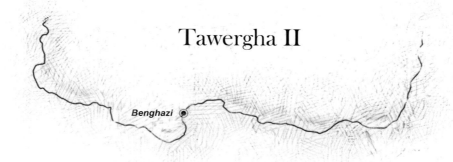

'I was in a car with my sister and her fiancé, on the road from Misrata to Sirte. In front of us, a lorry pulled across us so we had to stop. It had Misrata written on it. I didn't read the rest because then men came out of the truck.

'They grabbed my sister's fiancé and pulled him out of the car. My sister was screaming. I shouted out once but one of the men grabbed me on my mouth.

'They killed my sister's fiancé with a hammer. They hit him and hit him and hit him.

'There was blood everywhere.

'It was so cruel and so cold.

'You can't kill anyone that way. We had left our home. That was what they wanted.

'But they killed him with a hammer.

'I have a friend from Misrata, she is 11 like me. When we left Tawergha, she called me on my mum's mobile phone and said she was sorry for what had happened to me and that she would miss me.

'I said it would be OK and we would see each other when I came home. But she said we could not because her father had said she was not allowed to call me anymore or see me. I was sad because I liked to see her. And her dad was always nice to me.

'My oldest brother was 22 years old. He was in the army and he was killed. He was taken prisoner, but then someone told us he had died in prison. We do not know what happened to him.

'I miss them all. And I miss my home.'

You are at Benghazi's Garyounis Camp,* the second largest centre in the city for 'internally displaced people' (IDPs) – people who have left their homes because of conflict and have remained within Libya's borders.

Garyounis Camp is a small concrete former industrial estate near the centre of Benghazi, separated by tall iron gates from the main road it sits on. Surrounded on all sides by buildings, it has an open central square, with similar smaller spaces branching off to the left and right. It had previously been used as a loading area for trucks. The Tawerghan community live here in tents whose poles had been driven into the concrete, though some temporary buildings are also in use.

During the Civil War, thousands of people fled their homes as NATO bombing and shelling from khetibas and pro-Ghaddafi soldiers destroyed buildings and took lives.

Those who could, went east, towards the places – of which Benghazi was the biggest – which had fought and won freedom from Ghaddafi's rule.

Tens of thousands arrived between March and October, sleeping where they could while war raged behind them, in many cases sweeping away all they had known, their homes, businesses and communities.

Since you arrived in Benghazi, you have found it at times to be self-sufficient to the point of coldness, but in this it has never failed to impress you: its people did not just welcome the cold, scared and desperate from other parts of Libya – regardless of which side they were on – it is proud to have done so, and to continue to now.

Almost all Libya's IDPs have now either returned home, found work and a place to live in or around Benghazi, or left the country altogether.

One group remains: the Tawerghans.

On the way here, your translator and driver, who also helps run this camp, had offered you a warning: 'I know you have been to Tawergha. I have never been there, but I am sure it is a difficult place to see. But in this place, there are 2,700 people. Most of them are women or children, as almost every man over the age of 15-16 has been killed or imprisoned.* And they all want to return home.

* *At this stage, HRW estimated 2,000 Tawerghans had been imprisoned by Misrata katiba members, and another 2-3,000 were 'missing'. Ominously, in 2014, when this account was written, the figure had changed almost not at all.*

'They keep telling us they wish to return, and threatening they will march home. But they will die.* If they do not die on the march, they will be killed by Misrata khetibas if they try to re-enter Tawergha.

At about 781km, many people might have managed the walk, providing the weather stayed on their side and they had not encountered the Misrata khetiba (the latter being almost an impossibility heading West from Benghazi). But the oldest and youngest would have struggled to survive.

'If they manage to enter, they will find – you know – that there is nothing left that they could live in, and that all their possessions are gone. And even if, after all of this, they somehow decided to stay where they were, they would be hunted and killed, or arrested and tortured.

'How do you tell somebody that about their homes? Even when they hear that their town has been destroyed, they think about Sirte, and that they can rebuild. They cannot.'

You sit with a group of boys and girls who are playing a version of Ludo. As she flips a counter into a cup, one looks at you, still smiling at her success, and you watch her face change as she says: 'I miss Tawergha.'

You look at her, unsure of what to say. She begins again: 'There are good things about this place. People are kind to me here, and I have new friends.

'But I had to leave my home on 11th August when Misratans came. They hit rockets into my house and they fired guns until we came outside.

'We ran away because they told us to. We had no guns, so we could not fight. And I didn't want anyone to fight. I just wanted to be at home.

'We went first to Hayshah,* but we were chased away by Misratans.

Al Hayshah is the closest town to Tawergha, 18km to its south and east. It was a logical first stopping-point for the fleeing Tawerghans, but also a town held by Ghaddafi loyalists, and so a legitimate 'target' for Misratan khetibas to attack next.

It was perhaps coincidence that it was also now the place with the largest black-skinned population in all of north Libya.

They entered the town on 17th August, six days after the 'cleansing' of Tawergha, and took it within hours.

The movement of the majority of Tawerghans – those who headed east, away from Misrata, rather than west, hoping to pass the town and reach safety beyond it, in Tripoli – followed a simple pattern: Al Hayshah; Sirte; Jufrah; Brega; Benghazi.

Each time the tired, panicked population stopped, it was either caught again by the Misrata khetibas, caught by the war, or forced to leave by residents of each town. They were welcomed only in Sirte, which soon became unsafe because of NATO bombing, and finally, in Benghazi.

'Then we went to Sirte, and we stayed there for a little while. Many people were kind to us there, but we had to run away again after a few weeks and we went to Jufrah.* But everywhere we went, Misratans chased us and killed us.

Jufrah, the region of an oasis in the Sahara 250km south of Sirte, was taken by khetibas on 23rd September. Its fall confirmed the khetiba's conquer of Fezzan, the least wealthy of Libya's three historic regions, entirely desert, without a port.

'My father stayed in Sirte. He said he had to fight the Misratans. He said he did not care about Ghaddafi but he had to fight the Misratans because they would never stop chasing us and shooting at us.

'They killed him in Sirte.

'I have not seen him, I did not see him die and I will never see him again.

'One day, we had to leave Jufrah as well. I do not know why. But this time my brother said he would stay. He said the same as my father. He said he had to fight because they would keep chasing us wherever we went. We did not know yet that my father was dead.

'They killed my brother. Someone in the camp says he saw him, that he was captured and they pointed many guns at him all at the same time and he died. He was 26.

'We travelled across lots of places. In some people were kind, but in some they were very hard to us.

'One day, we were walking along on a long road and we were captured by Misratans. They separated our group into men and women. They told the women to be silent and then they lined all the men into a line.

'Then they shot all of the men at once. All of the soldiers fired and they fell down. I think some of the women wanted to scream, and I wanted to. But my mother clung onto my hand and I could tell she did not want me to. I was crying but I was quiet.

'Then they told us we must leave, or be put into a prison.

'So we walked for several days and then we arrived here. It was in October.

'I live here now with my mother. And I have made friends with other children here. We learn English and Arabic, and we learn music and singing, which I like the most.

'On some nights we have visitors who sit up and play games with us and eat and sing with us. That is fun and I like that.

'But I want to go home. I want to be back in my home, with my family.'

A boy has been waiting to speak to you, while the girl was talking and now shows you a photograph, but pulls it away before you can look at it properly.

'My dad is in prison,' he says. 'He is in the military so now he is in prison. I do not see him, but I know he is in a prison here because I know people who have seen him, so he is alive.

'He fought in Sirte. I do not really know why. I know that some people did not like Muammar Ghaddafi, and other people did like him.

'I think my dad liked him because he joined into his army when he was 15. That's just four years older than me, so he must have liked him.

'But we were in Sirte together and he told me that he did not really want to fight anybody but he had to because it was his job and it was why we could eat food. He said that he wouldn't like to fight any more but that other people didn't like Ghaddafi and they were fighting about it.

'But now he is in prison. I am glad that he is alive, but I do not know why he is there. I would like to see him. Maybe he didn't do his job properly so they put him in prison. I hope that they will let him out very soon, because there is my mother and me and my brothers and sisters but they are smaller than me and there is no-one else, because all five of my uncles are dead now. Three were killed on the same day, and that makes me feel sad.

'I am also sad because we had to leave our home, and I loved the TV and the PlayStation. I want to go home to get them and bring them here. I would like that and I think other people would like it as well. We could all play. I like to play outside, too, but it is hard here because there is not very much space to run and play.

'I think I have lost my enjoyment and lost my playing. I have no guns and I have nothing in this world. I would just like my father to come. If they move him to a prison that is not a military prison I will ask if I can live with him there.'

A little while later, a girl in her late teens comes across with coffee and sits down with you to watch the children play.

'I do not really want to talk very much about what happened after we left our home. Some things happened that I would not like to tell anybody. But I will tell you about when we had to leave Tawergha. When the town was attacked, we could not move. Behind us were the soldiers. But they were not our friends. And in front of us were the volunteers who fought against the soldiers. But they were not our friends either.

'We had to wait and to listen to the missiles and the bombs. It was so hard to stay. But if we went outside the soldiers and the volunteers would both shoot at us. So we stayed in our homes and listened to the bombs.

'Our neighbours were killed. We thought the bomb had hit us, but it had hit their home and we ran out and the soldiers started to shoot at us but we didn't care. We tried to save them but it was too late. They were dead and they were on fire and so we ran back into our house so that no-one would shoot at us again.

'If you take a look around this camp here you will find that everyone here has had things happen to them that should not happen to anyone.

'Now, here, I look after the children. I like to, because it helps me to be happier. I think when I return home I will become a teacher because of this.

'The children are good, but they have also seen and experienced bad things. They have seen people die, and been pushed around, made to feel small by men with guns and rockets.

'Even now, you can see that when the khetibas outside fire happy shooting, the children hear the shots and they cringe and shrink.'

At the exact moment she says this, a round is fired, outside the camp, but relatively close by. You are less certain than the girl that the round is happy shooting – you have been warned that some of the khetibas have become 'more active' in recent days. In any case, you immediately see that the girl is correct: the children hear the sound and their shoulders hunch, some of them glancing around them, but others staring fixedly at the floor.

The girl reaches out, and strokes the head of one of the younger girls. In turn, she seems to relax and hugs a small boy near her. Little by little, the tent returns to 'normal', and the children continue to play, read or paint as before.

'This is not a good place to live,' the girl opposite you says, leaning back and setting down her coffee cup. 'We are grateful to be here: we are all grateful to be anywhere. But it is not a place where people should be for a long time.

'We must return home. It is so very hard to be living in a place like this, so far from home, and with no idea when you can return.'

In one of the temporary buildings dotted around the central square, a man clears some books so you can sit down. He apologises as he does so, showing you the rolled-up bedding for seven people which is piled against the walls. 'It is not really an office,' he says. 'More a bedroom for many people where I sometimes try to work.'

He sits beside you, glances up and grimaces at the sound of further 'happy shooting' outside the camp, and places his hands on his knees.

'I must say to you that I do not really know how I am still alive,' he begins.

'I am in my 40s now, and almost every man from Tawergha has been shot or put into prison and tortured. I am the oldest man in this camp and although I know there are other men in other camps in this city and in Tripoli, there are not very many of us.

'I do not know how I have survived, and I do not know what I have done to deserve to be alive when so many other people from my home have been killed.'

The man was a Science teacher in a Tawerghan school when the war started. He tells you that he knew many of the boys who grew up to be soldiers in Ghaddafi's army: they were keen to help a man they believed would help them, he says, but he had warned them that to be a soldier was not an easy life.

'I do not think they all understood what I meant,' he says. 'Some of them, maybe, understood a little. I did not mean the training and the life of a soldier. I mean that it is hard to kill people.

It is hard to know that is what you have done. I do not envy the soldiers, or those firing guns outside now who are the new soldiers of the new Libya.'

He left Tawergha with everyone else, he tells you.

'There is nothing unusual about my story. I stayed at my home for as long as I could stay. I watched the bombs from the NATO planes falling, and heard them strike my neighbours' homes, the school, businesses and the clinics.

'Then I heard the gunfire and I realised we had to leave. That I would very soon be dead.

'I lined up with everybody else. The men were pulled out of the line and taken away. But I was not taken. I do not know why. They just left me standing with the women and the children. I could not move. I could not understand it.

'We walked then to Al Hayshah, but the khetibas from Misrata caught up with us there. I knew that they would do, so I tried to make everyone leave sooner. But many believed and hoped that they would be allowed to stay there, or that the Misratans would be defeated and they could return to their homes in Tawergha.

'We went then to Sirte, and then on to Jufrah. It is in the desert. There are not many things there, even though it is an oasis. Many Tawerghan people are angry about Jufrah, because people there forced us to leave, saying that there is nothing for Tawerghans there, that they would not give us any food.

'It makes me sad, and I admit that I feel angry a little as well. But I think they were afraid. Not of us, but that if we were there they might run out of food in the war and that maybe we would cause the Misratans to come and they would kill everyone.

'We went to Brega, and then arrived here. I do want to say – to tell everybody – that I am very, very grateful to Benghazan people. All Tawerghans are grateful to them.

'They have welcomed us and helped us. They have asked us what we need and tried to provide it. With the charities from overseas they have showed us kindness when we most needed it and I want – we all want – to be able to repay them for what they have done.

'I know that many people think that all Tawerghans supported Muammar Ghaddafi, and so it is even more wonderful that Benghazi, where most people hate him, has helped our people so much.'

He stops, looks at the calendar on his wall, which contains a picture of trees in blossom.

'It is hard to explain how we feel about what has happened. You must remember something. In all of the newspapers in Tripoli and Benghazi, and on all of the televisions, there has been a lot of people talking about how we have got rid of Ghaddafi and we are free. But Tawerghans are not free. We are still being punished. We cannot go home because we were chased from our homes. Most people in Tawergha were not fighters for Ghaddafi. They were poor people who tried to make a living.

'Ghaddafi's soldiers came, and the khetibas came and we were caught in the middle. But now that the war is won, we cannot return home because Misratans say it is now their home. It is because we are black people.

'It does not make sense. Before the war, we knew each other. We worked together and some of our families lived in Misrata. I think all people are the same as one another, but Misratans say we are black, so we are outsiders. It is very very difficult to live outside your culture and your community. And why should we have to?

'Look at where we live. And we are here only because of the kindness of the people of Benghazi. They recognise that black or white, we are all brothers.

'But this is not freedom, it is not OK. Our children have seen terrible things, things no person should ever have to see. And now they live in tents and sleep on the ground.

'We do not just want to return home. We must return. Because we cannot live like this. The people of Misrata must accept that we can return, that we have to be allowed to be in our own town and live in peace. But we are afraid of what Misrata will do to us.

'A lot of bad things happen in this world. But we miss Misratan people. Before the war, they were our friends. We lived side by side.

'We know we have to rebuild our homes, that everything has been stolen and burned. We have even heard that the water sources have been poisoned. But we were chased out on 11th August and it's a very long time to be away.

'We just want to return home, to stop living like we have broken the law, to stop being punished and to be allowed to start to rebuild our homes, our town and our lives. Anything else is just cruel. It does not make sense.'

Libya, November 2011-April 2012: Bani Walid

Bani Walid ◉

There are some pieces of advice that you vow to hand down to your children and grandchildren. Things you have learned through experience, and as a result, you hope they will never have to live through themselves.

In Bani Walid, you learned one of these: never lean into a vehicle while being led by a heavily-armed militiaman – even if it is to put down a tube of crisps.

Nine hours ago, you landed in Tripoli after spending a few days in Casablanca. The city was very much in its off-season, but its quiet grandeur, cafes and bars made a welcome change from the devastation you had recently experienced in Libya (one mark of the effect of this continual exposure to part- and wholly-destroyed buildings was that a taxi driver had to inform you that a block of apartments you had taken to be war-damaged was in fact being constructed, not repaired).

With no transport of your own, you had organised with a contact that his uncle would drive you the 463km from the capital to Sirte.

After some negotiation, you agree a price of 30 Libyan dinar for the journey. By any measure, this is remarkable value for money: less than 1p (UK) per kilometer. But it also means waiting for three hours until the small people-carrier he drives is completely full.

You sit and read, until you are taken out of the car and in a combination of your almost non-existent Arabic, your slightly better Italian and his five words of English, engage in debate over the route you will take.

The final five passengers to take seats in the taxi – two men, two women and one child – are black Africans (you later learn that they live in Sirte and have been visiting friends and family in Morocco).

Understandably, they do not wish to travel through Misrata, meaning that instead you will have to take a road into the Sahara, hooking north only after passing the town.

In one way, this is a good thing: by increasing your journey some 80-100km, the price you have agreed is arguably even better value for money.

In another, it equals an exchange: your security and safety risked to ensure the security and safety of five others in your car. Because the new route means you must travel through Bani Walid.

Bani Walid, and Sirte were the last two 'pro-Ghaddafi' strongholds, holding out longer than any other centres of support for the regime.

This was in part because Bani Walid is the traditional 'centre' of the one million-strong Warfalla tribe, one of the two major tribal allies of Ghaddafi's Qadhadfa tribe, and which benefited in terms of power and prestige from the dictator's regime.

But unlike Sirte, Bani Walid remains supportive of the deposed regime, and is the only place in Libya where fighting continues between khetibas and the remnants of the former government's support.*

* Bani Walid's own community leaders (the town is the major traditional centre of the million-strong Warfalla tribe, one of the strongest supporters of Ghaddafi during his reign) deny the charge that they were 'pro-Ghaddafi'.

In hindsight, it is possible to accept – if not entirely to believe – this claim. But over the course of two days in January 2012, when the town used violence to remove all khetiba presence, just three months after it had been 'defeated' in its defence of Ghaddafi's rule, it seemed likely that the town was expressing a political position.

On 23rd January 2012, the May 28 Brigade, which was the major khetiba in charge of the town, arrested a group of what it described as 'armed supporters of Ghaddafi'.

In response, a group of 100-150 people gathered to protest against the arrests, alleging that the brigade was torturing the prisoners, and demanding that they be released.

The earliest reports from the town repeated the May 28 Brigade's claim that these protestors had been carrying the old green flag of Libya, leading to speculation that the protest was an attempt to overthrow and remove the National Transitional Council (NTC) from the town.

Within hours, a large number of the protestors, calling themselves Brigade 93, had turned the protest into an armed attack on the May 28 Brigade, killing four and wounding 20 of the khetiba's members.

The attack succeeded in removing the NTC khetiba from the city, which was again taken as a signal that pro-Ghaddafists were launching a counter-attack against the new Libyan regime.

Mohamed Bashir, Bani Walid's Mayor, told the media that Ghaddafi loyalists had taken control of the town, and this speculation was further fuelled by claims that the old Libyan flag was raised over buildings across Bani Walid. But in fact most eye-witnesses rejected such claims, with outside observers and journalists confirming that they had seen no green flags raised, but many of the 'new' black, green, red and white banners flying.

And it is worth noting that the Libyan defence minister Osama al-Juwaily, and Bani Walid's tribal elders, were united in denying that the 'revolt' had any link to pro- or anti-Ghaddafi feeling, as well as the fact that, contrary to pessimistic predictions in some quarters, the Bani Walid uprising did not spark a single similar activity anywhere else in Libya.

Soon after the taxi ride recounted in this chapter, the NTC sent khetibas from Misrata, part of the NTC Misrata Shield, to cut off all routes connecting Bani Walid to the rest of the country. But on 24th January, a meeting of 200 tribal elders had 'officially' abolished the NTC council in the town, announcing plans to appoint a new government in its place.

On the same day, the leader of the now-defunct Bani Walid NTC council, Mubarak Al Fotmani, spoke in Misrata, claiming again that pro-Ghaddafists were behind the 'coup'. Local tribal elders responded by repeating their earlier claim that the arrest and torture of Bani Walid residents by the May 28 Brigade had sparked the uprising. They added that they were in negotiation with NTC national chairman Mustafa Abdel-Jalil, and meeting leaders from the towns of Zintan and Sabratha.

On 25th January, the Libyan defence minister al-Juwaily held talks with the Bani Walid elders, announcing within the town that the new tribal council was now recognised as legitimate, replacing the ousted NTC authority. The announcement was not universally popular: on 28th January, protestors demonstrated outside the Prime Minister's office in Tripoli against what they described as the Defence Minister 'siding with Ghaddafi's supporters'.

But for a month, the situation remained stable: the tribal elders' council ran Bani Walid, and khetibas sat at checkpoints 30km outside the town, on every road connecting it to the rest of Libya. Such a precarious balance could not hold for long: Bani Walid was effectively an 'independent' township in the centre of a state with a recently-formed new regime, and it was surrounded by heavily-armed, severely under-regulated young men.

More than that, although many Bani Walid residents were supporters of Libya's new regime, many others had told the press that privately, they missed the Ghaddafi government. They stated clearly that they were resigned to and accepted the fact that it would not return, but tensions remained high in one tiny region of the Libyan Sahara.

On 26th February, reports began to circulate that people still loyal to Ghaddafi, wanted for arrest by the NTC, were hiding out in Bani Walid, with the agreement of the town's leaders.

Jalil announced publicly that the NTC would send forces into the town to find the fugitives, but in common with the NTC's repeated requests and demands for the khetibas to hand over their weapons and disband, the warnings were ignored without punishment.

The stand-off continued, with occasional incidents of violence and bloodshed.

On 12th May, two members of the Misrata Libyan Shield Brigade were killed by Bani Walid brigade members, while other fighters from the town were alleged to have arrested four Zliten council members: in a state almost entirely without a police force, such allegations are hard to prove or disprove.

On 7th July, when national elections took place, (elections after which the NTC officially handed power to a General National Congress, GNC), Bani Walid residents voted, but its leaders prevented government officials from entering the town to oversee the voting process.

Perhaps in response, the GNC's Integrity Commission, set up to exclude and remove Ghaddafi-era representatives from politics, expelled every single independent candidate elected in Bani Walid, as well as all those from Ghat, and some from Bayda, Baten al-Jabal, Abu Salim, Hay Al-Andalus, Sabha, Tarhuna, Ubari, Wadi al-Shate, and Zliten. In the following eight months, only one of the 'vacated' seats was filled.

On 11th September, interim President Mohammed el-Magarif visited the town, in what was hoped to be the first step towards enabling Bani Walid to re-integrate with the rest of Libya, but was certainly also an attempt to negotiate the release of Omran Shaban, who had been captured and was being held in the town.

Shaban, a Misratan khetiba, was made famous after being filmed apprehending Muammar Ghaddafi shortly before the dictator was shot. He became a government member, popular within his home city and beyond.

He was kidnapped close to Bani Walid in July, while returning home from calming anti-government tensions in the south of Libya. He was not seen again, until interim President el-Megarif interceded for his release from Bani Walid.

He was released, but had bullet wounds in the lower half of his body, and despite being flown to a Paris hospital, he lasted only a few days longer, dying on 24th September.

He was 22.

Even then, the khetibas held their line, retaining siege positions rather than launching an attack on the town.

But on 2nd October 2012, nine months after Bani Walid had effectively declared its independence from Libya (though all the while protesting that it had done nothing of the sort), hostilities began again. Forces from Bani Walid struck against khetibas at Mordum, 20km north east of the town, and killed one person.

Thousands of khetibas massed outside Bani Walid, without permission from the GNC, and on 8th October, an attack was launched. Thirty people were injured, of whom 26 were alleged to have been gassed by the pro-GNC forces.

The GNC denied gas had been used, saying that gas could have been released from buildings struck by missiles, or because of corrosion. Eight days later, khetibas from Misrata, Mizda and Gharyan, again without orders or permission from the Libyan Chief of Staff Yousef Mangoush, attacked again, from three sides of the town, this time resulting in 11 deaths and 94 injuries by 18th October.

At this stage, the Libyan army was sent to Bani Walid, 2,000 troops taking part in an attack the government stated would 'reinstate the writ of government' and justified by its Resolution No.7, which called for the arrest of those responsible for the death of Omran Shaban, and anyone suspected of links to the Ghaddafi regime.

The offensive appeared to have failed when on 19th October, Megarif announced that 'parts of Libya' had still not been 'fully liberated'. But fighting continued, with dozens killed and arrested, and within days, Bani Walid was declared officially 'free' of Ghaddafi, almost a year after he had died.

Frustration remains in the town, however. Many people are still angered that when Misratan troops entered the city centre, they erected large posters of Shaban and Ramdan Swehli, a Misratan who had fought against Italian colonists, in its central square – images that the town believes were intended as symbols of conquest.

Bani Walid is now an official part of the wider Libyan state, but resentment simmers, and fears remain that what its residents now regard as 'humiliations' by the rest of Libya may spill over into excuses for 'revenge' if and when the town feels strong enough to restake a claim to control its own future.

Travel through Bani Walid is more dangerous, to you, than travel through Misrata. It is possible that should you agree to the change of route, you could be imprisoned, or even killed, by someone too keyed up by recent events, or nervous about their immediate surroundings, to make a reasoned, logical, judgement.

But on the other hand, you have been in Libya for months. You have lived in Sirte, a place where NATO's bombardment has made being a Westerner into being a target of disappointment at best, justifiable anger at worst. And you are taking this trip to return there: to refuse to travel through Bani Walid when your desired destination is Sirte is only slightly less perverse than if you were to refuse to travel through Sirte to reach Bani Walid.

More than that, you know that most people in Libya (at this moment) have no great interest in you as an individual, other than some curiosity about why you are here: you know that when you have spoken to them, every one has been polite, interested and helpful.

And you want to go to Bani Walid. You have seen the TV images of the latest rebellion. You have discussed with Libyans, and with Moroccans, Czech rig-workers and French accountants in Casablanca hotels what it means. You want to be there because it is the place where the Libyan revolution is still playing out. It is, almost, the reason you are here.

Finally, it is a choice between one person's probable safety and five people's definite risk. Even though you are the one person, it is no competition. Of course you agree to take the desert route, and visit Bani Walid.

It takes about an hour and a half to get out of Tripoli, the roads heavily congested even on a Wednesday in mid-afternoon, but when you do finally leave the city and then turn off the Roman Road, even in a packed people-carrier, there is a sense of incredible freedom.

Much of the journey is new to you. It is the first time since you arrived in Africa that you have been more than two miles from the sea, and it is the first time you have been able to see first-hand just how thin is the fertile strip of green within which most of Libya's largest cities and towns sit.

But the Sahara, which now opens up ahead and either side of you, is not quite the quiet deadzone that you, as a Northern European, had imagined it could be.

As you speed through the miles of sand, you are watched by hundreds of camels, travelling in a cross between lurch and prance to search for plants and liquid. On dunes, small movements of sand and shadow betray animals darting for insects or patches of cooler sand, and every so often, birds of prey wheel overhead.

And then there are the checkpoints.

In common with every major highway in Libya, this road is punctuated by roadblocks built from cargo containers, manned by men younger than you, most carrying weapons taller than you are.

Unlike the rest of the state, however, the further you travel on this road, the more interest you inspire in the militias.

Your experience so far has been that most checkpoints will wave you through without stopping, maybe one in five will ask to see your passport and let you through after you wind down the window and show your photograph and visa, and maybe one in every 15 will make you pull over, have a brief conversation and then wish you well. You realise your experience is unusual, but it is a pattern you have become used to.

This road is significantly different.

Before you set off, everyone in the car handed their passports to the taxi driver, and at each checkpoint he spreads the passports like a hand of cards at a poker table, flashing them to the khetibas through the window.

This is never enough, so he then winds down the window. Occasionally, that suffices, but more often, as he does so, six khetibas run across, four taking position at the corners of the car, and two staring through the passenger window directly at you, while the original two glance at the Libyan and Moroccan documents and study your own passport.

It is hard to know what to do while two armed men stare at you through a car windscreen and two others read every page of your passport, glancing at one another as if there was something of genuine interest within it.

You feel it would be too rude simply to read or pretend to read a book, you fear that too much direct eye-contact could simply wind the men up, while none at all would raise suspicion, and you certainly do not feel it would be fair to have a high-spirited conversation with your fellow passengers (in any case, by the third checkpoint you really only feel capable of saying 'Asif' to each one of them, 'sorry for me making us stop for 15 minutes every few miles').

At the first couple of stops, you looked up briefly and smiled at the two men.

But at the third stop, one of the khetibas smiled back and called 'Ahlan!' ('Hello!'), only to be elbowed by his companion-at-arms, who scowled at you, so from then on, you felt too uncomfortable even to do that much.

At the sixth stop, the driver is ordered to leave the car, and enters into a ten-minute conversation with two uniformed men. One soldier knocks on your window and motions for you to wind it down.

You smile, and do so, at which point he says something you do not understand (it is a mark of how different Libya's north coast is from the rest of the state that you had never before heard anyone say to you 'Get out of this car!', rather than, 'Sorry, sir, please could you talk to me out here for a moment?').

As you look blankly and start to say you cannot understand, the young man sat next to you says something across you. The khetiba answers, and for the next few moments, the pair converse, the armed man's expression seeming to soften with every sentence.

He actually shakes your hand before he leaves to speak to his superior, who in turn smiles, waves at you and shakes hands with the taxi driver.

You turn to the young man: 'I just said you were here to help', he said. 'I am a student at Sirte University and I know the driver's nephew. He has told me about you before, and I have seen you in town.'

As he speaks, you realise that you had been far more tense about this journey than you had known – a state of mind helped not at all by the continued stops and scrutiny you experienced.

The next stops are comparatively easy. You wind down the window as the khetibas approach, and say hello, talking to them about where they are from, how soon before they return home. You still feel guilty about the fact that your fellow passengers' journeys are being greatly extended, but they seem almost as relieved as you at the change in atmosphere at each checkpoint.

After about three hours, you reach a stopping-point on the edge of Bani Walid. You each leave the car to use the toilet, and then buy coffees and food from a small shop next door.

You have finished your drink – a short coffee so strong and so sugary you are pretty sure you could stand a walking stick in it – by the time you reach the door, dropping the paper cup into the bin. But as you step outside, your way is blocked by a short-ish khetiba, holding a gun at an angle you suspect is designed to show you it is taller than he is, but without actually towering over him.

He points at you – no mean feat given that there is less than 50cm between you – and crooks his finger to beckon you to follow him.

He walks backward, waving you in the same direction as him, as if you are a large vehicle reversing into a narrow parking space, with one hand tightly on his gun.

You are feeling more than a little uncomfortable, not only because every eye in the immediate vicinity is now trained on you, but also because you are beginning to think that in whatever negotiation is likely to follow, you will not be best placed to state your case convincingly while holding a bright red tube of crisps.

Bearing this in mind, it is unfortunate that the moment at which the khetiba trusts you enough to turn his back and lead you is the same moment at which you realise you are parallel with the window of the taxi.

You lean in to put down the tube of crisps, and freeze as you hear to your right the sound of boots scraping on gravel and sand, and the sweep and clicks of a large weapon being readied to fire.

You pause.

You are not alone. As you use the second or so available to decide exactly how slowly to step backwards so your head, chest and right arm are no longer within the car without 'encouraging' several gunshots to be fired in your direction – as well as attempting to work out how to show your hands are raised in a space where raising your hands is physically impossible – you are acutely aware that everyone else has also stopped moving, that people are holding their breath, waiting to see what will happen next.

You step backwards, slowly, hands above your head, then turn, very slowly, and smile.

'Asif, Sorry,' you say, softly. 'Crisps.' You do not nod, let alone point, in their direction.

He keeps his gun trained on you, glances towards the window, slowly lowers his weapon and shakes his head, as a father may do to show his disappointment to a toddler, albeit a father dressed in uniform and carrying a huge assault rifle.

You walk seven yards further.

'Stop', he says. You stop.

He walks across the road, into a large, single-storey building, and emerges, accompanied by another man, after a couple of minutes.

It is clear that the second man is his superior.

Each one looks and points at you at various intervals (it is at this point that you surprise yourself by wondering whether you would have been better wearing something less conspicuous than a suit, a shirt, and scarf lent to you by your fiancé: on balance, you decide it probably wouldn't make any difference whatsoever) and then both men move at once.

The man who has so far 'guided' you walks back across the road towards you, while the other also crosses the road, but on such a long diagonal that he stops at a point at least 500 yards away from you, forcing you to walk several steps further simply for the honour of talking to him.

You grin, wondering what the first man would have done had you – as you wished – applauded.

Your guide looks at you, with an expression midway between wary and exasperated, and jerks his head for you to follow.

You cross the distance between you with very little actually on your mind: you see to your right that the dune rising beyond the road contains far more gravel than most you have so far seen. You do not look left, but ahead, beyond the 'officer' awaiting you, you see Bani Walid itself. It looks peaceful, from a distance.

'So, you are from Northern Ireland, yes?'

This is a problem you have encountered before. Even people who read and speak English well cannot often be bothered to read the full name of 'The United Kingdom of Great Britain and Northern Ireland' from the front of a passport.

And for Libyans, whose country-name as represented on its passports is: 'al-Jamahiriyah al-Arabiyah al-Libiyah ash-Sha 'biyah al-Ishtirakiyah al-UZZma' (Great Socialist People's Libyan Arab Jamahiriya), choosing one or two words from a collection seems a sensible bet.

'No,' you say. 'I'm from England. Liverpool.'

'Oh! I have been to Liverpool!' the man says. 'Steven Gerrard, yes? He is a great footballer for Liverpool.'

You smile, open your arms: 'I am sorry,' you begin. 'I am not a Liverpool fan. I support Everton.'

Even as the words leave your lips, you ask yourself 'What are you doing? You are standing in the desert, close to the town most likely of all in Libya to contain people who might actually wish you harm, more than 2,000km from home, and an almost equally uncrossable 500 metres even from ten or so people who you have known for only a few hours and you choose to refuse a potentially friendly conversation with an armed and powerful man on the grounds that he's chosen a footballer you don't like?'

The man looks at you, narrows his eyes, and says: 'You are a brave man.'

You are not feeling particularly brave. You feel like an average man in an unusual situation, who has declined to stay on good terms with someone who heads a heavily-armed, battle-hardened khetiba on the edge of Libya's most dangerous town, and holds your passport in his hand. On the other hand, you do not think now would be the right moment to 'correct' him.

'Do you like it in Liverpool?', he asks.

You tell him that yes, you like it, that its buildings are pretty if you remember to look up, that you like the sea and you like the fact that there is always something happening.

He smiles: 'I like the sea also. When I was in England, I went twice to the Lake District. I saw Windermere and Coniston. They are very beautiful, do you think?'

'Windermere and Coniston are excellent,' you say. 'I have been many times to Coniston.'

'Did you walk up the hill there?' He asks. You nod. 'I was not able to. The person who took us said it was dangerous. I would like to climb it one day.'

You look at him, a man slightly taller than you, with a handgun in a holster, and a brigade under his command, stood in the Sahara, wistfully thinking of the day he was told by a guide that he could not climb the Old Man of Coniston. You can almost see the rain in his eyes.

'I will return,' he says. 'And climb it. You should come. Are there other Lakes that I should visit as well?'

'Yes, there are,' you say, delighted that Steven Gerrard appears not to be likely any longer to be the major contributory factor to your early death, or at least imprisonment. 'The north Lakes are very beautiful. They are a little more stark, but they are striking. You would like them.'

'Then I will come. I will climb the hill at Coniston, the "Big Man"? Ah, yes, the Old Man. I will climb the Old Man, and we will go to the northern Lakes.'

Actually, given his enthusiasm at the idea, you really want to. It also crosses your mind to tell him that he may have to change out of his uniform and leave his gun behind, but you decide that this time, it may be better to say nothing.

'So, where are you going to today?'

'Sirte.'

He raises an eyebrow: 'Sirte can be a very dangerous place,' he says.

You look over his shoulder at Bani Walid behind him. He smiles again: 'You are right, But even so, Sirte is a dangerous place for people like you who are not from Libya.

'And why are you going there?'

You explain, that you have come because you are a journalist, that you are working with international charities which have arrived to attempt to help Libya recover from its revolution and Civil War, that you are speaking to people about their lives and their recent experience, about what has happened to them, why and how it happened, what will happen next and what they need, to tell people in the West what is happening, so that they don't think that just helping to overthrow Ghaddafi and bombing towns and cities is enough, that Libya must be helped to take the steps to recover and…

You stop.

'You wonder what I think about that,' he says. 'Well, this is what I think. It is a good job that you do, and you are right about Libya. We will do all we can to make this new country work, but those of us who have travelled here in the last few months, and who have had time to think, we know that this country cannot exist alone.

'People already disagree what should happen next, towns and cities are broken, there is not enough money to fix them and until they are fixed no more money will come.

'But you have to be careful. You have to stay alive if you want to tell people what is happening here.

'You should not be trying to travel through Bani Walid. Why have you not travelled through Misrata? That is a safer way, you must know that.'

You explain about the five black Africans and their fears over travelling through the city.

'You are a brave man. This is a good thing. Please remember that many of us who have weapons and have killed people do not agree with all of the things that Misratan khetibas have done. They are brave, and powerful, and they believe in Libya. But they go too far. They should be controlled by wiser people, but instead they try to control.

'You were right to come this way.

'You can pass through this checkpoint, but tell your driver not to stop in Bani Walid. People are peaceful there now, but nobody can tell how long that may last. Do not stop, just return to Sirte.'

He hands you your passport, and shakes your hand.

'If you are ever in any trouble,' he says. 'Send word to Bani Walid and ask for the Zliten Brigade. We will come.'

You walk back to the taxi, and climb in. The student smiles, at you, and the Moroccan girl hands you your tube of crisps. Her mother laughs.

You drive through Bani Walid, which seems quiet, and continue almost due East, towards Sirte. Later that evening, you are delighted to see your first true Sahara sunset, the endless golden sand appearing to change colour to blues and blacks as the sun slips behind the dunes, and behind your taxi as you drive into the darkness.

Hours later you enter Sirte once more.

You never did have to call on the Zliten Brigade

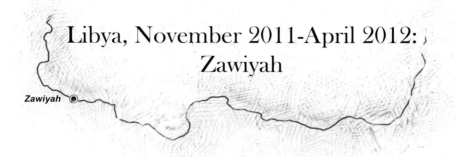

Libya, November 2011-April 2012: Zawiyah

Zawiyah ◉

Between a cracked, chipped white stone bench and an eight-storey building scorched black by flames, sits an arch of flowers.

The blooms' white petals gleam in the early-afternoon sunlight, standing out against the pale blue sky, the green of the stems and leaves, and the black of soot and holes punched through the walls of the surrounding buildings.

It is a quiet, eloquent, tribute to those who died here, in the main square of Zawiyah, the focal point of one of the Libyan Civil War's most important struggles.

You had passed through Zawiyah, Libya's fifth-largest city, on your way to Sirte – its position on the Roman Road between Tripoli and Tunisia was one of the two things which made the city a vital strategic target during the Civil War – but you had not had a chance to visit properly until today.

You were taken from Tripoli by a driver and a young woman who had offered to show you the town and translate for you (she had overheard you speaking Arabic the previous day, laughed, complimented you on being a white person 'who tries to make sentences correctly' and then informed you that because Libyans speak Libiyano, most Libyans would react to you as English people would to someone using Shakespearean English: you were sold).

On the 45km journey from Tripoli, she had warned you that Zawiyah had been severely damaged during the war: 'The centre is especially bad,' she said. 'But there are parts in other places, too. Some people who have not seen it…'

She paused, smiled. 'You have been in Sirte. I do not know Sirte well, and I do not know how the damage in Zawiyah compares. I think you will be OK, though.'

You are driven into the centre of the city, where the Central Square (now named Martyrs' Square) is surrounded by buildings in various states of dilapidation and collapse.

'This was a central point for all that happened in Zawiyah,' your translator says. 'This square was where people gathered and where many were killed.'

But the battles for Zawiyah did not begin here.

Your translator pointed to a mosque: 'Over there is the first place that Ghaddafi's troops attacked,' she said. 'It was a place where a protest was being held, to support rebels in Benghazi. It was 24th February when the government soldiers struck it with missiles.'

You are surprised. Though the Benghazans had used mosque loudspeakers to relay tactical advice to the khetibas in the city, this is the first time anyone has ever stated that a mosque was either a centre of protest or a target of attack during the Civil War.

In one way, you can understand each position: Ghaddafi's regime, as an 'Islamic secular' state, attracted opposition from Muslims keen to replace it with a religious government. This may be why they allowed their mosque to be used as a centre of peaceful protest.

And there is no suggestion that any of the protestors had claimed asylum within its walls, and Ghaddafi may have had no more qualms about attacking a mosque than he had about attacking any other building. But it is yet another inexplicable decision by Ghaddafi in the early stages of the Libyan popular uprising.

Not only is it unacceptable to use firearms (automatic weapons and an anti-aircraft gun, in this case) against peaceful protestors and against a mosque, it is also very difficult to understand why Ghaddafi might have ordered such an attack: the protestors were peaceful, and so did not 'need' to be attacked, and striking at a mosque could only make him yet more unpopular with traditionalist Muslims and those who feared their leader was violent and insane.

That night, thousands of people gathered in the town's central square, yards from the mosque, once again, peacefully, but in far greater number than those who had protested and been attacked by government forces.

The protest continued for 48 hours, with people sleeping in the Square. But on 26th February, soldiers loyal to Ghaddafi opened fire on the protestors.

'People could not go anywhere,' your translator begins. 'They were stood in the Square and soldiers surrounded them and opened fire. They could not run, and many were killed here on that evening.'

But most of Zawiyah was by then under the control of the city's khetibas, with most of Ghaddafi's forces at hastily-built checkpoints on the major routes linking it to Tripoli in the East and Tunisia in the West.

Ghaddafi needed Zawiyah. Every city in Libya was a huge potential loss – and treated as such by the regime – but Zawiyah was not only vital to continued trade with Libya's most valued neighbour (a history of violence between Libya and Egypt, combined with the fact that Benghazi was almost immediately 'off-limits' to the regime within days, effectively blocking all trade from the east, meant links to Egypt, by preference and necessity, were less important than those to Tunisia in the west), but also is Western Libya's most – and the entire state's second-most – busiest oil refinery and port.

And on 28th February, Ghaddafi sent 200 soldiers west to attack the city, but they were fought to a standstill by the rebels.

Your translator has started to speak to a lady who has also stopped at the central square: 'For two days, Ghaddafi's soldiers were surrounding the city. We carried on as normal, because there was nothing else to do. People had to mourn their friends or families who had been killed, and people had to eat.

'But it was also strange, to know that just a short distance from here, there were soldiers waiting to attack. It is more frightening to be attacked, of course, with bombs falling and gunshots, but it was also frightening to wait and wonder what would happen next. It was a hard atmosphere to be in.'

The stand-off did not last long: food and medical supplies were already running low in Zawiyah when, on 2nd March, Ghaddafi's forces attacked again.

'This time, they fired missiles into the centre of the city. There was fighting happening all around and it was very very frightening. Most people did not leave their homes, because it was dangerous on the streets. It was dangerous to stay at home as well, but there was nowhere else to go.'

Two days later, Ghaddafi's forces launched what they hoped would be a decisive strike. They forced the rebels back into the city's Main Square, where you now stand, killing the khetibas' Commander, colonel Hassan Darbouk along with 50 others. A further 300 khetibas were injured in the most costly day of fighting up to that date.

But what was expected to be a 'last stand' for the khetibas actually lasted for four days, with Ghaddafi's soldiers expelled from the city centre on two occasions.

The woman points to the buildings around the square: 'Both sides were fighting with everything they had, and the city centre was ruined. Worse was to come, but many of these holes in these buildings were created by those four days of fighting. The city was ruined.'

By 8th March, Ghaddafi's force had retaken the city centre, including the Main Square, but fighting continued throughout its suburbs.

'I think that that was some of the hardest fighting,' the woman says. 'Because the khetibas had to fight to stay alive and to free Zawiyah from Ghaddafi, but Ghaddafi knew if he fought as hard as them, he would win,' she pauses, looks at the ground, then smiles, sadly. 'Sometimes, it is nice to feel that you live in an important place. But at other times you wish you could just be left alone in peace and quiet.'

By 11th March, Ghaddafi had 'secured' the city, and with it the vital trade route to Tunisia, as well as the oil his regime needed. But guerrilla attacks continued throughout April and May, and on 11th June, khetibas launched a major assault, closing the Roman Road and engaging Ghaddafi's soldiers for two days.

Despite this, Ghaddafi retained control of the city, and was confident enough to bus reporters from Tripoli to Zawiyah late on 12th June, in a display of his control over the region.

The woman and your translator talk for a little while, about the suburb in which she lives, and the school her children attend, while you walk around the Square. Unlike Sirte's Saha Markazee, Zawiyah's Miden Shohada (Martyrs' Square) is literally and figuratively the centre of the city.

Though devastated today, it is easy to see that before the Civil War, the buildings here, this hotel, this mosque, these shops, were in a prestigious area. And the Square, which existed before Ghaddafi had taken power, had been designed with leisure in mind.

To your left, for example, sits a fountain. Cracked, and without water today, it sits next to empty flowerbeds and more broken white benches carved into the low white wall which surrounds the Square's central space. Once, it would have been a pleasant place to sit.

After the June offensive failed, life continued in Zawiyah much as before: people become used to even the most shocking destruction, and despite claims by the khetibas that 'thousands' of Zawiyans had been 'taken from the city' by Ghaddafi and that Ghaddafi's soldiers had killed and buried several Zawiyans at Martyrs' Square (no bodies were ever recovered), a man with whom your translator has started a new conversation casts doubt on that.

'When you two are as old as me you will know that even people who you agree with do not tell the whole truth, all of the time,' he shrugs. 'We all say what we think will help our cause the most.'

But Zawiyah's strategic importance actually increased through the summer of 2011. Having lost most of the east of Libya to the khetibas, trade with Tunisia was more important to the regime than ever, while the city's oil port was the only one which remained in government control.

In August, the khetibas launched another attempt to pry the city from the regime's hands.

Their first attacks, on 12th August, were remarkably successful. One group of khetibas managed to pass through defences in the West of the city, and reached the city centre, and other groups who entered were cheered by some Zawiyans, in some cases swelling their numbers with locals joining them to fight against the government.

But as khetibas pushed to the city centre from the west, government forces prepared to attack from the east, and NATO air strikes, designed to support the rebels and 'free' the city from Ghaddafi's rule, rained destruction from the skies.

'Those were some of the worst days,' the man says. 'The fighting was particularly strong, and buildings were struck from the ground. It was made worse in effect by the NATO aircraft. They were there to help us, but some of the worst damage which was done to the city was done in the nights that NATO was bombing us.'

By late afternoon on 14th August, amid a storm of misinformation from both sides (government forces claimed the attack was a 'suicide mission', easily dealt with, while NATO and the rebels claimed '70 per cent' of Zawiyah was under khetiba control: neither claim appears to have been backed by any actual evidence – and neither was actually true), television footage showed the rebels had achieved a symbolic victory, gaining control of the Roman Road and by implication, trade with Tunisia.

On 15th August, a series of government artillery strikes, followed by street fighting, pushed the khetibas out of the city centre once again. But the rebels claimed to have taken 80 per cent of Zawiyah.

That evening, the khetibas arrested a group of people they claimed were 'foreign mercenaries', though most of those arrested said they were in fact Nigerian guest workers and were not involved in the fighting at all.*

In the same month, August 2011, Amnesty International reported that half of all those detained by khetibas during the Civil War were black Africans, referred to as 'mercenaries' even though the vast majority of them had never been involved in fighting.

On the same night, using claims that missiles were being launched at Zawiyah from Janzour, a Tripoli suburb which neighbours the western city, NATO bombed Janzour. On 16th August, NATO claimed that rebels had taken the city centre – a remarkable assertion given that the khetibas themselves announced the same thing a full three days later.

But on 17th August, the khetibas struck at Zawiyah's oil refinery. They closed down oil pipelines through which fuel was carried to Tripoli, and 200 khetibas advanced as far as the refinery's gates, being stopped by the 100 pro-Ghaddafi fighters within the complex itself.

The khetibas announced at this point that almost all of the 100 pro-Ghaddafi soldiers making this desperate last stand were 'mercenaries', this time from Chad (interestingly, by this point there were actual soldiers who had been flown into Libya from Chad, but they were Libyans who had left during the 1980s, and returned by Americans, in American aircraft and land vehicles to assist the revolution).

Whatever the truth of this claim (and it would appear that in order for all of the allegations about 'mercenaries' to be true, Ghaddafi's forces must have contained at least 70 per cent of soldiers with non-Libyan nationality, and that the number of Libyans registered within the state's armed forces must have dropped by a similar percentage – there is absolutely no evidence to support such a scenario), what happened next is in no doubt.

After five hours of fighting, the khetibas made a decisive breakthrough, forcing the retreat of the government soldiers. NATO responded by bombing the boats carrying the retreating forces, drowning at least one boat-load of men. The UK's chief of Defence Staff Major General Nick Pope made the announcement the following day, saying: 'They were observed to use a tugboat... Since it was clear from their actions that these troops continued to pose a threat to the local population, the RAF engaged the ship.

'Although a challenging target, a direct hit was scored with a laser-guided Paveway bomb which sank the vessel.'

Despite finding time to name the missile and the technology which enabled the boat-load of men to be destroyed, Major General Pope did not have time to mention exactly how many of the retreating soldiers were killed by the strike.

It is surprising that at the congratulatory press conference, not one reporter thought to ask whether it is now NATO policy to kill retreating soldiers once they have been defeated in battle. Perhaps somebody should do soon, as by Major General Pope's logic, killing is always justified, on the grounds that as long as a soldier remains alive, they remain capable of attacking your forces, or civilians.

Also on 17th August, fighting continued in Zawiyah city centre, with particular attention paid to the city's main hotel, where loyalist snipers had created a point of attack.

Today, the hotel is just another of the ornate buildings which now have black holes punched into their walls, and fire damage smeared across their previously pristine, multi-coloured fronts.

The man gestures towards it: 'You can see the difference here,' he says. 'This has had missiles shot towards it from above as well as from below, and the destruction is greater. But, there is no longer a sniper in this building, or in any other.'

The last major exchange took place on 19th August, by which point the khetibas had taken the centre of the city, including Martyrs' Square, and had announced that the Zawiyah refinery would reopen within days to provide the khetibas with oil. On 20th August, the fighting ceased: Ghaddafi's troops would never return to Zawiyah.

You spend the rest of the afternoon driving through the suburbs of the city, walking and talking with its residents and watching children play in the rubble and detritus of war.

You return to Zawiyah's pockmarked, cracked city centre and walk once again through Martyrs' Square. An old man stands next to the arch of flowers, muttering something as he bows his head.

Across the Square, a woman carries shopping bags towards a western exit road. Aside from some distant traffic sounds, all else is silent.

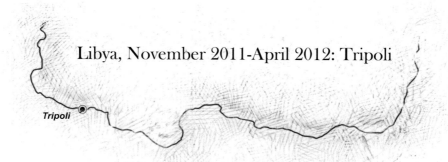

Libya, November 2011-April 2012: Tripoli

Tripoli

Guns

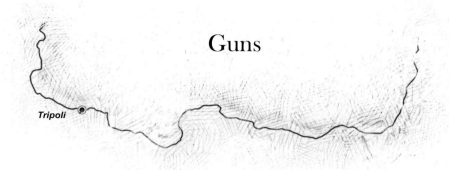

Tripoli

'One evening, I opened my door to find two men waiting for me. One walked towards me, gritted his teeth and told me that the next time someone was sent, they would be there to rape me.

'They were not soldiers, just people who supported Ghaddafi. They were sent to intimidate me because I am a young woman, I was born in Misrata, and most importantly because along with my younger brother, I was running guns to the khetibas here in Tripoli.

'As a girl, I did not expect to be in Tripoli as a gun-runner and an outlaw.

'My father's work as a diplomat for the Ghaddafi government meant I spent five years living in Morocco, five in Venezuela and eight in Jordan. Although I was born in Misrata, I did not live there for very long and I have lived in Tripoli for two years.

'But I spent my life with Libyan people around me, and many of them would talk about what was happening in my country. I also spent two months of every year here and I could compare it with the other countries in which I lived. I knew that Libya was sick, and we lived in the dark ages.

'The first week the revolution began, I was out of Libya. I was crying when I heard what was happening and I rushed to get home.*

* The first Tripoli uprising, in February 2011, followed a similar pattern to those in other cities. The city's main square (then Green Square, now Martyrs' Square) filled with protestors, and within hours fierce fighting broke out.

The anti-Ghaddafi marchers burned the People's Hall of the General People's Congress (the main meeting place of the government's legislative arm), police stations and the Justice Ministry building.

But the army crushed the uprising, through force of arms, by shutting down the internet, meaning protestors could not connect with one another, and through fortune, as the city's historic development meant its disparate suburbs made combined rebellion difficult.

Hundreds of people on both sides were killed.

But in March, the UN's no-fly zone, which NATO interpreted as permission to fly its aircraft over Libyan airspace, came into effect, and Tripoli was bombed regularly.

On the ground, resistance to Ghaddafi's regime continued with guerrilla fighting taking place most nights, and large areas of the city becoming de facto rebel-run areas, 'falling' to the rebels on an almost street-by-street basis.

'I was lucky. I caught the last plane to land in Tripoli airport.*

* *The UN was addressed on 21st February 2011 by the defected Libyan deputy Permanent Representative, Ibrahim Dabbashi. He stated: 'We are expecting a real genocide in Tripoli. The airplanes are still bringing mercenaries into the airports.'*

But no airplanes were bringing mercenaries into the airports. Instead, people were desperately attempting to travel home to their loved ones in a time of great danger.

Equally, and fortunately, no 'genocide' was delivered on Tripoli, even by Ghaddafi's notoriously merciless army, let alone by non-existent mercenary hordes.

'But when I landed, the phones had been cut off, and there was no internet. For a few days then, the city was quiet. I could not tell my family I was here, so I walked across the city, alone. It took two hours.

'It was very strange in Tripoli then. Ghaddafi was here, of course, and people very quietly took sides.

'It meant that you couldn't talk to anyone: even in your family, you could not be sure who thought what.

'That did not stop my brother though. He began to collect guns from other parts of Libya and take them into Tripoli for khetibas here. It was dangerous, crossing lines of soldiers and fighting.

'When I found out, I was angry at first. Not because of the danger he was in, but because he had not told me.

'But at this point, it was getting harder for boys and men to move easily in Tripoli. The government was becoming clever and was stopping them when they drove across the city. It was very serious to be stopped with weapons in your car.

'But it was also difficult if you were stopped by people who opposed Ghaddafi, and they were stopping people and searching their vehicles, too. You could tell them who you know and where you are going, but it was hard to check.

'For a woman, it was easier. People would not stop a woman, or suspect her. And this is how I became a gun-runner here in Tripoli, carrying weapons from khetibas outside the city to those inside it.

'Once or maybe twice each week, I would drive out of Tripoli, to a place we had arranged. Often it was a town but sometimes it was not. I would meet a man, who would load boxes into my car, and I would cover them with blankets and bags, and drive back to Tripoli.

'I did not always know where the weapons came from. Some of them I know were stolen from the army, but others had been dropped from planes for us from outside the country.

'I was almost never stopped by the khetibas or the army. I am a Libyan girl and even though there is risk and danger, I think neither of them really thought about women being in a war.

'It is funny to think of it, because women worked and still work in many other roles, but in a car, during a war, suddenly I was not the same, not involved.

'The revolution happened for a lot of reasons. Life was bad for many people: Libya has materials and could do much better, but the only people who seemed to do well were those who stole.

'Even worse was that most people could not find food to eat. The revolution came from very small, very quiet words: "we must be free from all this".

'Very soon after the revolution started, videos showed what was happening, killings and arrests, things like that. You could not just sit at home, waiting to see if something was going to happen to you. It is my country, I thought. I must be there, outside, helping to make things happen.

'Bombs were falling and guns firing. It was very frightening, but it was most strange because that soon became almost a normal thing.

'People had no fuel for their cars, because lots of oil comes from Benghazi and what was left was being used by Ghaddafi to fight. People began to say that they wished they had got out, but it was not possible any more. There were three-day queues for oil and when there was some you could get, it cost 200-300 Dinars* for 18 litres. It was crazy.

* Even in the immediate post-war period, oil in Libya was remarkably cheap: to fill the tank of a pick-up cost around £5, or 30 Libyan Dinar.

'Eventually, I left Tripoli. In August. I did not want to, but every time I left the flat I was staying in, I wondered whether the men I saw had been sent to rape me. I think I would have stayed anyway, but one of the guys I was moving guns for said I didn't have to, that I had done enough to help them and that he could help me get out.

'I travelled south by road into Chad, and then flew to Jordan. I stayed with friends for about a month, until Tripoli was very close to being liberated, and I realised I had to be there. It is the capital of my country, and I had worked to help things to happen there.*

* In mid-August, the moves which were to enable the khetibas to take Tripoli began. Striking from the Saharan Nafusa Mountains, the khetiba brigades took Sorman, Sabratha and Zawiyah, cutting the Ghaddafi regime's connections to Tunisia, as well as Gharyan, and its main links to the pro-Ghaddafi city of Sabha, in the south of the country.

On 20th August, the khetibas won the 27km Bridge at Janzour (so-called because of its distance West of the centre of Tripoli), and prepared to attack the following day, a date rebel leaders claimed they had chosen because it marked the 20th day of Ramadan, the anniversary of Mohammed's conquest of Mecca.

Meanwhile, the National Transitional Council, khetibas and the French government agreed on 120 targets for NATO aircraft to strike during the attack.

Within the city, khetiba members took over the Ben Nabi Mosque, cancelling prayers and broadcasting chanted anti-Ghaddafi slogans from its loudspeakers. Ghaddafi regime troops arrived, but were beaten back and by the end of the evening four further suburbs were won by the khetibas. Arms smuggled into the city in the weeks and months before made the uprising possible, and the 'zero hour' for this action was a speech by NTC leader Mustafa Jalil, broadcast across Libya, in which he claimed that 'the noose is tightening' around Ghaddafi.

That night, the government sent text messages to Tripoli residents, asking them to 'eliminate the armed agents'. Students at Fateh University rose up against armed guards loyal to Ghaddafi, who had been stationed there since February's rebellion, and chased snipers from its towers.

Fighting continued into the night, and the following morning khetibas set out for Tripoli from Zawiyah. Others arrived by sea from Misrata and Zliten.

Throughout the day, the khetibas achieved and reported victories across the city, with some surrounding Tripoli's international airport and others confirming their aim was the Bab al-Aziza military compound, where Ghaddafi lived.

Khetibas also freed prisoners from military bases and jails as they went, sweeping through four more neighbourhoods during the morning and fighting for control of three more in the afternoon.

The khetiba arrived from Zawiyah in the evening, after some fighting on Tripoli's outskirts, and headed east towards the city centre with no resistance – some eyewitnesses claiming they were met by cheering, flag-waving crowds.

Later reports suggested that they met so little resistance because Mohammed Eshkal, who led the government's Mohammed Megrayef Brigade, supposed to defend the city from the khetibas, ordered his troops to surrender immediately to them, because his cousin had been killed by Ghaddafi's regime five years before.

Equally, General al-Barani Ashkal, commander of Ghaddafi's forces at Bab al-Aziza, and several other senior military members who sympathised with the khetibas but had remained undercover, ordered their soldiers to abandon their posts when the khetibas approached.

That night, a government spokesman claimed 1,300 people had been killed and a further 5,000 wounded, blaming NATO for the deaths.

Around the same time, a new text was sent from the base of the Libyana mobile phone company, which the khetibas had taken that afternoon. Tripolitans received the message: 'Allah Akhbar. We congratulate the people of Libya on the fall of the Ghaddafi regime.'

It may be suggested that this was a strange message for Libyan troops to have sent one another, and indeed it may not have been drafted by a Libyan: it later emerged that in direct contravention of all United Nations Security Council Resolutions, Qatari troops, as well as British, American and French soldiers, were on the ground when Tripoli fell.

By 1am on 22nd August, rebels announced they controlled 90 per cent of Tripoli, including Green Square. Within hours, it was clear that this statement was about as reliable as every other issued by the khetibas, NATO and Ghaddafi's spokespeople (one of whom had described the fighting on 20th August as 'isolated scuffles').

Not only did another rebel leader say that he estimated 15-20 per cent of Tripoli remained in Ghaddafi's hands, TV cameras later that day showed khetibas marching on Green Square with rocket-launchers, which would mean they were aiming to take the Square they had 'controlled' just hours before.

The khetibas did take the state TV broadcast centre that afternoon, however, with all broadcasts within the city temporarily ceasing as a result. On 23rd August, with Green Square, along with Tripoli's main ports, international airport, and the city's entrances and exits, under rebel control, the khetibas advanced on Bab al-Aziza. A fierce battle ensued, but khetibas swiftly took control of one gateway, from which they advanced steadily, and entered the main building.

As members fired into the air in celebration, the flag of King Idris, adopted by the khetibas, was raised above the building. Once again, confirmation later arrived that Qatari troops, illegally operating as a ground force in the war, had attacked Ghaddafi's compound with the khetibas.

But Ghaddafi was nowhere to be found, and later that day claimed that he had left Bab al-Aziza as a 'tactical move'. If tactics were the reason he left the compound, nobody had informed his troops, who then opened fire in an attempt to retake it.

Fighting continued on 24th August, and at one point Ghaddafi's forces managed to push the khetibas back to the compound's exterior wall, but while NATO airstrikes continued overhead, *and with the assistance of Qatari, British and US soldiers, the khetibas held their ground and eventually took the base.*

In the aftermath, a golf buggy was reportedly found where it had smashed a hole into a wall. Speculation suggested Ghaddafi had used this as his escape-route from the compound.

Fighting was also taking place outside the Rixos Al-Nasr hotel, where reporters had been held by Ghaddafi's forces as a human shield for several days.

At 5pm, with water and food running very low, the hotel's doors were finally unlocked and the reporters allowed to leave in four Red Cross vans. Fighting continued the following day, focused on the airport, which Ghaddafi's forces were trying to win back, and two areas of Tripoli, which the khetibas were trying to prise from their grip.

On 26th August, 'eyewitnesses' claimed that Ghaddafi troops had killed prisoners, after 160 people escaped from their detention. In common with all such claims, no bodies have yet been found in connection with this incident.

On the same day, Ghaddafi, his son Khamis and daughter Ayesha, met at another of Tripoli's military bases. It was the last time Ghaddafi would see his daughter, as he and Khamis were taken by military convoys towards Sabha, the former capital of Fezzan, still loyal to Ghaddafi, and 400 miles south of Tripoli. They did not make it to the city, which itself fell to the khetibas in September 2011, and Ghaddafi moved instead to Sirte, while Ayesha, her mother and some of her remaining brothers fled to Algeria.

Khetibas announced Khamis had been killed by a NATO airstrike on 29th August. NATO refused to confirm this, but it is now accepted as truth. He has never been seen again.

On 28th August, the official final day of the 'Battle of Tripoli', khetibas attacked the last regime-friendly base in Salaheddin, south of the city. After seven hours it, and so symbolically the city, fell.

'I went to Lebanon, and from there I flew to Tunisia. It was not possible to land anywhere in Libya, and so I took a taxi from Tunisia into Tripoli.

'The city had changed very much. Everything that had been painted green before was now the black, green, red and white of our new flag, and people were out on the streets again, celebrating. Everyone was so happy, and then local khetibas left to help Sirte, so everyone here was waiting and hoping for Sirte to be freed.

'When Ghaddafi was caught, some people wondered why he had been killed and why he had not been arrested and taken to a court where he could be tried, but everyone was very happy because he was gone and our country was free.

'But looking back to those days now, it is possible to say that was when problems began to start again.

'We do have problems here. And not all of them are just Ghaddafi's fault. 'If you walk around you can see that there are many destroyed buildings here. I have been to other places, to see my family in Misrata, for example, and I know that some of them are more damaged than Tripoli. But that does not mean it is OK for Tripoli to be damaged.

'And even here, the government does not help. It cannot. So things are only fixed if people do that themselves.

'It is also bad because men with guns are still on our streets. They should not be there. Many of these men are heroes, and they did a very good thing for Libya. And maybe they should be

rewarded for that. Perhaps some of them could be elected. But it is not right for them to be here on our streets now.

'We are not at war and it is not right. War is more likely if people are carrying guns and belong to khetibas who disagree with each other and with the government. They have to leave, but they refuse. They should leave.

'And there are groups of people here in the city who have even more problems than others. The Tawerghans who are here have to live in camps. Not only do they have no homes to live in and no town to live in any more, they must also be kept safe from the Misratans.

'Even in Tripoli, they are not completely safe and so they live away from the city. But they are still not completely safe. Now, I work with children and young people at the camps, trying to help them learn, and stay safe and healthy. They should not have to suffer, because we all fought for all of Libya to be free.

'But even when we all work hard, we cannot do enough. The children should be in their houses, with their families. And they should have schools to go to, and a community to live in. Sometimes, I fear for their safety, because they are still threatened, even here. And they will be here for a very long time. There are so many problems, so we have to work hard to help make things better.

'In the city here, we have to teach young people. They need to be taught about guns, very urgently. It has become very easy for young people to have guns. I have met and spoken to boys who have been caught at schools or football pitches shooting guns and they just say that they have been given them. They do not understand how dangerous they are. When you talk to boys here in Tripoli they say it is good to play with guns.

'They have seen so many people with guns that it's not beginning to be normal, it is already normal for them. Guns are a normal thing. My brother's friend is 15. He came over one day and he told me that he and his friends got bored, so they just went into each other's houses and took all the guns, shooting them into the sea. Adults were there and did not do anything.

'If nothing is done then not just here but across the whole country we will be overrun by criminal gangs with guns.

'We have a nation full of children who have seen men called heroes while they hold and use guns. We have a society full of guns and our children want to hold them and to use them, even though they do not understand them.

'So many people have died since Ghaddafi was killed – because of happy shooting and because of deliberate killings. It shows how dangerous and damaging guns are and why we must educate children and teach them not to use them.

'Only a couple of weeks ago, a girl of 15 was shot and killed. She was eating dinner with her family and she was shot dead by someone outside. The person with the gun did not even mean to kill her. But she is dead.

'We are a country that has not been as good as it could have been. The revolution means we have a new chance. But it also means we have many new challenges. I do not know if we can do this alone. Some groups are here and helping us. But at some time, they will leave. I do not know what sort of a country they will leave then.'

The Toss of a Coin
Part Three: Days of Life in Libya

We entered Libya through Kufra in the South East, and we were put in the houses of the Libyans. But that wasn't the end. They came to me and they told me they wanted money. But I had no money. 'How much money?', I asked. $800, they told me.

'But I have no money,' I told them. 'I have no money and I have no-one where I am from who can send me any money.'

They sent in a man, who hit me. He had a large key sticking between the fingers of his fist.

He cut open my face and then walked out. Another man came and said 'I will show you how to get money.' He hit me, then four other men came in and beat me. 'Get money sent here,' they said. 'You will have to kill me,' I said. 'I have no money and there is no-one who can send me money.'

The Somalians I had arrived with tried to help me, and some others who lived there. They all gave $15 each, not to pay to the Libyans, but so that I could escape by car to Tripoli.

I arrived in Jalu in the North East, paying drivers the Somalians' money to get there.

It was 2009, and I hoped now I was in Libya I could find work and pay to travel by boat across the ocean to Europe.

Each day I would wake up and go onto the street looking for work to do. I saw that all the black people like me, and all the Egyptians, would sit on the street from about five or six in the morning, and so because I didn't know anybody, or know what to do, I would sit down with them and wait.

They took me to work with them. They gave me a job. It was lucky to have a job, and to know I would get some money. They sat me down, told me where to sit and took me with them when they worked.

In the weeks that followed, I would arrive on the roadside at 6am, sit with the others and at 7am we would be taken to a building site. I worked there until 5pm each day. My job was to make cement.

I had been promised 20 dinars for each day, but at the end of the first week, when I asked for money I needed for food and clothes, the Egyptians gave me a handful of cents.

I asked them why they had given me cents and they told me it was 100 dinars. But I knew it was just cents and they were keeping the money they had been given for my work.

I asked them please give me the money I have earned. I need it or I cannot eat. It was difficult because I could not speak their language well. But they said 'No. We will not give you more, you are a Somalian.' I said 'I am not.' But they wouldn't listen to me. At that moment, the Egyptians and the Libyans seemed the same to me.

But that night, I met a man who had come from Somalia in 2007. He said: 'They are playing with you because they can do. They do it when they think people do not know things because they do not speak their language.'

So, the next week, the Somalian who knew how to speak the Libyan language came to work with me, and at the end of that week they gave me $13, not cents. I was so happy.

I bought a pair of trousers and a t-shirt – my first new clothes I had bought for myself in all the time since I left Ethiopia. I also paid for my breakfast and lunch through the whole week. I was very happy.

I continued like this for a long time, working on building sites and buying what I needed, saving a little all the time. I started to learn the Libyan language, too. It was difficult, but I needed to learn so I could get a better job and talk to the people around me.

Near to where I slept, I met a man who said he had seen me waiting for work each morning. He asked me what I did and why, so I told him. When he heard I could do Tae Kwan-Do, he asked me if I would like a job which was more secure and for more money. Of course I said yes, so I started to work for this man.

There were two main parts to the job: I was mainly a security guard, but he also wanted me to wash his car every day after he got home. I was very happy. The hours were long, but he paid me 315 dinars per month, nearly four times what I earned on building sites.

With the extra money, I was able to save quickly, and because I had time to learn, I also managed to finish learning to speak the Libyan language.

I found someone who said he could help me cross to Italy on a ship, so I gave him $800. He moved me into a house, where I stayed until more people arrived, and then the next night we got onto a boat. It was quite full, but not too full, so we were happy when we set off.

But only a short time later, we were told we had been caught in Tunisian water, and we were returning to Libya. We were going to be arrested. Soldiers came, and began to prepare to take us away when the ship stopped. But I didn't want to be arrested and beaten again, so I jumped off the boat and into the sea.

It was hard. I didn't know how to swim and the sea was more strong than I had thought it would be. It pulled me out, away from the coast, and I had to struggle to be able to breathe. But it got a bit easier for me, and I was able to float, and to kick my legs.

After a long time, I got back to the coast, a few miles away from where the soldiers had been waiting, and I got out of the sea. Because I had lost my job when I tried to get to Italy, I had to look for more work.

I could speak the Libyan language now, so it was more easy to get a job.

I worked in a shop which sold perfume. I opened the shop every morning at 7am and then closed it again at 10pm. I was paid 400 dinars every month, but it was too hard. I worked every day and I was very tired. I still wanted to escape, to go to Europe.

I had to get to Italy, but I wanted to live in Norway, because life is good there, or in England because I love football and I love the Premier League. Chelsea are my favourites, but I also like Manchester United and Arsenal and Liverpool. I love football and they are very good teams. I loved to see them when I was near a television and I wanted to go to the country where they played. I still do.

I had saved up $1,000, because I could sleep on the floor of the shop and I didn't buy clothes and I didn't eat many meals so I could escape. They charged me $500, so I still had $500 in my clothes. I thought this would be good and could help me when I got to Italy, but instead we were caught by the police in a boat when we were still in Libyan waters.

This time, I couldn't jump. We were a long way from the land and the boat was too full and I couldn't get to the edge to jump. Instead, the police caught me and put me into prison.

I made a deal with the biggest police man. I gave him money and said: 'Let me out please.' I gave him $200. But he said it had to be more money. I told him I had no friends and no family, but I would try to get him some more money.

Everybody always thought I was Somalian, even though I am not from Somalia, so I said if he could get me to the Somalian Embassy, I would talk to my friends there and I would give him more money because they would give it to me. I didn't have any friends in Somalia, but I told him I would give him $200 more.

He said: 'You must pretend to be sick. If you do that, I will make sure you get to the Embassy.'

I pretended to be sick. I stayed in bed for four days, and I did not eat. I was sick by the end of it, because I was so hungry. But instead of taking me to the hospital, like he told the other cops, he took me to the Somalian Embassy. I told him I couldn't get the money, but he was angry and said he would make me go back to jail, so I gave him 200 more dollars.

But now I only had $100, not enough to get across the ocean to Italy, and no job. So, I had to find work again.

I met a man from France who was rich. I told him I needed a job and he said he could give me work and I would save money fast. So I worked every day from 7am to 1pm, cleaning houses he owned and washing his car. Then, I worked from 6pm-1am as a security guard for his houses and his garage.

I could have left Libya sooner, because I was earning a lot of money. He paid me $500 per month. But I made friends with some of the Somalian people who lived in Tripoli, and I met a lady. I liked her a lot, because I was coming to the age where you like ladies.

I told her I had money. I said we could get on a ship together, so we paid for a ship and we left Libya. I thought it is my third time and it will be lucky for me.

But we left Libya and then the ship broke. Its engine wouldn't work. I am not sure which country owned the ocean where we were. But we were stuck in the ocean, in a boat with too many people on it, with no food and no water to drink.

People were afraid. Some jumped off the boat, but I don't know what happened to them. I didn't jump because I cannot swim and we were too far from land and the ocean was too strong for me.

After four days, people were sick and some of them were crying. The children were asleep most of the day, but when they woke up they were crying.

But then a boat came. The people on the boat were not police. They said they would take us home, to Libya. But they took us to Libya, then took us to prison and they were given money by the prison guards.

The lady went home. She was a Libyan so they didn't want her to go to prison. So I had to escape.

I found out from some Somalians who had been in the prison longer than us that there had been some Eritreans there, who had escaped by loosening all the window catches. I checked the windows that night and the catches were still loose.

The next night, I escaped with one other friend from the boat. I tried to get the other Somalians to come, but they were afraid of what would happen if they were caught.

But we ran into the night and no-one came after us. We were back in Libya and we laughed together and said we would stay as friends.

I needed to find another job. Because I wanted to escape, but also because I thought I might marry the lady and either we could go to Italy together or we could stay in Libya, where she came from and I could get a job and we could live together.

So I got a job building roads in Libya. They paid me 600 dinars a month. It was less than my other job, but it was enough for me.

I went to see the lady. I told her I loved her. She said we should just be friends. I told her I needed to marry her. She said we should be friends. But then I told her my friend from the boat had said because I had escaped from a war in my country that I could get papers to be allowed to live in Libya and I said I would get papers.

She told me OK, get the papers and we will see.

So I went to the offices to get the papers I needed, so I could marry the lady.

My appointment was on January 1st 2011. But the office was closed when I went there. There were some people nearby who told me the office was closed forever. But they didn't say why. I was afraid and I didn't know what to do next.

I went home to the lady and she said that it was OK, she was still going to marry me. But I still needed papers.

Because I had left my country because of war, I was allowed to get papers and they would let me live in Libya with my wife or maybe cross the ocean with her.

We waited for two weeks and we visited the office each day, but it was closed. My wife said we could find the office in Egypt, which we thought would be open and could help us. Or if not that office we could go from there to Tel Aviv. I agreed. I decided that place was not good for us.

I knew other people – Somalis – who also wanted papers, or wanted to leave Libya, so we went together.

There were 16 of us who went. Me, my wife, three Somalis including my friend from the boat and the rest were Egyptians. We drove across Libya from Tripoli to the Egyptian border. It is a long road and goes from Tunisia to Egypt. But the cars we were in broke down before we crossed the border.

We tried to fix the engines but we couldn't. We still had to cross the border, but it was close, so we decided to walk across. We went off the road because without papers we could not cross at a road crossing where we would need a passport, so we walked across the land instead.

But because there had been fighting between Egypt and Libya before,* one of the two had left landmines in the land.

*A four-day border dispute between the two states in 1977. Even 37 years later, the battlefields remain strewn with landmines.

We started to walk across, one Egyptian leading the rest of us. But it did not work. I heard a clicking noise and then there was a massive explosion. I was thrown to the ground. I opened my eyes and I thought I was lucky, because I could have been the one to step on the mine, or been thrown into one by the explosion.

I sat up. I had blood in my eyes and I was bleeding, but I wiped the blood away. I looked for my wife. She had been knocked down by the blast and she was shaking, but she had not been hurt. So, I picked her up in my arms and carried her.

But my friend was hurt. He was crying out. I found him and he was lying down. He had lost his right leg and he was bleeding very much. 'Please don't leave me,' he said. But I could not carry him and my wife too. I had to leave him. But he was my friend. I knew my wife and I could get over the border but my friend would definitely die if we left him.

I gave him some water and told him I would find a soldier at the border. The soldiers would arrest us, but my friend could stay alive.

I carried my wife, and we walked across. To my right, another Egyptian man stepped on a mine. I saw the explosion but it did not knock us over this time. He lost his left arm and many ribs. I went to him, but he was already dead.

I carried my wife to the border. I was sad. I could just walk across but I knew my friend would die if I left him with no leg and bleeding. I looked at my wife. She shook her head and we walked along the border. It took 30 minutes to find a soldier. He told other soldiers to find my friend, and he arrested us.

I was beaten by the soldiers. At first on the border, and then on the way to the prison in Basra and then at the prison. They hurt me and they made me bleed, but I was already bleeding and I had not stepped on a mine and they did not push a bullet into my arm so I was hurt but it was not the worst I had experienced.

We were there in the prison for two months. There was no way to escape. The soldiers had already taken our money and there were no ways to break the windows or walls.

But at the start of the third month we were there, in March 2011, another group of soldiers came. They told us we were free to go, and gave us ID cards. I do not know why they did that. But they told us we had to get new cards every three months and told us we had to get them from the government offices. Then they said 'you are free' again and they let us out.

I travelled to Tripoli. But I was afraid of what would happen next. There was fighting going on across the country. I didn't know why, but I knew what fighting meant in my own country. And the government had given me an ID card even though I didn't ask for one. Even though I wanted one, and I was pleased, I was worried because it would run out in three months and there was fighting all around us.

We had tried to escape by the ocean, and to escape to Egypt. This time, my wife and I crossed to Tunisia, and that is why I am here at the Choucha Camp.

Security

'I think that Tripoli is a good place. The best place in Libya, I think.

'Maybe that is not fair. I work with people from Benghazi and from Misrata, Sirte and Zawiyah. They all tell me good things about their homes and I am sure that they are good.

'But Tripoli is where I was born and where I have always lived, and I think it is a good place to live. There is history, and there are many shops and places to go, and things to do. There are some bad things as well, but not so many as the good.*

Tripoli has been continuously occupied for at least 2,700 years. It was founded by the Phoenicians, though its earliest recorded name, Oea, is Berber, suggesting it was in fact built on a pre-existing town. In common with each of Libya's major northern cities, its history is far more closely tied to the Mediterranean than to the majority of the African continent, which was far harder for it to influence or be influenced by because of the vast Sahara which stretches to its south.

After 500 years of rule by the Phoenicians and then Carthaginians (with a brief spell under the Greek rulers of Cyrenaica), it was overtaken by Romans, and became part of Regio Syrtica, in the province of Africa.

Another half a millennium later, in the Third Century AD, an administrative restructure saw the district renamed Regio Tripolitana, the region of the three cities, referring to Oea, Sabratha and Leptis Magna. The region was raised to the status of province by Septimus Severus, who was a native of Leptis Magna.

Leptis and parts of Sabratha are now extensive and impressive Roman ruins, but in Tripoli, always inhabited, little evidence remains of the Roman presence: almost all Roman buildings have been broken down for materials, or built over in the 1700 years since the Empire fell, though one imposing structure remains, the Marcus Aurelius arch, which is surrounded now by restaurants, shops and cafes.

Tripoli suffered close to a century of Vandal raids from the Mediterranean, before being taken decisively by Muslims from Egypt in 642-643 (the 22nd year of the Hijra).

Egyptian rule lasted roughly 500 years, followed by Tripoli's subsumation into the Almohad Empire, which sprang from the Atlas Mountains, Morocco, in the 12th Century, and at its height included vast swathes of modern Morocco, Algeria, Libya and Spain.

When the Almohad Empire fell, Tripoli was for around three centuries a regional capital under the Hafsids kingdom, ruled from Tunisia and including Algeria, Tunisia and western Libya.

In 1510, Tripoli was once again 'connected' to Europe, when Don Pedro Navarro, Count of Oliveto, perhaps in an attempt to 'prove' Spain's strength as a nation following centuries of Muslim rule, conquered it and claimed it for his country.

Just 13 years later, Spain handed the city to the Knights of St John, who had been chased from Rhodes by the Ottoman Turks.

The Knights were charged with stopping piracy on Christian shipping lanes in the Mediterranean (Tripoli had previously been a centre for the Barbary pirates) and worked hard to fortify the city. They are credited with the earliest work on the Red Castle, which now sits overlooking both the city's coast and its 'Martyr's Square'. But the city was unsettled under Christian rule, and in 1551, facing rebellion from within and attack from without, the Knights surrendered it to the Ottomans.

The Turks treated Tripoli well, building the city up until it became a leading North African metropolis. They also turned a blind eye to the activities of the Barbary pirates, whose actions not only benefited the Ottomans' own naval ambition but also, by the 17th Century, acted as a block on English trading of Catholic and Muslim slaves throughout the region.

One of the earliest English strikes on the city was led by John Narborough in 1675. He hoped to crush piracy to enable English interests to flourish. But his effort was foiled almost as much by indifference as by action on Tripolitans' behalf.

In 1711, Ahmed Karamanli killed the Ottoman ruler of Tripoli and by 1714 had completed a deal with the Ottoman Empire in which 'his' Tripolitania was effectively independent from Ottoman rule, in exchange for a tax to the Empire's Sultan.

By then, Tripoli's rulers were actively using the Barbary pirates, allowing piracy to take place unless a state paid the city to protect its ships. But in 1801, the city demanded that the US government should pay more than the $83,000 per year it had been paying since 1796 for this 'service'. The Americans refused, and entered a four-year war against the North African city.

Tripoli had the better of the sea battles, and could probably have defeated the USA if not for a land attack by William Eaton. He led a force of US Marines, Greek, Arab and Turkish mercenaries, and also containing an elder brother of Tripoli's ruler, who promised to accede to all American demands if placed in power.

The force crossed the desert from Alexandria and took the city of Derna, at which point Tripoli's ruler accepted $60,000 in exchange for ending the war.

In 1835, the Ottomans seized back control of Tripoli following a Civil War in the region. This time, the city was made capital of 'Tripoli' which included the entire Mediterranean coast between Tunisia and Egypt, including Cyrenaica, as well as Fezzan, and four desert oases. Effectively, the state of Libya came into existence for the first time, with Tripoli as its capital.

Two rebellions were crushed in the next ten years, but after this Tripoli was at peace until 1911, when Italy invaded the city, claiming they did so to 'protect' Italian citizens from Ottoman rule.

After World War One, Italy officially granted Libya sovereignty, but in fact increased its colonisation of the region. By 1938, 39,000 of Tripoli's 108,000 inhabitants were Italian.

Many of the city's more modern features – including its first modern hospital – were built or begun by the Italians, whose occupation also fostered an increased interest in both football and motor-racing.

In football, with which Ghaddafi's family was obsessed, Tripoli's club sides have excelled, and in the winter of 2013, the city wildly celebrated Libya's triumph in the Cup of African Nations, the tournament in which only African-based players can take part.

The city remained under Italian rule until 1943, when the British took control of Tripolitania and Cyrenaica. After independence from Britain in 1951, Tripoli and Benghazi co-existed as dual capitals, of the new Libyan state, but when Ghaddafi seized power in 1969, he made Tripoli sole capital of Libya.

This may have been in part because of the symbolism attached to moving 'control' from King Idris' home city, but it was also because Tripoli was Libya's largest city by far (with 2.2m inhabitants, it is now more than twice the size of Benghazi) and because of its long history as capital of its province, region, and state. But as in previous eras, Tripoli's prominence has been a curse as well as a blessing.

In 1986, the US government claimed to have intercepted telex messages from Libya's Embassy in East Berlin (then still a Communist city, under the wider auspices of the Eastern Bloc and Warsaw Pact) suggesting Ghaddafi had been involved in a nightclub bombing.

President Ronald Reagan ordered the bombing of Tripoli, killing at least 60 people. Some commentators suggested this strike was motivated as much by a desire to remove a 'left-wing' ruler from an oil-producing state as by any desire to bring the perpetrators of the nightclub attack to justice. Ghaddafi's adopted daughter, Hannah, was one of those reported dead as a result of these strikes.

Economic sanctions remained in place for 17 years until 2003.

Prior to Libya's Civil War, Tripoli had become an increasingly busy trade and tourism centre, with a number of ambitious construction projects newly- or part-finished.

Today, along with Benghazi, Misrata, Sirte and others, and entirely in keeping with the rest of its history, it remains to be seen whether the city's international connections are on balance to its credit or detriment.

'I did want to leave during the revolution, though. It was hard to be here. I was not a fighter. I am a dental technician and I worked at a pharmacy. I studied hard to get a degree and I liked my job. I kept doing it for as long as I could.

'But things became bad during the revolution. Large parts of the city had no electricity or water, because there was no oil. My family were lucky, and we lived in a place where the water kept working, and most of the time the electricity kept working.

'But all over the city, there were shortages. It was very difficult to buy food, because in Libya we import so much food and we did not get any imports. Here in this city, we were not bombed so much as other cities were, but we could not eat. And we were bombed. On the streets there were gun battles and fighting and bombs were dropped from aircraft.

'The first battles were intense and they did not stop, they only became smaller, and then the second battles were much harder.

'With the bombing as well, it was very frightening. Anyone who was not fighting stayed at home all day and all night. It was too dangerous on the street.

'I was not involved in the revolution. But like many people here I wanted it to end quickly and to end well. I wanted Ghaddafi to be gone, although people here did not all want that, because he had done some things they thought were good for them and for the city.

'And some good things have happened since then.

'I have a job with an international organisation which is helping to make sure Libya is a better place to live in. It is a good feeling, because I organise things and those things help to make my city and my country a better place to live.

'But there are things which are not better.

'People still stay at home here in Tripoli, because everybody has a gun on the street.

'Anyone can deliver any threat they want to, because they have a gun and there is no-one to stop them.

'It is a bad thing. We opposed Ghaddafi's police because they did bad things and they were a bad police force. But now we have no police and it is even worse.

'As a woman, here in Tripoli I felt comfortable to walk home alone from a friend's house at 10pm, well after it was dark.

'But today, I and other women here do not feel we can do so any more.

'We rush to get home before 7pm.

'It is not what the revolution was for. For many of us today, our city is worse: it is good that Ghaddafi has gone, but the buildings are damaged, and there are guns everywhere. I do not always feel safe.

'But I work – all of us do – to make things better.'

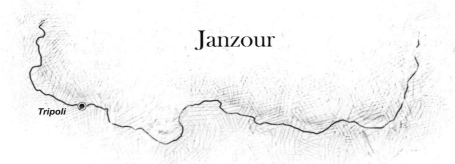

Janzour

You arrive early in the afternoon, pausing briefly at the gates while your documents are checked before driving slowly into the compound.

A brisk wind is blowing in off the sea, causing the blankets, shirts and trousers hanging on the makeshift washing lines to crack and snap as if banners championing the cause – and victory – of domestic life.

At every sandstone building – each perched a few metres above the sea – there is a sign of activity, from the washing lines strung from building to building, to singing from several of the small open windows, the songs mingling and mixing with the wind to create something more melancholy than any individual singer intended.

This is Janzour Camp, a former naval academy full today not with cadets – the effective disbandment of Libya's sea force ending also the need for immediate training in sea warfare – but with civilians, men, women and children, who cannot go home.

Though not everyone here is a civilian. Lining the compound's walls, and manning its entrance and exit points are armed, uniformed men: 'They are the government's soldiers,' your driver tells you. 'They are here to make sure the people here are safe from attack by the Misrata khetiba. They do not want the Tawerghans to be here.'

There are 1,500 Tawerghans at Janzour Camp, one of three Tripolitan locations converted into emergency accommodation for the victims of the greatest war crime of the Libyan Civil War* – the ethnic cleansing of Tawergha.

*Early in the war, there were allegations that Ghaddafi's forces had been ordered to rape civilians, but several human rights organisations, and NATO – though in the latter case only after repeating the allegations in international media – reported that they had found no evidence such orders existed or that such systematic rape had taken place. Similarly, claims that Ghaddafi's forces had committed acts of mass murder have so far remained evidence-free, in contrast to some episodes in which khetibas killed pro-Ghaddafi prisoners.

You are here as an invitee of one of the women you have interviewed in Tripoli, who currently works with the children and young people in the camp.

'They need a school,' she tells you. 'And we cannot provide them with that. But we work hard, and the children do too. We teach them Maths, English, Arabic, Music, Art and some other things, and we organise activities like playing and acting. But they are stuck here. They cannot go to school because their parents fear that they will be abducted, and we cannot be sure that they are wrong.

'We have to keep safe, but they really need to go to school each day.'

You are looking at some paintings on the wall when a young girl walks over and asks your name. She shows you her painting, which shows a man behind bars.

'That's my brother,' she says. 'He is sad because he is in Misrata in prison. He has been there since August when everyone had to leave our home. My mother says he will be OK but I know that she has not spoken to him because I heard her say so to one of my friend's mothers a week ago. But I hope he is OK.

'We left because the people from Misrata came and they made us all go away from our houses. We went to Haysha and then Tripoli, but here I have met people who went to Jufrah then to Tripoli.

'Sometimes I think the people who went to Jufrah were the luckiest ones because when we went to Haysha it was only good for a short time because then the Misratans came and forced us to leave there as well. That was very frightening. It meant that they knew where we were and it was not enough for them to make us leave our homes and then leave us alone.

'But other times I remember that the people who went to Jufrah tell me that people there made them leave and were not kind to them. So maybe it was more bad for them.

'It is nice here. It is good to be so close to the sea. We can climb down some rocks and put our feet in the sea. I like to do that.

'And it is good to learn here. I like to learn English and find out new things. I do not know where any of my friends are who I was friends with in Tawergha. But I have made new friends here and I like to play with lots of the girls. They are nice to me and I am nice to them.

'But sometimes I think about my home as well and it makes me sad. I want to go home.'

The girl introduces you to a young man; 'He is my favourite teacher,' she says. She sits and listens for a while as the two of you speak, eventually asking if she can leave to play with her friends.

'I left Tawergha on 11th August,' the man begins. 'It was the same day that almost all of us left, the day that Tawergha was killed.

'We had to leave because the town was full of bullets being fired and full of bombs being dropped on our homes.

'I first walked into the desert. I had no car, and I knew that if I stayed any longer the Misratans would arrest me or shoot me, so I just walked into the sand.

'But then some people helped me. First, the army helped me. They gave me some water and some food to eat, and I needed it because I was thirsty and hungry. And then they told me which direction to walk in so I went the way that they said and I met some people who were helping each other and they let me ride in their car.

'They took me to Haysha. I met some people who walked all the way, but I did not have to.

'I stayed there for three days, but then the Misratans followed us and I had to leave Haysha. I went to Tripoli. Tripoli is the best place we have found. It's OK. I feel like I can live here.

'Before the revolution, I was studying Medicine at University in Misrata. I knew friends there and I hope God will fix what has happened to us all in Tawergha.

'But I enjoy working with young people here. If I could not come here to help to teach the children I would feel weird. I would be wondering what I would do and why I was living here. So I volunteer here and I work here in the morning and the afternoon.

'It is very important that the children here can be taught. They have done nothing wrong and they need to learn and not have their education spoiled. I love to help them, and when I am here I forget everything outside: all the problems and all the issues.'

A little later, after a brief indoor football game, involving the volunteer teacher and a large group of boisterous boys and girls, a 13 year-old boy talks to you.

'I am here with my mum and dad and my brothers,' he says. 'That is not the same as lots of other people. It is because we left Tawergha when NATO bombed our town the first time, in April. We left then because we thought things would get worse.

'We went to Haysha, and stayed there until August, but then we had to leave again. Lots of other people came from Tawergha to Haysha when the Misratan soldiers came, and we thought that we were safe but we were not, because they arrested people and made everyone else from Tawergha leave Haysha. I did not think that was fair, but I was scared so I did not tell anyone.

'My uncle helped us to get here and I like it here. I love it because everyone here is close to everyone else. Everyone brings food to everyone else and because we know that the government is bringing things that we need to us so we feel happy about the government and I want to help the government.

'I come to this centre here every day and I love to learn and to take part in the activities here. I love to do acting and play football. But I also like to know lots of things so I work hard at learning. I love to read the Qur'an.

'My mother and father are not as happy as me. But I have been scared in Tawergha when NATO bombed us, and I was scared in Haysha when the Misratan people came and fired guns at us all.

'I am not scared here. I like to live here. I hope that I can get a job here and help the government when I am older.'

Two days after your visit, 20 members of the Misrata khetiba forced their way in to Janzour Camp. They killed six men, women and children, injuring others and taking teenage boys and men away with them, claiming they had 'arrested' them.

It was never revealed what 'crime' these young men, living in former naval cadet barracks, were supposed to have committed.

The Camp's armed guards had tried to stop the khetiba members entering, but were quickly overwhelmed.

The khetibas then placed guards at each exit and entrance point, and stormed the small living spaces of the Tawerghan families.

They opened fire as the homeless people protested against their actions, killing and injuring people regardless of age or sex.

One woman said: 'I tried to help my brother because he was shot in the head and neck. They then shot me in the leg.'

Fathi Bashaga, a member of Misrata's military council, perhaps with one eye on the khetiba's relations with the government following a strike on a guarded government safehouse for internal refugees, offered a not entirely convincing denial: 'There is no way Misratans were involved.'

But local people and Tawerghans at Janzour were in no doubt: 'They had Misratan accents, drove cars with Misratan plates and were here to arrest and hurt Tawerghans,' one Tripolitan said. 'Who else would it be but the Misrata khetiba?'

Your colleague sent you an e-mail: 'We knew that Misratans would come, and the government knew. And then they did come. Bashaga's denial is empty. It says nothing.

'This is how Libya is now. Scared people are helped by most of us, but those with the most guns and bullets will do as they please and then pretend they did not do anything. In Misrata, nobody is denying who did this. They know, and they are proud.'*

---

* *Things have still not improved for Tawerghans in Libya. In January 2014, thousands of Tawerghans were still housed in camps, including Janzour and Garyounis.*

They cannot return home, because the Misrata khetiba, the Libyan state's most powerful military organisation, and with the backing of the city's residents, simply refuses to accept that Tawergha even exists.

The Misratans have won: the ethnic cleansing of their small pocket of Libya has succeeded.

They have imprisoned more than 3,000 Tawerghans, none of whom have faced trial and almost all of whom are believed to have been tortured.

None have been charged, because who would risk charging the innocent? At that stage, the Tawerghans would have to be released, and the Misrata khetiba does not want that.

And the 24,000 who are not in prison and have not been killed are trapped in camps, unable to return to their ruined town because of the murder that lies in wait if they do, unable to accept that they will never be able to return, and unable to build a new life while the shadow of Misrata remains cast over them.

Tawerghans are Libyans, and remain in Libya. But they can never go home, because Misrata has renamed their ruined town 'New Tamini' and its khetibas stand guard to prevent their return.

As a result of the war crimes of one city, Tawerghans are Libya's landless, lost seemingly forever in their own land.

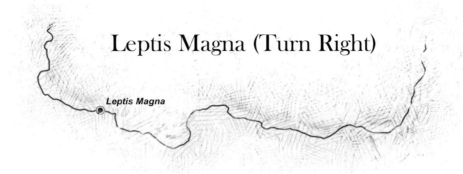

Leptis Magna (Turn Right)

Leptis Magna

I met a traveller from an antique land
Who said: 'Two vast and trunkless legs of stone
Stand in the desert...

On the vast Roman Road which links North Africa to the Classical and Mediaeval centres of European power and culture, there stands an impressive reminder of Libya's importance in the history of what is today known as 'Western' civilisation.

Although you had, before today, travelled almost the entire length of Libya's Mediterranean coast, using the vast highway which has for thousands of years carried soldiers, traders, farmers and slavers, you had never done what so many of those who came before you had done, and turned right.

Leptis Magna, one of the world's largest and best-preserved Roman ruins, sprawls, vast and imposing, 130km East of Tripoli, and 433km West of Sirte, the town you have early this morning left for the last time.

At one time, it was Africa's largest and finest city, greater than Libya's modern capital, whose name, which translates as 'three cities' is a reminder of Leptis Magna's vital past importance not only to the region, but the entire Roman Empire.

You walk through a car park, pass the small gift shop and walk towards the city itself. Leptis Magna had been a Berber and Phoenician town, then Carthaginian, before being taken over by the Romans. But it was not until 193AD, when one of its citizens rose to become Emperor of Rome, that it rose to international prominence.

Septimus Severus' capital was of course Rome itself, far vaster than Leptis and much better positioned to run the Empire. But he spent vast sums of time and money expanding and improving his birthplace, building theatres, public spaces and buildings, and developing its port, to improve its links to the European centres of power.

He made it, in reality, the 'capital' of Roman Africa, as well as one of the Classical World's greatest centres of business and trade – one of the six largest cities in the Empire. People from across the Empire worked and traded here, while Africans, at least those who could make it and were allowed in, came here to build reputations, trade links and maybe fortunes.

Having lived in Sirte, and learned a little of its recent history, it is hard for you not to draw comparison with Ghaddafi's project for the place of his birth, and attempt to create a 'capital' of Africa. Even further, perhaps, it is a comparison which could be drawn with all of 'Ghaddafi's' Libya. It certainly seems a comparison of which Ghaddafi was aware, and keen to draw attention.

The first Roman structure you come across, as you walk down the stony path towards the city and the Mediterranean beyond it, is a vast four-sided building – the Arch of Septimus Severus. Once the gateway at the entrance to the city, the arch would have been a centre of activity, where documents were produced and examined, and incoming visitors exchanged greetings with those leaving the city, to take to the Road and Morocco to the west, or Egypt, Byzantium, even Rome, to the east and north.

Today, you and your driver stand alone in the sculpture-covered structure, the silence all around you broken only by the sound of leaves rustling on the soft sea breeze.

Inside the arch, a stone-mounted sign added only three years before proclaims Ghaddafi's achievement in having Leptis Magna recognised as a UNESCO World Heritage site (in 1982), and commemorating its use for a son et lumiere performance in September 2009, part of a week-long celebration to mark the 40th anniversary of the revolution which toppled King Idris and made Ghaddafi Libya's leader.

Of course, gaining UNESCO recognition helped Ghaddafi present himself as a leader who was part of and connected to the wider world, but you cannot help wondering whether there was anything more to the dictator's deliberate evocation of Severus than simple power-play.

Your driver glances at the sign, smiling sadly, and shaking his head as he walks on. But you remain in the archway a little longer before following him down into the city.

...Near them, on the sand,
Half-sunk, a shattered visage lies, whose frown
And wrinkled lip, and sneer of cold command,
Tell that its sculptor well those passions read
Which yet survive, stamped on those lifeless things,
The hand that mocked them and the heart that fed.

The first thing that strikes you about Leptis Magna, as you wander down from the Arch of Severus, is its scale. The second is just how kind the weather and the march of time have been to it.

You are told that Pompeii is similarly well-preserved, but does not approach the sheer scale of this abandoned city: streets, temples, centres of trade, habitation and entertainment, all created from light stone, now bleached pale yellow and white by the sun, stretch almost out of sight, seemingly bound only by the sea to the North and the horizon to West and East.

Rome is of course far bigger. But its own Classical buildings are generally less intact, and are all, in any case, surrounded by more modern structures.

There is something remarkable about Rome's simultaneous ancient and modern city status, where business people enter offices in buildings around 2,000 years old. But in Leptis Magna, even allowing for the fact that its people, vehicles and animals are all now just figments of those who can imagine a past long left behind, you can feel you are actually in a Roman city, as designed and intended by its inhabitants and rulers.

Equally, it occurs to you that the devastation of Sirte, far younger yet bearing the marks of damage far more sharp and stark than where you now walk, further emphasises Leptis' remarkable condition in your mind.*

In fact, the Civil War came close to delivering devastation to Leptis in a way that more than 1,500 years abandoned to the elements had not.

Early in the conflict, Ghaddafi had claimed that the city was being bombed by NATO's planes – yet another false statement in the war of lies between Ghaddafi on the one side, and rebels and NATO on the other.

But NATO in fact specifically refused to rule out bombing the 3,000 year-old UNESCO World Heritage site, one of the greatest of the world's remaining Roman ruins, when the khetibas announced Ghaddafi was hiding missiles and military vehicles at the historic site.

Fortunately, lack of evidence – and perhaps lack of time – prevented NATO repeating in Libya its shameful activities in Iraq, where it destroyed ancient relics and buildings central to humanity's shared history and culture: in common with so many of the statements each side made about the other, the khetiba's claims were simply untrue.

You walk on paved streets, past walls, and columns in remarkable condition for a city uninhabited for almost 1,400 years. In many places, you can walk into the ground floor of structures still recognisable as houses, and walk down steps into cellars.

You pass circular, pillared buildings, one the city's former main market, others used for other business and entertainments, and to your right, closer to the sea, view vast storage warehouses.

And everywhere that you walk, past the city's Baths, and Roman toilets which remain in remarkable condition, you are reminded that this was a city once filled with people who thrived during one of the Western world's most famous, and arguably, for some at least, civilised periods.

Now, all is quiet. Even the breeze from the sea has died down, as you enter the circus, a vast open-air oval amphitheatre. Its steps face a raised platform where theatre or musical entertainments were staged. You climb and sit for a while, watching the sea, as small birds play in the pillars and columns. A short walk away is the forum, another large open space, this time rectangular, with high orange walls and lower down, part-ruined colonnades of arches.

At the top of each arch, where they are intact, large Gorgon faces, sculpted from white stone and with snakes instead of hair, are mounted.

This space was where politicians, philosophers, religious experts and others who felt they had something to say and needed an audience or an argument, gathered. No-one else is around, so you and your driver perch for a while, sharing cold rice and harissa, and slightly too warm Diet Cokes. Fittingly, though also predictably, since you and he have talked about little else since you met, he starts to talk about politics.

'I think we will need to have a right-wing government,' he says. 'Ghaddafi was left-wing and he was a bad leader and a bad politician. We must elect a government which will allow us to run businesses and not tax us.

'We need a good government to help us to become a good country.'

With Ghaddafi gone, most political conversations follow a line of debate similar to this: Ghaddafi was like this, so what we must do now is to have the opposite thing.

It is understandable. It is almost sensible.

And yet you can't help asking whether it is true.

The commonest problems – all justified, all good reasons to have removed him from power, and all to a greater or lesser extent true – which are levelled at Ghaddafi are as follows:

He favoured his tribe, and two which supported him, over all others. This was unfair.

But he was the member of a tribe, in a society based on tribal loyalty and which placed tribal obligation over state laws. Ghaddafi should have used his power to change that, but it is unlikely many others would have done so in his place.

He was a dictator; no-one had political representation in Ghaddafi's Libya.

But Ghaddafi was a military leader, who was welcomed when he took power from a King who had outlawed political parties. His own ideas of how a political state could run were never realised, perhaps through lack of desire on his part, but Ghaddafi was hardly the cause of a lack of popular representation in Libya, just its most recent manifestation.

He 'interfered' in the affairs of other states.

This is true. But he did not do so any more than the United States, UK, USSR or France during the period of his rule.

And in Chad, in the terrible 13-way War in the Democratic Republic of Congo, and in the spiralling chaos of Somalia, he was at least as arguably on the right side as any of his opponents, as he chose the democratically-elected ruler of each state, ahead of the armed insurgents who attempted to depose them: he chose the attacked-against, rather than the attacker.

In South Africa, too, he was on the 'right' side, supporting Mandela's ANC ahead of the apartheid state which oppressed the majority of its people.

The irony is not lost on you.

But if Ghaddafi was, as Ronald Reagan once put it 'A mad dog with designs on global domination', his designs often happened to coincide with acting in the interests of those facing aggression, rather than those who were the aggressors.

And Ghaddafi, unlike many other national leaders, also took steps to be part of the 'solution' to some of Africa's worst humanitarian and societal catastrophes.

He opened his borders to sub-Saharan Africa's discontented, desperate and unfree.

Hundreds of thousands of people – from Somalia, Eritrea, Ethiopia, Sudan, Chad and many other states – were granted citizenship by his regime (with perhaps a similar number 'passing through' en route to Europe), no small matter in a state containing a total of six million people (by comparison, Nick Clegg, the Deputy Prime Minister of the UK, a country of 62 million people, announced in 2013 that he had helped find space for less than 100 of Syrians fleeing a brutal three-year Civil War: the UN had asked the UK to take 30,000 of the 'most vulnerable' people).

He 'stole' money from the Libyan people and spent it on himself. Certainly true. But on the other hand, Ghaddafi's social policies saw Libyan quality of life rise to higher levels than that of most Middle Eastern oil-producers, let alone the African states to his west, east and south.

He used Libya's oil money for his own ends, and spent much of it on weapons to interfere in other states' affairs, but in 33 years he also helped Libya rise from a state where just one person in ten could read, to one in which almost nine in ten were literate, and in which life expectancy increased by 20 years on average, from 55-75.

He murdered people, tortured others, and without reason imprisoned others.

And that is it. Whatever the rights and wrongs of Ghaddafi's meddling internationally, spending Libyan oil money on himself, his family and his closest supporters, regardless of how many people he saved from torture or death in their own states, and regardless even of the ways in which his social programme helped millions of Libyans, he killed people, he tortured people, and he imprisoned people without reason.

Anything else is window-dressing.

That does not mean that smashing his country to pieces was the only possible – and certainly not the best – response (the images of his bloody face after he had been captured and shot on the outskirts of Sirte were described by some with glee as 'revenge' for crimes he had committed* and by others, with slightly more sensitivity, as 'grimly ironic'. But revenge is seldom a healthy political driving force, and irony is better served without shootings and blood – in any case, who now suffers as a result of the 'revenge' delivered to Ghaddafi?).

* *The Sun, a UK tabloid newspaper, brought news of Ghaddafi's death to its readers with a full, front page close up of his bloody face, and the headline: 'That's for Lockerbie'.*

Exactly how grateful the grieving relatives of those killed in a terror attack on an aircraft over Scotland were to The Sun, a newspaper which had falsely smeared the names and reputations of 96 football fans crushed to death in the UK's largest football stadium disaster, has not yet been definitively ascertained.

But equally, anything good, or even indifferent, achieved by Ghaddafi, is immediately wiped out by his record of tyranny. A murderer does not become innocent because they open a clinic.

You worry about Ghaddafi's legacy in more than one way, though. What he achieved for Libyan's 'quality of life' should not be lost, and to claim that his cruelty and indifference to human life were because he was 'left wing' seem to you to be a major threat to those achievements.

Being right-wing did not prevent Hitler, Pinochet or Franco from mass murder, and neither did it prevent the George W Bush administration in the US from opening and operating a torture factory at Guantanamo Bay (yet even today, only Africans have been tried by the International Criminal Court).

Neither the Left nor the Right says murder is acceptable: people, not ideology, do that.

Your driver nudges you, smiling.

'I would miss the hospitals and schools', he says, and begins to laugh.

You smile, and walk with him towards the end of the Forum. As you turn right at the 'exit', part of one Gorgon face, half buried in the sandy soil, looks up at you. Thanks to the way the shadows are cast by the arches, and the way the plants have grown up around it, from where you stand, it appears to be sneering. And on the pedestal these words appear –

"My name is Ozymandias, king of kings:
Look on my works, ye mighty, and despair!"

Immediately after the 9/11 terrorist attacks, it became clear to the more intelligent, and (slightly) less war-like members of the Bush administration that if Al-Qaeda could not be immediately defeated, it must be denied bases and places in which to thrive.

Though neo-liberal ideology actively prevents the kind of economic regulation which could have actively lifted the world's poorest, least powerful people – those most likely to be won over to radical, violent direct action against those they believe 'oppress them' – from poverty, there was at least some understanding that something had to be done.

It became clear very early on that wherever western states could 'reach out to' secular Arab and/or 'moderate' Muslim nations, this should be done, as to strengthen their regimes could severely lessen the chance that extremists and terrorists would grow in power in those places.

And so, in 2004, as a symbolic gesture of international rapprochement, Tony Blair visited and shook hands with Muammar Ghaddafi. It cannot be said that the moment really did either leader many favours. Having cheered – and then literally led – wars against Muslim states, Blair did not win plaudits by shaking one man's hand. And in the UK, where attitudes towards Libya and Ghaddafi in particular were soaked in negativity, it actually lost him popularity.

In Libya, the handshake was greeted more equably; this was part of a sequence which had already seen US sanctions against the state dropped after 17 years, and seemed to signify new opportunities for its people (those who oppose Blair's policies in the UK may counter that not everything was so positive. Ghaddafi was inspired by the meeting to open Academy Schools, for example).

And in international relations terms, the gesture seemed weighted with its own potential: perhaps the international community could use positive rather than negative measures to encourage states to act in a benevolent, rational, fashion – assisting and rewarding rather than warning and then raining death from above.

Less than a decade later, however, with Blair out of office in the UK, now bringing his direct experience of long, bitter warfare in remote locations (much of which was designed and delivered by his own hand) to bear on the Arab/Israeli peace process, NATO unleashed its weapons of shock and awe on Libya.

Ghaddafi is dead, and much of Libya in ruins.

Walking back through the remains of Leptis Magna (the buildings' once-jagged edges, now softened by plants and centuries of erosion, inspire you to think of Sirte viewed through a time and nature filter) – you recall the story of Leptis' demise.

In 439, the Vandals swept into north Africa, capturing Carthage, Tripoli, Leptis Magna and much of the rest of the African Roman Empire.

The Vandal leader Gaiseric, who had become the new King of the region, ordered Leptis' defensive walls dismantled, to discourage the city from attempting to stand against him.

But the now defenceless city was also vulnerable to attack from outside, and in 523, it fell once again, this time to a wave of Berber 'liberationists', attempting to purge their region of a ruler they did not want, and felt benefited them little.

It was the beginning of the end. Ten years later, the Byzantines seized the city, claiming it as a provincial capital of the Eastern Roman Empire, but it was never to recover: when, a century later, Arab Muslims arrived, fired with zeal to spread the messages of their new faith, nothing more than a small Byzantine garrison remained.

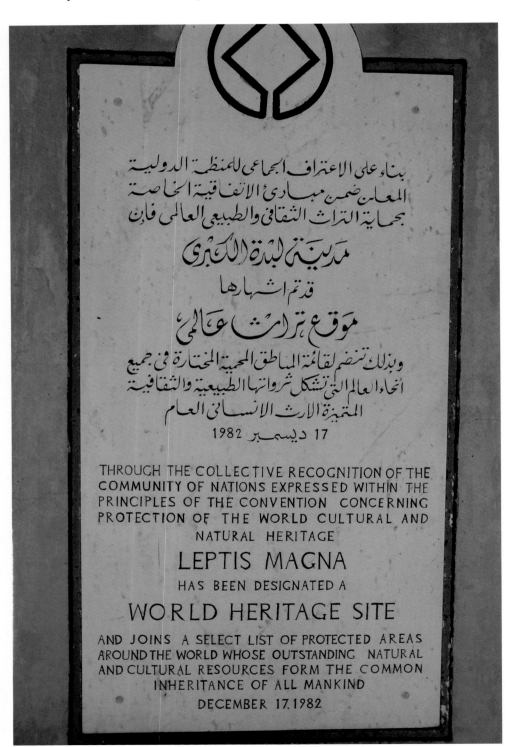

THROUGH THE COLLECTIVE RECOGNITION OF THE
COMMUNITY OF NATIONS EXPRESSED WITHIN THE
PRINCIPLES OF THE CONVENTION CONCERNING
PROTECTION OF THE WORLD CULTURAL AND
NATURAL HERITAGE

LEPTIS MAGNA

HAS BEEN DESIGNATED A

WORLD HERITAGE SITE

AND JOINS A SELECT LIST OF PROTECTED AREAS
AROUND THE WORLD WHOSE OUTSTANDING NATURAL
AND CULTURAL RESOURCES FORM THE COMMON
INHERITANCE OF ALL MANKIND

DECEMBER 17.1982

You know that Sirte, whose people are striving to rebuild their lives, should escape this fate.

But you cannot help comparing the enforced lowering of Leptis' walls with the enforced no-fly zone which Libya recognised and NATO did not.

You cannot stop yourself comparing the invasion of Berbers in the post-Roman years, of a city developed by a man who was born there, with the invasion by Berbers in 2011 of a city developed by a man who was born there.

Sirte is not Leptis Magna. You are sure that its people will not be defeated by the disaster rained upon them from the UK, France and the US, any more than the whole of Libya will be defeated by the War it fought to rid itself of Ghaddafi.

But there are more questions than answers in the 'new', 'free' Libya. And you fear that those who have reduced parts of the state to rubble have returned home, patting one another on the back and raising glasses as if their role is over.

A vacuum exists in Libya today. You do not know what can fill it.

Perhaps nothing will.

Nothing beside remains. Round the decay
Of that colossal wreck, boundless and bare
The lone and level sands stretch far away.'

You know that 'lone and level sands' are not all that remain in Libya.

But you have reached the end, for now, of your life in the North African state. And you wonder, with regret, at the things that might happen next, which you may not be able to see.

You walk, with your driver, back through the ruins of a city once envied by much of the world, and which now few are even aware of, towards the pick-up, the Roman Road, the airport and eventually, home.

The Toss of a Coin
Part Four: The Toss of a Coin

I have been here at Choucha Camp since the end of March 2011. Now it is November 2011. I do not know what will happen to me.

My wife has left and I will not see her again.

When we had been here only a short while, her uncle came. We were very happy. He said he had come to take her home so we prepared to leave with him, but he said to me: 'Not you. I am here only to take her home. You cannot come. I will not take you. You are not our family and I want you to leave her alone and stay here.'

I was very sad. I asked her what I could do and she said 'stay here'. Her uncle said I had to divorce her. I looked at her and she said 'divorce me'. I was very sad. I cried a little bit, but I said I would divorce her because that is what she wanted and I loved her.

And then she left. I know why she left. She did not have to be here. She had family and she had a place to go to. But I had none of those things. No family, no friends and no place to go to. I loved her, but I also think that I hated her a little because she knew that and she left me and made me divorce her.

She went to Libya. I did not see her again and I never will. It makes me sad but she chose that.

While I have lived here, I have helped with the children who are here too. I cannot teach them anything about education because I did not really go to school. But I have been teaching them Tae Kwan-Do and I play sports with them. It is good because this is not a good place to be if you are a child and it is good to see them smile, and to help them to smile.

I also met my uncle here.

It was a strange thing. One evening a man came to me and he told me my name and told me I had lost people 14 years ago. I did not know what to do.

He told me my grandfather's name and he said he was my father's brother. I hugged him and we talked. He said he had tried to find his brother, and my mother, brothers and sisters, but he never had found them. He showed me photos of my father and mother. I had not seen them for a very long time. But it was them. I cried a lot.

He told me my grandfather was trying to come to Libya, the same way I had come, by lorry from Sudan. So, we sent money and we waited for him.

But a few weeks later, people in the camp who also hoped their friends and family would come by lorry told us that he had died, because the lorry broke and was not found in time. We were sad, but at least I had an uncle. Before I had no family.

My uncle then said he was trying to get us papers to go to Kenya, from UNHCR who are in charge of this camp. I think Kenya would have been good to live in. I still wanted to go to Norway or England, but Kenya would have been a good place to live, if my uncle was there, too. But then one day he said it was taking too long, and we would not get the papers at all. That is what he thought, so he said we should get a boat and cross the ocean. The next day he said he had found out a boat was leaving and he had got a place. 'Only one place?', I asked. And he said: 'Yes. Only one of us can go, but the other one will send money back and so we can be together again.'

He had a coin. I looked at it for a long time. I called the side it would land on and we watched it as he flipped it up and it landed on the table under his hand. He looked at me and he pulled his hand away. I had lost.

'Please don't leave me here', I said. 'I will be here all alone. I will be so alone. I had no family, now I have an uncle and I do not want to lose my family again.'

But he said: 'It will be alright. I will cross the ocean and go to Italy. I will get a job and I will send you money. I will wait for you and when you come to Italy we will work and we will get to Norway or England.'

He left, and I was here in the camp. It was dark, and I was alone. I did not feel so alone before as I did then. I waited for him to call, because he had said he would get a mobile phone and he did call a friend at the camp who had a telephone. He told me he would get on the boat the next night and that he had met my wife and she was on the same boat and she had a plan to see me when I crossed the ocean.

I waited for two days to see if there would be a call. I waited two more days, then two more days, then on the next day, a man came to me and said that the boat his son was on had sunk in the ocean and that they were too far to be rescued. He said everyone had drowned.

I told him I was sorry and he said he was sorry too.

I looked at him again. He said: 'Your friend was on the boat.' He meant my uncle. He did not say anything about my wife. I do not think he knew her.

I chose a side of the coin and I lost.

And because I lost my uncle died and my wife is dead, and I am here alive. I do not know what to say about that.

Here at the camp, I help with the children. It helps me to feel happy and I hope helping other people will be a good future for me. I still hope I can live in Norway or in England and I hope I can help children and make them smile. I can teach them Tae Kwan-Do.

All the people here have a hard life. And their life before was hard. But we hope it will be better after this.

Sometimes I think about my home. There are other people from Ogaden here. But we have been told we cannot go back there. I do not know why. Nobody has told us why.

I still have the coins. The first one I earned and the one which landed on the wrong side, so I did not cross the ocean and I am still alive.

I will always keep them.

POSTSCRIPT

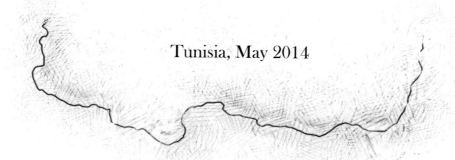

Tunisia, May 2014

Choucha

There is, officially, no longer a Choucha refugee camp.

This is not to say that where the unhappy tent-city once stood, white-ish above golden sand and beneath blue sky, now only desert stretches south from the Roman Road: just that according to its former operator, the camp no longer exists.

UNHCR declared Choucha closed in July 2013. But its tents still stand, testament not only to the thousands who lived here, lives on pause, while awaiting the international community to decide their fate, but also those who have been left behind, forgotten, while the world's focus is directed elsewhere.

Today, 90 people live in those tents, without electricity, water or food, and reliant on the kindness of the nearby residents of Ben Guardane, whose previous relationship with the camp has developed, today, into sympathy for those left behind.

None of the 90 grew up with a strange dream to exist in almost solitude, on the border of civilisation where only the generosity of strangers saves them from death. But they cannot go anywhere else. Denied refugee status, usually without explanation, they cannot simply go 'home' to Sudan, Niger, Somalia, because what awaits them there is death.

They have no papers, no permission to travel, and no money to do so, even if they had.

When asked by Al-Jazeera about the fate of the 90 who remain, UNHCR issued a statement.

Houda Chouchal, the head of UNHCR's protection department in Tunisia, said: 'Choucha doesn't exist anymore. That's our press line and it's not going to change.'

And so 90 people are stranded, in tents, in an unforgiving desert, lives still on pause, as they have been now since February 2011.

In November 2014, 90 people have been left to die in tents which have stood for close to three years.

Tunisia:
The State of Things to Come

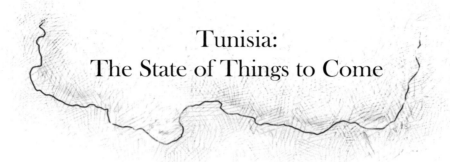

Even those at Choucha who had been found new places to live were not always content.

In April 2013, seven hunger-strikers, who had attempted to reach Tunis to take their complaints to the national government, were hospitalised.

They and 34 fellow hunger-strikers had been angered that instead of repatriation overseas, like thousands of fellow refugees who had left Choucha for Canada, the USA, Turkey, Jordan, Germany, France, the UK, Switzerland, Qatar, Norway or any number of other states, they were to become 'naturalised Tunisians'.*

This idea in itself would have been remarkable in 2011, when – perhaps with an eye on Ben Guardanian pressures and concerns – the Tunisian government had said its priority regarding Choucha was swift repatriation of refugees.

At the time – even though they were likely to be safer in Tunisia than either Libya or the sub-Saharan African states from which they had originally escaped – it was possible to understand some of their misgivings.

On 6th February 2013, Left-wing politician Chokri Belaid,* an Opposition member of Tunisia's legislature, the National Constituent Assembly (ANC), had been shot outside his Tunis home.

Belaid, a 48 year-old lawyer, had served as part of the legal team which defended Iraq's former President Saddam Hussein during his trial for crimes against humanity. He was a pan-Arabist, an outspoken critic of Ben Ali but also of Islamic fundamentalism. He was co-ordinator of the Democratic Patriots' Movement, which had one seat at the ANC.

Only the night before, he had spoken in the ANC, claiming that: 'All those who oppose Ennahda* become the targets of violence.'

Despite fierce criticism and scepticism from secular politicians, Ennahda describes itself as a moderate Islamic political organisation.

It won 1.5m votes in Tunisia's first ANC elections in October 2011, giving it 89 of the 217 seats in the legislative chamber. By comparison, the next largest party, the Congress for the Republic (CPR), a left-wing, secularist party, took 353,041 votes, and 29 seats. Just over four million valid votes were cast.

Ennahda immediately formed a government in coalition with the CPR and the next largest party Ettakatol, (284,989 votes, 20 seats), another social-democratic secular party (election turnout was 51 per cent, with 1.29m votes taken by Independents, standing for seats which were not allowed to be held by Party politicians).

In the arrangement, the Ettakatol Secretary General Mustapha Ben Jafar, with Ennahda and CPR support, was elected Speaker of Parliament, CPR's leader Moncef Marzouki was made interim President of the Republic and in turn, Marzouki appointed Ennahda's Secretary General Hamadi Jebali Prime Minister.

The assassination sparked protests in cities across Tunisia, with police using tear gas to disperse a large group which gathered outside the state's Interior Ministry building in Tunis. Ennahda's offices in El Kel and Mezzouna were burned to the ground, and in Gafsa, demonstrators broke into its office and ransacked it.

Ennahda's Secretary General, Tunisian Prime Minister Hamadi Jebali, described the murder as 'the assassination of the Tunisian revolution' and said he would create a caretaker government made up of technocrats, to govern until a new election could be held.

But the announcement was not enough to calm anger at the killing. On 8th February, the BBC estimated that more than one million people attended Belaid's funeral, and police battled protestors on Tunis' streets once again.

Ennahda, which in a statement issued on behalf of the whole party described Belaid's killing as a 'heinous crime' and criticised the killers as deliberately endangering the stability and security of Tunisia, blocked Jebali's attempts to create a government of technocrats.

Having won the 2011 election, and formed what it considered to be a centrist, moderate Islamic government, the Party's members were reluctant to hand over power to a technocratic regime, voting instead to retain a 'government of politicians'.

As a result, Jebali* resigned on 19th February 2013. He said: 'I promised if my initiative did not succeed I would resign as head of government. Today there is great disappointment among the people and we must regain their trust. This resignation is a first step.'

* Part of Ennahda's reformist wing, Jebali had been jailed by the Ben Ali regime for 'armed overthrow' despite arguing that he had known nothing of the alleged attempt to overthrow Tunisia's leader for which he had been arrested.

He was sentenced on 28th August 1992 to 16 years' imprisonment after a trial Human Rights Watch, the Lawyers' Committee for Human Rights and Amnesty International described as 'unfair'. The latter group also named Jebali a 'prisoner of conscience'.

He spent more than ten of the 14 years he served in solitary confinement, and undertook several hunger strikes against his treatment, two of which were reported to have lasted more than 36 days each.

He was eventually released in February 2006, on the 50th anniversary of Tunisian independence.

Two months before the assassination, the Ennahda-led Assembly had missed the deadline by which it was supposed to deliver a new constitution for Tunisia – a document which was supposed to lay the foundations for a new model of public participation in politics in the state.

And five months on, on 25th July, with a constitution no closer to being produced, another Left-wing, Arab nationalist member of the Assembly, Mohamed Brahmi, was shot dead.

Brahmi, 58, had founded the Nasserist Unionist Movement in 2005, which was declared illegal by the Ben Ali regime. He led the People's Movement – part of the same anti-Islamist Popular Front coalition to which Chokri Belaid's Democratic Patriots' Movement also belonged. The People's Movement had two seats at the ANC, having taken 30,500 votes, in October 2011.

He was shot 14 times outside his home in Ariana, Tunis, in front of his wife and children.

Though he belonged to the same coalition as Chokri Belaid, Brahmi was not a vocal critic of Ennahda, and in fact had several friends within the party.

But critics of Ennahda once again claimed the Party was responsible for the assassination, or allied to those who were.

Although there is no evidence that Ennahda played any part whatsoever in the killings (Tunisian authorities say the same gun killed both men and wish to question Boubacar Hakim, a Salafist* jihadist also believed to have smuggled weapons into Tunisia from Libya), the murder was almost enough to topple Tunisia's government.

* Salafist Muslims are part of the Sunni branch of Islam and take their name from the Arab word 'Salaf', meaning 'ancestors'. They believe that the purest form of Islam was that practised by the earliest Muslims (Mohammed once said: 'Those of my generation are best, then those who come after them, then those of the next generation.'). They are often associated, or confused, with Wahhabits – the sect to which Osama Bin Laden belonged, but in fact Salafis believe the term Wahhabi is insulting to them.

As an undeniably fundamentalist Islamic group, with some extremist members who claim that violent warfare against civilians is an acceptable act if performed to spread Islam, the word 'Salafi' or 'Salafist' is used by some Western commentators as if it were interchangeable with 'terrorist'.

But Salafist scholars and community leaders condemn the use of acts of violence, so Hakim is more accurately described as a 'Salafist jihadist'.

In Egypt, a Salafist political party, the Al-Nour, took 27.8 per cent of the vote, and 127 of the 498 available seats, in the parliamentary elections of 2011-12. Like the Muslim Brotherhood, whose Freedom and Justice Party took 235 seats in the same election, Al-Nour campaigned for an Islamic state including forcing all Muslim citizens to distribute alms.

Unlike the Brotherhood, Al-Nour refuses the right of women or Christians to hold political office, and takes an antagonistic position against Iran, based on the latter state's Shia Islamic leanings.

At Brahmi's funeral, thousands of protestors were again involved in street battles against police, in which the authorities used tear gas against the demonstrators. And 60 politicians withdrew from the ANC and staged a sit-in outside its Tunis headquarters, demanding the end of Ennahda's government.

By 6th August, the ANC had been suspended.

An outspoken, but small, protest group, Tamaroud, connected to an Egyptian group of the same name which had played a part in organising protests against the democratically-elected Muslim Brotherhood* in its own country, and paved the way for the repressive military dictatorship which replaced it, demanded that the ANC should be immediately dissolved.

The Muslim Brotherhood, which had already won 235 seats in the new Egyptian Parliament, also saw its candidate, Mohamed Morsi, elected President in 2012, with 51.73 per cent of the vote.

The Party had been illegal under the rule of Egyptian dictator Hosni Mubarak, and its rise to power was to prove the catalyst for a military coup which seems set to shape Egyptian politics for the next decade at least.

The Brotherhood intended to create an Islamic state, but did offer the opportunity for other political organisations to join it in government, to help draft a new Egyptian constitution. All refused.

The party passed some restrictive laws, including one making it illegal for a Christian or a woman to hold the office of President (though in doing so, it also alienated Islamic extremists, who had campaigned to prevent women or Christians holding any political office: instead, the Brotherhood insisted Christians and women must be able to hold any political office other than President: it is uncertain why the line was drawn where it was).

But there is little doubt that much of the opposition to the Brotherhood was politically – rather than socially – based. Political opponents, moderate Muslims, Christians and Liberals, gathered against Morsi, despite few sharing many views with one another.

The groups had some legitimate concerns: in late November 2012, Morsi had granted himself the temporary ability to legislate without judicial oversight, claiming he had to safeguard Egypt's new political system against a return of Mubarak-style dictatorship.

Unrest rose through the winter, and in April, when a series of fuel shortages and electricity outages struck across the state (the Brotherhood claimed to have evidence showing they were caused by supporters of the Mubarak regime), national demonstrations began.

Millions of Egyptians were reported to have taken part in the protests, which should have been the end of the Brotherhood's regime, though many thousands – reported by some media as millions – also marched in support of the President.

Unfortunately, the Brotherhood actually fell on 3rd July 2013, at the hands of Egypt's army, which claimed to be acting because Mohamed Morsi had 'unconstitutionally' attempted to change the law, by proposing to enable a sitting President to hold office for more than one electoral term.

In fact, Morsi had suggested the move, but withdrew the proposal in the face of parliamentary opposition.

The army, with depressing predictability, declared a month-long 'state of emergency' (even though it had been in power for more than a month already) which it used to raid Brotherhood premises, and to crush a pro-Morsi protest in Rabaa al-Adawiya square. More than 1,000 people were killed and 4,000 injured – the highest death and casualty count in Egypt's modern history.

The army arrested thousands of Brotherhood members, including its Supreme Leader Mohammed Badie – a step even Mubarak had never taken – and pushed for the group to be outlawed and its assets seized, a right granted by the courts on 23rd September 2013.

On 21st December, a car bomb attack which destroyed a police station and killed 14 people in Mansoura, inspired the government to declare that the Brotherhood was now officially a terrorist organisation. Remarkably, even when the terror group Ansar Bait al-Maqdis claimed responsibility for the bombing, the government refused to change its opinion, preferring instead to castigate the Brotherhood for the deaths.

UK Prime Minister David Cameron, at the prompting of the Egyptian coup leaders, promised to 'investigate' the Muslim Brotherhood in the UK.

Though his exact aims in announcing such an investigation remain unclear, it will be interesting to see how an investigation into a democratically-elected minority government which survived mass protest and then fell to a brutal military coup will be played out by a minority government which inspired riots in its major cities but remained in power.

In Egypt, General al-Sisi, whose armed forces seized power, and have smashed the government by force of arms, won a national election to remain President on 29th May 2014. Just 47.5 per cent of the population voted, even though Sisi had declared an extra day of voting, made the extra day a national holiday and threatened to fine anyone who did not vote.

He took a credibility-stretching 96.1 per cent of the votes cast, according to Egyptian government sources.

In Tunisia, the Tamaroud's concerns were different,* but also won less popular support.

* The Tamaroud in Tunisia expressed pleasure at what its 'sister' organisation in Egypt had achieved, but also admitted it had 'some reservations' about the new regime.

In part, this was perhaps because Ennahda in Tunisia had succeeded where the Muslim Brotherhood in Egypt had failed, and created a genuine coalition government.

Many people could support the Tamaroud's demands for the formation of a new government, the disbandment of the unpopular armed 'revolution protection committees' (which were similar to, but less powerful than, the Libyan khetibas) and the revelation of who had committed the assassinations of Belaid and Brahmi.

But few seriously wanted the ANC to be dissolved, or believed that the CPR leader, renowned and respected protector of human rights and President of Tunisia, Moncef Marzouki had become a 'blind ally of the Islamists' who must be deposed for the good of Tunisia, as the Tamaroud demanded after Brahmi's murder.

Ennahda members in fact did a convincing job of showing Tunisians that although they were generally opposed and criticised by secular politicians, they were little – if at all – more popular with the state's small Islamic extremist groups. But even though the Party could probably have survived the protests of summer 2013, it also recognised Tunisia's wider problems.

In 2011, a 13 per cent unemployment figure had been a major factor in the revolution against Ben Ali. By June 2013, it had risen to 16.5 per cent. Inflation had steadied at the high rate of 6.5 per cent, threatening once again to price food and other basics out of the reach of ordinary Tunisians. Youth unemployment, a major spark in each of the so-called 'Arab Spring' revolutions, was far worse at almost 32 per cent. Almost one in three young people was set to leave school or University with no prospect of finding employment.

In the centre, South and East of Tunisia, in towns such as Maknassy, and Sidi Bouzid, where the revolution in Tunisia began (and where Brahmi was born and had grown up), residents felt neglected, some claiming that the government served them no better than Ben Ali had done.

To make matters worse, a Transparency International poll, issued in July 2013, suggested that 80 per cent of Tunisians believed their country was more, not less, corrupt than it had been in 2010.

In short, it was small wonder that sub-Saharan Africans, having escaped war in their own land, then in Libya, and then having lived for more than two years in tents on the northernmost edge of the Sahara desert did not look forward to attempting to carve out a life in an economically-struggling Tunisia.

By no means all of these problems could be laid at the door of Ennahda, and neither did the party intend to shoulder all the blame. In the wake of Brahmi's assassination, Tunisia's new Prime Minister and Ennahda member Ali Larayedh urged the ANC to 'hurry and finish the constitution quickly'.

He had a point, though of course his party was the biggest single political entity in the ANC.

The constitution was by this point eight months late, and the country could not expect to recover from deposing Ben Ali without the political certainty such a document promised, especially after two major crises sparked by the murder of politicians in its capital city.

And unlike its eastern neighbour Libya, a significant part of Tunisia's economy is based on tourism, which had been severely damaged in the wake of the revolution.

In 2013, 6.5 million mainly French and Eastern European tourists visited Tunisia, still 15 per cent less than the 2010 figure.

One Ennahda member, International spokeswoman Yusra Ghannouchi, revealed she shared common ground with UK Chancellor George Osborne when she told the BBC, also in the summer of 2013, that as well as 'having to take into account the decades of injustice, oppression and instability we have inherited', part of Tunisia's economic difficulty was due to 'the economic crisis that is affecting Europe – Tunisia's main economic partner'. (Tunisia entered into an EU Association Agreement in 1998)

Ennahda only restarted the Tunisian government, and the drafting of the nation's constitution, with an announcement by Larayedh that he would step down as PM in advance of an election to be held on 17th December.

Although the date of the election was later pushed back to late 2014, on 14th December, Larayedh did announce his retirement, and that he would be replaced as Prime Minister by Independent technocrat Mehdi Jomaa.

One of Larayedh's last duties as Tunisian Prime Minister, alongside Marzouki and speaker Ben Jaafar, was to sign the new Tunisian constitution, on 27th January 2014.

It was by now 12 months overdue.

But when it arrived, three years and 23 days after trader Tarek al-Tayeb Mohamed Bouazizi's self-immolation outside the local governor's office in his hometown of Sidi Bouzid, setting in process uprisings not only in Tunisia but across the Maghreb and beyond, the constitution was internationally praised for its forward-thinking, progressive commitments.

So much so, in fact, that even those who noted its lateness conceded that the wait may have helped to make it a better document.

Amira Yahyaoui, of Tunisian independent political monitoring group Bawsala, told the Guardian newspaper: 'Writing this constitution to really transform the minds of the people needed time, and I absolutely don't regret those two years. I am happy we had time to discuss and think about the arguments.'

The constitution declares Tunisia a secular democratic state, with laws not based on Islam.

Though Islam remains the nation's official religion, the constitution guarantees specific rights of 'freedom of belief and conscience', meaning any citizen must be allowed to follow any religion – or none. It also protects those who speak out against any religion, including Islam, from violence or repression.

But the constitution, which was approved by 200 votes to 16 in the ANC, goes further than the granting of religious freedom.

Tunisia is now only the third state in the world to specifically commit to protect the environment from damage and combat climate change: 'Contribution to a sound climate and the right to a sound and balanced environment shall be guaranteed. The state shall provide the necessary means to eliminate environmental pollution.'

It also guarantees the 'conservation and rational use of water' as a state responsibility.

The state now promises to provide healthcare for all: 'Health is a right for every person. The state shall guarantee preventative health care and treatment for every citizen and provide the means necessary to ensure the safety and good quality of health services. It will provide free health care for those without support and those with limited income.'

On women's rights, uniquely in the Arab world (though ironically a similar approach had been taken by Libya), and unusually for any state in the world, the constitution is explicitly progressive: 'The state shall commit to protecting women's achieved rights and seek to support and develop them. The state shall guarantee equal opportunities between men and women in the bearing of all the various responsibilities in all fields.'

It also commits to balance the number of men and women serving in elected councils, and adds: 'The state shall take the necessary measures to eliminate violence against women.'

Ms Yahyaoui added: 'This is the real revolution. Many democratic constitutions do not even have guarantees of equality between men and women and a commitment by the state to protect women's rights, as ours does. It will have a real impact on the rest of the Arab world, because finally we can say that women's rights are not a western concept only, but also exist in Tunisia.'

Workers' rights are also guaranteed, including the right for all workers to join unions, and for all except members of the army and security services to strike, so long as they reject violence and abide by the law, and the constitution once again goes further than most others across the world, stating that: 'All citizens, male and female, shall have the right to adequate working conditions and a fair wage.'

The UN General Secretary Ban Ki-moon said: 'Tunisia can be a model to other peoples who are seeking reforms.'

I was in the UK when the Constitution was signed, and first became aware of it, while writing an earlier chapter of this book, when friends of mine in Tunisia began to post celebratory updates on facebook and twitter. I saw my Libyan friends – and other westerners I had met – post congratulations to them. I did so myself, thinking at first that the delighted nature of the posts reflected relief, as much as anything, that a document finally existed which would enable Tunisia to take its next steps forward as a state. But as I read the constitution, I realised the celebrations were something more: that they recognised just how remarkable a piece of statecraft the document is, and that it lays the foundations for the small North African nation not just to take a place, but a leading role in regional and international political affairs.

Tunisia's struggle is not over.

Unemployment is high, with youth joblessness at levels which threaten to create an entire 'lost generation' of Tunisian young people, and inflation at the current rate could yet, by threatening people's ability to purchase food, outweigh any constitutional guarantee of rights.

But the state has emerged from decades of dictatorship, a revolution inspired by suicide, political bickering and terrorist activity within its borders.

And if a constitution can be seen as a guide, a go-to document to be used to remind a people and its representatives of the fundamental ideas and ideals which unite them and to illuminate the state's forward travel, then although Tunisia's was two years in the making, it is a reliable and inspirational support to one of the world's newest democracies.

Election, 26th October 2014

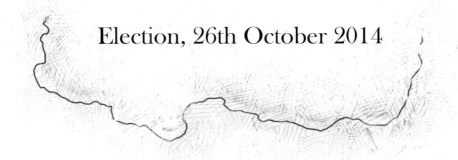

The results of Tunisia's second elections were announced on 30th October. Almost 3.6m people voted – a 69 per cent turnout (though some 80 per cent of 18-25 year-olds did not vote) – in a peaceful and fair ballot.

They handed most seats – 86 of the 217 in the Assembly of the Representatives of the People – to Nidaa Tounes, a party led by Beji Caid Essebsi, an 87 year-old former foreign minister and parliament speaker for the deposed dictator Ben Ali. Its other members include politicians from the dictator's regime, as well as businessmen and leading trades unionists.

Ennahda, the democratic Islamist previous party of government, finished second with 69 seats, having taken just over 947,000 votes.

The next three most popular parties, the 'business-focussed' Free Patriotic Union, the left-wing Popular Front and the centre-right secularist Afek Tounes party, took 16, 15 and eight seats respectively.

And so Tunisia's second election left no outright party of government, a worryingly low turnout among young voters, and a party of Opposition who some observers – perhaps inspired to fear by the word 'Islamist' – speculated might react violently to losing the popular vote.

But Ennahda's record to date has not been one of inspiring, encouraging, or carrying out, violent acts: in common with its Muslim Brotherhood equivalents in Libya and Egypt, it has entered its state's new system with enthusiasm, presenting its views to the public and accepting the response those views have received.

This time, its campaign was centred on 'change'. Against a backdrop of joblessness, a sluggish economy and continuing incidents of terror enacted by extremist Muslim groups and individuals, this was understandable.

But Ennahda was also changing internally, and in the end this process, unfinished and therefore confusing and discouraging to some voters, appears to have been enough to prevent it presenting itself as a viable government.

In the months before the election, the Party had altered its internal systems, so that Party members could suggest and vote for new policies, and its regional branches could choose candidates for the Assembly.

This was in direct contradiction to Nidaa Tounes, which is run by a small central executive of Ben Ali-era politicians and others who rose to prominence during the dictator's years in power.

Ennahda and Nidaa Tounes also differed on how the nation should be governed. The democratic Islamic Party's Leader Rachid Ghannouchi confirmed Ennahda wished to enter a coalition with opponents, including Left-Wingers and secularists.

He said: 'We hold tight to politics geared around consensus. We cannot govern with a majority of 51 per cent. That would be enough in a stable democracy, but we are in transition.'

He added that he hoped Tunisia could be an example to the world of a tolerant, moderate, democratic Islamic system.

If some voters found Ennahda's campaign confusing and unclear, Nidaa Tounes offered a simpler outlook, though one which was equally vague about its policies and plans for Tunisia's future.

Like the Christian Democrats in Italy (a party which also contained large numbers of members who had served as part of a dictator's regime), Nidaa Tounes defined itself by what it was not – religious, or Ennahda – rather than by what it was.

And like the Italian Party, which despite being Centre-Right served in coalitions with Socialists in order to prevent its major opponents – Italy's Communist party – from taking power, Nidaa Tounes was also clear that it would enter coalition with any Party except Ennahda.

Though many smaller parties offered clear policies and intentions, in the end the majority of voters sided either with a religious party which promised 'change' within and 'consensus' without, or a secular party made up of former Ben Ali acolytes which defined itself by what it was not, rather than by what it was.

It is not, perhaps, the ideal scenario. But the proof of Tunisia's success as a democratic state will not be the names of its politicians, or the ideas for which they claim to stand. And it will certainly not be the opinions held of those people or their ideas by outside observers, but the ability of Tunisians to choose who represents them in parliament.

And as everywhere else, the proof of Tunisian governments' success will be whether they manage to deliver a decent standard of living – in which economic comfort and human rights are provided and protected – to the Tunisian people.

Tunisia in 2014 still faces many of the problems it faced in early 2011: economic stagnation causing high unemployment (particularly among young people – a major reason why four-fifths of 18-25 year-olds in Tunisia did not vote in the second national election in the country's history) and significant levels of poverty; dissatisfaction with its political leaders, and justified impatience for matters to improve: for the revolution to deliver for the state and its people.

And to this can be added the new fear of religious insurgence and assassination. But it can still call on significant strengths. Its government has, so far, the approval of the public. The national Opposition has proven by any reasonable criteria to be reliable, committed to the democratic system, and eager and able to behave as a responsible, peaceful political organisation. And perhaps most importantly, Tunisia can rely upon its constitution – the single outstanding achievement of the North African state since its revolution sparked the feted, but elsewhere stumbling, 'Arab Spring' – and a document which could also serve as an inspirational guide for far older, longer-established democratic states.

It is the constitution, as much as anything else, which is the reason to believe the words of the former dance teacher who worked at Choucha Refugee Camp:

'I do not think we will go back to how it was before. We do not want to.

'We will stay with this system and make choices for ourselves.

'If we sometimes get it wrong at first, that is OK.

'We will keep trying, and our lives will be better.

'It is our first time, and we will get it right.'

Libya, 2014

A St Valentine's Day Charade

On 14th February 2014, three days short of the third anniversary of the start of Libya's revolution, a retired general issued an unusually threatening Valentine's Day message.

Khalifa Haftar, once described as 'the worst military leader Libya has known', made an 11 minute broadcast to the nation in which he called for the Libyan government and parliament to be suspended, and announced that he would take over the nation's political institutions.

He said: 'The national command of the Libyan army is declaring a movement for a new roadmap', and added that 'Libya must be rescued... from militias.'

Haftar, who as a 20 year-old had helped install Muammar Ghaddafi in power, before spectacularly falling out with him over a botched military incursion in Chad,* added that the army did not intend to take power, but instead would: 'appoint a president... and an interim civilian government.'

It was the Chad mission to which Libyan historian Fathi al-Fatdhali referred when he described Haftar as the worst military leader in Libya's history.

His comment, in full, was: 'The war was a scandal. Haftar is the worst military leader Libya has known. He didn't have a plan – even a withdrawal plan.'

Haftar was born in Benghazi in 1949, and was one of the small unit of soldiers who worked with Ghaddafi to deliver 1969's bloodless deposition of King Idris I. He remained in the Libyan military, rising to the rank of Colonel (on the basis of his service and achievements in the army, rather than as a 'gift' from the force, as was the case for Muammar Ghaddafi).

He also served as the nation's Chief of Staff, a role in which he led Libyan troops alongside Egyptian forces in the 1973 Arab War against Israel.

In 1987, at the height of Hissene Habre's US-backed efforts to complete his conquest of Chad, Libya suffered a series of catastrophic defeats at the hands of Habre's army, culminating in the battle of Maaten Al-Sarra – an airbase within Libya – by the end of which every Libyan soldier in Chad had been repelled or captured.

Among those taken prisoner were Haftar, the chief commanding officer of Libya's troops in Chad, and the 300 soldiers in his direct command. It was this defeat, among others, which led to al-Fatdhali's scathing criticism.

Ghaddafi was faced with a serious problem: he had assured the international community that he had complied with an earlier agreement under which he promised to withdraw Libyan troops from Chad, and that any fighting with Habre's force was being undertaken by Chadian rebels. As a result, he refused to recognise Haftar's presence in Chad, and declined to negotiate his return on the grounds that he had 'disobeyed orders'.

Left in a Chadian jail, furious with his former friend and political ally, Haftar was eventually freed only because of an agreement negotiated by the American CIA. He moved to Langley, Virginia, in 1990, and it is believed he received training from the CIA during the 21 years he lived there.

He visited Libya just once between 1990 and 2011, to lead the CIA-backed National Salvation Front for Libya in its failed 1993 coup attempt, though he did tell Maghreb media that he was working with the US government to build an armed force to 'eliminate Ghaddafi'.

Whether under his own initiative, or at the CIA's behest, he returned again in 2011, to take part in the Civil War.

His exact position in the hierarchy of khetibas was confused at the time: in March, one militia spokesman described him as 'commander of the military', but this claim was immediately denied by the National Transitional Council. In April, he was described as ranking third in the rebel forces' structure of command, behind Commander-in-Chief Abdul Fatah Younis, and Chief of Staff Omar El-Hariri.

After the Civil War's end, he was often discussed in Libyan media as a potential Defence Minister, but he achieved no position of power or public renown.

In an international context, the statement appeared laden with threat: Libya already had a government, elected by the people, and seven months earlier, the Egyptian military, led by General Abdel Fattah el-Sisi, had smashed its country's democratically-elected government from power and embarked on a spiteful, bloody killing spree.*

* From July 2013, when the Egyptian military seized control of the state from the Muslim Brotherhood, until 3rd June 2014, when the junta's leader General Abdel Fatah Al-Sisi was elected President (with an eye-wateringly improbable, but officially declared, 96.1 per cent of the vote), the state's apparatus was used by the army to kill more than 1,000 people on Egypt's streets.

It also injured 4,000, arrested 16,000 – including every member of the democratically-elected government it had shot out of power – and on 28th April 2014, the court it still runs sentenced 720 people to death for the murder of one police officer.

In Libya, however, the general reaction was one of bemusement. The nation's Prime Minister, Ali Zeidan, dismissed the retiree's call for a coup. Noting that Libya already had a Parliament, the General National Council (GNC), and a government, he said: 'Libya is stable. The army is in its headquarters, and Khalifa Haftar has no authority.'

He added that Haftar would face legal proceedings under military law.

In the maelstrom of Libya's post-revolutionary era, the former general's outburst seemed little more than a curiosity – a small, failed military man making a fool of himself on international television, only to be brushed aside by his country's Prime Minister.

And for several months, as if chastened, Haftar did disappear.

But before the year was out, he had supported a missile attack on Libya's Parliament, set up international airstrikes on Tripoli, caused both of Libya's major cities to be overrun by illegal militias, and created a stalemate in which two opposing governments – both utterly powerless – were forced to watch from either side of the country as chaos, violence and death once again reigned supreme in Libya.

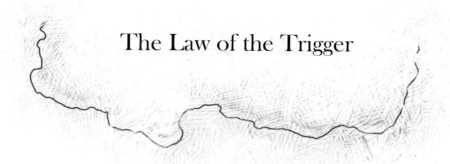

The Law of the Trigger

When Haftar called for Libya's government to be smashed from power, the country was far from happily – or effectively – run.

In fact, Libya's post-war political, legal and economic environment has been characterised by chaos – actually farcical in the few matters where it does not directly endanger people's lives and health.

For seven days before the former General's exhortation to violence, the state's government had existed solely because it voted for itself to remain in power beyond its legal mandate, having failed to draft – let alone enact – a constitution.

Its legal system relied on Ghaddafi's laws – some updated to restrict criticism of itself, rather than the dead leader – and was in any case so weak that people who might face trial anywhere else in the world know there is little danger they will ever have to answer for their actions.*

It is not only the case that few people were ever arrested for their crimes: even those who were seldom served their sentence.

On 26th December 2013, 40 prisoners escaped in a mass breakout from Ajdabiya jail.

And Ajdabiya was just one of many towns and cities suffering regular prison breaks, which were seemingly unopposed by poorly-paid, under-motivated staff. In July, 1,200 prisoners broke out from Kuwaifiya, Benghazi's major jail, and four jailbreaks were staged in 2013 in the Southern city of Sabha.

In a state awash with arms, and with borders – particularly in the South – open to drug- and people-trafficking, the lure of 'opportunities' for escapees far outweighed the tiny risk of capture and punishment.

Many of its roads, schools, and hospitals remained in the state they were after NATO helped smash them. Unemployment and poverty were rife, and in every part of the country, armed men – not government officials – held power because, simply, they controlled the guns and heavy weaponry.

All of these issues were connected, but the most prominent and obvious in most people's daily lives was the continued power of the khetibas.

In the aftermath of the Libyan Civil War, the tens of thousands of young men who had fought and with help defeated Ghaddafi's military* saw little reason to lay down their weapons.

Government figures suggest that there were at least 165,000 khetibas active in Libya as of January 2014: that figure is very unlikely to be comprehensive, but a sizeable proportion of the khetiba's membership is also believed to have signed up after, rather than during, the Civil War.

Most had been unemployed, or employed piecemeal, in jobs such as farm day-labouring, with little money and certainly no security to show for their efforts. The khetiba, with guaranteed wages, food and a sense of purpose and belonging, amounted to a huge improvement.

Equally, these were in the main young men who had been told they were serving the best interests of their nation, and believed that what they had done deserved specific reward, beyond the knowledge that they had helped remove a dictator from power.

On the other hand, Libya's civilian population had an at least equally legitimate expectation that the government would disarm and return to civilian life those who had deposed Ghaddafi.

In fact, the Libyan government was weak, relied upon the khetibas' support for its existence, and its national military was far smaller, weaker and worse-equipped than the combined khetiba force. The people's expectation was reasonable, but it was impossible for the government to live up to it.

The government had formed in August 2012, when the National Transitional Council (NTC)* stepped down, to make way for a new body, the General National Congress (GNC).

The NTC had formed in Benghazi on 27th February 2011, ten days after the revolution against Ghaddafi had begun. On 8th March 2011, with soldiers and khetibas killing one another across the country, it announced that it was 'the sole representative all over Libya' and 15 days later, it announced that it had created an 'interim governing body' tasked with preparing Libya for democracy.

In June 2011, Ghaddafi's son, Saif al-Islam, said his father would agree to an internationally-monitored general election in Libya, and to leave power if he lost, but the khetibas refused the offer, and the UN Security Council did not even consider it.

On 3rd August, with NATO and rebels still battling to remove Ghaddafi and his forces from most of southern, central and western Libya, the NTC issued its 'Constitutional Declaration'.

This laid out aspirations for a democratic Libya, with Islam as its state religion, and with laws based on the Sharia code. It guaranteed an independent judiciary, rule of law and basic human rights including freedom of religion and women's rights.

It set a deadline of December 2013 (later extended to 7th February 2014 due to delays in elections and in agreeing posts within government), by which time the state should be a Presidential republic with an elected national assembly (the General National Congress) and democratically agreed Constitution.

On 20th October, the day Ghaddafi was shot in Sirte, 100 countries severed relations with the Ghaddafi regime and instead officially recognised the NTC as representative of Libya, and on 23rd October, NTC Vice Chairman Abdul Hafiz Ghoga announced Libya was 'freed', marking the end of the Civil War.

Elections took place on 7th July 2012, in which 2,501 candidates contested the 200 GNC seats. Three hundred candidates were disqualified from the process on suspicion of 'sympathising with the previous regime' – hardly a hallmark of an inclusive democracy, but perhaps understandable given Libya's fragile state and the relatively short period since Ghaddafi's shooting ended the vicious, divisive and destructive Civil War.

Of the 200 seats, 120 were set aside for independents, leaving only 80 to be contested by 'party' members.

The idea behind this split was to attempt to ensure that no single party group would be able to 'carry the House' on any single issue – particularly important given that the Congress was never supposed to be a legislature. Instead, its role was to rebuild Libya's shattered infrastructure, lay foundations for a strong and trustworthy democratic system and oversee the creation of a national constitution.

But the political parties ignored the spirit of the restriction.

They ran their strongest candidates as 'independents' and weaker ones on their party list, creating a GNC overrun by large political blocs, with only a sprinkling of true independents, for whom the only way to gain backing for policies was to 'trade' votes with those blocs.

Of 2.865 million registered voters, 1.764m cast votes, a 61.58 per cent turnout.

The largest share of votes – by far – went to the National Forces Alliance, a 'Liberal' (though the Party, wary of scaring some sections of Libya's Muslim vote, shies away from the label) party which campaigned for a society inspired by, but not rigidly adherent to, Sharia Law.

The NFA's message of tolerance and the protection of rights for minority groups, non-Muslims and non-Libyans won 714,769 votes, 48.14 per cent of the total count, and 39 out of the 80 Party seats, as well as 25 of the 120 'independent' seats.

The next largest group, the Justice and Construction Party, is connected to Libya's Muslim Brotherhood.

Its 'moderate' Muslim approach (its spokesman Mohamed Ghair told media before the election that while the Party supported a legal system developed from Sharia Law: 'We do not wish to do the things that some people would associate with that view, such as banning women from leaving home: that is not rational.') won it 152,441 votes, ten per cent of the national total, and 17 seats in the GNC.*

The third party which proved influential in the first stage of Libya's post-Civil War politics was the National Front, which won 60,592 votes, 4.08 per cent, and just three seats.

Based upon an anti-Ghaddafi resistance movement (the National Front for the Salvation of Libya) set up in 1981 and almost immediately outlawed by the dictator, the National Front ran on a strong anti-Ghaddafi campaign, demanding the trial of all Ghaddafi-regime supporters to assist national unity. In this, it was also supported by the fourth largest party in the GNC, the Union for the Homeland. It also campaigned for stronger women's rights and economic growth.

The record of the group it grew from, and of its leader Mohammed Magarief (who had been an anti-corruption lawyer, then Libya's ambassador to India, before self-exiling to Morocco and then the USA), won it warm support from independents and 'opponents' alike.

Magarief was democratic Libya's first President, beating liberal-leaning National Party for Development and Welfare leader Ali Zeidan by 113 votes to 85.

Zeidan, a former colleague of Magarief's at Libya's Indian Embassy – and the man credited with convincing Nicolas Sarkozy to commit to joining the US and UK in bombing Libya during the Civil War – was elected Prime Minister in October 2012.

But the party also won 17 'independent' seats, and proved adept both at convincing independents – many of whom held moderate or extreme Islamic political views – to support its plans. It was also a far more cohesive group than the NFA, which was often riven by serious internal disagreement.

The GNC – and the government it created – did not begin altogether badly. It recognised, for example, that the presence of thousands of armed men, still relatively fresh from war and with no jobs to go to, posed a huge threat to the future of the state, and attempted to deal with the issue.

But it was hamstrung.

Its armed forces were weak, thanks to NATO's targeting of its hardware and bases (along with many civilian targets), the army's defeat by the khetibas and the reluctance and later prohibition of Ghaddafi's officers to contribute their expertise and experience to the force.

Even those who may have joined as new recruits could be tempted instead to join a khetiba, with the lures of better wages, (as the government's income from oil – worth more than 90 per cent of Libya's total annual revenue – was in the practical, if not legal, control of the khetibas who were on the ground, closest to the major oil fields and their ports), more active engagements and arguably greater purpose than that offered by service in the Libyan official military.

As a result, the Libyan army, funded by and loyal to the state, was actually incapable of standing up to, let alone displacing, the khetibas. And the khetibas themselves took an active role in promoting their own political priorities and preference.

The state's second largest group of khetibas, the al-Zintan Military Council, made up of 23 'brigades' (the largest of which has 4,000 fighters) based in the Nafusa mountains in Western Libya, was a strong supporter of the National Forces Alliance.

The Misratan Union, a far larger collective of khetibas – and Libya's largest by some distance – supported the Justice and Construction Party.

The Misrata militia, made up of more than 200 militias – about 40,000 fighters – is estimated to 'own' more than 800 tanks, at least 2,000 vehicles armed with anti-aircraft and machine guns and a large amount of heavy artillery.

Justice and Construction was also, rather ominously, supported by the state-funded khetiba collective, Libya Shield Force, which had been set-up as a 'temporary vehicle' in 2012, to try to engage the khetibas in working for the state on internal security matters.

The khetibas, which had up to then been a loosely-connected network of militia organisations, had effectively 'split' in the run-up to the July 2012 elections. Zintan and Misrata's brigades retained their commitment to a democratic Libya, but in Benghazi the elections sparked wildly divergent responses.

Most civilians within the city – and many khetibas – hoped for a successful, democratic and united Libya. But the 'Cyrenaica Transitional Council' had already been proclaiming the former Greek and Roman province a part of a non-existent 'federal Libya' for two months.*

* *Though largely peaceful, the Cyrenaica group's co-founder Abu Bakr Baeira stated at the group's declaration of the region's federal status: 'We hope they [the rest of Libya] don't force us to a new war and new bloodshed. This is the last thing we look for.'*

  Fortunately, rather than war and bloodshed, the Council was met with blank indifference as Libyans attempted to rebuild their nation.

And the election also inspired a more serious 'split' among the Libyan khetibas. Less than a month before the vote, the Ansar al-Sharia brigade, a Benghazi-based, anti-democratic Salafi* khetiba, with alleged links to Al Qaeda, paraded armed vehicles through Benghazi's streets to demand the immediate imposition of Sharia law across Libya.

* *Although the vast majority of Benghazans are neither Salafists nor jihadists, the city contains the largest number of people belonging to either group in all of Libya.*

  The reasons are varied, but connect to the city's belief in itself as the 'true capital' of Libya – formerly capital of Cyrenaica and then for almost two decades the 'home' of the Libyan monarchy (the same reason explains the strong separatist feeling within the city, among secular democrats and religious extremists alike).

  The monarchist ideal closely fits with Salafist political aspiration, of a religious and spiritual head of state chosen by Allah, though whether Salafism fed the monarchist ideal, or the city's traditionalist approach to governance attracted Salafists to the city is unclear.

  The third major reason was that whether inspired by Islam, or by socio-political character, Benghazi was throughout Ghaddafi's regime a 'rebel city'. It was the place where most protest took place, and from where most attempts to overthrow Ghaddafi's regime began.

  Because Ghaddafi stood against Islamic law, this made Benghazi a magnet for those Libyans who desired a state run on religious grounds, at the same time as becoming a place where political dissidents may at least remain undetected, if not ever entirely safe to campaign to topple the regime.

  The result was that many of the strongest political and Islamic resistance leaders against Ghaddafi followed the same route, from dissidence, to Abu Salim prison for political 'agitators', to Benghazi.

  Along the way, Islam and political resistance to Ghaddafi in eastern Libya became if not married, at least engaged in a serious, long-term, and often tempestuous relationship.

  So the strongest Islamic militias were formed in Benghazi, and in turn, attracted those young men – from across Libya and from other countries – who were most dedicated to the formation of an Islamic state to join them there.

  Unlike in Misrata, where the khetibas demanded a leading role for Islam in the Libyan state, some of Benghazi's most powerful khetibas – though not most of its civilians – demanded instead that if necessary, Libya should cease to exist, to make way for a new Islamic entity.

The demand was ignored, and the election went ahead, but the moment marked the end of 'unified' khetibas across Libya. Ansar al-Sharia's name gained international notoriety 34 days after the GNC's creation, when the US government denounced it as a terrorist organisation following the murder of Christopher Stevens, its Ambassador to Libya.

Mr Stevens, the US ambassador to Libya, was killed, aged 52, in an attack on the US consulate in Benghazi on 11th September 2012. Early reports, seized upon by Western press and the US government in the confusion following the murder, suggested that he may have been killed by a Benghazan mob, outraged at the posting on Youtube of an American film depicting the prophet Mohamed as a sexually-incontinent fool.

The film certainly existed, and in fact only a day previously, protestors against it took to the streets in Egypt, scaling the walls of a US government building and setting fire to the US flag.

But it soon became obvious that the use of rockets in the attack, and the attackers' seeming knowledge of the US government staff's safe-house locations made it more likely that an organised group had planned an operation to kill the diplomat.*

> ** One American-Libyan eyewitness of the attack on the US consulate asked the UK's Guardian newspaper: 'What demonstration? There was no demonstration. They came with machine guns, with rockets.'*

Stevens was later described by his friends and family as a dedicated official, with a genuine interest in and attachment to Libya. He had been a Peace Corps volunteer who taught English in Morocco, and was sincere in his professional aims of establishing a 'secure' Libya.

He had also been a strong proponent of the 'clean strike' policy, in which NATO would bomb Libya (disregarding the basic illegality of such an activity) to depose Ghaddafi without committing US troops to a long engagement in the state.

The policy was certainly attractive to NATO. To Libyans, who have since been forced to live with its consequence without even any NATO commitment to supply financial or practical assistance to the rebuilding of the country's ruined infrastructure, it may now seem slightly less ideal.

To whichever group committed the murder of Stevens (no group has claimed responsibility for the act, despite US government assertions of Ansar al-Sharia's guilt),* however, Stevens' advocacy of the clean strike may have made little difference: it was 11th September, and a chance arose to 'rid Libya' of Americans.

> ** Ahmed Abu Khattala, a commander of Ansar al-Sharia, was charged by the US government in July 2013 with playing a significant part in the attack. Eye-witnesses at the scene had named him as 'leading' the group which launched the strike on the US consulate. Libyan President, Mohammed Magarief, also blamed 'elements' of Ansar al-Sharia. But Khattala, who had been imprisoned at 19 by Ghaddafi and held at Abu Salim prison for his religious and political views, and who has also told the New York Times that he believed the United States worked 'for both sides' in the Libyan Civil War and that without NATO strikes 'God would have helped us' (to depose Ghaddafi), denied killing Stevens, or being part of the attack at all.*

In the hours immediately following the attack, the US State Department told international media that Mr Stevens and three other staff were killed in a rocket attack on the Ambassador's car. It said that it had sent a military plane to transport the bodies to Tripoli, and then back to the US. In the days that followed, it became clear that, like so many reports from Libya, this account was not entirely accurate. In fact, the attack on the consulate, and on Stevens, was more determined, and more meticulously planned. At 7pm on 11th September, a group estimated to contain 125-150 men carrying rocket launchers and machine guns, advanced on the US consulate.

At least one – possibly as many as three – rockets were fired at the building, and the group stormed it, setting it alight as they advanced. Libyan khetiba members – perhaps mindful of recent attacks on international organisations' staff* – mobilised to attempt to defend the consulate, but were forced back under heavy fire.

On 11th June 2012 (possibly as a direct response to the killing of Al-Qaeda's second in command, Abu Yahya al-Libi in Pakistan exactly one week earlier), the convoy of UK Ambassador to Libya, Dominic Asquith, was attacked with rockets in Benghazi. He escaped unscathed, but two of his bodyguards were injured.

As a result of the incident – and similar attacks on UK aid workers and International Red Cross staff – the UK government and many non-governmental organisations had ceased to maintain permanent presence in Benghazi. It remains unclear why Mr Stevens and his team were in the city during a period of heightened tension.

Mr Stevens was found alive by Benghazan civilians.

They had stormed the consulate, defying the force of the armed group which had set it ablaze, and discovered Stevens alone on the building's roof, where it seems he had collapsed due to smoke inhalation.

What happened after the Benghazans found Mr Stevens has become one of the least-accurately reported (at least by some Arabic and Western media, and by 'shares' on social media sites around the world) events in international journalism's recent history.

Inexplicably, reports began to surface that the civilians who found Stevens had used cattle prods to torture him, and raped him.

Only the media outlets responsible for this wild falsehood can ever explain why they claimed this took place. It did not.

The Benghazan citizens, who had risked their lives to find Christopher Stevens, carried him across the city to hospital, where he was discovered to have suffered cardiac arrest brought on by severe asphyxia.

Medical staff worked to resuscitate him, but Mr Stevens was pronounced dead at 2am on 12th September 2012.

Meanwhile, around 36 survivors of the attack were driven to a safe house in Benghazi, to await rescue by the US government. Eight US military and security staff arrived to assist their transit from the city, but were immediately attacked by armed men who surrounded the building and killed two more Americans.

The group finally escaped to Benghazi airport thanks to an escort manned by Libyan khetibas, and flew to Tripoli, then the US.

Including Stevens, five US government employees died in the attack and its aftermath.

Their killers have never been brought to justice. In response to Stevens' murder, the citizens of Benghazi decided to take matters into their own hands.

On Friday 21st September 2012, thousands of people swarmed into the buildings occupied by khetibas in the city, causing the armed groups to scatter. The New York Times described it as 'an angry mob demanding law and order'. They went first to the Ansar al-Sharia stronghold, then to the 'office' of the moderate Islamic Rafallah al-Sehati Brigade, where four members of the public were killed before the khetiba left.

In Derna, another hotbed of Islamic militarism, 290km East of Benghazi, the Abu Slim Brigade and Ansar al-Sharia left voluntarily, but ominously, took their weapons with them.

Two days later, on Sunday 23rd September,* Libyan President Mohammed Magarief ordered all khetibas which did not fall under the GNC's 'authority'** to disband. It was a well-meant attempt, but failed completely.

The date was one year and nineteen days after the NTC's first 'demand' that Misratan and Zintani khetibas should leave Tripoli. The khetibas had refused on the grounds that 'Islamists' were taking over the NTC.

It was also three months and 11 days before Magarief would survive an assassination attempt in the south-western town of Sabha. He was on a fact-finding mission, hoping to help the government restore security and crack-down on smuggling in southern Libya.

On 4th January 2013, his hotel was attacked by gunmen. Three of his personal bodyguards were injured in the ensuing three-hour-long battle, but Magarief escaped unharmed.

** *The government had realised it could not force the khetibas to disband. Neither could it defeat them in battle.*

Instead, it attempted to bring the khetibas, now victors in the only war in which they had ever fought, into the army which they had defeated.

But many who accepted the offer simply remained at the service of their khetiba commanders, many of whom never joined the Libyan military, meaning at best they served two 'masters'.

Others remained loyal to government forces only until an opportunity for more money, greater 'glory' or both arrived, and the majority simply refused the government's demands, carrying on much as before.

Some of those who refused, such as the major Misrata and Zintan khetibas, pledged themselves to 'serve' the GNC, but avoided any legal or enforceable loyalty or responsibilities, while others, including large numbers of Misrata's smaller militias, agreed in the wake of Stevens' killing to join the Libya Shield force. But though the Shield was supposed to be a semi-official, nominally government-controlled, national security force, it operated as its commanders, rather than the Defence Ministry, saw fit.

There were also problems within the army itself. During the Civil War, most of the most expert and experienced soldiers had been serving in defence of Ghaddafi, and refused to return to serve under the new regime.

Even those who did return have expressed grave reservations about 'sharing' the army with what they see as brash, largely untrained, and occasionally foolish young rebels. One Libyan colonel told a journalist for American publication The Atlantic: 'I would rather resign than share the army with these bloody idiots.'

Just how badly the GNC's attempt failed can be counted in the following ways: first, the khetibas remained in Libya's towns and cities long after 18th May, when Magarief lost his position as Libyan President. Second, nine foreigners were killed by armed operatives in Libya from October 2013 to March the following year, including seven Egyptian Christians found shot in the head on a beach just outside Benghazi in February 2014.

And third, on 15th-16th November 2013, Misratan forces in Tripoli killed 44 peaceful protestors, journalists and medical staff, and injured more than 500 others.

Thousands of Tripoli's workers and residents had responded to the calls of the Tripoli Local Council, the democratically-elected city authority, to march in protest against the continued presence of Misrata khetibas on its streets. The march was called after clashes between militias from Misrata and Tripoli within the city on 7th November had left several dead and wounded.

The demonstrators gathered at al-Quds Square and marched in peace to Gharghour, where the Misrata khetiba lives in homes formerly owned by Ghaddafi-regime officials.

They chanted 'Tripoli is free, militias should leave', and 'We want the army, we want the police, Libya is in a mess'.

In response, and even though Human Rights Watch reported that none of the demonstrators was armed, the Misrata khetibas opened fire on the crowds, using assault rifles, machine guns and heavy weapons. They killed 43 people, injuring 460.*

On 8th June 2013, Benghazan citizens had experienced similar 'justice' from the khetibas. They had marched to the city's compound of Libya Shield One (considered the less loyal of the two Shield units to the Libyan government), calling for the Libyan government to abolish the khetibas, disband the Shield and replace them with a real police force.

The Shield opened fire, killing 32 people. Its leader, Wissam bin Humayd, who had earned plaudits as commander of revolution's Ahrar Libya Brigade, fled to Tripoli, then Misrata. He remains at large.

Among those killed on 15th November were a doctor treating a wounded woman in an ambulance, eight students from Tripoli University, and photographer Saleh Ayad Hafyanaa, who was covering the protest for the Fasatou press agency.

Libyan Prime Minister Ali Zeidan told media the following day that police and Libyan armed forces were under orders not to intervene, because 'they are weaker than the khetibas'.*

Zeidan himself had had direct experience of the khetibas' strength, a month earlier, when he had been kidnapped by the Libya Revolutionaries' Operations Room (LROR), a group which had been set up by, and was under direct orders from, the state's President Nuri Abu-Sahmayn.

Abu-Sahmayn, an Independent, had won the Presidency on 25th June 2013, after Mohammed Magarief, Libya's first President of its post-Civil War period, had stepped down in anticipation of the introduction of Libya's 'political isolation' law.

The law, which barred all Ghaddafi's political employees and associates from holding public office, was deemed to apply to Magarief because of his role as Libya's Ambassador to India under Ghaddafi – even though he had exiled himself from the state after dedicating himself to attempting to root out corruption under the regime.

Abu-Sahmayn, a Sunni Muslim who had a record of supporting the Justice and Construction Party in the GNC, formed the LROR from khetiba members. It is largely Islamic in outlook, and was supposed to ensure Tripoli's security, but instead, in the early hours of 10th October 2013 (the first anniversary of Zeidan's election as Prime Minister), kidnapped the Libyan Prime Minister from the Corinthia Hotel.

The LROR said it had acted in response to Zeidan calling in September 2013 for international assistance to build a Libyan police force and army, and the Libyan government's alleged involvement in the American arrest of Tripoli-born Al Qaeda computing specialist Anas al-Liby on 5th October.

Al-Liby is accused of masterminding the 1998 US Embassy Bombings which killed hundreds of people in Dar es Salaam and Nairobi. US Army Delta Force operators arrested him in Tripoli and deported him under military custody to the US.

Ali Zeidan denounced his kidnapping as being a Justice and Construction Party plot against him – a confirmation that the Independent PM's relations with one of the GNC's most powerful groups had collapsed. The LROR has retained its role in Tripoli without censure or punishment for kidnapping the Libyan Prime Minister.

The Misrata khetiba was chased out of Gharghour by the protestors, but the following day, bolstered by reinforcements, it returned and seized control of the area once more.

On their way into Tripoli from Misrata, the reinforcements were engaged at Tajoura, an eastern suburb of Tripoli, by Tripolitan fighters.

One man was killed and dozens more injured as the Misratans battered their way back into the city.

Also on 15th-16th November, in what is believed to be an unrelated attack, several men claiming to be members of the Misrata khetiba broke into the North Tripolitan al-Fallah camp, which is still home to 1,200 Tawerghans. They opened fire on its residents, killing one and injuring three others.

The condemnation and anger caused by the series of killings eventually proved too much even for the Misrata khetiba to weather, and on 22nd November, 14 months and 18 days after the National Transitional Council had first demanded they remove themselves from the Libyan capital city, the Misrata khetibas withdrew from Tripoli.

They, too, retained their weapons, and remained the single most powerful military organisation within Libya, allied to one political party, but with no official loyalty or responsibility to any part of the Libyan government.

The South: Oil and Water

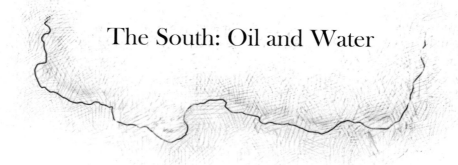

In the South of Libya, the landscape is different in every sense.

Unlike in Tripolitania and Cyrenaica, where sea is separated from desert by a green strip of land, on which almost all the large cities sit, in Fezzan, the landlocked southern region, a small number of oases and a few roads are all that punctuate thousands of square miles of golden sands.

Fezzan sits on reservoirs of oil (though many are, as yet, untapped) which could help it to become rich as an independent state. But most within the region recognise that the oil can be transported only from sea ports, making unity with a wider Libya preferable to any attempt to go it alone.

Equally, the Fezzan region has relatively few people, and even less fertile land on which to grow crops. Independence is not a serious option here: Fezzan can potentially supply oil, and in return it receives food.

It is hard to see how it could be any better off outside a united Libya than within it, and few here believe the dismantling of Libya would be a positive step.

At ground level, the region is striking and moving for visitors – miles and miles of sand, blown into varied patterns and shapes, and covering every surface as far as the eye can see.

Major roads tail off into desert tracks, which head south towards the heart of the vast African continent. The clear blue skies of day slide almost imperceptibly into almost pitch-black nights speckled with bright stars and dominated by often vast, haunting moons.

For those who live there, it is also harsh, and somewhat boring.

Sand is not a friend to human beings, and when most of us are faced with a real choice between running water and plentiful food or a remarkable sunset, it is likely most would choose the sunset only once or twice in every ten or so opportunities.

The region's largest town is Sabha. Set in one of the Libyan Sahara's oases, it sits in the south west of the country, straddling a road which carries on only a hundred kilometres or so before becoming a track through the desert towards Niger and Chad. It has roughly 200,000 inhabitants, and was also the place where Muammar Ghaddafi attended Secondary School, after his father moved from Sirte to work for the Saif Al Nasr family.*

* The family, part of the wider Awlad Sulieman tribe – arguably its leaders, in fact – gained particular acclaim for its battles against the Ottomans who ruled Libya in the 19th Century, and the Italian colonists in the early 20th.

As a schoolboy, Ghaddafi staged an anti-government demonstration within the school, followed by a second demonstration at a hotel owned by the Saif Al Nasr family, the reward for which was his expulsion from school.

Since the Civil War, the town also became a refuge-post for a wide group of northern and central Libyan families who now find life in their hometowns intolerable, or even impossible.

In Sirte, for example, Al-Jazeera in October 2013 broadcast members of Islamic khetibas performing public whippings for 'crimes' including drinking alcohol at home and swearing in the street. Reports from residents suggested that groups from outside the city were ignoring any remaining Libyan law to arrest and incarcerate people with little justification greater than their superior firepower.

Most of these recent migrants have settled well in Sabha. But one ethnic group, which has lived in the town far longer than the new influx of Northerners, has found it less easy to settle.

The Tebu, a part of the Teda ethnic group, make up by far the largest single group of people living in Sabha's Tauri district.

Traditionally desert warriors from the southern and eastern Sahara, most of the Teda live in the harsh Tibesti Mountains, on Libya's desert border with Chad. In Sabha, the majority of Tebu are regarded – and see themselves – as a people without a nation.

They are described by other tribes and ethnic groups as liars and petty thieves, but it should be noted that the Teda, who controlled the caravan routes through their territory and made most of their money through slave-trading and plunder, have defeated in battle all the groups which surround them, including the Tuareg, within the last two centuries.

Today, although they live by a combination of farming, pastoralism, date-growth and smuggling, they are perceived by much of the rest of Sabha's population as 'non-Libyans' trying to take over their home.

In part, this results from the fact that much of South Libya, and the state's borders with Chad and Niger, are dominated by Tebu militias.

This gives them a stranglehold over everything from goods and food trade to arms dealing, drug sales and people-trafficking. And it made them an obvious – and often accused – culprit for the attempted killing of Libyan President Mohammed Magarief in January 2013.

In common with almost all armed offences committed in Libya since 2011, no-one has admitted responsibility, and no-one has been arrested for the attempted murder.

And early in 2014, steadily increasing tension between the Tebu and Awlad Sulieman tribe members spilled into violence. In clashes which broke out on 8th January, 21 people were killed and 45 wounded. The situation was further confused by the actions of pro-Ghaddafi fighters, who hoped to use it to start a counter-revolution, two years after the ruler's death. They snatched Sabha's airport, and were then besieged by Tebu forces, who had earlier seized several Awlad Sulieman compounds.

Khetibas from Tripoli, Misrata, Zintan, and the Jebel Nafusa (a collective of Berbers based in Western Libya, who, like the Tebu, demand that their tribal rights must be explicitly safeguarded in Libya's constitution, whenever it is created) were ordered by Libyan Prime Minister Ali Zeidan into Sebha after four days of fighting. The khetiba force from the north and west of Libya put down the Ghaddafist uprising, and calmed the fighting between the Tebu and Awlad Sulieman militias.

But though the incident was over, at least in the immediate-term, it highlighted two large concerns for Libya's future.

First, that in parts of Libya, pro-Ghaddafi feeling remained strong enough to encourage Ghaddafists to strike at the nation's infrastructure.

But second, more ominously, that the Libyan government, seeing armed violence between tribal militias in a poor southern region awash with weapons which have come from NATO, been traded for drugs, people and food, or stolen from soldiers, decided its own military was not capable of travelling 476 miles to calm it.

Instead, it turned for help to the sole true military power in Libya: the khetibas.

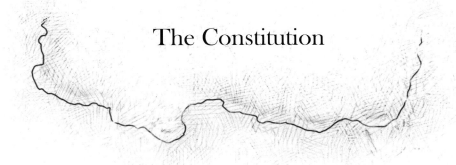

The Constitution

If the activity of the khetibas posed the greatest threat to Libya developing successfully, it was clear by the time Haftar attempted to incite nationwide conflict that inactivity in other places was also jeopardising any hopes for a successful post-Ghaddafi future.

The GNC, at its creation in the NTC's Constitutional Declaration, was charged with one responsibility: to write a constitution for the new Libya.

Whatever else it achieved, the GNC's entire purpose – according to the Declaration which created it – was to have written the guidelines for Libya's future political and social structure within 20 months of its election: by 7th February 2014.

Not only had it not completed the document by 7th February, it had not even begun to write it.

But the date did not pass unmarked. Because instead of completing and enacting a constitution to guide Libya, the GNC decided after two years and seven months of bickering, to extend its own period in power until December 2014.

Despite failing in its sole serious purpose, the GNC, without any kind of public consultation, let alone a national vote, chose to reward itself a longer period in power than the NTC's Declaration – at that point the only written agreement guiding Libyan political activity – allowed it.*

Twenty members of the body walked out in disgust at this decision, never to return, making it ten per cent harder for the body to reach the 120-member attendance rate necessary to legally pass laws and decisions.

It did, however, finally organise elections for the Constitutional Assembly – the body which would be charged with drafting a Libyan constitution. They took place on 20th February 2014, 13 days after the document – which was expected to take 20 months to develop, was supposed to be completed and in operation.

Though Haftar's call for a coup was vastly out of proportion to the crisis at hand, many Libyans were at least able to agree that the GNC's behaviour constituted a political crisis. On the face of it, it is then small wonder that despite the Constitutional Assembly election's central and vital import to the entire future of Libya – indeed, the election was arguably the most important in Libyan history – just 500,000 people, roughly 15 per cent of the potential electorate, turned out to vote.

As Claudia Gazzini, a senior analyst for the International Crisis Group, put it: 'People are saying "What happened?". They are saying "I'm not going to dip my hand in the ink this time."'

Immediately after the Civil War, most Libyans welcomed the idea of a new democratic system, and welcomed the GNC's creation.

But they expected – as they had every right to – that the 'new' Libya should be an improvement on the harsh days of Ghaddafi's rule, and on the chaos, destruction and devastation of the war which removed him.

In fact, by February 2014, little had truly improved. Armed gangs still patrolled Libya's roads; hospitals, schools, apartments and businesses smashed from street level or flattened by NATO's relentless bombing remained in ruins, Libya's streets were holed, and its ships remained broken and battered in city ports.

Unemployment was higher than it was in 2011, while the state's income had plummeted and prices for food and other staples increased.

The continued refusal of the khetibas to disband certainly contributed to most of these factors, but in truth, the Misrata and Zintan brigades' support of opposing groups in the GNC actually helped the body survive (though simultaneously preventing it from working in Libya's best interests, by promoting and prolonging disagreement within it). Equally, the militias' continued existence was not only a cause, but also a symptom of the nation's wider failings.

At the most basic level, the GNC and the temporary constitutional system set up to guide it were fundamentally flawed, making it unable even to lay the foundations of Libya's transition from dictatorship to democracy.

And the reason was the Constitutional Declaration. The best and worst thing which can be said about the Declaration is that it was short. It set just one target, and that was clear and understandable – the completion of a constitution for Libya, within a clearly set deadline of 20 months after the GNC's election, and 18 from its first meeting.

But in their strict adherence to brevity, its authors forgot to include any guidance about the respective roles and responsibilities of the bodies in charge of ensuring the constitution's delivery, or any indication about how and when they should interact.

The Declaration stated that the GNC should nominate members to form a government, but did not state what either the GNC or the government's responsibilities should be.

As a result, the GNC, which was never intended to be Libya's government, repeatedly elected Prime Ministers from within its ranks, only to then undermine them, and refuse to accept the Cabinets it is the PM's right to select.

The GNC had, in effect, toppled more governments in the 20 months to February 2014 than the total number of governments to have existed in Libya in the previous 60 years.

A clear – and very early – example of the way in which the GNC was prepared to disrupt Libyan politics came on 7th October 2012, when it voted to remove the Prime Minister it had elected less than a month earlier, Mustafa Abu Shagour.

Abu Shagour, an Independent, was elected Prime Minster on 12th September 2012 with a majority of just two (96-94).

He had beaten the popular leader of the National Transitional Council Mohamed Jibril, when the Justice and Construction Party and its Independent allies threw their support behind him because of Jibril's 'association' with the Ghaddafi regime (his three and a half year spell as head of Libya's National Planning Council and National Economic Development Board were seemingly more important than his leadership of the NTC through the Civil War which deposed the dictator).

But he was then dismissed on the grounds that his proposed cabinet did not include representatives from Zawiyah (protestors led by khetibas had attempted to storm the GNC building when this became known) and also that it did not include prominent members of the GNC's largest group, the National Forces Alliance.

To an extent, it is understandable that the latter factor caused concern, as the NFA was the largest elected group in the GNC. But the fact remains that the GNC chose a Prime Minister who was supposed to have control over the cabinet he selects, yet removed him from his role when he attempted to exercise this most basic of his powers.

The GNC's power to appoint and remove Prime Ministers and cabinets – an attempt to prevent any one group becoming all-powerful (even if it wins the majority of votes in an election) – also led to politically-motivated stalemate.

Ali Zeidan, who succeeded Abu Shagour, having defeated the Justice and Construction Party's favoured candidate Mohammed Al-Harari by 93 votes to 85, proved more careful than his predecessor, choosing a cabinet containing members of Justice and Construction, the NFA and Independents, as well as from a wide range of geographical locations.

Six of its members were investigated for alleged links to the Ghaddafi regime, but all six were cleared. But Zeidan, an avowed liberal, was unpopular with some of the GNC's Muslim groups and Independents, and on 1st January 2014, 72 members tabled a motion to withdraw confidence in him.

This had been tried before several times, but each time the motion of no confidence to remove Zeidan had failed to achieve the necessary 120 votes to be passed.

The January attempt appeared to have won liberal support for the first time, however, when Mohamed Jibril admitted that the removal of the Prime Minister and cabinet was 'being considered' because of alarm that Zeidan had – despite a GNC-set deadline of 24th December – failed to solve a crisis posed by a Cyrenaican separatist movement's theft of Eastern Libya's oil ports.*

At this stage, Libya's oil production had fallen from 1.4m barrels per day in May 2013 (and from its 2010 peak of 3.1m per day) to 300,000 per day – a massive drop for a state which relies on oil for more than 90 per cent of its income.

In common with all those which had preceded it, the motion failed. Too few liberals supported it, in part because they and the GNC's Muslim groups could not agree on a suitable successor to Zeidan.

But at a moment when three quarters of Libya's major income source was being stolen, and when that income was desperately needed to rebuild schools, hospitals, roads, homes and businesses destroyed by khetibas, Ghaddafi's soldiers and NATO's bombs in a Civil War which had ended more than two years before, the GNC had created a 'lame duck' government: too strong to be removed, but too weak to pass laws.

Political division, supposed to safeguard against one group becoming too powerful, had instead created a single, all-powerful body whose internal divisions prevented any decisive action at all.

And on the few occasions when the GNC did pass or update laws, they hardly increased confidence in its ability to deliver 'Libya Hora', a free state where human rights were recognised and protected for all.

On 5th February 2014, 12 days short of the third anniversary of the revolution against Ghaddafi, the GNC altered Article 195 of the Penal Code left by the Ghaddafi Regime.

This law had banned all criticism of the Libyan state, its emblem, flag, the Great Fateh revolution, which brought Ghaddafi to power, and its leader, Muammar Ghaddafi.

Breaking this law carried a three to 15-year prison sentence as punishment.

In the new Libyan political climate, such a law was unacceptable. The GNC amended it so it became – and remains – illegal to criticise the 17 February Revolution, the GNC, the President or the Libyan judiciary.

The law still carries as punishment three to 15 years' imprisonment.

Nor was this a merely symbolic gesture. In 2013, Amara al-Khattabi, a journalist who published the names of 84 judges he alleged were corrupt, was arrested under the terms of this law. A student who was studying outside of Libya during the Civil War and described the khetibas as 'rats' was charged with 'insulting the revolution'.

Hassiba Hadj Sahraoui, Amnesty International's Middle East and North Africa Deputy Director, asked: 'What is the difference between not being able to criticise Ghaddafi's "Al-Fateh Revolution" or the "17 February Revolution"? It is a flagrant attempt to undermine freedom of expression.'

It is possible, of course, that this was yet another attempt to reward and placate Libya's khetibas, but it was the co-option of a dictator's lunacy for new ends.

And it raised the possibility that, for some people at least, the toppling of Ghaddafi may have been less about a 'brave new Libya', or the 'Libya Hora' the graffiti proclaimed, and more about the creation of upheaval and chaos to enable a straight power-grab.

As a result, the GNC's decision to extend its period in power despite not delivering a constitution, appeared to be further evidence of its lack of commitment to Libyan democracy. And it inspired considerable anger.

Demonstrations against the extension – and the way it had been delivered – were held at Tripoli's Martyr's Square and in central Benghazi.

They passed peacefully, but the level of tension felt within Libya over the issue – fuelled in part by the Zintan militias mobilising very publicly in the wake of the GNC decision – was indicated by Ali Zeidan's timely plea for peace just before they took place:

'I urge all citizens to be committed to peaceful means. All demands can be implemented peacefully and through dialogue. The government is at the will of the people. We will implement the people's will no matter what it will be.'

The GNC did appear to take some notice, and set up a committee, which brought the date for national elections forward from December to 25th June 2014.

The February Committee, which set the date, comprised 15 members, six elected from the GNC itself, and nine others, mainly jurists.

It was handed responsibility for the design of a new legislature for Libya, as well as for the process by which it would come into being.

The Committee proposed that the 25th June elections would create a new legislative body – the House of Representatives (HoR) – which would sit in Benghazi. Elections for the 200-seat House, which would be officially created in Tripoli with a symbolic handover of power from the GNC, would be open only to independents.

The HoR would, like the GNC before it, choose a Prime Minister from within its ranks, but would not be allowed to appoint a President, who would instead be chosen by a full public election.

The Committee set 13 responsibilities for the President, including representing Libya internationally, appointing ambassadors, officially appointing the HoR's choice for Prime Minister, issuing laws passed by the HoR, and to dismiss the Prime Minister in consultation with the HoR, and government ministers in consultation with the Prime Minister.

The proposals were announced on 6th March, by the Committee's leader, Dr Al-Koni Abboda. He wryly admitted the process had not been without disagreement, saying: 'We are not concerned with satisfying the GNC, but with satisfying our consciences and meeting the needs of the nation. We sometimes differed, but didn't hit each other with shoes.'

Almost everyone welcomed the Committee's plan: for the GNC, it went some way to sanitising its extended mandate, and delivered time for its members to prepare for re-election, while for the public and the GNC's opponents it set a definite date on which the politicians with whom they disagreed could be removed.

The khetibas, always looming in the background, saw little reason to topple a parliament whose members were kept in position largely through its support, and so Haftar's cries for the government's violent overthrow was the only move made to unseat the GNC.

In the event, the GNC voted to accept the election date and creation of the HoR – though it rejected the recommendation for a publicly-elected President – not at its next available plenary session, on 9th March, but 21 days later.

It had used its 9th March session instead to launch another failed vote of no-confidence in Ali Zeidan, and to vote on rights for minority groups, including the Teba in the South, and also the Amazigh – or 'free ones' – in Libya's West.

The 'Free Ones'
The West, and the Oilfields

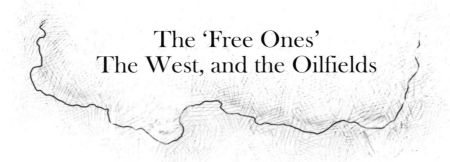

When only 500,000 people voted in the 20th February Constitutional Assembly election, it seemed clear that huge numbers of people in Libya were losing faith in their fledgling system.

Early enthusiasm and interest had, over the 28 months since Ghaddafi's death, slowly been ground down.

Lawlessness, the continued defiance of the government by illegal militias, the government's own infighting and inability to even begin to draw up a constitution, and the fact that all across the country, holes which gaped from ruined roads, and homes, businesses and schools reduced to rubble were not just a reminder of war, but of the failure to recover, had driven the belief in a better future from the Libyan people.

But it was only part of the story. Because although only 500,000 people actually voted, one million people had registered to do so.

This is only a third of those old enough to register, but the fact that half of those who still carried enough belief in the system to register did not vote, suggests other factors may have contributed to the astonishingly low turn-out.

And in the West of Libya, the experience and activities of the 'Free Ones' offers some insight into what those factors might be.

In 2011, the western region's Berbers, who in their own Tamazight language call themselves the Amazigh ('Free Ones'), had enthusiastically joined the Civil War to battle against Ghaddafi, who had made using their language a criminal offence, and prevented them even from expressing and teaching their culture and traditions within their own communities.

In the aftermath of the war, they were celebratory, enjoying the first opportunity in more than 40 years to teach children, advertise and speak together in Tamazight.

In Zuwara, a largely Amazigh community, the local council began hiring native Tamazight speakers from Morocco and Algeria to teach in local schools.

But since those early post-war days, the Amazigh, like the Tebu in Libya's south, and in common with groups in many Libyan towns and cities, felt neglected.

Their polite requests that the new Libyan constitution – whenever it was produced – should include strong measures to include Amazigh culture and the Tamazight language, developed, after being repeatedly ignored, into ever-louder demands. And still no promise was granted.

In late October 2013, the Free Ones took matters into their own hands. Sailing coastguard boats they had seized during the Civil War, 51 people, led by former army officer Adel al-Falu, boarded two oil tankers loading at Mellitah port, 100km west of Tripoli.

They hoisted banners and flags, declared the port 'seized' and set up camp there, preventing the export of oil. Two weeks later, on 12th November, the Amazigh closed the pipeline which carries natural gas from Mellitah to Italy.

The gas pipeline closure lasted only until 17th November – long enough to show the Amazigh were serious, but brief enough to show they did not wish to seriously damage Libya – and though some among the Amazigh favour devolved powers in a federal state, the act was largely an attempt to safeguard their rights within a united Libya. But the seizure of a vital oil port by a 'force' of just 51 men was a further embarrassment to the government.

And the Amazigh were not alone in having taken control of parts of the west's oil production from the ineffective Tripoli government.

The Petroleum Facilities Guard (PFg)* in the west of Libya – whose oilfields produced 500,000 barrels per day during their post-Civil War peak – was never under true government control, but rather that of the Zintan khetiba.

The PFg was another Libyan government initiative to attempt to convince khetiba members to serve the Libyan state, putting their weapons and organizational capabilities to use protecting the nation's vast oil exports.

Even during the Civil War, Ghaddafi and the khetibas who overthrew him shared a recognition of the importance of oil to Libya's economy (in 2010, the 3.1m barrels of Libyan oil sold on the international market each day accounted for more than 90 per cent of its annual income).

Both sides deliberately avoided targeting oil facilities during the war, and the post-war regime continued to protect oil production by paying khetibas to form the PFg, with the aim of guarding the fields and securing a reliable oil supply. The plan failed spectacularly.

By February 2014, the Zintani brigades appeared to be the best of a very bad bunch. They were undeniably illegal armed militias, brigands and highwaymen with heavy weapons, but since October 2011, they had been less bloody than the Misrata khetibas, less extreme in their religious and social outlook than Ansar al-Sharia, and in general largely loyal to the Libyan government.

Even so, it was an illegal militia, and held control of wide stretches of the west of the country. And it did not hesitate to use its military power to disrupt oil supplies in the region, citing grievances that too little money, aid and attention were being given to rebuild and improve its buildings and infrastructure.

A combination of oil's overriding importance to the Libyan economy, and the government's incapacity to seriously threaten any armed group within its borders, meant the Zintan khetibas felt untouchable in their western stronghold – potentially facing greater threat from the Amazigh than from the Libyan government.

In practice, this proved to be exactly the situation: oil ports were regularly seized from July 2012, and from September 2013, the western Libyan oil ports were effectively 'swapped' between Amazigh and Zintani groups, with the government reduced to a helpless bystander.

For the Amazigh, the Constitutional Assembly elections were another opportunity to make their increasingly desperate calls for constitutionally-protected rights: they threatened – and then carried out – a boycott of the elections.

It may appear counter-intuitive for a group demanding constitutional rights to block the production of a constitution, but the Amazigh set a promise of constitutional guarantees as a starting-point for their involvement in the election and the constitution-drafting process which was to follow.

And they had some power over the process. The Amazigh were granted two of the Constitutional Assembly's 60 seats – too few to force the inclusion of Amazigh rights in the constitution, but enough, the community believed, to make the Assembly illegitimate if they remained unfilled.

In the event, the Amazigh refused to put up any candidates (a total of 660 candidates across Libya did run in the 20th February election), and were joined in this by the Tebu, who also had a two-seat allowance on the Assembly, meaning a maximum of 56 of the 60 seats could be filled (The Tuareg, the third and final ethnic minority group guaranteed two seats on the Assembly, did take part in the election).

Instead, the Amazigh announced a 'Day of Mourning' in which community members demonstrated against 'these false elections'.

In other parts of Libya, the election process was subverted by unhidden violence.

Attacks by armed groups across the state forced a total of 81 polling stations to close.

In Derna, part of the Cyrenaica province, Islamic khetibas carried out bomb attacks on six polling stations, preventing votes being cast for the city's three Assembly seats.

And in Kufra and Sebha, where 95 per cent and 97 per cent of stations did open, vehicles carrying ballot papers to the stations were hijacked and prevented from being delivered to the stations, leaving polling booths open, but without any possibility that votes could be cast.

It is believed Tebu gunmen were responsible for this.

The violence and disruption meant that the election filled only 47 of the Assembly's 60 seats.

In response, the increasingly desperate head of the Libyan High National Elections Commission, Nuri Elabbar, pledged to hold elections in the affected areas on the following Wednesday, 26th February, but the Amazigh and Tebu communities maintained their boycott, while militias in Derna and other cities made it impossible for people to vote in safety.

On 1st March, Elabbar criticised the government for 'ignoring' the HNEC's repeated requests for security for the elections. The following day, he resigned.

Thirteen of the 60 seats on Libya's Constitutional Assembly remained – and still remain – unfilled. Almost a quarter of the body which is supposed to create a constitution on which the rest of Libya's political and social future relies was, two and a half years after the end of the Civil War which 'freed' Libya, empty.

Not only was the constitution, which was supposed to have been in place by 7th February 2014, not written, it was not even possible to see how it could be started.

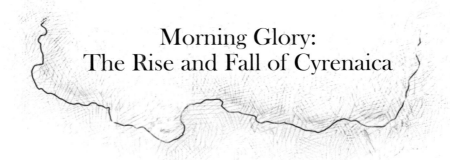

Morning Glory:
The Rise and Fall of Cyrenaica

In the Spring of 2014, Libya was governed by an illegitimate parliament, which was paralysed by its internal battles, and by its members' ongoing attempts to depose a Prime Minister powerful enough to retain his position, but not powerful enough to pass any laws.

Its President's personal militia had kidnapped the country's Prime Minister and gone unpunished, and it had sidestepped a coup only because the armed forces were weaker than bands of heavily-armed militias. It faced ethnic, tribal and political unrest in Fezzan, and was unable to prevent Amazighs and Zintan khetibas alternating control over Libya's oil fields in the West.

But the biggest threat to Libya's future was posed by a group of 20,000 irregular troops, headed by a man in his early 30s, who claimed to own 60 per cent of the state's oil.

In the summer of 2013, a strike by armed guards at Libya's oil fields over pay and conditions (the government responded with an offer of 67 per cent pay increases, seemingly to no effect) developed into a full blockade of many oil production facilities. One man, Ibrahim Jadhran, seized upon the strike and steered it to make a completely different demand: the 'freedom' of eastern Libya. Jadhran, who spent seven years in the Abu Salim prison for 'political opponents' of Ghaddafi, had led a khetiba battalion in the east of Libya during the Civil War.

The post-war Libyan regime rewarded him by making him chief of the Petroleum Facilities guards (PFg) in eastern Libya. But instead of safeguarding the nation's oil supply, Jadhran (who was at this point 33) used the strike to take control of not only eastern Libya's oil fields, which produce almost three-fifths of Libya's oil, but also the putative governmental structure of the region of Cyrenaica.

Almost two months before, on 1st June, the latest iteration of the 'Cyrenaica Transitional Council' – now led by King Idris' great-nephew Ahmad Zubayr al Senussi, who himself had served 31 years in Libyan prisons after attempting a coup against Ghaddafi in 1970 – had declared that it would govern Cyrenaica as part of a 'federal Libya', an entity which did not, and still does not, exist.

But after Jadhran led 17,000 PFg East members, and around 3,000 other armed men to seize the region's major oilfields and ports, gaining an arrest warrant for insubordination against the Libyan army and state in the process, he displaced the 'Transitional Council' and on 17th August announced he was leading a Political Bureau which would campaign for an autonomous Cyrenaica. Jadhran's public statements often seemed to oscillate between a desire to lead Cyrenaica to break away from Libya altogether, and to set Cyrenaica as a federal state within a wider Libya. But on announcing the Political Bureau, he said: 'The process is unavoidable: we have already declared our independence from Libya financially. After being ignored and neglected by the current government, we need to be free to create our own administration and to be in charge of our own budgets.' He would never achieve this aim. But what he did in the next five months was enough to cause a major international incident, inspire armed conflict in Sirte, and topple Libya's government.

Jadhran was aware that his – and Cyrenaica's – main strength was oil, (though an offshoot of his control over oil in the east was that whichever of Zintan and the Amazigh happened to control the west's major oilfields, controlled 60 per cent of the nation's income), and he intended to use it not only to bring cash to his rogue state, but also to deliver de-facto trade recognition: a state which buys oil from Cyrenaica, the argument went, must therefore recognise Cyrenaica exists.

On 7th January 2014, the Political Bureau issued a letter to the international media, in which it promised to protect any ship attempting to purchase and load oil from the ports the Bureau was occupying. It read: 'The official government of Cyrenaica* will fully ensure the security and safety of any ship or tanker that will enter Libyan waters for oil lifting in the port of Sidra. Any warning or statement by the Central Libyan government is considered as not applicable to ports under full control of our government.'

The statement brought to mind Thatcher's comment that 'Being a powerful person is like being a lady: if you have to tell someone that you are one, you are not.'

Oil traders rejected the letter as 'not credible' – not least because it had been inspired not by an empty warning from the Libyan government, but by the Libyan militias firing on a Maltese tanker which had attempted only days before to dock at Es Sider, Libya's largest oil port.

But on 1st March, a group of armed men boarded the MV Morning Glory, a 35,000 tonne oil-tanker, which had once belonged to Liberia and was heading for Tunisia under a North Korean flag. They turned off the ship's satellite transponder, causing it to disappear from world shipping maps, and on 9th March 2014, docked at Es Sider.

Despite a series of warnings from Ali Zeidan's government – to the ship's crew and to Jadhran's proto-government – Morning Glory prepared to leave on 11th March, with a cargo of 234,000 barrels of oil: US$20m stolen from the Libyan state.

The government was determined to prevent Morning Glory leaving Es Sider, but was once again embarrassed by weakness. Ghaddafi's major warships had been destroyed by NATO's bombs in 2011, and the government had neither the cash, nor the power, to replace them.

Its air force (many of whose planes were relatively undamaged during the Civil War because unlike NATO, Ghaddafi obeyed the 2011, UN-imposed no-fly zone over Libya) refused to follow government orders to launch, due to a dispute over its leadership. And so, once again, the government turned to the khetibas – this time, the Libya Shield, specifically one of its Misrata brigades – to attempt to defend the state's possessions and perhaps its continued existence.

The brigade commandeered a tug, to which it lashed anti-aircraft guns and a jeep mounted with rocket-launchers. It set sail for Es Sider, where Morning Glory was already facing heavy seas, heavy rain and high winds. The tug did manage to engage the tanker: a TV crew aboard the 'Libyan government' vessel posted videos of the Shield firing rockets at Morning Glory. One appeared to hit the ship, but then its crew* broadcast a distress plea:

It later emerged that Morning Glory was crewed by six Pakistani sailors, all of whom were returned safely home, without any suspicion they had committed any crime.

'Don't fire, don't fire. We have security on board, we cannot do anything.'

(Shield captain) 'We are not firing. Could you change the course to Misrata, please? Have you taken your map to see Misrata port please?'

'I cannot do anything. The security on the bridge, the security on the bridge, with guns. They cannot let me do anything. Please don't fire, please don't fire.'

Morning Glory, its size better enabling it to handle the rough seas and adverse winds, soon ploughed away from the tug, and into international waters.

The rogue, stateless* ship, had escaped.

Though Morning Glory been had registered as a North Korean vessel, the East Asian state announced during the attempted theft that it had 'cancelled and deleted' the vessel's registration, for 'violating its contract that prohibits it from transporting contraband cargo'. Even the world's pariah state could not be convinced to recognise Cyrenaica.

But the Morning Glory crisis had provided Ali Zeidan's government with cover for a land advance on Sirte, parts of which Jadhran had seized only a week before.

Though their comrades at arms had failed at sea, Libya Shield retook Sirte's Ghardabiya airbase, and forced Jadhran's army out of Eastern Sirte with relative ease: no injuries were reported and the Shield seized several weapons from the PFg.

And by 12th March, the Shield force was 5,000-strong, after three Tebu battalions and others from the South and West joined the Misrata brigades. But celebrations were muted – and not just because Morning Glory had escaped the Libyan government.

First, when the Shield arrived in Sirte, it opened fire on the headquarters of the Zawiyah Martyrs' Brigade, which had been in control of the city's 'security' for the previous ten months. The khetiba's leader Colonel Jamal Al-Zahwi commented, with admirable restraint: 'We were surprised at this.' (the Misratans apologised for their mistake).

Second, it could have escaped no-one's notice that this was the first time since October 2011 (and the second time ever) that gunfire had been exchanged over the 'ownership' of Sirte – and 'victory' only served to move Jadhran's usurper state back East by a matter of a few kilometres.

But third, and most damning, the 'liberation' of Sirte was achieved not by the government, but by khetibas from Misrata – also home to the militias which had killed 77 Libyan civilians and injured hundreds more in the previous nine months. The city which arguably defended Libya's unity was regarded with justified suspicion by most non-Misratans.

Morning Glory: Repercussions

It took only a few hours for the first effect of the Morning Glory escape to be felt: Libya's Prime Minister, Ali Zeidan, was removed from power.

The deposition had been coming – and was clearly foreseen by Zeidan himself, because despite state prosecutors' remarkable speed in declaring him guilty of 'corruption' (only hours passed between his deposition and the guilty verdict), which enabled the GNC to issue an order banning Zeidan from leaving Libya, it emerged that he had already gone. His plane had stopped for fuel in Malta, en route to Germany.

Zeidan claimed the process removing him and his government had itself been illegal, arguing that the 120 votes needed for a vote of no confidence to pass had not been reached.

The GNC responded that 124 of its members had backed the no-confidence motion, arguing with some justification that this made its decision not just a fait accompli, but also genuinely legal. And the Council's frustrations with Zeidan had been, if not entirely fair, at least understandable, and based on perceived failures of the Prime Minister and his cabinet, including their failure to meet the 24th December deadline to solve the crisis caused by Jadhran's blockade of Eastern Libya's oil ports.

Zeidan responded from Germany that his deposition was an attempt by the Muslim Brotherhood to 'take over' and that the group was using Islam as 'a political tool'. But Morning Glory had dealt a severe blow to his immediate political career, and thanks to GNC manoeuvring, made an elected liberal representative of the Libyan people Libya's first new political exile since late October 2011.

In the immediate aftermath of Zeidan's removal – and the lack of governance which resulted from it* - Libyan President, GNC chairman, Nuri Abu-Sahmayn, ordered the Misrata khetibas, now assisted by the Tebu and other militias, to advance South and East of Sirte, where they removed Jadhran's forces from the oil fields of Zeutina, Al-Ghani and Al-Fida.

---

* The GNC provisionally announced a new PM, the former defence minister Abdullah Al-Thinni, but he and his caretaker government – itself only a temporary arrangement before he presented his chosen government for GNC approval – had not had time to acclimatise to their new role, let alone get to grips with the challenges which faced them.

Four members of the Zawiyah Martyrs' Brigade were killed on the same day the advances were made, 12th March 2014, in an incident the exact details of which are still unclear. What is certain is that a rocket struck one of the khetiba's vehicles, incinerating all four men within it. Their bodies were taken to Benghazi, where three of the four had grown up.

Early reports suggested the attack was the result of another mistake by the Misratan Shield force, but later speculation also raised the possibility that Ansar al-Sharia – a major force in Sirte since the Civil War – had struck against members of a khetiba it regarded as a rival to its ambitions.

It is equally possible that another of the fundamentalist groups who, like Ansar, had overrun Sirte and were dispensing roadside 'justice' there, may have struck against a militia with which it shared little common ground following Ghaddafi's death, or that the Cyrenaican force itself had launched the rocket during its retreat from Sirte.

In any case, images of the burned men were combined with accusations of Misratan responsibility and used in Benghazi to raise a force made up not only of Jadhran's rebels, but also Benghazan militias nominally loyal to the government, as well as some Ansar al-Sharia gunmen. This new collective took up position at Wadi Lahmar, 90km east of Sirte, at the traditional border between Cyrenaica and Tripolitania. It prevented further Misratan and Tebu advances east.

In Libya's west, the Zintan khetibas maintained their support for Zeidan. They declared his sacking illegal and blockaded Western oil and gas production – effectively taking over from the Amazigh, who had on 8th March ended their blockade and agreed to take part in the Libyan municipal elections (though it continues to boycott the Libyan Constitutional Assembly).

Morning Glory, meanwhile, had travelled east, and on 16th March, the USS Roosevelt intercepted the ship in international waters off Cyprus. US Navy SEALS boarded the tanker and piloted it back to Libya. Along with the six crew members, the SEALS found just three armed Libyans aboard – it takes few people to steal US$20m of oil, provided they are in the right place and carry the right weapons.

The detention of three men on Cyprus – two Israelis and a Senegalese national – on Saturday 15th March may have delivered some clue as to Morning Glory's target destination. But a court at Larnaca declined to issue arrest warrants for the three men because Cypriot authorities had no evidence any offence was committed in its waters.

Ibrahim Jadhran described the US Navy's actions as 'theft', stating both that the oil belonged to the people of Cyrenaica and that any cash made from its sale would have been shared between 'Cyrenaica, Tripolitania and Fezzan'. He added that some of the cash would have been used to 'improve security in Benghazi and Derna' and called on the Arab League and international organisations to intervene and return the oil to his proto-statelet. But his words, spoken after a land defeat to the Shield, and a sea defeat which proved his impotence on the international stage, were mere sabre-rattling. The Arab League did not intervene, and international organisations allowed Morning Glory to return to Libya without complaint.

Jadhran's precariously-formed border alliance with Benghazan khetibas and Ansar al-Sharia remained in place, but how long that could continue seemed to depend solely on how long its component groups regarded the Shield as a genuine threat to people's safety. The attempt to win Cyrenaica international status had fallen at the first hurdle.

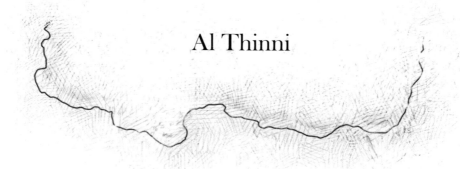

Al Thinni

Despite Cyrenaica's failures on land, at sea, and in international diplomacy, the Libya Abdullah Al-Thinni was now expected to lead was not really any better-off than that from which Zeidan had been chased.

'Victory' over Cyrenaica had 'liberated' three oil fields, but most of the state's oil remained under Jadhran's control. It had removed Jadhran from Sirte, but only pushed his troops back 90km, where a newly-unified Cyrenaica force, stronger than Jadhran's PFg alone, waited on the region's historical border.

Even under these terms, the 'victory' had been won not by Libya's army, but by the Shield's khetiba forces, loyal first to their immediate command, then to their city, and only finally to the government. And in this case, the Shield was made up of armed men from a city whose khetiba members had slaughtered 77 Libyan civilians in Benghazi and Tripoli within the last 12 months.

Not only that, the Zintan khetibas' closure of the pipes linking the Sharara oilfield to its ports had effectively ended oil production in much of Western Libya.*

Sharara produced 340,000 barrels of oil per day, out of a national total of 500,000 once the Cyrenaica fields had been snatched.

That closure was perhaps a less immediate threat to the state than the khetibas' military control of most of Libya, the creation of 'Cyrenaica' and battles in the south, but it held the potential to be much greater than any of them.

On 4th February, Zeidan and his Deputy Minister for Finance, Maraja Ghait, had announced that the government had presented a six-month budget to the GNC for approval.

But on 18th March – when al-Thinni was already a week into his 'interim' Prime Ministership (he was awaiting confirmation from the GNC that he could continue longer than the fortnight for which they had appointed him) – Libya's acting Finance Minister Souhail Abu Sheikha, revealed the Budget had still not been approved.

The Libyan state was now without a Prime Minister or a government, was operating under an Executive which had sacrificed its legitimacy by re-electing itself, facing a stand-off against newly – if probably temporarily – unified religious, regionalist and Cyrenaican separatist forces, under a 'government' working to break away from Libya, and had no financial plan.

Not only that, Abu Sheikha confirmed that he could only 'guarantee' that Libya had enough money to survive for three or four months.

The Libyan Central Bank had loaned the state-owned electricity production company one billion dinar to 'help solve the difficulties it faces', but Mohammed Abdallah, head of the parliamentary budget committee, admitted that the government had incurred a deficit of 3.785 billion dinar in January and February 2014 alone.

Al-Thinni was not an economist. Nor had he much experience in politics. But a long military career* had at least given him the ability to act tactically and effectively.

Al-Thinni, then 60, was originally from the north-west Libyan town of Ghadames, and had graduated from Military College in 1976. He was stationed in Tobruk, in the far East of Libya, and fought in the state's war against Egypt.

After the war, he served for seven years as a professor at Libya's Military College, but his position became more difficult after his brother – a Libyan Air Force pilot – stole an air force plane and escaped to Egypt, from where he became a vocal critic of the Ghaddafi regime's engagement in Chad.

Abdullah Al-Thinni, still a professor at the Military College, had risen to the rank of Colonel. But he was jailed by the Ghaddafi regime for his brother's activity and statements. He was released, and returned to his professorial post, but was detained on a number of other occasions – always because of his close family links to a dissident – and took early retirement from his post in 1997.

He had been appointed Libya's Defence Minister by Ali Ziedan in August 2013, after his predecessor in the role was sacked in June because of public dissatisfaction with the state's failure to respond to increased violence and killings across the country.

As Defence Minister, Al-Thinni was an outspoken defender of the Libyan army, telling NPR: 'The army is in the beginning of its inception. The world wants Libya to become a state in a night and a day. That's impossible.'

Nor was he a stranger to the power of Libya's khetibas. Though he had not yet been targeted by the state's illegal and semi-legal armed groups, his son Muhammed had been kidnapped on 24th September by armed men, who he said dragged him from his car when he visited Janzour.

He was released almost four months later, on 14th January, telling reporters he did not know why he had been kidnapped, or where he had been held, beyond the fact that he had been 'moved to different hiding places'.

In an interview with NPR (published on 26th February, just six weeks after his son's four-month kidnap ordeal), Abdullah Al-Thinni offered a view on the khetibas which had been publicly stated too little: 'As soon as (the militia members) are assured the state is strong and the army is strong, they will hand over their arms and return to their affairs. But Libya is going through a difficult phase with many challenges.'

In the short-term, Al-Thinni ignored the precarious nature of his Prime Ministership, sidestepping the necessity to propose a medium- to long-term cabinet and relying instead on the 'transitional' group of politicians installed by the GNC.

He also paid no attention to the questionable legal status of the khetibas, and focussed on the unquestionable illegality of the Jadhran regime, and its possession of Libya's oil.

Al-Thinni did not engage the forces sat on the historic border between Cyrenaica and Tripolitania, but opened direct negotiations with Jadhran. Whether as a measure of his negotiating abilities, his military experience and tactical brain or simply because Jadhran was in a position where he could no longer believe Cyrenaica could defeat a Libya which wanted it to remain united with it, the decision paid off.

On 6th April, the two smaller oil ports seized by the Cyrenaica rebels, Zuetina and Hariga, were handed back to the Libyan government by Jadhran. Ras Lanuf and Es Sider, both far larger* would be handed back after further negotiation.

Zuetina and Hariga combined produced roughly 200,000 barrels of oil per day: Ras Lanuf and Es Sider, 500,000 barrels per day, at the levels of May 2013. According to the GNC, the eight-month blockade of the four ports, combined with the irregular blockades in the West, has cost Libya US$18bn in income.

Jadhran spoke to a Cyrenaican broadcaster at Zuetina, saying: 'We did this out of goodwill to build trust, have a dialogue and solve all problems between Libyans by peaceful means. We will undertake more measures to strengthen these intentions provided the government fulfils its part. We serve Libya's interests.'

On the Libyan government side, Justice Minister Salah al-Marghani restrained himself to reading out the agreement the two sides had reached. He said: 'The ports Zuetina and Hariga will be handed over to the state with the signature of this agreement. The protestors are banned from returning, or obstructing work at the ports.'

Jadhran's own powers of negotiation should not be underestimated. Al-Marghani also confirmed that all charges would be dropped against the rebel secessionist and the PFg, and that all members would continue to receive their Libyan government salary, as well as that a committee would be set up to investigate financial and administrative corruption in Libya since Ghaddafi's death.

However, the agreement did not mention Cyrenaica's main demand: a greater share of oil revenue for the region. Nor did it include any suggestion of regional autonomy for the Eastern area.

Nine days later, on 15th April, the Italian tanker the Aegean Pride docked at Hariga to become the first vessel in more than eight months to legally load oil from an East Libyan port.*

Though it was to take another ten weeks, Jadhran's deal was completed, and on 2nd July 2014, the Ras Lanuf and Es Sider oil terminals were officially re-opened and put back into operation.

Al-Thinni moved swiftly to capitalise on his success. He returned to the GNC to request security for his position, saying in a letter delivered to the body: 'The events that this country is witnessing require quickness in executive decision-making. Thus, the interim government will take responsibility only as a government with full authority without interference from the legislative power.'

It was a deliberate swipe at the GNC and its committees, but on 8th April, Al Thinni was confirmed as 'permanent' Prime Minister by the GNC.

The vote caused immediate controversy. Suad Ganur, a GNC member returned by Sabha, pointed out that having received just 42 votes (only 76 members were present at the GNC to vote on the appointment of the new Libyan Prime Minister), the decision could not be legal, having fallen way short of the required 120 vote threshold.

Her – entirely reasonable – qualms were swept aside. Fellow GNC member Tahar Al-Mokni told the AFP news agency that 120 votes were not necessary, because Al-Thinni had been appointed temporary Prime Minister on 11th March with 124 GNC votes.

But the vote could hardly be considered an overwhelming expression of faith in Al-Thinni either.

Omar Hmidan, the GNC's official spokesman said: 'He was chosen after legislators failed to reach consensus on another candidate.' He did add, however, that Al-Thinni would remain in power until the election of a new Parliament to succeed the GNC.

He was given a week to form a new government.

Instead, within five days, he tendered his resignation.

On 12th April, gunmen opened fire on Al-Thinni and his family as they rode in convoy close to their home in Tripoli.

They escaped unharmed, but further intense gunfire broke out before the unidentified armed men left the area.

In a letter to the GNC, posted on the legislative body's website, Al-Thinni described the attack as 'cowardly' and 'a shooting that terrified people in a residential area and endangered the lives of some'.

He added: 'I do not accept a single drop of blood be shed because of me* and I do not accept to be a reason for fighting among Libyans because of this position. Therefore I apologise for not accepting my designation as Prime Minister.'

---

* Even if he were a 'cause' of bloodshed in Libya, Al-Thinni was certainly not alone. In fact, for the khetibas, it was pretty much 'business as usual' in Libya.

On 17th March, a car bomb exploded at a Benghazi military college's graduation ceremony, killing 14 people and injuring more than a dozen. On the same day, a second bomb exploded in Benghazi, killing a soldier as he drove through the city's Birkah district.

The killings were unusual mainly for their ferocity: security forces are attacked on an almost daily basis in Libya, but they and civilians are more often shot than blown to pieces.

And on 15th April, three days after Al-Thinni's family was attacked, gunmen in Tripoli opened fire on the convoy of the Jordanian Ambassador to Libya, Fawaz Aitan. The hooded men, riding in two civilian cars, wounded Aitan's driver, and abducted the Ambassador. It came four months after armed men had kidnapped five Egyptian diplomats. They had been released after several hours.

Aitain was eventually released on 13th May, but only as part of an exchange for a Libyan terrorist, Mohammed El Darsi, who had been jailed for life in 2007 for the attempted bombing of the Queen Alia International Airport in Jordan's capital, Amman. In common with almost all of the daily killings across Libya, no-one has been brought to justice for the attacks.

However, Al-Thinni's letter also stated that he made his decision to: 'protect the interests of the country and so as not to drag different sides into fighting when there can be no winner', and added that he would stay on as head of the Cabinet until a replacement could be appointed by the GNC.

The statement offered an intriguing possibility – that Al-Thinni had read the political situation in Libya and at the GNC, and was trying to strengthen his position.

All Libya knew that the GNC would struggle to agree on any alternative candidate for Prime Minister, and that he could therefore expect to remain not as GNC-appointed Prime Minister, but as head of the Cabinet – a post of necessity, rather than of prestige.

And in the event, that is exactly what happened.

Seven candidates to replace Al Thinni were nominated by the GNC's different political groups. One, Ahmed Maetig, a Misratan representative and former businessman supported by the Misrata khetiba and the GNC's Islamic bloc (including the Justice and Construction Party), emerged as clear favourite.

But although Maetig won the first ballot with 123 votes, he received just 83 in the decisive second round.

As a result, the First Deputy President of the GNC, Ezzidden Al-Awami, the man in charge of the process, instructed Al-Thinni to remain in post as PM.

Al-Thinni's spokesman Ahmed Lamin told the Libya Herald: 'The First Deputy has sent us a letter saying that the election of Maetig did not reach the required number of 120 votes and that accordingly Al-Thinni was to continue in office. We only deal with formal letters sent to us from the GNC.'

Within the GNC, questions were also raised about whether it would even be worthwhile for another Prime Minister to be appointed, as elections now must take place either at the end of June, just before Ramadan, or at the beginning of August, just after Eid.

Abdulmonem Alyaser, GNC member for Khoms, said: 'Electing a Prime Minister for a maximum of three months makes little sense. What kind of vision could possibly be enacted over such a short period of time?'

The question was not one which Maetig appeared to consider with any great seriousness. With the backing of the GNC's Muslim groups, he proceeded to assemble a Cabinet, and on 2nd June, accompanied by heavily-armed members of the Libya Shield and LROR (though neither group fired a shot), he forced his way into the Prime Minister's offices, where he held his first Cabinet meeting.

Al Thinni and his own Cabinet left Tripoli in the face of this violence, and was in Bayda when, nine days later, the Libyan Supreme Court, which had been ordered to pass judgement on Maetig's election as Prime Minister, ruled that it had been illegal.

It ordered that Maetig could not be considered Libya's PM on the grounds that the GNC had not been quorate – that although he had received enough votes to take the post, too few people had actually been in the GNC chambers to debate and vote on his accession.

Maetig and the GNC accepted and abided by the decision, which left Al Thinni – a man who officially abdicated his post as Prime Minister in April – as head of the Cabinet as Libya approached its June 2014 elections.

Libya's Future and Libya's Past

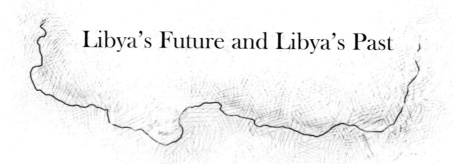

Even as Al Thinni manoeuvred to a positon in which he could lead a cabinet, Libya's day-to-day challenges continued much as before.

On 20th April, Justice Minister Salah al-Merghani moved to calm fears over Libya's oil supplies, announcing that Zuetina port, in East Libya, which had been expected to re-open at the same time as Hariga, remained closed only due to 'damage' sustained during the Jadhran-led secession attempt, not due to any breakdown in negotiations with the Cyrenaican 'administration'.

Nevertheless, with negotiations with the Zintan khetibas so far proving fruitless, this meant only one of Libya's seven oil ports was open and operating at anything close to full capacity.

The following day, the GNC admitted that oil production had fallen to a record low of 140,000 barrels per day in the first quarter of 2014.

As a result, Muhammed Abdullah, head of the Budgetary Committee, announced that the state's budget, drawn up in February to last just six months, but still not in place more than two months later, would have to be slashed from 68.6bn Libyan Dinar to 44bn.

He admitted that the cut would hit wages and infrastructure redevelopment plans, the two elements of most pressing importance to Libya's now long-suffering civilian population, adding: 'It is very difficult to launch a development plan in the absence of a government.'

Al-Merghani was in the public eye for another reason in April 2014, when ghosts from Libya's past cast shadows over the country's present and future.

On 14th April, the trial was expected to begin of 39 high-ranking officials from the Ghaddafi regime, including former Prime Minister Baghdadi al-Mahmoudi, ex-spy chief Abdullah al-Senussi, and two of Ghaddafi's sons, Saif al-Islam and Saadi Ghaddafi.

This was supposed to be Libya's 'trial of the century' – drawing a final line under the worst activities of the Ghaddafi regime by bringing some of its most prominent members to face real justice, in a properly-run court, following due process.

It was a chance for justice to succeed, to show how far things had progressed in the new Libya – Libya Hora. Instead, it was a farce.

Even before the trial began, Human Rights Watch had raised concerns over issues including the state limiting defendants' access to lawyers.

A spokesman for the organisation, Hanan Salah, said: 'Militias and criminals have harassed, intimidated, threatened and in some cases assassinated judges, prosecutors, witnesses.'

Its International Justice Director Richard Dicker added: 'The case has been riddled with procedural flaws right from the beginning. Putting Ghaddafi-era officials on trial without fair trial guarantees should not leave anyone satisfied that justice is being done.'

Concern over due process increased in April when prison guards shot and released a video in which – apparently without a lawyer present – Saadi 'confessed' to the crimes of which he was accused. And serious questions remain unanswered about Libya's legal right to try Saif al-Islam and Abdullah Al-Senussi at all.

Unlike Saadi Ghaddafi and the 36 other defendants, Saif Al-Islam and Senussi were charged by the International Criminal Court. Judges at The Hague ruled that Saif Al-Islam must stand trial at the ICC, while Senussi's lawyers were appealing against a decision made by the same judges that he could be tried in Libya: no trial against him should take place there until the appeal was completed.

Senussi's ICC legal team were prevented from visiting their client by 'Libya' – in fact by the Zintani khetibas who arrested him and have refused to hand him over to the Libyan government. His testimony was to be heard by satellite link from Zintan, as the khetibas refused even to allow him into Tripoli to stand trial.

Amal Alamuddin, part of the ICC legal team charged with handling Senussi's case, asked: 'How can you have a fair trial if they don't let the lawyers visit Senussi or even speak to him by phone?'

Questions could be asked, also, about the charges laid against the 39.

Libya filed more than 40,000 pages of evidence with the ICC, and accused Saif al-Islam, Saadi and the 37 others (who, perhaps not coincidentally, make up almost all of the surviving high-ranking members of the Muammar Ghaddafi regime) of orchestrating a campaign of murder, torture, and bombardment of citizens during the Civil War.

Of course, any member of Ghaddafi's regime who actually committed these crimes, and any who ordered them, must face justice, but there was an uncomfortable crossover between the accusations made solely against Muammar Ghaddafi (many of which, including mass killings at Tawergha, the issuing of Viagra to soldiers to enable rape and plans for 'genocide' have yet to be backed by any evidence at all) and those now made against his sons, other family members and his political associates.

And in the case of Saadi Ghaddafi, many Libyans have expressed scepticism about all of the charges.

Saif Al-Islam was known in the West for his social life, having enjoyed hospitality at Buckingham Palace and being linked to Prince Andrew and Tony Blair. But Saadi is best known in Libya and overseas for his love of football and 'good-living' – particularly his attempts to make it as a professional footballer in Italy.

He was actually signed by three Italian Serie A sides, but played just twice in total – for Perugia and Udinese. Sampdoria, for whom he was registered for one year, never used him in a competitive fixture.

And in 2010, he was fined €392,000 by an Italian court for an unpaid hotel bill run up in Liguria in 2007.

While these may not be great qualities in a leader, they are also far from being the mark of a man preparing to continue his father's brutal record of terror and torture.

Saadi's public appearances during the Civil War are also hardly the stuff of hard-nosed brutalism. On 24th August 2011, he told CNN that he had authority to negotiate on the regime's behalf, and called a ceasefire to be discussed with the US and NATO.

Seven days later, he appeared on Al Arabiya, telling the broadcaster his father was ready to step down, and calling for dialogue with the NTC.

On both occasions, he was ignored.

He waited just five days before trying again, this time offering on 5th September to mediate between his father and the NTC from a 'position of neutrality'.

Once again, Saadi's offer fell on deaf ears. But being poor at negotiations and publicity is not the same as being a torturer or murderer.

On 11th September, more than a month before his father was killed, Saadi fled to Niger. Two months later, the Niger government confirmed it had offered him asylum, on the grounds that he would face persecution, and possible torture and death were he to return to Libya.

But on 5th March, the Libyan government announced he had been extradited from Niger and was being held in Tripoli.

As one social media commentator put it: 'I can believe that Saif and Senussi could have done what is alleged. But I cannot believe that Muammar Ghaddafi would have let Saadi anywhere near the War. He was a bad football player, and he liked cars and hotels. No-one could have thought he was clever enough to run a war.'

A more believable charge, considering his life pre-2011, was one also laid against Saif Al-Islam: using state funds to pay for extravagant lifestyles abroad.

Despite the reservations of human rights organisations, on the morning of 14th April, journalists gathered for the trial at the maximum-security al-Hadba prison.

The hearing was an abject failure. Only 23 of the defendants were present.

Saif Al-Islam, of course, was expected to be absent, as the Zintan militia had agreed he would testify by satellite link.

But Saadi was also not there, without explanation, and then an announcement was made from Misratan khetibas that they 'demanded' the same 'privileges' as those granted the Zintan militias, and would only allow the seven defendants in their custody to take part in the hearings by video link – even though they were detained in Tripoli.

The video link from Zintan showed no sign of Saif Al-Islam, either, only an empty courtroom.

Al-Senussi, 64, did attend the court. The UK's Guardian newspaper described him as 'lean and haggard, unrecognisable from the once-rugged figure accused of terrorising the population for three decades.'

He faces charges of murder, torture, kidnapping, false imprisonment, embezzlement and incitement to rape.

At one point he rose, telling the court that he had only just been granted a lawyer, six months after one was supposed to be appointed.

'I get treated completely differently to my fellow cellmates,' he began. 'Five days ago I signed a paper with a defence lawyer.

'I want to be treated like other prisoners. I want visiting rights. And I want to see my lawyer.'

Judges demanded an explanation, and prosecutor Siddiq al-Sur said: 'He was allowed visits. He was allowed to see his daughter, his cousins. We were looking for lawyers to defend him. We have asked him for his lawyer's name.'

The judges took just one hour to adjourn the case – to 25th May 2014. Tellingly, their parting comment was to order that defence lawyers must be able to examine copies of the evidence against their clients.

Ashraf Abdul-Wahab, chief reporter of the Libya Herald, commented after the hearing: 'This is not a trial, they shouldn't call this a trial. This was a test for justice in Libya, and it's a test Libya failed.'

On 21st May 2014, the International Criminal Court reaffirmed that Saif al Islam must stand trial at the Hague, not in Libya, expressing concern that he was not charged with the same crimes in Libya as he was by the international community.

And by that point, circumstances had already conspired to make the 25th May court hearing an impossibility.*

---

* *The trial re-started in Tripoli on Sunday 16th November. Saif al Islam was amongst those not to attend, even though the Zintan khetiba had, on 12th November, refused the ICC's demand to hand him over. Sanussi was, once again, forced to appear.*

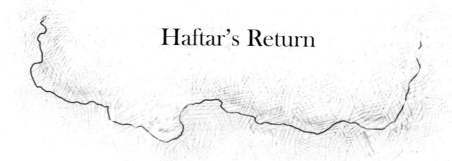

Haftar's Return

Khalifa Haftar had not appeared in public since the bombast of his Valentine's Day call for a 'new roadmap' for Libya had been punctured by Ali Zeidan.

But on 16th May, a force he commands, which he originally attempted to call the Libyan National Army (the name did not catch on), launched a strike on Ansar Al Sharia buildings in Benghazi.

Two days later, Zintani militias, who had allied with Haftar, attacked the GNC parliamentary buildings in Tripoli, ransacking the building, kidnapping ten people and killing two.

They declared the GNC 'suspended' and when some members of the parliament attempted to meet in another location to vote on matters including the state's budget and ongoing Prime Ministerial problems, the building they were in was attacked with rockets.

In total, the Tripoli and Benghazi strikes left 80 people dead and 160 injured.

Haftar, who masterminded both, claimed to be operating a plan he has designed, under the name Operation Libyan Dignity,* in order to remove 'Islamists'** from Libyan political life.

Though the name sounds American, this may well be solely because of the 20 years Haftar spent in Virginia. US State Department spokeswoman Jen Psaki responded to Haftar's activity with the following statement: 'We do not condone or support the actions on the ground and nor have we assisted with these actions', adding a plea for dialogue between opposing forces.

**Haftar and his allies' use of the term 'Islamists' has devalued the term to such an extent that it has become almost meaningless. In its public statements, his 'force' – effectively a united band of khetibas and parts of Libya's military – has equated violent extremists, such as Ansar al-Sharia, with the elected politicians of the Justice and Construction Party.*

While both groups were undeniably 'Islamist' in that they felt Libya could be organised and run on religious, Muslim, guidelines, Ansar advocates the use of violence to attempt to destroy democracy and replace it with a caliphate, in which one man rules the entire state, while Justice and Construction's politicians are active democrats, partaking in the democratic system with enthusiasm, if not always expertise.

The Misrata khetibas, while certainly not peaceful, also claim to support democracy, and their violence since Haftar's attacks has been no greater or less than that used by the 'liberal' Zintan khetibas.

As a result, any time the term 'Islamist' is used in the chapters which follow – outside of direct quotes – it will always be coupled with either the word 'extremist', used to denote those who wish to use violence to smash democracy, or 'moderate', describing Muslim people or organisations which hope to operate within a democratic system.

The extent of the support for Haftar within Libya was not immediately clear. Military aircraft fired on Benghazi, indicating some support from the state's armed forces, and he was enthusiastically backed by the Zintani khetibas (in itself not especially surprising: as a supporter of the National Forces Alliance, the Zintani brigades could naturally be expected to ally with a man claiming to want to rid Libya of 'Islamists', as the Justice and Construction Party's moderate Islamists represent the greatest opposition to the NFA in Libyan politics).

He was also publicly-backed by Libya's UN envoy Ibrahim al-Dabashi, who claimed: 'The campaign is not a coup, but a nationalist move.'

This view was not shared by Al Thinni, who on 16th May described the attacks as: 'illegal… an attempted coup. Those who attack Benghazi do not have legitimacy from the state.'

Definitely ranged against him – and the victims of his first attack – are the Ansar Al Sharia and February 17 Brigades.

Both groups are part of the Shura Council of Benghazi Revolutionaries, which was set up in response to the US government's arrest of Abu Khattala under suspicion of the murder of Christopher Stevens, and both are backed by Al Qaeda.

The Misrata khetiba, more powerful than the Libyan military and Zintani khetibas combined – and the main backer of the Justice and Construction Party at which the shocking strike on the GNC was aimed – made no reaction to the strike on Benghazi.

But it responded to the Zintan khetiba's attack on the GNC with typical force, pushing the Zintanis back to their Tripoli airport road stronghold.

The opinions of Libya's civilian population were also divided. Most supported the idea that extremist Islamists should be prevented from killing and terrorising, but were also concerned by Haftar's motives.

Tripoli-based lawyer Abdullah Banoun summed up the feeling when asked by Associated Press on 21st May. He said: 'If Haftar wants to take over power, we won't accept more coups. Ghaddafi terrorised us for 42 years. The alternative to Ghaddafi is civilian rule, nothing less than that.' And Haftar's actual statements on the matter – beyond his mantra of the need to remove 'Islamists' from Libya – were wildly inconsistent.

In little more than a fortnight, he assured people he did not wish to lead a coup, recommended the arrest of democratically-elected representatives of the people, publicly supported the missile attack on Libya's Parliament, proposed that the Constitutional Assembly should take power until August (even though that body has still not filled any of its 13 vacant seats) and offered to head a military council which will hold power until elections could be held.

Taken as a whole, this array of proposals bring to mind the criticism levelled by historian

Fathi al Fatdhaldi of Haftar's Chadian command: 'He didn't have a plan – not even an exit plan.'

And the proposal of a military council is worryingly close to the pattern followed by Egypt's blood-stained dictator Sisi, who also repressed Islamic political groups, then staged his impossible amassing of 96.1 per cent of the vote in order to retain the power he had seized with guns.

It is also hard to understand why anyone who wished to clear the way for peaceful, fair elections would have chosen to attack the Libyan Parliament on 18th May, just one month and one week before the nation was due to choose its representatives at the new HoR.

Early polls in the run-up to the elections were particularly promising to those who wanted Justice and Construction removed from power, suggesting the Party was set to take just 14 per cent of the vote, compared to the NFA's projected total of 70 per cent.

Haftar's strikes on the Al Qaeda-aligned Shura Council of Benghazi Revolutionaries were, in a sense, at least in the spirit in which the fundamentalist militias have themselves behaved – refusing democracy and choosing instead to attempt to rule by fear, weapons and death.

But Justice and Construction – like the wider Muslim Brotherhood movement throughout the Maghreb – deliberately chose the ballot box to attempt to achieve its ambitions. And the party was on course to be wiped out in Libya's next elections.

Even if Haftar believed it was a negative factor in Libya's political environment, it was concerning that he would rather use weapons to smash away a democratically-elected group of politicians than simply wait five weeks for the Libyan public to do it by voting.

On 18th May, his spokesman Mohammed Al Hegazi told the TV broadcaster Alahrar: 'The aim (of the attack on the GNC) was to arrest Islamist bodies who wear the cloak of politics. This Parliament supports extremist Islamist entities.'

But for all its faults, the GNC – and the Justice and Construction Party within it – did not support either Ansar Al Sharia or the February 17 brigade.

The Muslim Brotherhood in Libya is firmly tied to the Misrata khetibas, and to claim links between either the GNC or Justice and Construction and Islamist extremism raises serious questions about the person making such a claim.

The GNC was populated by politicians. Many of them – on both sides of the Muslim Brotherhood/secular divide – were of dubious competence, but they were peaceful participants in a democratic system. Haftar ordered his allies in an illegal militia to smash the national parliament with missiles, killing two people in the process.

Whatever his motives, that was an inexcusable perversion of 'saving the Free Libya' or of protecting the aims of the Revolution.

Haftar's next strike in Benghazi, on 1st June, sparked reprisals from the city's Shura Council.

Using Libyan air force planes, Haftar bombed buildings being used by Ansar Al Sharia in the Hawari and Gunfuda areas of Benghazi.

The following day, the Council's militias bombarded Benghazi's Air Base 21, said to contain elite special forces, killing and wounding soldiers inside.

In total, across the two days, 18 people were killed and 39 injured.

Two days later, a suicide bomber drove a car packed with explosives into Haftar's Benghazi home. Three people were killed, but Haftar himself survived.

Al Qaeda in the Islamic Maghreb called for Libyans to fight Haftar, describing him as an 'enemy of Islam, carrying out a crusader campaign'.

It was a reminder of the weakness at the heart of Haftar's campaign.

In March, Libya had been faced with a separatist movement which planned to end the state, and take vast amounts of oil with it. Al Thinni and Abu Sahmayn, politicians of sound mind and some strategic ability, had recognised that the strongest military organisations in Libya were the khetibas, and encouraged them to overcome their political differences and stand together to defend their nation.

They succeeded.

Haftar, by contrast, attacked a council of militias backed by an international terror organisation, and at almost exactly the same time split Libya's khetibas with an unjustified, illegal and inexplicable attack on the country's parliament. In doing so, he made himself and his allies not only enemies of the Benghazi Shura Council in the east, but also the Misrata khetiba – Libya's strongest military force – in the west.

He compounded his error by pretending that the moderate, elected, Islamic political party Justice and Corruption was the same as the violent and illegal militia Ansar Al Sharia, which kills innocent people on a daily basis.

In doing so, and by painting 'Islamism' rather than extremism, as his and 'Libya's' enemy, he began to force Muslims within the state to choose not between moderation and violence, but between Islam and taking part in Libyan political life.

It is still not too late to avoid turning Libya into what Syria is today – a battleground where international jihadists fight bloodthirsty militarists, destroying, and likely ending, the lives of anyone who would rather not be either – but Haftar's illegal attack on Libya's two largest cities, and his abject strategic failure were at that point the two largest steps ever taken in Libya towards delivering that nightmarish outcome.

25th June 2014: Voting Under Fire

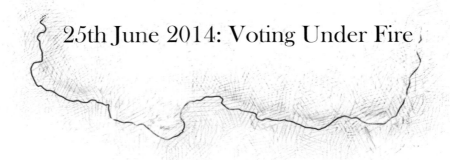

The most surprising thing about Libya's 25th June national election is that it took place at all.

Haftar's attacks on Benghazi and Tripoli had created not so much a country at war, as a nation hosting several wars at once.

In Tripoli, the Zintan and Misrata khetibas were battling one another on a sporadic, street-by-street, and day-by-day basis, rather than in an all-out assault on one another, but in Benghazi Haftar's 'Libya Dignity' illegal army was engaged in full, open warfare against Benghazi's extremist, Al Qaeda-backed Shura Council. The signs were that 'Dignity' was losing ground almost every day.

In Derna, to the east of Benghazi, Islamist extremists had controlled daily life for many months, and showed no signs of reducing their aggressive repression of those they regarded as their opponents – effectively, almost anybody or anyone who was not actually a member of Derna's Islamic Youth Shura Council. And in Libya's south and west, minority groups and political dissidents battled for rights, as well as for money, water and food.

Under such circumstances, the GNC could have been forgiven for postponing the elections, which would have been an ironic outcome of Haftar's assault – though it would perhaps also have handed him 'justification' by pushing the GNC to extend its expired mandate yet further.

Instead, the parliament ordered that the ballot must take place as scheduled, and in doing so proved it had learned nothing from the experience of February's Constitutional Assembly election. Turnout on the day was just 18 per cent: 630,000, out of 3.4m registered voters. Once again, no voting was able to take place in Derna, as the Youth Council threatened to bomb polling stations, and to shoot anyone who attempted to enter them.

In Benghazi, five people were killed and 30 injured when militia members opened fire on a building being used as a voting centre, and later that day, human rights activist and mother-of-three Salwa Bughaighis* was killed on returning home from casting her vote in the city.

* Bughaighis, 50, had been an outspoken critic of Ghaddafi, and had taken part in some of the earliest demonstrations against him in Benghazi in 2011. She was a founder member of the National Transitional Council, resigning in protest at a lack of female representation within it, and she went on to become a mentor to aspiring female politicians and campaigners.

She had supported Libya's secularist political movement, but her brother was a member of the Justice and Construction Party. Since 2012, she had been an outspoken opponent of the continued presence of armed groups on Libya's streets.

On her return home on 25th June, five men – four masked and all wearing military fatigues and hoods – fought their way into her house, shooting and stabbing her to death. It is believed the five, who also kidnapped Mrs Bughaighis' husband Essa Al-Gariani, belonged to Ansar Al-Sharia. They have not been arrested.

In Kufra and Sabha, people were also prevented from voting, and ballots which had been cast were prevented from being sent for verification and counting. The Amazigh, Tuareg, and Teba all boycotted the election.

The result was that only 188 of the 200 seats was filled, and in many places, candidates took seats having received fewer than 1,000 votes, leading many Libyans to question the validity of representatives who had won only a tiny fraction of the available votes.

However, as in every election, only those who actually vote – even if many of those who did not were prevented from doing so with missiles and bullets – are able to choose the government. Calls for a re-election were ignored – after all, when would Libya be peaceful enough to stage a better plebiscite? – and so it was that on 22nd July, the House of Representatives' first composition was announced.

Under the criteria set out by the February Committee, the candidates for the HoR elections were not allowed to stand on a Party platform, but in the event, predictably, that is exactly what many did.

The results handed 50 seats to the National Allied Forces, the secularists who had also held the majority in the GNC until 7th February.

Justice and Construction took 30 seats, and Cyrenaican Federalists and separatists, despite the unmitigated failure of their independence attempt just three months before, scooped a remarkable 25 seats.

The remaining 83 seats (12 remained unfilled) went to 'independents' but unlike the GNC elections of 2012, most of these were secularist-leaning, and considered to be unlikely to side with Justice and Construction.

It was not quite the secularist rout that the polls predicted – though the 'independent' vote pushed it very close to being so – but the election, despite being questionably representative of Libya as a whole, had delivered defeat to Justice and Construction. The international community swiftly congratulated – and officially recognised – the new parliament.

However, the HoR was almost immediately thrown into controversy as a direct result of the war Haftar had started to remove Islamic influence from Libyan politics.

The February Committee had stipulated that the GNC must hand power to the HoR in Tripoli, and that from then, the new parliament would sit in Benghazi. The former was set to take place on 4th August, the latter at the soonest available opportunity following that date.

Both were self-evidently problematic. Sporadic gun battles and missile strikes in Tripoli led many of the politicians who had been elected to the HoR reluctant to return to the city, while Benghazi was gripped by an ongoing all-out war, making it impossible for parliament to sit there.

Instead, the HoR announced it would be unable to attend a handover in Tripoli, and that it intended to hold its first parliamentary session on 4th August 2014, in Tobruk, Libya's eastern-most city, around 100km from the Egyptian border.

In response, the members of the Justice and Construction party, as well as some independents, refused to attend the HoR. That some did so to attempt to neutralise an electoral outcome they disliked, is undeniable.

Immediately, it became clear that this very public stand-off was feeding into an already divisive situation, once again pitching moderate Islamists against secularists, instead of the arguably more appropriate grouping of supporters of democracy against extremist murderers.

Smaller, but also significant, outcomes were the elevation of the Cyrenaican Federalist movement to a position as Libya's official Opposition, and making it harder for the HoR to achieve the 120 votes it needs to pass laws, in line with the Constitutional Declaration's requirements (regular attendance, by September, was around 115 politicians per session).

Both factors had the effect of handing casting votes on proposed laws to 25 people who hope Libya will cease to exist.

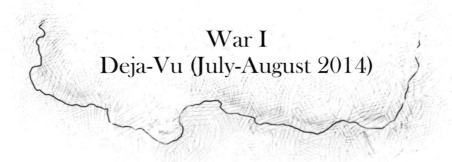

War I
Deja-Vu (July-August 2014)

The summer of 2014 was supposed to be a turning-point for Libya.

In the minds of the country's February Committee, and its politicians, the election of the HoR – and the ongoing existence of a fully-elected, restructured parliament with a full public mandate – was to stand as a shining example for the nation as a whole, a symbol that progress, though gradual, was real.

Instead, Libya's summer began with a sickening sense of deja-vu.

In the west, gun battles and rocket-fire punctured sleep, and made travelling to work, school, or to the shops into a potentially life-threatening experience, while in Benghazi, a member of a formerly revolutionary cadre of army officers was hammering the city with aircraft and ground troops.

NATO was not there (though it was only to be a matter of time before it was invited to return) but apart from that all the pieces were in place, and seemed ready to stage a particularly convincing reconstruction of Libya's 2011 Civil War.

At the time of writing (mid-November 2014), it has become fashionable in certain quarters to claim that the battles between the Misrata and Zintani khetibas began only after the HoR elections removed Justice and Construction from power.

It is a view which is comforting for those, like Haftar, who wish to paint secularists as Libya's saviours and 'Islamists' as its enemy, but it is incorrect.

The Misrata khetiba was always more bloody than Zintan's equally-illegal cadre of gunmen, but had nonetheless managed to remain relatively peaceful since its re-entry into Tripoli after Haftar's Valentine's Day call for a coup.

It was still preventing Tawerghans from returning to the homes it had forced them from, and its members should have been facing war crimes trials for its ethnic-cleansing of that small town.

Equally, it should have been awaiting censure and punishment for the massacre of 43 peaceful demonstrators in Tripoli the previous November.

And it is certainly unclear how long the Misrata khetibas, by now in the fourth consecutive year of a war they have arguably never truly left behind, and labouring under the belief that they should be rewarded for removing Ghaddafi, would have allowed the Tripoli détente to last.

Perhaps their part in the defeat of Jadhran's separatists could have helped them integrate finally, into the society they believed they had created almost single-handedly. Or maybe they would, as they always had done in the past, allow their anger to spill into rage and the spilling of blood.

Whichever was more likely to happen, if we are to accurately record the cause of the 'Battle for Tripoli' of 2014, we must start with the Zintani khetiba's inexcusable attack on serving politicians in the GNC.

If the Misrata khetibas were waiting for an excuse to attack, this was it. Under the pretext – perhaps honestly held – of protecting the GNC, they pushed the Zintani militias back to Maetiga, Tripoli's international airport, which had been held by the Zintan brigades (despite repeated government requests for its return) since 2011.

From there, a series of street skirmishes took place until, on 13th July, nine days before the national election results were to be announced, the Misratan khetibas – by now unified with Libya Shield forces under the name 'Fajr' ('Dawn') – launched an attack on the airport itself.

The intensity of the fighting increased from there. On 27th July, five days after the HoR election results had been announced, almost all international diplomats had withdrawn from Libya. Three days later, British and French expat workers were evacuated, and the following day the Philippines government became the last to remove its citizens from the state.

As that evacuation was underway, huge numbers of Libyans and Egyptians began to flee west, attempting to cross into Tunisia. The Tunisian government closed its border – albeit temporarily. It appeared that almost all of the ghosts of Libya's Civil War had returned.

News from Benghazi was less easy to come by – and harder to verify. Most news carriers within and outside of Libya overlooked the reports from the Shura Council of Benghazi Revolutionaries, leaving only the statements of Haftar's 'Dignity' force as updates from the battles. From those broadcasts, it became clear that even though Haftar was attempting to win a war of information, he was being heavily defeated on the ground.

And on 31st July, reports confirmed that the Council had effectively defeated 'Dignity' in Benghazi, having added the city's main police station and the barracks of the 'Dignity'-aligned Saiqa army unit to its 14th July capture of the main army base.

Haftar's force still held on at Benina – Benghazi's international airport – but defeat was looming for 'Operation Dignity' – and a massive morale boosting victory handed not just to members of the Shura Council, but to violent extremists across the state.

On 8th August, watching with increasing horror from its Tobruk base, the HoR voted to call for Western intervention – perhaps hoping NATO would oblige in assisting Haftar in the same way as it had helped the khetibas in 2011.

The call was largely ignored, except within Libya, where Abdul Raof al-Mannai, an elected member of the HoR who was by that point boycotting the parliament, claimed it was unconstitutional. On the same day, with Tripoli experiencing food shortages as a result of fighting (money and petrol were already unavailable) the UN mission in Libya (UNSMIL), led by the mission's special envoy Bernardino Leon, attempted to open negotiations to end the fighting.

Though the negotiations failed to end the conflict in the city, elders from communities in and around the metropolis managed to reach an agreement to reduce the disruption of supplies and services, enabling money to reach banks, fuel stations to reopen, and the provision of food to shops. And in what seemed like a small signal that things may be returning to something like normality, Tripoli's bus services restarted operations on 12th August.

But with Haftar all but chased from Benghazi, the House of Representatives met again on 13th August, this time deciding by 111 votes out of 124 to call for UN intervention in Libya.

Secretary General Ban Ki-Moon was later to respond that any intervention could only happen as a result of a Security Council vote in favour, and the matter was not taken any further. At the same session, the HoR passed a motion by 102 out of 104 votes calling for all illegal militia organisations in Libya to disband. The demand was treated as all previous ones had been: across Libya, khetibas lined up against one another and fought, while in Tobruk, the HoR was left to watch, powerless to prevent them.

But while Libya's illegal militias were ignoring the HoR, and the UN was quietly distancing itself from its requests, Abdul Raof al-Mannai was strongly engaged with its activities.

The day after the parliament's call for UN intervention, he submitted a request to Libya's Supreme Court for a ruling on whether the HoR is a legitimate organisation under the Libyan Constitutional Declaration, inspired, he said, by the suspicion that the HoR's calls for foreign involvement in Libyan affairs had been made contrary to the Declaration's criteria.

In the context of the ongoing fighting – and the very real possibility that conflict could escalate further – the request seemed of limited importance.

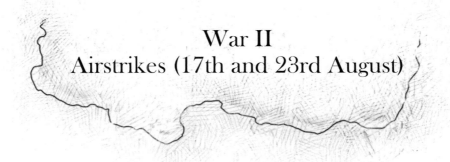

War II
Airstrikes (17th and 23rd August)

Even disregarding Haftar's undeniable strategic and battlefield shortcomings, and his deficiencies of leadership, the war he chose to fight was always likely to be an uphill struggle.

He had cobbled together a force of demoralised, poorly-trained, poorly-armed, and exhausted troops from the Libyan army, ill-prepared and ill-disposed to enter a new civil war so soon after the last, some members of the national air-force and Libya's second-strongest khetiba.

Their opponent in Benghazi, the Shura Council of Benghazi Revolutionaries, is relatively small, but well-drilled, well-rooted in Benghazi, with experience of fighting and killing on its streets, dedicated to the death of its enemies and the crushing of democracy in Libya, motivated by Salafist Jihadism, funded from Saudi Arabia and with a near-continuous supply of members from across Libya and beyond.

Even under those circumstances, if the Zintan khetiba had been able to join the rest of 'Operation Dignity' in Benghazi, it is possible the force might have overcome the Shura Council. But because Haftar decided to open a war on two fronts, pretending that serving politicians were no different from extremist militias and ordering the attack on the GNC, the Zintani brigades had been caught in a battle against Fajr, and so unable to assist their ally in the east.

Haftar had been chased from Benghazi, a humiliating reversal. But if the Zintan khetiba had been able to defeat Fajr in Tripoli, it may have been able to mobilise to help Haftar swiftly counter-attack, and perhaps even have inspired 'Dignity' to defeat the Shura Council.

Unfortunately, by mid-August, the Zintan khetibas' weakness relative to Fajr was beginning to show. Though it had proven almost impossible to dislodge from Maetiga airport, it had lost ground in every other part of the city, and as Fajr advanced towards the airport, it was clear that a decisive defeat for Zintan was by far the most likely outcome.

Faced with certain defeat in the east, and almost certain failure in the west, Haftar fell back on his American training.

In the most shameful act of the 2014 conflict so far, he called in airstrikes on the capital city of Libya. Two aircraft, flown by Libyan air force pilots under the command of Khalifa Haftar, entered Tripoli's airspace during the night of 17th August 2014.

The bombs they dropped killed six people, injuring 30 more.

In the immediate aftermath, speculation on social media and official news sources alike attempted to make sense of what had happened. Fajr sources claimed – predictably – that 'Dignity' had launched the strikes, while Haftar's supporters in Tripoli countered that Libya did not have aircraft capable of making such a strike in darkness.

They were both correct. The aircraft were Egyptian, flown by 'Dignity' pilots and the mission had been funded by the government of the UAE.*

> * *Egypt originally denied involvement in the strike, but anonymous US government sources confirmed within days that the craft were owned by the Egyptian air force. They also claimed the US government had warned Egypt and UAE not to engage in the conflict in Libya. No action has yet been taken by the US against either state.*
>
> *The reasons for Egypt's involvement are relatively easy to understand: General Sisi, having designated the Muslim Brotherhood a terrorist organisation while slaughtering its members and supporters on the streets of Egypt's cities, had no desire to see the capital of a neighbouring state overtaken by its supporters.*
>
> *The factor driving the UAE's engagement are a little more complex. The UAE's government is extremely closely allied to that of Saudi Arabia, which opposes the Muslim Brotherhood not for its Islamic views but because the Brotherhood opposes monarchical rule. In effect, the airstrikes on Tripoli were the Saudi regime indirectly assisting Haftar in west Libya, while at the same time directly funding his enemies in Benghazi.*

Later reports have suggested that Egyptian troops have also been sent to assist Dignity forces in Benghazi. Haftar's air defence commander Saqer al-Jouroushi, confirmed: 'We, the Operation Dignity, officially confirm to have conducted air strikes on some militias' locations belonging to Misrata militias.'

The strikes – apart from horrifying Libyans and angering the US government – had little effect. Fajr continued its seemingly-relentless advance on Maetiga airport, and the Zintan brigades were no more likely than before to defeat them when they arrived.

Never one to give up on an idea simply because it is clearly not working, Haftar tried again – the same combination striking Tripoli from above again on 23rd August, this time without killing or injuring anybody.

The 23rd August strikes were exactly as effective as those launched on 17th August, and later that day, Fajr defeated the Zintan khetibas, taking Maetiga airport, and the rest of Tripoli with it.

Khalifa Haftar, the least competent military leader Libya had ever produced, had proclaimed his mission 'Operation Libyan Dignity'. In his relentless campaign for Libyan unity, he had started a civil war, which he was losing. And in his quest for Libyan dignity, he had drawn on his CIA training and emulated his American teachers, by launching air strikes on Libya's capital city, and most populous urban area.

Dignity is perhaps a word with many meanings.

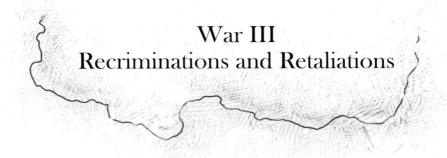

War III
Recriminations and Retaliations

'Operation Libyan Dignity' had failed to prevent Tripoli falling to its foes, and had been chased from Benghazi.

And Khalifa Haftar had achieved what even his former comrade Muammar Ghaddafi had not: the bombing of Libya's capital.

It was unclear how – and in fact whether – he would be able to recover in the east, while in the west, Fajr began to stamp its authority onto Tripoli and the Zintan khetiba it had defeated to snatch the capital.

In Tobruk, the increasingly nervous and desperate HoR denounced Fajr as terrorists. It had reason: Fajr is an illegal group of armed gangsters who had seized the capital city of Libya in clear defiance of the government's wishes.

Not only that, on the same day the announcement was made, Fajr members had attacked the Tripoli home of the nation's Prime Minister Abdullah Al-Thinni. He was not at home, instead serving at the HoR, but his family were forced out of the property at gunpoint, and then the house was looted and set ablaze.

The previous day, Fajr members attacked a TV station, Alassema, setting fire to equipment, kidnapping three employees, targeting journalists' homes and threatening them with further violence, attempting to justify this by claiming Alassema was 'biased' against it.

On 27th August, Fajr khetibas set fire to the home of Libya's acting transport minister, Abdelgader al-Zintani, burning it to the ground.

With these, and other greater or lesser acts of petty violence, designed to intimidate and punish crimes it had invented or perceived, Fajr revealed that the HoR's denouncement was correct: Fajr was certainly capable of committing terrorist acts.

But in the hopelessly divided Libya created by Haftar's folly, the statement was bound to draw a response. Because if Fajr was a terrorist organisation, then how could Haftar, who had launched attacks on Libya's two largest cities – the first of which the country's PM had described as an illegal act – escape the same censure?

And within Tripoli itself, Fajr had snatched the international airport, but it had taken it not from the government, but from another illegal band of gunmen, who had for almost three years refused repeated requests to hand it back to the state.

Human Rights Watch, in a statement it issued on 8th September about the days immediately following Fajr's defeat of the Zintan khetibas, was clear that both groups should be regarded with caution.

Its Middle East and North Africa director Sarah Leah Whitson said: 'Commanders on both sides need to rein in their forces and end the cycle of abuses or risk being first in line for possible sanctions and international prosecution. All warring parties, as well as the Libyan government, should respect their obligation to protect civilians at all times and to hold their forces accountable when they commit crimes.'

The HoR was a body from which every non-secular politician had walked out, leaving only a group of anti-'Islamist' men and women, perched at the country's easternmost edge, forced to look on in horror as Libya was tearing itself to pieces.

It is understandable that it sought something to blame, and that what it found was the Muslim Brotherhood-aligned Fajr movement in Tripoli. But when Libya needed unity, and the HoR was the sole democratically-elected power base in the country, it is hard not to conclude that by choosing a side, parliament failed the people.

Also on 25th August, while the HoR was voting to conclude Fajr was a terrorist group, the GNC was reconvened for the first time since the election of 25th June.

The Congress met in Tripoli, some three weeks after the handover of power between it and the HoR had been scheduled to take place. It argued that as HoR had refused to follow the steps mapped out by the February Committee, it had rescinded its right to govern, and that the GNC had no choice but to reform, as Libya's sole legitimate government.

It also stated that HoR was responsible for the airstrikes on Tripoli, and, more plausibly, that its calls for foreign intervention in Libyan affairs, made early on 8th and 13th August, were unconstitutional.

At the same session, it named Omar Al-Hassi* as Libya's Prime Minister. Al-Hassi was elected unanimously, but as only 88 politicians were at the session, there are clear questions about the legality of the decision.

* Al-Hassi, a lecturer in political science at Benghazi's Garyan University, had been a losing candidate in the elections for PM which had seen Maetiga – briefly – elected in place of Abdullah Al Thinni.

In response, the United Nations stressed that it recognised only the HoR as Libya's legitimate government. But Libya, which in March had appeared to unite and solve its most pressing challenge, was, by the end of August, a country in which at least two wars were taking place (though with Khalifa Haftar central in both), with two rival governments, each in thrall to illegal militias which it could never hope to control.

More than that, one of the governments was awaiting the result of a Supreme Court hearing which would decide whether it was legitimate, and the other had formed only a few days before, and in its first session had named as national Prime Minister a man who had received 32 votes fewer than necessary to legitimately ascend to the position.

The national capital was run by a militia denounced by one of the country's two governments as a terrorist organisation, and its second city was overrun by another which was denounced internationally as such. The United Nations estimated that by the end of August, the fighting in Tripoli and Benghazi had led to 100,000 people fleeing their homes to stay elsewhere in Libya, while 150,000 fled the country altogether.

In Tripoli, 12,600 families were displaced. Haftar, at this stage, was conspicuous by his absence from the public eye. Despite all of this, and as an indication of the ways in which the experience of the general public can be at odds with the wider political situation, life in Tripoli marginally improved.

By 27th August, petrol stations had reopened, and gas shortages had been remedied, though in both cases, this was an effect of conflict ending, rather than any expertise or innate talent of Fajr for governance.

Also on 27th August, Fajr demanded that the Zintan khetibas should lay down their weapons and hand over Saif Al-Islam, who was still imprisoned by the illegal militia. The Zintani brigades, which were by now safe in the Zintan mountains, simply ignored the demand.

In the east of the country, and four days after his Tripoli home had been ransacked and burned by Fajr members, the HoR's PM Abdulla Al-Thinni resigned, along with all of his Cabinet, in order, he said, to enable the HoR to elect a 'more inclusive' government. Whether his intention was to lure Justice & Construction party members back to the HoR, or to attempt to ensure the HoR itself began to understand the challenges it faced – including the scheduled Supreme Court judgement – the end result was actually to weaken the parliament.

On 1st September, Al-Thinni was re-elected, taking 64 of 106 votes. This meant that Libya had two Prime Ministers, neither legitimate according to the electoral rules of their respective parliaments.

Back in Tripoli, on 30th August, the Misrata khetibas continued their systematic victimisation – and slaughter – of Tawerghans. Though almost all of the 1,000 people who lived at the three Tripoli camps for displaced Tawerghan people – al-Fallah, Airport Road and the Naval Academy – had escaped between mid-July and the end of August, fearing victimisation should Fajr take control of the capital, armed men drove into al-Fallah on the morning of 30th August and fired indiscriminately on the few people who remained.

They seized six men, including one they had injured by firing on the camp, and took them to their base elsewhere in Tripoli. Members of the Tawergha community were later able to negotiate the release of five of the men, but the sixth, Irheel Abdelsalam, died as a result of the bullet wound he had received at the camp.

Fighting continued sporadically in Benghazi, with rare moments of violence in Tripoli, including an airstrike in the Gharyan area on 15th September* ('We attacked positions of the Libya Dawn,' commented Saqer al-Jouroushi), taking Haftar's total to three aerial attacks on Tripoli with little or no effect.

---

* This strike, like the previous ones, had almost certainly been carried out with Egyptian craft, and UAE funding.

The previous day, Al-Thinni claimed to have received evidence that an aircraft laden with weapons had been sent from Qatar to the Fajr forces in Tripoli. The Sudanese government had also been implicated in trafficking weapons to Fajr – an accusation it denied. Such claims increased fears that Libya was becoming a battle-ground for proxy warfare between regional powers.

And on 29th September, as Haftar began to increase the intensity of his attacks on Benghazi, desperately seeking a way back into the city after being routed a month earlier, the United Nations began negotiations for a ceasefire across Libya.

The talks, in Ghadames, north-west Libya, were amicable, and almost immediately saw the 22 parties – including representatives of both the HoR and the GNC – agreeing that a ceasefire was necessary.

However, no documents to this effect were signed, and the call would in any case have been unlikely to succeed because none of the khetibas had been invited to take part, even though they were the only ones to hold any power within Libya, and were the only ones fighting.

The main reason for this was that the HoR, as the sole governing body recognised by the international community, had been invited to suggest attendees.

It had accepted the need for GNC members to take part, but had refused to allow Fajr, which it had already denounced as a terrorist organisation. From there, it was increasingly difficult – and effectively pointless – to invite the Zintan brigades, or Haftar, while if Fajr was excluded as a terrorist organisation, it would have been impossible to allow Ansar Al-Sharia to take part.

It is unlikely that all parties would have attended even if invited (though Fajr's statement 'We do not recognise these talks' was made only after the event, and seemed like an attempt to save face rather than a serious dismissal of the concept of negotiation). But to fail even to make the attempt doomed the talks to failure even before they had begun.

By mid-October, Haftar and the Operation Dignity forces' attempts to re-enter Benghazi had met only limited success, but the campaign was in a healthier position than at the end of August.

It had taken a number of strategic positions around the city, and had managed to enter areas within its boundaries. In an attempt to generate a bridgehead – and enable a 'surge' of troops into the city – he called for Benghazans to stage a popular uprising. The response was muted. Some citizens welcomed the Operation's soldiers, but in other places they were greeted not with hostility, but with silence.

Three days later, having retaken roughly 30 per cent of the city, Haftar showed he was still determined to win the media war, announcing that he was 'very satisfied' and 'near to victory' in a city in which he had suffered ignominy just six weeks before.

Perhaps one of the reasons for Benghazans' reluctance to flood the streets was the sheer impact the continued fighting was having on them and their city.

On the same day Haftar expressed his 'satisfaction', 18th October, the Libya Red Crescent reported that fighting and suicide bombings were having a crippling effect on Benghazi, and posted on its facebook page a desperate plea for a ceasefire 'even if only for one hour' to enable injured and at-risk citizens to escape.

Haftar and the Shura Council united for the only time to date, in order to both ignore the request.

Back in Tripoli, were Fajr was now comfortably in control, the Supreme Court was expected on 20th October to deliver its verdict on the legitimacy of the HoR. But one day before, gunmen took positions surrounding the Court's headquarters. Fajr claimed it had dispatched the armed men to 'protect' the Court from extremists, to enable it to safely announce its findings.

Instead, on 20th October, the Court issued a statement postponing the announcement of its decision to 5th November. As if in echo of Haftar's request to the Benghazan public, the HoR called on 21st October for a 'public uprising' in Tripoli.

The parliament announced that it had ordered the army to 'liberate Tripoli from armed groups,' and called on young Libyans in Tripoli to 'join hands with the army to liberate yourselves, your families and your city,' as well as requesting citizens to begin 'a civil disobedience campaign until the arrival of the army'.

The requests did not spark a revolution in the capital, perhaps not in defiance of the HoR's request, but in recognition that the parliament was not capable of freeing Tripoli. As troops had not arrived a month later, Tripoli's citizens may have made the correct decision.

During the same session, the HoR continued to increase its aggressive stance against its Tripolitan rival, pledging to prosecute the GNC-appointed PM Omar Al-Hassi, who it claimed was 'staging a coup'. Khalifa Haftar continued to attempt to 'liberate' Benghazi, without comment on this development.

In Ghadames, peace talks continued, without input from the khetibas, the only groups who could conceivably bring about peace.

On 23rd October, Misratan politician Fathi Bashaga, who represented the members of the HoR who were boycotting the parliament, said: 'The talks are an attempt to mend excesses and mistakes. When we determine to go the route of negotiations, we understand that compromises must be made in order to reach consensus.'

On the same day, a Joint Statement by the governments of France, Germany, Italy, the UK and US for the first time noted the detrimental role Khalifa Haftar had played in Libya's recent past.

The statement read: 'We condemn the crimes of Ansar Al-Sharia entities and the ongoing violence in communities across Libya… We are also concerned by Khalifa Haftar's attacks in Benghazi. Libya's security challenges and the fight against terrorist organisations can only be substantially addressed by regular armed forces under the control of a central authority, which is accountable to a democratic and inclusive parliament.'

It was the first time Haftar's repeated contempt for international law had been criticised since Al-Thinni had done so on 17th May. His Operation Dignity continued without offering any comment.

Three days later, in Derna, flags of the extremist Islamic State group were flown by the city's Shura Council of Islamic Youth, which had previously been assumed by outside observers to be allied to Al Qaeda.

The Council's repressive rule of Derna had continued. It had removed rights for women, and installed a penal system which included beatings for possession of alcohol.

Two days later, 28th October, a car bomb was detonated close to the security headquarters in Tobruk – the first time any direct attack was made on the HoR's home city. Nobody was injured in the blast.

In Benghazi, Haftar's forces had stepped up their campaign with mixed results. As much as 50 per cent of the city had been seized from the city's Shura Council, but the khetibas were pushing back, and in the ten days from 16th-26th October, at least 130 people had been killed (by comparison, between 16th May and 30th July the Libyan Health Ministry reported 214 people had been killed, and a further 918 injured across the country, though the organisation Libya Body Count estimated the number of deaths was likely to be higher than 400).*

* *Aside from the difficulties of providing accurate casualty figures while conflict is still going on, the figures are further complicated in Benghazi by the Shura Council's refusal to share information about the number of deaths and injuries within its ranks. As a result, the figure of 'at least' 130 deaths quoted above could be as little as half the true figure.*

And the city's Garyounis University briefly became a focus of the conflict, with Dignity forces firing grad missiles into the building, causing large fires to break out.

But despite increasingly fierce resistance, Haftar's advance continued. By 3rd November (at which point the death toll since 16th October had risen to more than 200), with heavy fighting taking place at the city's port, a little less than 60 per cent of Benghazi was estimated to be under the retired general's control.

It is hard to be sure whether this reinforced his 18th October claim that Dignity was 'near to victory'.

On the same day, Omar Al-Hassi, the GNC's Prime Minister, gave an interview to Agence France Presse, calling for new Libyan elections, and accusing the HoR – which had claimed Hassi was staging a 'coup' and should be arrested and prosecuted – of lacking legitimacy.

Also within the article, released just two days before the Libyan Supreme Court was set to deliver its judgement on the HoR's constitutional status, he claimed that Haftar was staging a coup, wresting control of Libya from politicians to rule Libya himself.

He said: 'This parliament is no longer accepted in Libya. It has lost its legitimacy. We need new elections. The poll must take place under the supervision of (elected) local councils.

'The revolution has been stolen. We are in the process of getting it back again. Haftar is a coupist who's trying to convince Libyans and the international community that he's the country's saviour and will rid it of Islamist groups.'

In the south, too, skirmishes continued. On 5th November, Tuareg militias stormed and seized the El Sharara oil field, close to the city of Owbari. The oilfield had been guarded by Tebu fighters acting on behalf of the Zintan khetibas – and, by implication, also the HoR – and was producing around a quarter of Libya's oil output of 800,000 barrels per day. But the Tuareg unit – rumoured to have been made up of veterans of the battles following the setting up of Mali's Islamic state in 2012 – swept in almost unopposed.

Most of its members left soon after, taking every single weapon and vehicle at the facility with them, but a small number – possibly connected to the Fajr force in Tripoli – remained, signalling yet another 'changing of the guard' in ongoing battles for control of Libya's resources.

Nobody was injured in the attack. As the battle for oil took place in the south, the Supreme Court quietly announced it would delay its announcement for another 24 hours.

Matters of Legitimacy
6th November 2014

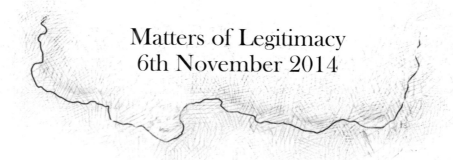

When judgement finally came, it was a surprise.

Many people in Libya accepted that, were the Supreme Court to invoke the exact wording of the February Committee's criteria for the HoR's existence, it would have no choice but to announce the Tobruk parliament illegitimate.

Its supporters hoped that the Court might make the judgement that a power handover in Tripoli had, in August and September 2014, been all but impossible, and that Benghazi – still a war-zone – was an inappropriate host city for a government, and set new dates for a handover, along with a requirement for HoR to move to Benghazi once fighting was over.

Its opponents argued that exceptions could not be made – if the GNC could operate in Tripoli then it must only have been HoR's preference for the Zintan khetiba and Operation Dignity over the politicians of Justice and Construction and the Fajr militia, which kept them in Tobruk. But what the Supreme Court announced on Thursday 6th November went far beyond a statement on the technicalities of the parliament's location.

The gathered judges told the Libyan and international media who had gathered in Tripoli that the HoR was not a legitimate government because the elections of 25th June had themselves been invalid, because, in turn, the February Committee itself, set up by the GNC to solve the problems of its own dubious legality, was not constitutionally legitimate.

If the announcement had an air of finality, that was entirely appropriate: 'This decision,' it ended. 'Cannot be appealed.'

Technically, the Court was correct. The GNC had not been quorate during the session in which the Committee had been set up. But the Court's statement, which made vague reference to the requirement for future elections to be held, left the GNC – which had itself created the problem and was now a body which had not itself achieved quorate status since June – as the national government.

It may not have been intended as a reward for incompetence, but in handing power to the exact body which had created the problem to begin with, that was how it appeared. Reaction, as is to be expected in a state as deeply divided as Libya, was wildly divergent. On the streets of Tripoli and Misrata, people spilled onto the streets, firing guns into the air in celebration (though of course, many more – particularly in Tripoli itself – did not).

That response may be explained in part not by any great desire to see Libya cast into yet deeper labyrinthine political complications – which was the one certain outcome of the Court's announcement – but because as far as Fajr and the Misratan public were concerned, the HoR was little more than the public face of its enemy in war: few people care enough about complex constitutional judgements in themselves to celebrate them with gunfire on the streets.

But the celebrations certainly seemed to overlook the fact that not only was the GNC the body which caused the elections not to meet the minimum criteria to be legal, it was also led by a Prime Minister who had himself been elected when the Tripoli parliament was inquorate.

The response of the HoR was equally predictable.

Its members pointed to the fact that it, not the GNC, was the internationally-recognised Libyan parliament, as if this might override the state's own rules.

They added that the Court had been forced to make its decision not only in Tripoli, the stronghold of the GNC and Fajr, but also surrounded by armed men who are assumed to have wanted the HoR disbanded (nobody has made any allegation of a specific threat made to the Court's members, but the presence of several heavily-armed militia members may in itself perhaps be considered such a threat).

Abu-Bakr Baeira, one of the HoR's Cyrenaican Federalists, who had announced in 2012 that he hoped the Cyrenaican Transitional Court's illegal announcement of a federal state of Cyrenaica would not be opposed because he hoped not to be 'forced into a new war', dismissed not only the Court's decision, but also the idea of Libya as a whole.

He said: 'We are calling a meeting for leaders in eastern Libya and we are going to – maybe – announce a separate government and parliament here. We cannot make a federal system with such criminals [GNC and Fajr]. No – it will be a separate state in eastern Libya.

'If our colleagues in the south will join us, we can create a new Libya composed of east and south. We will leave Tripoli and Misrata alone – let them enjoy what they are doing.'

Few others within the HoR were quite as keen to immediately write off the idea of Libya as a united state, or to cut off those in Tripoli (to say nothing of those in Zintan, Zawiyah and the rest of west Libya) who did not consider themselves supporters of Fajr.

But the Tobruk parliament's line was uncompromising. Its official statement, delivered to the media by member Adam Abu Sakhra, read: 'The ruling was taken under the threat of arms, because the capital is ruled by outlaw militias.

'The House of Representatives rejects the verdict under these conditions and says it is still functioning.'

In the immediate aftermath of the surprise ruling, few people stopped to ask why, on 5th November, the Supreme Court had postponed its announcement by 24 hours. Its statement at the time had claimed the delay was intended to allow judges to hear 'appeals one final time', but on 14th November three judges, Faraj Maarouf, Abdulsalam Abhiih and Bashir Al-Ziani, suggested another reason.

The trio, all Supreme Court members, claimed that two judges had resigned on 5th November, in an attempt to prevent the Court's final session from taking place. Replacements were appointed, they claimed, by the GNC's Minister of Justice. If true, this would be an act in direct contradiction of the Libyan Supreme Court's own constitution, which states that judges must be appointed by the Supreme Judicial Court, which meets just once every three months.

The possibility is, therefore, that in November 2014, Libya's parliament, whose Prime Minister was elected in contravention of its own rules, was declared illegitimate and power handed to another parliament, which has not been quorate since June 2014 at the latest, and whose Prime Minister was also elected in contravention of the parliament's regulations, by a Supreme Court which itself was invalid when it passed the ruling.

Haftar re-entered Benghazi in person for the first time on the following day.

He has yet to comment on the Libya he has made.

Sirte

In Sirte, once a small village derided by the Nazis, an increasingly – and depressingly – familiar situation was developing.

On 24th January, Ansar al-Sharia announced its leader, Mohamed al-Zehawi, had died as a result of wounds suffered in battles with Haftar's forces the previous October. The organisation announced he was buried in Sirte, though it is unclear whether he died in January, October, or at any point between the two.

In the same city, on Valentine's Day 2015, IS announced it had taken control and was set to create a 'Caliphate' in Sirte, similar to that which had been imposed by a small band of gunmen on the reluctant citizens of Derna.

It remains unclear whether IS had in fact any widespread control over Sirte, aside from one radio station from which it was certainly broadcasting its claims of control. But the following day, men claiming to belong to the armed group released a video of the beheading of 21 Egyptian Coptic Christians on Sirte beach.

Among them were at least two men you had previously worked with – part of the gangs of men who sat on the roadside early each morning, waiting for work.

In which case, IS murdered people who were responsible for some of the repairs and rebuilding in Sirte – some of its recovery. Though IS does not particularly care, it is to be hoped the people of Sirte, though currently powerless to show it, remember the service they performed.

In response, General Sisi in Egypt ordered airstrikes, which hammered Libya on the morning of 16th February. It was a very typical military response to terrorism: meeting a perceived 'need to respond' while having almost no effect on the group responsible for the outrage.

IS' 'rise' in Sirte had not been widely predicted. But with the benefit of hindsight, and some small knowledge of IS' progression into other parts of the world, perhaps it was predictable.

In Yemen, Ansar al-Sharia had had a meaningful and threatening presence, only to lose many of its younger members to IS after the latter began to recruit there.

It is almost impossible to imagine that IS 'invaded' Sirte, as to get there from Derna the organisation would have had to have battled through Benghazi and Ajdabiya.

But it is perfectly possible that a couple of its members, backed by the grim 'publicity' which its videoed murders bring, were able to effect a similar recruitment process.

It does not, after all, take many more than 21 people to carry out 21 decapitations.

And so Sirte beach, recently the place where the leftover weapons of a recent war were moved to keep the city's residents safe, became, three years later, the stage for the latest in a list of Libyan atrocities.

And given the failure of Haftar to overcome Ansar in Benghazi, or IS in Derna, it seems that short of a multilateral decision to lay down arms, only the Misrata khetibas may have the capacity to prevent one or both of the militias advancing even further West.

The once tiny fishing outpost, turned into a city by its most famous son, has already been the location of the final battle of a Civil War. It may soon find it is transformed again into the battleground on which Libya's future is decided.

It is a fate no city deserves.

Failure?

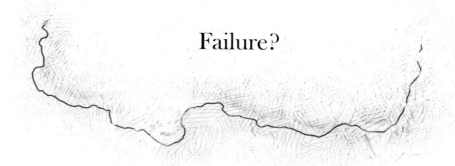

In the late Spring of 2014, it was fashionable among Libyan officials and observers of the state to claim that Libya was not a failed state; just one which had not yet emerged.

For this to be true, Libya would have had to have been entirely unique in global history: a defined, named, geographical region, containing people with a shared language, culture and history, and long experience of being governed as one nation – albeit by dictators – and yet still a state which had 'not yet emerged'. It was a remarkable claim. But at least, until Haftar's attacks in May 2014, there could be some debate, and some clear reason for optimism.

Libya had recently drawn together its opposing illegal militias, to work under its democratically-elected government, and removed the greatest threat to its existence as a unified state.

It had a Prime Minister intelligent enough to sidestep conflict with opponents within parliament and outside it, and it had designed a new legislative body, as well as setting a date on which it would be elected.

It would be foolish to pretend that there were no problems facing Libya before Haftar's intervention. Its six million people lived in a state which had been wrecked by war.

The combined efforts of Ghaddafi, the khetibas who overthrew and killed him, and wave after wave of NATO strikes on vital 'military targets' including Ibn Sina hospital, apartment blocks, schools, Ehemmet's café and the entire town of Tawergha, meant they lived their lives in the shadows of ruins.

And the only possible source of the cash it desperately needs to repair its ruined homes, businesses, medical centres and universities – its oil – was regularly swapped between heavily-armed, illegal warlords who 'liberated' it, some of whom have committed crimes against humanity, and others who aimed to destroy either Libya itself, or to install another dictator of a different religious and political outlook.

In fact, oil production had fallen by 97 per cent since February 2011. And despite the plans for a new government, its people could not depend upon the one they had, which even at its strongest moments was hamstrung by a legislative body which had failed to deliver a constitution and failed even to move Libya any closer to a position where a constitution could be completed.

But before Haftar, whose strategic incapabilities saw him divide the only force which could have helped defeat extremists in the east, and back the HoR when it came into being, there was at least a promise that Libya could one day enter the light at the end of its very long, dark, tunnel.

To a certain extent, Haftar's ineptitude – like the weakness of Libya's military – is a positive in Libya. A quick, decisive campaign in Benghazi (where at least 400 people were killed in the three weeks up to 8th November) would have been far preferable to the drawn-out, stumbling comedy of errors and humiliating defeats the retired, disgraced general has overseen in east and west. But in Egypt, where a strong military led by a charismatic and efficient general has snatched power, the results have been disastrous.

Sisi's Egyptian regime denounced the previous government as terrorists, and unleashed a wave of bloodshed and political repression which should have – but has not yet – been met with international horror and censure.*

On 28th April 2014, the same day the last of the 720 death sentences for the murder of one police officer were ordered, by Egypt's court, prosecutors also symbolically destroyed the last hopes of Egypt's Arab Spring. It outlawed the April 6 youth movement, not an Islamic political organisation, and far less a terror group, but one of the liberal collectives which had led Egypt's 2011 revolution against Hosni Mubarak.

The group's spokesman Ahmad Abd Allah said: 'It shows it's not just the Islamists that are being targeted, it's also liberal groups like us. And the government will continue all the way to close down all democratic forces.

'What else did you think would come from a military regime that has killed thousands more? And it's just the beginning.'

Libya has, as yet, not quite fallen so low.

But such an outcome is not impossible. Haftar may yet be defeated in Benghazi, which would leave the city – and the wider eastern region – in the control of extremist terrorists, some backed by Al Qaeda, others associated with IS. The people of Cyrenaica could possibly find that even their current perilous existence gets worse.*

From 10th-12th November, three car bombs were detonated in Cyrenaica. The first, in Shahat, north-eastern Libya, exploded while Al-Thinni was meeting UN special envoy to Libya Bernardino Leon in the town.

No-one was injured in that blast, but on 12th November car bombs, in Al Bayda, close to Shahat, and in Tobruk, killed nine and injured at least 25 people.

Tobruk is home to the HoR, while Al Bayda is the city in which the Libyan Constitutional Assembly is based. The Derna Islamic Youth Shura Council is suspected to have been behind all three attacks.

Also on 12th November, three human rights activists, Mohamed al-Mesmari, Siraj Ghatish and Mohammed Batu, all aged 19-21, were found beheaded. Each had used social media to criticise the Youth Shura Council, documenting floggings, the Council's separation of men and women in public places, and public executions.

And if Haftar were to win, what then? Would he move to attack Tripoli? If victorious there, where would he stop?

Comparison with Libya's Eastern neighbour invites comparison with the state to its West.

One cannot blame 'Islamists' for Libya's problems, the way that Tony Blair and others blamed them for Egypt's difficulties, and Haftar has attempted to do in Libya, because in Tunisia, those 'Islamists', part of the same Muslim Brotherhood which backs Libya's Justice and Construction Party, helped to write an inspirational constitution.

In today's Libya, the division between 'Islamists' and 'secularists' is certainly real, and has become the major driver for conflict within the state.

But this was not a foregone conclusion, even in Spring 2014. Libya's major problems then were not caused by religiously-motivated politicians struggling to overcome their secular counterparts, but by the state's weakness, and the khetibas strength.

Even on 16th May, when Haftar attacked Benghazi, it was not clear that the result would be war across Libya.

Had he any tactical sense, he could have engaged both Zintan and Misrata khetibas to oppose Benghazi's Shura Council. He need not have spoken about the GNC (which he had already publicly called for a violent uprising against), and he may have carried Benghazi, setting the stage for peaceful, meaningful elections on 25th June.

It is far from clear whether this is what Haftar actually wanted.

Based on what he said – and what he did – it seems more likely that his motivations are one or both of the following: the prevention of moderate as well as extremist 'Islamists' from holding power (an anti-democratic and unjustifiable aim), or to take power for himself.

Whatever his motivations, he has failed, abjectly.

In choosing to ally with only the Zintan khetiba – itself an illegal military occupier of areas of Tripoli – calling the GNC's politicians criminals and sanctioning a rocket attack on them, Haftar drove the divide in Libya wider than it has ever been: not between extremists and moderates, but between moderate secularists and all sections of Muslim society in the state.

He saw Misrata khetibas – a dangerous, violent conglomerate of bandits, with much to answer for, but Libya's strongest military force, and one a more intelligent man could have put to use crushing Ansar Al-Sharia, before bringing its members to justice – and inexplicably decided that with his limited abilities and equally limited military resources, he would fight against them and Ansar Al-Sharia at once.

Haftar's war on two fronts against a dangerous band of Saudi-funded, Al Qaeda-aligned extremist terrorists in the east, and Libya's strongest armed organisation on the other side of the country, was a novice's mistake.

But he did not stop there.

With every word, and every action – his violence towards peaceful serving politicians and his statements, claiming moderate Islamists were Libya's enemy – Haftar has also kept driving a wedge between people who could have worked together, the moderate Islamists and secularists whose unity was Libya's greatest realistic hope for a better, more peaceful, future.

Haftar's words, and Haftar's actions, have led Libya to the brink.

Tripoli, the nation's capital, is now under the 'protection' of the Misrata khetiba: an organisation which has, in the last four years carried out at least one act of ethnic cleansing, and at least one massacre of peaceful demonstrators. Haftar's 'war' was the circumstance which made that possible.

Haftar's allies, the Zintan brigades, are no more legal than the Misratan force (though to date they have been less brutal) and neither force should be perched in Tripoli, waving guns and dispatching mob justice as and when it sees fit.*

> * *The Derna Islamic Shura Youth Council is not the only organisation in Libya capable of acts of terror. On the morning of 13th November, car bombs were exploded outside the Egyptian and UAE embassies in Tripoli. In contrast to the attacks in Cyrenaica, these were timed to minimise the risk of casualties, and no deaths or injuries resulted.*
>
> *But these were clear attacks on organisations – the Egyptian and UAE governments – which Fajr regards as enemies, following the airstrikes on Tripoli both took part in, in August.*
>
> *GNC Prime Minister Omar al-Hassi condemned the attacks, and promised his government would repair all damages.*
>
> *Fajr's leadership also issued condemnations, but considering how closely the attacks fitted with its own outlook – both in terms of the enemy chosen and the violence aimed at it – it is hard to believe it was not responsible. The only likely alternative – at least as worrying – is that Fajr's leadership, having conquered Tripoli, no longer has control over the troops it is supposed to command.*

Nor has Haftar's illegal war improved Libya's political system.

Instead of one paralysed government, unable to control the illegal khetibas within it, but at least led by a man of intelligence and ability, there are now two: both regarded as illegitimate (HoR under Libya's internal legal system; GNC by the rest of the world); both led by Prime Ministers who were elected counter to their parliament's own rules; and both sat, powerless, at either end of the nation, while illegal armed groups kill civilians and one another.*

> * *It is possible that the Supreme Court's ruling could have at least some positive short- to medium-term effects.*
>
> *Although the HoR has a far greater claim to legitimacy than the GNC in Tripoli, it is hard to escape the fact that it has abused that privilege.*
>
> *Its decision to declare one group of illegal militias – the Misrata khetibas and Shield, under the name Fajr – terrorists, while seeming to tacitly support the equally-illegal Zintan khetibas, and Haftar's 'Dignity' army, which had started the conflict, was irresponsible, and unbefitting a national government.*
>
> *Haftar's airstrikes on Tripoli were an outrage, yet the HoR remained silent. Neither of these things reduce HoR's legitimacy (though arguably the failures of the GNC in February do) and they do not make its competitor parliament in Tripoli any more deserving of recognition, but they were grave, unnecessary, and in some cases spiteful errors.*
>
> *But the most damaging decision by the HoR was almost certainly not driven by spite. Its choice to request that the Misrata khetibas were kept from the United Nations-led negotiations at Ghadames (still ongoing as this book goes to press) was understandable. Unfortunately, it was also an error.*

Fajr and Dignity (as well as the Zintan khetiba) are the only organisations which can possibly ensure there is peace in Libya. Neither the HoR or GNC have any ability whatsoever, at this stage, to prevent them from fighting – indeed, both arguably rely on the illegal groups for their continued existence.

Unless they are allowed to the table, the UN negotiations are pointless.

If HoR is regarded as less powerful as a result of the Supreme Court's decision, this could open the way for that to happen. And that, in turn, might open the path to greater co-operation and rapprochement between groups across the country.

In fact, Haftar's war has solved nothing, while making other matters far worse than they had been before.

One year after the failed general's televised call for a coup, his vanity project – his attempt to smash Libyan democracy – has left the state with two governments, neither of which are legitimate (a decision made by a Court which may itself be invalid); four opposing armed forces (including his own); hammered by airstrikes (many called in by him); and with two cities overrun by the world's most dangerous terrorist organisation: the maniacal, murderous, lunatics of IS.

Libya still has no constitution; it has two governments; unemployment is high; wages are low; minorities have no recognised legal rights; people continue to be murdered on the street; khetibas are the most powerful actors in the state; the systematic murder and abuse of the Tawerghans continues; Tripoli is under the control of illegal gunmen; Benghazi is a war-zone, contested by terrorists and a failed, incompetent, retired general, illegally commanding the remains of Libya's pitifully weak armed forces; neither of its two governments has any power over any part of Libyan life, including the production and sale of oil;* and , three years since its Civil War ended, large parts of the country are still rubble, smashed and destroyed by NATO's campaign of Shock and Awe.

* On 12th November, in retaliation for the Tuareg's theft of the El Sharara oilfields, the Zintan khetiba shut the pipeline to its terminals and ports at Mellitah and Zawiyah, shutting off a quarter of Libya's production capability with one small act. Five days later, the pipeline remained closed.

In peacetime, one may look at Libya and see the potential it holds.

In peacetime, it would be possible to see that some of Libya's gravest political problems since 2011 have been caused by the fact that no-one – including serving politicians – has ever before experienced a working democracy. And this can be addressed, by training those politicians and civil servants in the skills they need to perform their roles.

In peacetime, it would be possible to see that some of Libya's gravest social and economic problems since 2011 have been that the country lies largely in ruins, following NATO's relentless bombing and, using the tenet that 'if you break it, you pay for it', call for donations of cash and construction expertise from France, the UK and US to spark the reconstruction the state needs.

In peacetime, it would be possible to look at the fate of Libya's surviving Tawerghans, trapped in camps in Tripoli and Benghazi, never sure when Misrata khetiba members may come to torture or kill them, and demand it stops, immediately: that Tawerghans must be allowed to return home, and live their lives, unmolested and in peace. In fact, that cannot wait. That must happen now. In peacetime, it would be possible to use Libyan oil revenue for public projects, ranging from strengthening its military and legal systems, to making education and health services among the best the world has to offer.

And in peacetime it would be possible to encourage Libya's other strengths to return to the fore: its role as a safe haven for those fleeing violence and terror in their own states, and perhaps further down the line, becoming an outspoken advocate at regional and UN level for the rights of people across the continent at whose head it sits geographically, if not yet socially.

In other ways, too, a Libya at peace could hope one day to lead its region. With 90 per cent of its land harsh desert, unusable for crop growth or extensive animal rearing, and with its talented, highly-educated population it could, with investment and time, export energy derived from the sun, rather than from oil. And it could – should its people desire it – use the opportunity of its 'reset' in 2011 to harness modern communications technology to develop a new, genuinely direct, democracy – perhaps of the sort Ghaddafi claimed to desire, but did not deliver.

But at present, what Libya needs most is peace. Instead, it is mired in a war which is at best the product of Haftar's own lack of self-awareness, combined with vanity vanity – the least competent military leader in Libyan history taking it upon himself to 'rescue' the state from its own democratic decisions.

At worst – and it is certainly possible – Haftar, a former close friend and ally of Muammar Ghaddafi, is attempting an all-out military coup.*

* On 17th November, reports from Libya suggested that members of the HoR were calling for a 'military council', led by Haftar, to take power, a disconcertingly similar suggestion to that made by Haftar himself several months previously.

Whatever his intentions, Haftar saw his country in trouble, staggering towards its second democratic elections, and instead of helping it over the line, he has kicked its legs out from under it. Libya's future hangs by a thread. While warfare continues, no rebuilding can take place. All the training in the world can only work within a stable, functional political system. And all the goodwill available to the human race will not improve the lives and safety of the Libyan people.

If Libya is to survive, and its population is to have any decent standard of living – as it should and must – then Ansar al-Sharia and IS must be defeated and deported. But let us make no mistake: Haftar's delusions and determination to use bullets where the ballot was poised to succeed, caused this latest of Libyan disasters.

Four years after the revolution and then civil war which removed Ghaddafi, and one year after his former friend took to national television to demand a coup, Libya is experiencing the darkest moment in its history. There is still potential for a true Libya Hora, even after the current state of Libyan horror. But if it is to emerge, the state requires more than the defeat and deportation of Ansar and IS. Al-Fajr – and perhaps most importantly Haftar, who created this disaster – must at the very least be de-fanged, never to torment Libya and its people again. Libya deserves peace, and to be rid of those who prevent it.

ACKNOWLEDGEMENTS

Many thanks to Hygge Media – especially to Shay O'Donnell for his amazing artistic input, to Ruth Shedwick for her great design work and for pushing this over the line, and to Alex Stacey, whose work from start to finish and steadfast persistence through a sea of challenges (not all caused by me) has made sure a collection of shorthand notes has become something much more.

Also thank you to all the people I met in Tunisia and Libya, for talking to me and looking after me, as well as to the people I knew before I went there, including members of my family who were kind enough to worry about me.

Finally, a massive thank you to the operators of the stretch of railway between Brighton and London Bridge. Had your services run on time, ever, I would have had far fewer hours to type up my notes…

ABOUT THE AUTHOR

After 15 years in journalism, during which he covered floods, riots, General Elections, economic crises, war, housing and immigration, **Rory O'Keeffe** moved to Tunisia, then Libya, late in 2011, to perform political analysis and raise awareness of the humanitarian crisis caused by the Libyan Civil War.

Since then, he has worked in an advisory and communications role for a UK political party, and simultaneously in communications and political analysis for international aid organisations.

ABOUT THE ILLUSTRATOR

A self taught artist with training in architectural design, Shay O'Donnell graduated with a Ba(Hons) in Architecture from the University of Manchester in 2013. He has since followed his heart as a designer and illustrator, publishing online and exhibiting his creative work to varying audiences.

Shay works in a creative range spanning both traditional and online media, with a particular love for painting portraits- a passion that, at the age of 17, earned him an outstanding achievement award in recognition of his work in a summer school organised by the Lincolnshire Artists' Society, a collective who would later that year invite him to join. Professionally, Shay now works as a graphic designer in and around Manchester, freelancing and taking commissions in his spare time.

Hygge Media

Hygge *['hyga]* */HUE-gah/* is something we all seek – but seldom find. It is a Danish word meaning a "complete absence of anything annoying, irritating or emotionally overwhelming, and the presence of and pleasure from comforting, gentle and soothing things". It is especially associated with Christmas time, barbeques on long summer evenings and sitting around a cosy fire surrounded by lit candles on a cold, rainy night. There's nothing more hygge than gathering round a table with loved ones and a glass or two of wine, discussing the big and small things in life…

Hygge Media is inspired by the essence of hygge, creating a warm friendly atmosphere and enjoying the good things in life with good people. Hygge Media is a boutique publishing and design consortium, specialising in producing high quality specialist and technical magazines and books.

The philosophy of Hygge Media is to only work with people we want to work with; people whom we trust; highly skilled people who are invested in the projects we are working on.

Our team is comprised of professional, passionate people drawn from our professional networks. People that we have either worked with in former roles or who have been recommended to us by trusted colleagues and friends.

Working in this way means that we will only ever offer the best service possible.

Acknowledgements

Publisher	Alex Stacey
Graphic Design & Typesetting	Ruth Shedwick and Adam Thomas
Cover & Illustrations	Shay O'Donnell
Proof Reading	Dr Michael Mellors

Enquiries

info@hyggemedia.com
www.hyggemedia.com